Shakespeare's Comedies

University of

Blackwell Guides to Criticism
Editor Michael O'Neill

The aim of this new series is to provide undergraduates pursuing literary studies with collections of key critical work from an historical perspective. At the same time emphasis is placed upon recent and current work. In general, historic responses of importance are described, and represented by short excerpts, in an introductory narrative chapter. Thereafter landmark pieces and cutting-edge contemporary work are extracted or provided in their entirety according to their potential value to the student. Each volume seeks to enhance enjoyment of literature and to widen the individual student's critical repertoire. Critical approaches are treated as 'tools', and not articles of faith, to enhance the pursuit of reading and study. At a time when critical bibliographies seem to swell by the hour and library holdings to wither year by year, Blackwell's *Guides to Criticism* series offers students privileged access to and careful guidance through those writings that have most conditioned the historic current of discussion and debate as it now informs contemporary scholarship.

Published volumes

Shakespeare's Comedies

Edited by Emma Smith

Blackwell
Publishing

350 Main Street, Malden, MA 02148-5018, USA
108 Cowley Road, Oxford OX4 1JF, UK
550 Swanston Street, Carlton, Victoria 3053, Australia

First published 2004 by Blackwell Publishing Ltd

Library of Congress Cataloging-in-Publication Data

Shakespeare's comedies / edited by Emma Smith.
   p.   cm. – (Blackwell guides to criticism)
   Includes bibliographical references and index.
   ISBN 0-631-22011-9 (hb. : alk. paper) – ISBN 0-631-22012-7 (pbk. : alk. paper)
   1. Shakespeare, William, 1564–1616 – Comedies.   2. Comedy.   I. Smith, Emma,
1970-   II. Series.

PR2981.S495   2003
822.3'3 – dc21

                                                                      2003040322

A catalogue record for this title is available from the British Library.

Set in 10 on 12.5pt Caslon
by SNP Best-set Typesetter Ltd., Hong Kong
Printed and bound in the United Kingdom
by MPG Books Ltd, Bodmin, Cornwall

For further information on
Blackwell Publishing, visit our website:
http://www.blackwellpublishing.com

Contents

Preface

This *Guide to Criticism* has two purposes. First, it offers a narrative overview of pre-twentieth-century responses to Shakespeare's comedies, including generous extracts from major commentators. It then presents twentieth-century criticism, divided into thematic sections: 'Genre', 'Language', 'Gender and Sexuality', 'History and Politics' and 'Performance'. Each of these sections includes a short overview of criticism in the area, and then reprints in full two significant recent studies. Thus the *Guide* stands as a substantial critical history and collection of recent criticism, reprinted in a single volume for ease of reference. Secondly, through the overview introductions to each section, and through the extensive bibliographies, the *Guide* also offers those readers who have access to further critical reading some suggestions about how to navigate the great sea of secondary literature on Shakespeare, by indicating key debates or interventions in the critical history. Some of the editorial material is not specific to the comedies, and therefore overlaps with the companion volumes, *Shakespeare's Tragedies* and *Shakespeare's Histories*.

The *Guide* is not, nor could it be, definitive or exhaustive, nor is it intended to canonize those authors and arguments included; rather, it is intended to be indicative of the range and vitality of Shakespearian criticism over four hundred years, from the earliest sixteenth-century responses to the new playwright up to the end of the twentieth century.

Editorial references to Shakespeare's plays use the Oxford edition, *William Shakespeare: The Complete Works*, ed. Stanley W. Wells and Gary Taylor (Oxford: Clarendon Press, 1986).

Acknowledgements

The editor and publisher wish to thank the following for permission to use copyright material:

Penny Gay, '*As You Like It*: Who's Who in the Greenwood' in *As She Likes It: Shakespeare's Unruly Women* (1994), pp. 48–85, Routledge. Reproduced by permission of Routledge Inc., part of The Taylor & Francis Group.

Kim F. Hall, 'Guess Who's Coming to Dinner? Colonization and Miscegenation in *The Merchant of Venice*', *Renaissance Drama*, vol. 23, edited by Mary Beth Rose (1992), pp. 87–111, Evanston, IL, Northwestern University Press. Copyright © 1992 by Northwestern University Press.

Lisa Hopkins, 'Marriage as Comic Closure' in *The Shakespearean Marriage: Merry Wives and Heavy Husbands* (1998), pp. 16–33, Macmillan, reproduced with permission of Palgrave Macmillan.

Carol Rutter, 'Kate: Interpreting the Silence' from *Clamorous Voices: Shakespeare's Women Today*, ch. 1, ed. Faith Evans, published in Great Britain by The Women's Press Ltd, 1987, 34 Great Sutton Street, London EC1V 0LQ, is used by permission of The Women's Press.

David McCandless, 'Helena's Bed-trick: Gender and Performance in *All's Well that Ends Well*', *Shakespeare Quarterly*, 45: 4 (1994), pp. 449–68, copyright © Folger Shakespeare Library. Reprinted with premission of The Johns Hopkins University Press.

Russ McDonald, 'Here Follows Prose' in *Shakespeare and the Arts of Language* (2001), pp. 108–36, Oxford University Press. Reprinted by permission of Oxford University Press.

Katharine Eisaman Maus, 'Transfer of Title in *Love's Labor's Lost*: Language, Individualism, Gender.' Copyright 1991 from *Shakespeare Left and Right*, edited by Ivo Kamps, pp. 205–23. Reproduced by permission of Routledge, Inc., part of The Taylor & Francis Group.

Annabel Patterson, 'Bottom's Up: Festive Theory' in *Shakespeare and the Popular Voice* (1989), pp. 52–70, Blackwell.

Valerie Traub, 'The Homoerotics of Shakespearean Comedy' in *Desire and Anxiety: Circulations of Sexuality in Shakespearean Drama* (1992), pp. 117–44, Routledge. Reproduced by permission of Routledge Inc., part of The Taylor & Francis Group.

Robert N. Watson, 'False Immortality in *Measure for Measure*: Comic Means, Tragic Ends', *Shakespeare Quarterly*, 41: 4 (1990), pp. 411–32, copyright © Folger Shakespeare Library. Reprinted with permission of The Johns Hopkins University Press.

Every effort has been made to trace copyright holders and to obtain their permission for the use of copyright material. The editor and publisher will gladly receive any information enabling them to rectify in subsequent editions any error or omission.

1

The Development of Criticism of Shakespeare's Comedies

1590–1660

Contemporary mentions of Shakespeare are thin on the ground. It is striking – and salutary – for an historical account of early Shakespearian criticism to have its starting-point in Robert Greene's disparaging remark about the young playwright as 'an upstart Crow, beautified with our feathers' (1592), but perhaps Greene's animosity was prompted by emerging jealousy of the new-comer's literary powers. By the time Shakespeare's narrative poems *Venus and Adonis* (1593) and *The Rape of Lucrece* (1594) had been published their author was routinely included in lists of eminent Elizabethan authors. Francis Meres's commonplace book *Palladis Tamia* (1598) praises Shakespeare's generic versatility:

> As *Plautus* and *Seneca* are accounted the best for Comedy and Tragedy among the Latins so Shakespeare among the English is the most excellent in both kinds for the stage; for comedy witness his *Gentlemen of Verona*, his *Errors*, his *Loves Labours Lost*, his *Loves Labours Won*, his *Midsummer Night's Dream* and his *Merchant of Venice*: for tragedy his *Richard the 2. Richard the 3. Henry the 4, King John, Titus Andronicus* and his *Romeo and Juliet*. (Meres, 1598: 282)

In 1602 the law student John Manningham reported on a performance of *Twelfth Night* at the Middle Temple, noting: 'a good practice in it to make the steward believe his lady widow was in love with him, by counterfeiting a letter as from his lady, in general terms telling him what she liked best in him, and prescribing his gesture in smiling, his apparel, etc., and then when he came to practise, making him believe they took him to be mad' (Schoenbaum, 1975: 156).

Ben Jonson was less impressed by Shakespeare's comic style: the Induction to *Bartholomew Fair* (1614) asserts that its author 'is loth to make Nature afraid in his plays, like those that beget *Tales*, *Tempests*, and such like drolleries' in an apparent reference to *The Winter's Tale* and *The Tempest*. At the end of *The New Inn* (1629) there is a scathing reference to 'some mouldy tale / Like *Pericles*'. Jonson's work is characterized by its frequent use of prefatory material often containing literary commentary: this is almost non-existent in Shakespeare's canon, although the 1609 quarto of *Troilus and Cressida* carries an – apparently unauthorial – Epistle to the reader which identifies the play as a comedy:

> this author's comedies, that are so framed to the life, that they serve for the most common Commentaries of all the actions of our lives, showing such a dexterity and power of wit, that the most displeased with plays are pleased with his comedies. And all such dull and heavy-witted wordlings, as were never capable of the wit of a comedy, coming by report of them to his representations, have found that wit there that they never found in themselves, and have parted better wittied than they came: feeling an edge of wit set upon them, more than ever they dreamed they had brain to grind it on . . . It deserves such labour as well the best comedy in Terence or Plautus.

Other scattered references in the period exist, but the first substantial act of memorializing and shaping of Shakespeare's critical reputation was the publication in 1623 of a substantial folio volume collecting together thirty-six plays as *Mr William Shakespeares Comedies, Histories and Tragedies* (often known as the First Folio, or abbreviated to F). The title of the work reveals one of its most significant critical legacies: in dividing the plays into three genres in its catalogue, the First Folio established the major critical categories still in use today: 'comedies', 'histories' and 'tragedies'. Thus the plays listed as comedies in 1623 are, in their order, *The Tempest*, *The Two Gentlemen of Verona*, *The Merry Wives of Windsor*, *Measure for Measure*, *The Comedy of Errors*, *Much Ado About Nothing*, *Love's Labour's Lost*, *A Midsummer Night's Dream*, *The Merchant of Venice*, *As You Like It*, *The Taming of the Shrew*, *All's Well that Ends Well*, *Twelfth Night, or What You Will*, and *The Winter's Tale*. To these are often added *Pericles*, and the collaboration with John Fletcher *Two Noble Kinsmen*, not included in the Folio, and some assessments of comedy, following the quarto epistle, have also included *Troilus and Cressida*.

John Heminges and Henry Condell, Shakespeare's fellow-actors and the men responsible for the publishing of his collected plays, addressed their prefatory epistle 'To the Great Variety of Readers':

> It had been a thing, we confess, worthy to have been wished, that the Author himself had lived to have set forth, and overseen his own writings; But since it hath been ordained otherwise, and he by death departed from that right, we pray you do not envy his Friends, the office of their care, and pain, to have collected

and published them; and so to have published them, as where (before) you were abused with diverse stolen, and surreptitious copies, maimed, and deformed by the frauds and stealths of injurious impostors, that exposed them: even those, are now offered to your view cured, and perfect of their limbs; and all the rest, absolute in their numbers, as he conceived them. Who, as he was a happy imitator of Nature, was a most gentle expresser of it. His mind and hand went together: And what he thought, he uttered with that easiness, that we have scarce received from him a blot in his papers. But it is not our province, who only gather his works, and give them you, to praise him. It is yours that read him. And there we hope, to your diverse capacities, you will find enough, both to draw, and hold you: for his wit can no more lie hid, then it could be lost. Read him, therefore; and again, and again: And if then you do not like him, surely you are in some manifest danger, not to understand him. And so we leave you to other of his Friends, whom if you need, can be your guides: if you need them not, you can lead yourselves, and others. And such Readers we wish him. (Wells and Taylor, 1986: xlv)

The playwright Ben Jonson contributed an elegy:

> He was not of an age, but for all time!
> And all the Muses still were in their prime,
> When like Apollo he came forth to warm
> Our ears, or like a Mercury to charm!
> Nature herself was proud of his designs,
> And joyed to wear the dressing of his lines!
> Which were so richly spun, and woven so fit,
> As since, she will vouchsafe no other wit.
> The merry Greek, tart Aristophanes,
> Neat Terence, witty Plautus, now not please;
> But antiquated and deserted lie
> As they were not of nature's family.
> (Wells and Taylor, 1986: xlv)

In his *Timber, or Discoveries*, first published in 1640, Jonson again addressed Shakespeare's reputation, referring back to Heminges and Condell's 'To the Great Variety of Readers':

I remember the players have often mentioned it as an honour to Shakespeare, that in his writing, whatsoever to be penned, he never blotted out line. My answer hath been, 'Would he had blotted a thousand'; which they thought a malevolent speech. I had not told posterity this but for their ignorance, who choose that circumstance to commend their friend by wherein he most faulted; and to justify mine own candour: for I loved the man, and do honour his memory, on this side idolatry, as much as any. He was, indeed, honest, and of an open and free nature; had an excellent fantasy, brave notions, and gentle expressions; wherein he flowed with that facility that sometime it was necessary he should be stopped. '*Sufflaminandus erat*' ['Sometimes he needed the brake'], as Augustus said of Haterius. His wit was in his own power, would the rule of it had been so too. Many times he fell into those things, could not escape laughter: as when he said in the person of Caesar, one speaking to him, 'Caesar, thou dost me wrong'; he replied 'Caesar did never wrong, but with just cause'; and such like: which were ridiculous. But he redeemed his vices with his virtues. There was ever more in him to be praised than to be pardoned. (Donaldson, 1985: 539–40)

1660–1720: 'Good in Parts' – Texts in Print and on Stage

It is to post-Restoration culture that we need to look to see the establishment of many now-familiar preoccupations and approaches to Shakespeare. As Michael Dobson notes, in his study of the 'extensive cultural work that went into the installation of Shakespeare as England's National Poet' between 1660 and 1769:

> so many of the conceptions of Shakespeare we inherit date not from the Renaissance but from the Enlightenment. It was this period, after all, which initiated many of the practices which modern spectators and readers of Shakespeare would generally regard as normal or even natural: the performance of his female roles by women instead of men (instigated at a revival of *Othello* in 1660); the reproduction of his works in scholarly editions, with critical apparatus (pioneered by Rowe's edition of 1709 and the volume of commentary appended to it by Charles Gildon the following year); the publication of critical monographs devoted entirely to the analysis of his works (an industry founded by John Dennis's *An Essay upon the Writings and Genius of Shakespeare*, 1712); the promulgation of the plays in secondary education (the earliest known instance of which is the production of *Julius Caesar* mounted in 1728 'by the young Noblemen of the Westminster School'), and in higher education (first carried out in the lectures on Shakespeare given by William Hawkins at Oxford in the early 1750s); the erection of monuments to Shakespeare in nationally symbolic public places (initiated by Peter Sheemaker's statue in Poets' Corner, Westminster Abbey, unveiled in 1741); and the promotion of Stratford-upon-Avon as a site of secular pilgrimage (ratified at Garrick's jubilee in 1769). (Dobson, 1992: 3)

Ben Jonson's half-praise, half-sneer in his elegy about Shakespeare's classical knowledge – 'small Latin, and less Greek' – was an early suggestion of one of the obstacles to Shakespeare appreciation in post-Restoration culture. The Restoration aesthetics of neoclassicism favoured poetry as imitation of classical, especially Roman, authors, and the idea of the writer as educated craftsman following ancient generic rules. Thus Thomas Fuller identifies Shakespeare among *The Worthies of England* in 1662, but is preoccupied with his subject's education, or lack of it:

Plautus, who was an exact Comaedian, yet never any Scholar, as our Shakespeare (if alive) would confess himself. Add to all these, that though his Genius generally was *jocular*, and inclining him to *festivity*, yet he could, (when so disposed), be *solemn* and *serious*, as appears by his Tragedies, so that *Heraclitus* himself (I mean if secret and unseen) might afford to smile at his Comedies, they were so *merry*, and *Democritus* scarce forbear to sigh at his Tragedies they were so *mournful*. He was an eminent instance of the truth of that Rule, *Poeta no fit, sed nascitur*, one is not *made* but *born* a Poet. Indeed his Learning was very little, so that as *Cornish diamonds* are not polished by any Lapidary, but are pointed and smoothed even as they are taken out of the Earth, so *nature* it self was all the *art* that was used upon him. (Fuller, 1662: 126)

The introduction of nature as a term of cultural valorization to balance against art is key to the recuperation of Shakespeare in this period. When, for example, Margaret Cavendish defends Shakespeare in one of her *Sociable Letters* of 1664, she argues that it is the vitality of his characters that is crucial to his success:

So well he hath expressed in his plays all sorts of persons, as one would think he had been transformed into every one of those persons he hath described; and as sometimes one would think he was really himself the clown or jester he feigns, so one would think, he was also the King and Privy Counsellor . . . nay, one would think he had been metamorphosed from a man to a woman, for who could describe Cleopatra better than he hath done, and many other females of his own creating, as Nan Page, Mrs Page, Mrs Ford, the Doctor's Maid, Beatrice, Mrs Quickly, Doll Tearsheet, and others, too many to relate? (Thompson and Roberts, 1997: 12–13)

Early in this process of recuperating Shakespeare for the Restoration period is John Dryden's important statement of neoclassical aesthetics, his essay *Of Dramatic Poesie* (1668). Dryden's essay takes the form of a discussion between four interlocutors: Eugenius, Crites, Lisedeius and Neander, generally believed to represent Dryden himself. While others of the conversationalists praise Ben Jonson as 'the greatest man of the last age' because of his adherence to classical rules, particularly the unities of time, place and action (Dryden, 1969: 14), Neander favours Shakespeare for his untutored but instinctive, intuitive expression. Shakespeare is to be praised for his natural learning, despite his flaws:

he was the man who of all Modern, and perhaps Ancient Poets, had the largest and most comprehensive soul. All the Images of Nature were still present to him, and he drew them not laboriously but luckily: when he describes anything, you more than see it, you feel it too. Those who accuse him to have wanted learning, give him the greater commendation: he was naturally learn'd; he needed not the spectacles of Books to read Nature; he look'd inwards, and found her there. (Dryden, 1969: 47–8)

In the comparison with Ben Jonson – and in particular with his comedy *Epicoene, or the Silent Woman*, considered an especially perfect dramatic construction – which was to be the touchstone for the nascent literary criticism of Shakespeare in the Restoration period, Neander's emotional loyalties are clear: 'If I would compare [Jonson] with *Shakespeare*, I must acknowledge him the more correct Poet, but *Shakespeare* the greater wit. *Shakespeare* was the *Homer*, or Father of our Dramatic Poets; *Johnson* was the *Virgil*, the pattern of elaborate writing; I admire him, but I love *Shakespeare*' (Dryden, 1969: 50). Elsewhere in his works, Dryden twice praises *The Merry Wives of Windsor* for its plotting and structure, and that play enjoyed particular popularity in the Restoration theatre.

In his preface to the first scholarly edition of Shakespeare's works (1709–10), the poet laureate and tragedian Nicholas Rowe advocates a more historically informed appreciation of Shakespeare's apparent divergence from classical precepts:

> as Shakespear lived under a kind of mere light of nature, and had never been made acquainted with the regularity of those written precepts, so it would be hard to judge him by a law he knew nothing of. We are to consider him as a man that lived in a state of almost universal license and ignorance: there was no established judge, but every one took the liberty to write according to the dictates of his own fancy. (Rowe, 1709–10: xxvi)

Rowe argues that writing outside the constraints of literary tradition allows Shakespeare's imagination free rein:

> I believe we are better pleased with those thoughts, altogether new and uncommon, which his own imagination supplied him so abundantly with, than if he had given us the most beautiful passages out of the Greek and Latin poets, and that in the most agreeable manner that it was possible for a master of the English language to deliver them. (1709–10: iv)

He also recognizes the generic hybridity of many, even the majority, of Shakespeare's plays:

> His plays are properly to be distinguished only into comedies and tragedies. Those which are called histories, and even some of his comedies, are really tragedies, with a run or mixture of comedy amongst them. That way of tragicomedy was the common mistake of that age, and is indeed become so agreeable to the English taste, that though the severer critics among us cannot bear

it, yet the generality of our audiences seem to be better pleased with it than with an exact tragedy. *The Merry Wives of Windsor*, *The Comedy of Errors*, and *The Taming of the Shrew*, are all pure Comedy; the rest, however they are called, have something of both kinds. 'Tis not very easy to determine which way of writing he was most excellent in. There is certainly a great deal of entertainment in his comical humours; and though they did not then strike at all ranks of people, as the satire of the present age has taken the liberty to do, yet there is a pleasing and a well-distinguished variety in those characters which he thought fit to meddle with. In *Twelfth Night* there is something singularly ridiculous and pleasant in the fantastical steward Malvolio. The Parasite and the Vain-glorious in Parolles, in *All's Well that Ends Well*, is as good as any thing of that kind in Plautus or Terence. Petruchio, in *The Taming of the Shrew*, is an uncommon piece of humour. The conversation of Benedick and Beatrice, in *Much Ado about Nothing*, and of Rosalind in *As You Like It*, have much wit and sprightliness all along. His clowns, without which character there was hardly any play writ in that time, are all very entertaining . . . To these I might add, that incomparable character of Shylock the Jew, in *The Merchant of Venice*; but though we have seen that play received and acted as a comedy, and the part of the Jew performed by an excellent comedian, yet I cannot but think it was designed tragically by the author. (1709–10: xvii–xx)

A final, seventh volume appended to the series in 1710 added a more extensive critique of the dramatic qualities of the plays in 'An Essay on the Art, Rise and Progress of the Stage in Greece, Rome and England' by Charles Gildon. Gildon, like many of his contemporaries, is particularly concerned with Shakespeare's tragedies and with defending the playwright against the charges of neoclassical critics, although he does add a short commentary on comedy:

Comedy participates in many things with the rules of tragedy, that is, it is an imitation both of action and manners, but those must both have a great deal of the ridiculum in them . . . Ben Jonson is our best pattern, and has given us this advantage, that though the English stage has scarce yet been acquainted with the shadow of tragedy, yet have we excelled all the ancients in comedy.

There is no man has had more of this *vis Comica* than our Shakespear, in particular characters and in *The Merry Wives of Windsor* he has given us a play that wants but little of a perfect regularity. (1709–10: lvii)

In the end, Gildon's view of Shakespeare is mixed:

Shakespeare is indeed stor'd with a great many Beauties, but they are in a heap of Rubbish; and as in the Ruines of a magnificent Pile we are pleas'd with the Capitals of Pillars, the Basso-relievos and the like as we meet with them, yet how infinitely more beautiful, and charming must it be to behold them in their proper Places in the standing Building, where every thing answers the other, and one Harmony of all the Parts heightens the Excellence even of those Parts. (1709–10: 425)

Gildon expanded this view in his book *The Complete Art of Poetry* (1718), in which the final chapter offers 'Shakespeariana: or Select Moral Reflections, Topicks, Similies and Descriptions from Shakespear' – the first book of Shakespearian quotations.

It is easy to see how the idea of a Shakespeare good in parts also reflects contemporary stage practice. What Gildon is attempting critically – the sifting of worthy from unworthy elements of the plays – scores of stage-plays attempted dramatically, in adapting, rewriting and recombining Shakespeare's works to suit the tastes of new audiences. These adaptations are themselves works of criticism; often, in prefatory material and epilogues, explicitly so, although, again, it is Shakespeare's tragedies which attract most interest during the period. Among the comedies, *The Tempest* is a favourite subject with adaptations by John Dryden and William Davenant in 1667 and Thomas Shadwell in 1674; John Lacy produced *Sauny the Scot, or, the Taming of the Shrew* in 1667; George Granville adapted *The Merchant of Venice* as *The Jew of Venice* in 1701; and John Dennis adapted *The Merry Wives of Windsor* in 1702, correcting its 'strange defects' of style and plotting, since 'in comedy, which is an image of common life, everything which is forced is abominable' (Vickers, 1974: II, 163). Dennis also wrote an extensive criticism of Shakespeare in his *An Essay on the Genius and Writings of Shakespear*, published in 1712, in which he argues that 'Though *Shakespeare* succeeded very well in comedy, yet his principal talent and his chief delight was tragedy' (Dennis, 1712: 27).

By the second decade of the eighteenth century, therefore, both Shakespearian textual scholarship in the form of Rowe's edition of 1709–10, and literary criticism in the contributions of Gildon and Dennis, were both established and contested fields. Divergent impulses towards the canonizing and concretizing of the Shakespearian text, on the one hand, and towards disintegration on the other, are key to eighteenth-century approaches.

1720–1765: Editions and Editors

Alexander Pope's edition of 1725 described itself on its title page as 'Collated and Corrected by the former Editions'. Pope's 'Preface of the Editor' evades the task of the critic in favour of that of the new, humanist textual scholar, the editor. Rather than entering 'into a Criticism upon this Author', Pope sets out to 'give an account of the fate of his Works, and the disadvantages under which they have been transmitted to us. We shall hereby extenuate many faults which are his, and clear him from the imputation of many which are not' (Pope and

Rowe, 1725: I, i–ii). Pope also acquits Shakespeare of the charges that neoclassical critics had laid at his door: 'To judge therefore of Shakespear by Aristotle's rules, is like trying a man by the Laws of one Country, who acted under those of another' (1725: I, vi). Rather, Pope repeats the critical orthodoxy that Shakespeare 'is not so much an Imitator, as an Instrument, of Nature; and 'tis not so just to say that he speaks from her, as that she speaks thro' him' (1725: I, ii), and makes a particular feature of Shakespeare's characterization:

> His Characters are so much Nature her self, that 'tis a sort of injury to call them by so distant a name as Copies of her . . . Every single character in Shakespear is as much an Individual, as those in Life itself; it is as impossible to find any two alike; and such as from their relation or affinity in any respect appear most to be Twins, will upon comparison be found remarkably distinct. To this life and variety of Character, we must add the wonderful Preservation of it; which is such throughout his plays, that had all the Speeches been printed without the very names of the Persons, I believe one might have apply'd them with certainty to every speaker. (1725: I, ii–iii)

Pope praises Shakespeare's 'Power over our Passions' (I, iii), and also his intellectual control of 'the coolness of Reflection and Reasoning' (I, iv).

Many of Shakespeare's perceived faults are in fact, Pope proposes, errors of the printing and publication process. He surmises that Shakespeare did not authorize or check those of the plays that were published in quarto editions during his lifetime, and that therefore:

> how many low and vicious parts and passages might no longer reflect upon this great Genius, but appear unworthily charged upon him? And even in those which are really his, how many faults may have been unjustly laid to his account from arbitrary Additions, Expunctions, Transpositions of scenes and lines, confusion of Characters and Persons, wrong application of Speeches, corruptions of innumerable Passages by the Ignorance, and wrong Corrections of 'em again by the Impertinence, of his first Editors? (I, xxi)

In 1726, a volume appeared with the descriptive title *Shakespeare Restored: or, a Specimen of Many Errors, as well Committed, and Unamended, by Mr Pope in his Late Edition of this Poet: designed not only to correct the said Edition, but to restore the true Reading of Shakespeare in all the Editions ever published. By Mr Theobald.* Its author, Lewis Theobald, proposed numerous new readings and emendations, particularly of *Hamlet*, many of which were plagiarized by Pope for his second edition which appeared in 1728. Pope pilloried Theobald in the first edition of his mock-epic poem the *Dunciad* published a few months later, mocking his pedantry in footnotes wondering whether 'Dunciad' should be spelt 'Dunceiad' and pitying 'hapless Shakespear, yet of Tibbald sore, / Wish'd he had blotted for himself before'. Theobald's riposte was his own Shakespeare edition of 1733, *The Works of Shakespeare: in Seven Volumes. Collated with the Oldest Copies, and Corrected; With notes, Explanatory and Critical.*

Theobald's style is effusive:

> No Age, perhaps, can produce an Author more various from himself, than Shakespeare has been universally acknowledg'd to be. The Diversity in Stile, and other Parts of Composition, so obvious in him, is as variously to be accounted for. His Education, we find, was at best but begun: and he started early into a Science from the Force of Genius, unequally assisted by acquir'd Improvements. His Fire, Spirit, and Exuberance of Imagination gave an Impetuosity to his Pen: His Ideas flow'd from him in a Stream rapid, but not turbulent; copious, but not ever overbearing its Shores. The Ease and Sweetness of his Temper might not a little contribute to his Facility in Writing: as his Employment, as a Player, gave him an Advantage and Habit of fancying himself the very Character he meant to delineate. (Theobald, 1733: I, xv)

His view of his predecessor and literary rival Pope is clear; Shakespeare studies has its first real personality clash: 'He has acted with regard to our Author, as an Editor, whom Lipsius mentions, did with regard to Martial; *Inventus est nescio quis Popa, qui non vitia ejus, sed ipsum, excidit.* He has attacked him like an unhandy Slaughterman; and not lopped off the errors, but the Poet' (1733: I, xxxv–xxxvi). Theobald's is not, however, the last word in this particular bibliographic and personal spat. In 1747 Pope, together with his collaborator William Warburton, brought out an edition to trump Theobald: *The Works of Shakespear in Eight Volumes. The Genuine Text (collated with all the former Editions, and then corrected and emended) is here settled: Being restored from the Blunders of the first Editors, and the Interpolations of the two Last: with A Comment and Notes, Critical and Explanatory.*

Theobald's edition establishes and promulgates his own theory of the editor's task. This covers three activities: 'the Emendation of corrupt Passages; the Explanation of obscure and difficult ones; and an Inquiry into the Beauties and Defects of Composition' (1733: I, xl). He elaborates on his editorial principles:

> Where-ever the Author's Sense is clear and discoverable, (tho', perchance, low and trivial;) I have not by any Innovation tamper'd with his Text; out of an Ostentation of endeavouring to make him speak better than the old Copies have done.
>
> Where, thro' all the former Editions, a Passage has labour'd under flat Nonsense and invincible Darkness, if, by the Addition or Alteration of a Letter or two, I have restored to Him both Sense and Sentiment, such Corrections, I am persuaded, will need no Indulgence.

And whenever I have taken a greater Latitude and Liberty in amending, I have constantly endeavoured to support my Corrections and Conjectures by parallel Passages and Authorities from himself, the surest Means of expounding any Author whatsoever . . . Some Remarks are spent in explaining Passages, where the Wit or Satire depends on an obscure Point of History: Others, where Allusions are to Divinity, Philosophy, or other Branches of Science. Some are added to shew, where there is a Suspicion of our Author having borrow'd from the Antients: Others, to shew where he is rallying his Contemporaries; or where He himself is rallied by them. And some are necessarily thrown in, to explain an obscure and obsolete Term, Phrase, or Idea. (1733: I, xliii–xliv)

Further editions, including those by Hamner and Capell, appeared throughout the eighteenth century as each editor claimed to be improving on the text of his predecessors.

Shakespeare's most significant and influential eighteenth-century mediator was editor and critic Samuel Johnson, whose annotated edition appeared in 1765. Johnson sets out 'to inquire, by what peculiarities of excellence *Shakespeare* has gained and kept the favour of his countrymen' (Johnson, 1765: I, viii). The answer, for Johnson is that:

Shakespeare is above all writers . . . the poet of nature; the poet that holds up to his readers a faithful mirrour of manners and of life. His characters are not modified by the customs of particular places, unpractised by the rest of the world; by the peculiarities of studies or professions, which can operate but upon small numbers; or by the accidents of transient fashions or temporary opinions: they are the genuine progeny of common humanity, such as the world will always supply, and observation will always find. His persons act and speak by the influence of those general passions and principles by which all minds are agitated, and the whole system of life is continued in motion. (1765: I, viii–ix)

For Johnson, Shakespeare is a philosopher and teacher, filled with 'practical axioms and domestick wisdom', but he argues strongly against the recent tendency to find Shakespeare's greatness in particular passages: 'he that tries to recommend him by select quotations, will succeed like the pedant in *Hierocles*, who, when he offered his house to sale, carried a brick in his pocket as a specimen' (1765: I, ix). Verisimilitude, the quality of creating recognizable individuals, dialogue and scenarios, is key to Johnson's appraisal of Shakespeare's work. Thus '*Shakespeare* has no heroes; his scenes are occupied only by men, who act and speak as the reader thinks that he should himself have spoken or acted on the same occasion', he 'approximates the remote, and familiarizes the wonderful', and his reader can benefit from 'reading human sentiments in human language' (1765: I, xi–xii).

Johnson's approach to Shakespeare's genres is radical:

> *Shakespeare's* plays are not in the rigorous or critical sense either tragedies or comedies, but compositions of a distinct kind, exhibiting the real state of sublunary nature, which partakes of good and evil, joy and sorrow, mingled with endless variety of proportion and innumerable modes of combination; and expressing the course of the world, in which the loss of one is the gain of another; in which, at the same time, the reveller is hasting to his wine and the mourner burying his friend; in which the malignity of one is sometimes defeated by the frolick of another; and many mischiefs and benefits are done and hindered without design. (1765: I, xiii)

While this, Johnson admits, is 'a practice contrary to the rules of criticism', 'there is always an appeal open from criticism to nature'. Unlike the classical authors set as exemplars by neoclassical critics, '*Shakespeare* has united the powers of exciting laughter and sorrow not only in one mind but in one composition' (I, xiv). Johnson defines genres historically, so that, for Shakespeare's audience: 'An action which ended happily to the principal persons, however serious or distressful through its intermediate incidents, in their opinion constituted a comedy. This idea of a comedy continued long amongst us, and plays were written, which, by changing the catastrophe, were tragedies to-day and comedies to-morrow' (I, xiv). Johnson exonerates him from the charge of neglecting the classical unities, arguing that spectators are not so literal-minded as to require the stage to represent a single place or continuous time: 'the truth is, that spectators are always in their senses, and know, from the first act to the last, that the stage is only a stage and that the players are only players . . . Where is the absurdity of allowing that space to represent first *Athens*, and then *Sicily*, which was always known to be neither *Sicily* nor *Athens* but a modern theatre?' (I, xxvii).

Unlike Dennis, Johnson sees Shakespeare's true talent as for comedy:

> In tragedy he often writes, with great appearance of toil and study, what is written at last with little felicity; but in his comic scenes, he seems to produce without labour, what no labour can improve. In tragedy he is always struggling after some occasion to be comic, but in comedy he seems to repose, or to luxuriate, as in a mode of thinking congenial to his nature. In his tragic scenes there is always something wanting, but his comedy often surpasses expectation or desire. His comedy pleases by the thoughts and the language, and his tragedy for the greater part by incident and action. His tragedy seems to be skill, his comedy to be instinct. (I, xvii)

Johnson's awareness of Shakespeare's 'excellencies' makes him equally clear about his failings. Shakespeare's tragic plots prompt moral objections, in his comedies he 'is seldom very successful when he engages his characters in reciprocations of smartness and contest of sarcasm; their jests are commonly gross

and their pleasantry licentious' (I, xxi). Shakespeare is rebuked for the violation of chronology and his use of anachronisms, and for occasionally strained
or wearisome rhetoric, but Johnson reserves his most lengthy, and famous,
censure for Shakespeare's wordplay:

> A quibble is to *Shakespeare*, what luminous vapours are to the traveller; he follows
> it at all adventures; it is sure to lead him out of his way, and sure to engulf him
> in the mire. It has some malignant power over his mind, and its fascinations are
> irresistible. Whatever be the dignity or profundity of his disquisition, whether
> he be enlarging knowledge or exalting affection, whether he be amusing
> attention with incidents, or enchaining it in suspense, let but a quibble spring
> up before him, and he leaves his work unfinished. A quibble is the golden apple
> for which he will always turn aside from his career, or stoop from his elevation.
> A quibble, poor and barren as it is, gave him such delight, that he was content
> to purchase it, by the sacrifice of reason, propriety and truth. A quibble was to
> him the fatal *Cleopatra* for which he lost the world, and was content to lose it.
> (I, xxiii–xxiv)

Like previous commentators, Johnson allows for a mixture of good and bad
qualities in Shakespeare's work: 'he has scenes of undoubted and perpetual
excellence, but perhaps not one play which, if it were now exhibited as the
work of a contemporary writer, would be heard to its conclusion.' Rather,
Johnson argues, 'it must be at last confessed, that as we owe everything to him,
he owes something to us; that, if much of his praise is paid by perception and
judgement, much is likewise given by custom and veneration' (I, xlvi).

1765–1800: Stage and Page

Johnson's interest in the texts of the plays did not extend to an interest in their
theatrical performance. Sandra Clark describes the eighteenth century's
preference for adapted Shakespeare on the stage as a 'paradox whereby
Shakespeare's works achieved the status of "classics" in the study while for a
long period on the stage the divine Bard (as he came to be called) was often
represented by plays only a small proportion of which he actually wrote' (Clark,
1997: xliii). Shakespeare's position in the theatre during the eighteenth century
was largely dependent on his tragedies, with *The Merchant of Venice*, *The Merry
Wives of Windsor* and various adaptations of *The Tempest* and *The Taming of
the Shrew* lagging behind *Hamlet*, *Macbeth*, *Othello*, *King Lear*, *Romeo and
Juliet*, *Richard III* and *1 Henry IV* in relative performance figures (see Hogan,
1952: II, 715–16). Bell's Acting Edition of 1774, dedicated to David Garrick,
'the best illustrator of, and the best living comment on, Shakespeare' (Bell,
1969: I, 3), presents itself as 'a companion to the theatre' (I, 8) rather than

a critical edition. It prints the texts with the standard performance cuts and emendations, proposing that these changes allow 'the noble monuments he has left us, of unrivalled ability, [to] be restored to due proportion and natural lustre, by sweeping off those cobwebs, and that dust of depraved opinion, which Shakespeare was unfortunately forced to throw on them' (I, 6). Bell's edition also presents itself as an alternative to the increasingly scholarly and specialized writing on Shakespeare, as a forerunner to self-consciously peda- gogic or introductory volumes popular in the twentieth century:

> it has been our peculiar endeavour to render what we call the essence of Shake- speare, more instructive and intelligible; especially to the ladies and to youth; glaring indecencies being removed, and intricate passages explained; and lastly, we have striven to supply plainer ideas of criticism, both in public and private, than we have hitherto met with.
>
> A general view of each play is given, by way of introduction.
>
> Though this is not an edition meant for the profoundly learned, nor the deeply studious, who love to find out, and chase their own critical game; yet we flatter ourselves both parties may perceive fresh ideas started for speculation and reflection. (Bell, 1969: I, 9–10)

The edition's particular stress is on theatrical representation, and it finds many of the plays wanting. *The Winter's Tale* is prefaced: 'that Shakespeare was particularly right in his choice of a title for this piece, very imperfect criticism must allow, for it has all the improbabilities and jumble of incidents, some merry, and some sad, that constitute Christmas stories; there are many beau- ties even in wildness; it is a parterre of poetical flowers sadly choked with weeds' (1969: I, 151); *Twelfth Night* is 'in its plot very complicate, irregular, and in some places incredible. The grave scenes are graceful and familiar: the comic ones full charged with humour; but rather of the obsolete kind . . . Action must render it more pleasing than perusal' (I, 315); '*The Comedy of Errors* does not very obviously produce a moral, but we may deduce from it, that Providence can happily regulate the most perplexed and unpromising cir- cumstances, and change a temporary apparent evil, into a real and lasting good. Patience and submission are herein justly and properly inculcated' (I, 81).

While Shakespeare criticism looks to be a male preserve, women were also increasingly involved. Elizabeth Montagu's *An Essay on the Writings and Genius of Shakespear, compared with the Greek and French Dramatic Poets* (1769) was extensively reprinted and translated. Montagu scorned as narrow-minded critics who criticized Shakespeare's learning:

> For copying nature he found it in the busy walks of human life, he drew from an original, with which the literati are seldom well acquainted. They perceive his

portraits are not of the Grecian or of the Roman school: after finding them unlike to the celebrated forms preserved in learned museums they do not deign to enquire whether they resemble the living persons they were intended to represent. (Montagu, 1970: 17)

It is Shakespeare's facility in drawing recognizable characters that Montagu most admires: he 'seems to have had the art of the Dervise, in the Arabian tales, who could throw his soul into the body of another man, and be at once possessed of his sentiments, adopt his passions, and rise to all the functions and feelings of his situation' (1970: 37). Elizabeth Griffith, in her *The Morality of Shakespeare's Drama Illustrated* (1775), described Shakespeare as a 'Philosopher' whose 'anatomy of the human heart is delineated from *nature*, not from *metaphysics*; referring immediately to our intuitive sense and not wandering with the schoolmen' (Griffith, 1971: ix), and thus, perhaps, uniquely accessible and applicable to contemporary women largely denied a classical education. Like Montagu, Griffith is able to claim authority to write on Shakespeare by wresting him from the enervating grasp of the scholar and reinstating him as the poet of everyday life.

Character study was to be the dominant theme of Romantic criticism of Shakespeare. There were, however, other, now familiar strands emerging. In 1794 Walter Whiter published *A Specimen of a Commentary on Shakespeare. Containing I. Notes on As You Like It. II. An Attempt to Explain and Illustrate various passages on a new principle of criticism, derived from Mr Locke's doctrine of The Association of Ideas*. Whiter explained John Locke's idea of 'association' as 'the combination of those ideas, which have no natural alliance or relation to each other' (Whiter, 1972: 65). Whiter argued that critics had hitherto been preoccupied by discovering:

> the *direct*, though sometimes perhaps obscure allusions, which the poet has *intentionally* made to the customs of his own age, and to the various vices, follies, passions and prejudices, which are the pointed objects of his satire or his praise. But the commentators have not marked those *indirect* and *tacit* references, which are produced by the writer with *no* intentional allusion; or rather they have not unfolded those trains of thought, alike pregnant with the materials *peculiar* to his age, which often prompt the combinations of the poet in the wildest exertions of his fancy, and which conduct him, unconscious of the effect, to the various *peculiarities* of his imagery or his language. (1972: 71–2)

Whiter's careful exposition of linguistic details – his use of analogues from contemporary writing and from elsewhere in Shakespeare's lexicon – marks an early example of something twentieth-century critics as diverse as Caroline Spurgeon and Patricia Parker (see chapter 3 on Language) have developed.

1800–1840: Romantic Critics – Schlegel, Coleridge, Hazlitt

Whereas one major current in eighteenth-century Shakespeare criticism was to sift the plays for their beauties and point out their weaknesses, Romantic critics such as August von Schlegel argued for their 'organic unity', a structural organization intrinsic to the literary work which 'unfolds itself from within' and is not imposed by a framework of rigid classical aesthetics. As Bate (1992) argues, the continuing influence of this method, taken up by I. A. Richards as 'practical criticism', can still be seen in the many educational contexts in which close reading aimed at uncovering organic form is taught and examined (Bate, 1992: 5). In his lectures, translated into English in 1846, Schlegel identifies characterization as one of Shakespeare's most dominant qualities:

> Never, perhaps, was there so comprehensive a talent for characterization as Shakspeare. It . . . grasps every diversity of range, age and sex, down to the lispings of infancy . . . the king and the beggar, the hero and the pickpocket, the sage and the idiot, speak and act with equal truthfulness; not only does he transport himself to distant ages and foreign nations . . . He gives us the history of minds; he lays open to us, in a single word, a whole series of their anterior states. (Schlegel, 1846: 363–4)

His characterization is ironic:

> Shakspeare makes each of his principal characters the glass in which the others are reflected, and by like means enables us to discover what could not be immediately revealed in us . . . Nobody ever painted so truthfully as he has done the facility of self-deception, the half self-conscious hypocrisy towards ourselves, with which even noble minds attempt to disguise the almost inevitable influence of selfish motives in human nature. This secret irony of the characterization commands admiration as the profound abyss of acuteness and sagacity; but it is the grave of enthusiasm. (Schlegel, 1846: 369)

Schlegel praises the comedies' 'powerful impression on the moral feeling' while avoiding the pitfalls of sentimentality or invective (1846: 384). His discussion of individual plays brings out some interesting observations: he judges the Induction to *The Taming of the Shrew* 'more remarkable than the play itself' (1846: 382); in *All's Well that Ends Well*, Parolles is seen as second only to Falstaff in Shakespeare's comic characterization; and of *Measure for Measure*: 'The piece properly takes its name from punishment; the true significance of the whole is the triumph of mercy over strict justice; no man being himself so free from errors as to be entitled to deal it out to his equals.' 'The most beautiful embellishment of the composition' is the character of Isabella; the Duke 'unites in his person the wisdom of the priest and the prince' (1846: 387–8).

Schlegel's enjoyment of the subtleties of Shylock's 'light touch of Judaism in everything he says or does' as he directs his revenge at 'those Christians who are actuated by truly Christian sentiments' requires 'the finished art of a great actor' (1846: 389). *As You Like It* has little plot, 'or rather, what is done is not so essential as what is said', but 'whoever affects to be displeased, if in this romantic forest the ceremonial of dramatic art is not duly observed, ought in justice to be delivered over to the wise fool [Touchstone], to be led gently out of it to some prosaical region' (1846: 391, 392). Schlegel considers *The Tempest* and *A Midsummer Night's Dream* together: Caliban is judged 'in his way, a poetical being; he always speaks in verse' (1846: 395). *The Winter's Tale* Schlegel glosses as:

> one of those tales which are peculiarly calculated to beguile the dreary leisure of a long winter evening, and are even attractive and intelligible to childhood, while animated by a fervent truth in delineation of character and passion, and invested with the embellishments of poetry lowering itself, as it were, to the simplicity of the subject, they transport manhood back to the golden age of imagination. (1846: 396)

Samuel Taylor Coleridge's important observations on Shakespeare are scattered through his papers and the extant accounts of his lectures. In his 'Notes on the Tragedies of Shakespeare', Coleridge argued that the unities of time and place are unnecessary inconveniences which can be dispensed with, and that 'a unity of feeling pervades the whole of his plays' (Hawkes, 1969: 112). Coleridge argues that generic labels based on classical drama are inappropriate in connection with Shakespeare's plays, which are 'in the ancient sense neither tragedies nor comedies, nor both in one, but a different genus, diverse in kind, not merely different in degree – romantic dramas, or dramatic romances' (Hawkes, 1969: 58). Shakespeare's strength is seen in his verisimilitude of character: 'The ordinary reader, who does not pretend to bring his understanding to bear upon the subject, often feels that some real trait of his own has been caught, that some nerve has been touched; and he knows that it has been touched by the vibration he experiences – a thrill which tells us that, by becoming better acquainted with the poet, we have become better acquainted with ourselves' (Hawkes, 1969: 99). This recognition is perhaps epitomized in Coleridge's own claim to 'have a smack of Hamlet myself, if I may say so' (1969: 158).

Coleridge argues that whereas for other writers the main character is also the main agent of the plot, 'In Shakespeare so or not so, as the character is itself calculated or not calculated to form the plot. So Don John, the mainspring of the plot, is merely shown and withdrawn' (Hawkes, 1969: 115). He distinguishes between the titles of the tragedies and those of the comedies, 'when the total effect is produced by a co-ordination of the characters, by a wreath of flowers' (1969: 159). Writing on individual plays, he considers *Love's Labour's Lost* a 'juvenile drama' with characters 'either impersonated out of his own multiformity, by imaginative self-position, or of such as a country town and a school-boy's observation might supply' (1969: 125). He reserves high praise for *The Tempest* as a 'specimen of romantic drama':

> It addresses itself entirely to the imaginative faculty; and though the illusion may be assisted by the effect on the senses of the complicated scenery and decorations of modern times yet this sort of assistance is dangerous. For the principal and only genuine excitement ought to come from within – from the moved and sympathetic imagination; whereas, where so much is addressed to the mere external senses of seeing and hearing the spiritual vision is apt to languish, and the attraction from without will draw the mind from the proper and only legitimate interest which is intended to spring from within. (Hawkes, 1969: 224)

Measure for Measure is 'the single exception to the delightfulness of Shakespeare's plays. It is a hateful work, although Shakespearian throughout. Our feelings of justice are grossly wounded in Angelo's escape. Isabella herself contrives to be unamiable, and Claudio is detestable' (1969: 274).

William Hazlitt's *Characters of Shakespear's Plays* published in 1817 sets out to extend Schlegel's analysis and to illustrate Pope's remarks on Shakespeare's distinctive characterization: 'every single character in Shakespear, is as much an individual as those in life itself' (Hazlitt, 1998: I, 85). His accounts of individual plays cover comedies as well as tragedies: 'Shakespeare's comedy is of a pastoral and poetical cast. Folly is indigenous to the soil, and shoots out with happy, unchecked luxuriance. Absurdity has every encouragement afforded it; and nonsense has room to flourish in' (I, 222). Discussing *Twelfth Night*, Hazlitt suggests that it is 'perhaps too good-natured for comedy. It has little satire, and no spleen. It aims at the ludicrous rather than the ridiculous. It makes us laugh at the follies of mankind, not despise them, and still less bear any ill-will towards them' (I, 221). But it is the serious aspects of comedy that engage Hazlitt most: 'if his inclination to comedy sometimes led him to trifle with the seriousness of tragedy, the poetical and impassioned passages are the best parts of his comedies'. 'Much as we like catches and cakes and ale', Viola is 'the great and secret charm' of *Twelfth Night* (I, 222). Of *The Merchant of Venice* Hazlitt feels 'the desire of revenge is almost inseparable from the sense of wrong', and that we can 'hardly help sympathising' with Shylock (I, 228); *The Winter's Tale* is 'one of the best-acting of our author's plays' (I, 233); the interest of *All's Well that Ends Well* is 'more of a serious than of a comic nature' (I, 237); the chapter on *Love's Labour's Lost* begins: 'if we were to part with any of the author's comedies, it should be this' (I, 240). Hazlitt judges *Much Ado About Nothing* the height of the 'middle point of comedy . . . in which the ludicrous blends with the tender, and our follies, turning round against themselves in support of our affections, retain nothing but their humanity' (I, 246). *As You Like It* emerges as an essentially Romantic drama, in which 'the very air of the place [Arden] seems to breathe a spirit of philosophical poetry: to stir the thoughts, to touch the heart with pity, as the drowsy forest rustles to the sighing gale. Never was there such beautiful moralising, equally free from pedantry or petulance' (I, 247). *The Taming of the Shrew* is the only play to have a 'downright moral': 'how self-will is only to be got the better of by stronger will, and how one degree of ridiculous perversity is only to be driven out by another still greater' (I, 250).

Like many Romantic critics, Hazlitt did not have a high regard for the plays in performance, arguing that 'We do not like to see our author's plays acted' (I, 148), and illustrating this with an account of *A Midsummer Night's Dream*:

> Bottom's head in the play is a fantastic illusion, produced by magic spells: on the stage it is an ass's head and nothing more; certainly a very strange costume for a gentleman to appear in. Fancy cannot be embodied any more than a simile can be painted; and it is as idle to attempt it as to personate *Wall* or *Moonshine* . . . When ghosts appear at mid-day, when apparitions stalk along Cheapside, then may the *Midsummer Night's Dream* be represented without injury at Covent-garden or at Drury-lane. The boards of a theatre and the regions of fancy are not the same thing. (I, 158)

However, in Hazlitt's dramatic criticism published as *A View of the English Stage* (1818), a number of Shakespearian productions are discussed, including Edmund Kean's performance of Shylock, a 'travestie' (Hazlitt, 1998: III, 64) of *The Tempest* at Covent Garden, and a production of *Measure for Measure* which prompts him to reflect that Barnadine is 'what he is by nature, not by circumstance . . . he is Caliban transported to . . . the prisons of Vienna' (III, 115). This repeats, almost word for word, his comments in *Characters of Shakespear's Plays*: here and elsewhere criticism of performance and text cross-fertilize.

Also concerned with characterization is Anna Jameson's *Characteristics of Women, Moral, Poetical, and Historical* (1832), although, as the title of her book suggests, its aims extend beyond Shakespeare criticism and to a defence of female character *per se*. Her first set of heroines are described as 'characters of intellect' (I, 68), including Portia, Isabella, Beatrice and Rosalind. In the trial scene of *The Merchant of Venice*, Portia 'shines forth all her divine self. Her intellectual powers, her elevated sense of religion, her high honourable principles, her best feelings as a woman, are all displayed' (I, 77). Among characters of 'passion and imagination', Jameson includes Helena, whose idolization of a man unworthy of her would be untenable 'if it never happened in real life' (I, 213); Miranda is a combination of 'the purely natural and the purely ideal' (I, 283); Hermione is one of the 'characters of the affections'. Throughout,

Jameson is sympathetic to the heroines' plight, willing to see them as moral exemplars, as accurate portraits, and sometimes, ideally, both.

1840–1905: Bardolatry, Biography and the Division of the Comedies

The worship of Shakespeare's powers which George Bernard Shaw would later dub 'Bardolatry' had its most famous mid-century expression in Thomas Carlyle's 'The Hero as Poet', a chapter in his influential *On Heroes, Hero-worship, and the Heroic in History* (1840): 'here, I say, is an English King, whom no time or chance, Parliament or combination of Parliaments, can dethrone! This King Shakspeare, does not he shine, in crowned sovereignty, over us all, as the noblest, gentlest, yet strongest of rallying-signs; indestructible' (Carlyle, 1993: 97). Like his Romantic predecessors, Carlyle stresses Shakespearian characterization:

> it is in what I called Portrait-painting, delineating of men and things, especially of men, that Shakspeare is great. All the greatness of the man comes out decisively here. It is unexampled, I think, that calm creative perspicacity of Shakspeare. The thing he looks at reveals not this or that face of it, but its inmost heart and generic secret: it dissolves itself as in light before him, so that he discerns the perfect structure of it. Creative, we said: poetic creation, what is this too but *seeing* the thing sufficiently? The *word* that will describe the thing follows, of itself, from such clear intense sight of the thing. And is not Shakspeare's *morality*, his valour, candour, tolerance, truthfulness; his whole victorious strength and greatness, which can triumph over such obstructions, visible there too? Great as the world! No *twisted*, poor convex-concave mirror, reflecting all objects with its own convexities and concavities; a perfectly *level* mirror. (Carlyle, 1993: 97)

In 1844, Matthew Arnold wrote in his sonnet 'Shakespeare': 'Others abide our question. Thou art free. / We stand and ask – Thou smilest and art still, / Out-topping knowledge.' As the Victorian period continued, there were different attempts to escape Arnold's sense of the ultimate unknowability of Shakespeare, and instead to explicate aspects of his writing. Many of these were influenced by the new quasi-scientific methods of bibliographic scholarship expounded by the New Shakspere Society, founded in 1874. The society's aims were set out by its director, F. J. Furnivall, in the prospectus:

> To do honour to Shakspere [Footnote: This spelling of our great Poet's name is taken from the only unquestionably genuine signatures of his that we possess . . . Though it has hitherto been too much to ask people to suppose that Shakspere knew how to spell his own name, I hope the demand may not prove

too great for the imagination of the Members of the new Society], to mark out the succession of his plays, and thereby the growth of his mind and art; to promote the intelligent study of him, and to print Texts illustrating his works and his times, this *New Shakspere Society* is founded. (Furnivall, 1874: n.p.)

Furnivall made explicit the connections between this new branch of literary criticism and the scientific temper of the age:

> Dramatic poet though Shakspere is, bound to lose himself in his wondrous and manifold creations; taciturn 'as the secrets of Nature' though he be; yet in this Victorian time, when our geniuses of Science are so wresting her secrets from Nature as to make our days memorable for ever, the faithful student of Shakspere need not fear that he will be unable to pierce through the crowds of forms that exhibit Shakspere's mind, to the mind itself, the man himself, and see him as he was . . . (Furnivall, 1874: n.p.)

This methodology is developed in R. G. Moulton's study, first published in 1885 as *Shakespeare as a Dramatic Artist: A Popular Illustration of the Principles of Scientific Criticism*. Moulton argued that 'literary criticism should follow other branches of thought in becoming inductive' (1885: 1), and that 'interpretation in literature is of the nature of a scientific hypothesis, the truth of which is tested by the degree of completeness with which it explains the details of the literary works as they actually stand' (1885: 25). Moulton's study discusses *The Tempest, As You Like It* and *Love's Labour's Lost* as part of his thesis that criticism should aim to discover a 'Central Idea' which 'should be shown to embrace all the details of the play [and] it must be sufficiently distinctive to exclude other plays' (1885: 329). This approach would supersede generic considerations: in place of comedy and tragedy Moulton proposes 'Action-Drama' and 'Passion-Drama', arguing that 'the so-called "Comedies" of *The Merchant of Venice* and *Measure for Measure* contain some of the most tragic effects in Shakespeare. The true distinction between the two kinds of plays is one of Movement not Tone' (1885: 372–3).

Furnivall also wrote an introduction to an influential account translated from the German of G. G. Gervinus, *Shakespeare Commentaries* (1877). Gervinus's commentaries covered all the plays. *The Comedy of Errors* and *The Taming of the Shrew* Gervinus allocates to Shakespeare's youthful apprenticeship. The 'love-plays' depict the 'many-sidedness of love and its manifold bearings and effects upon human nature' (1877: 151, 152). In order that Helena in *All's Well that Ends Well* avoid the reader's 'repugnance' at 'such bold and masculine steps', the skills of 'a great actress' are required (1877: 185). Gervinus, in marked contrast to critics writing earlier in the century, urges 'the necessity of seeing Shakespeare's plays performed, in order to be able to estimate them fully' (1877: 201). Gervinus places *All's Well that Ends Well* between

Love's Labour's Lost and *A Midsummer Night's Dream*, a play in which action is motivated by 'caprice' rather than 'character and circumstance' (1877: 188). His account of *The Merchant of Venice* argues that the love affairs are peripheral to the action, which favours 'the most unselfish spiritual love' as the friendship of Antonio and Bassanio: 'for even sexual love, in its purest and deepest form, through the addition of sensual enjoyment, is not in the same measure free from selfishness as friendship is, which, as an inclination of the soul, is wholly based upon the absence of all egotism and self-love' (1877: 237). The central comedies focus on female characters who 'all have more or less something of unwomanly forwardness in their nature, something of domineering superiority; and therefore the men in contact with them play more or less a subordinate part' (1877: 421). What unites these plays is their preoccupation with 'exposing self-love, its self-deceptions and its attempts to deceive others, with unveiling the discrepancy between real and feigned character, with unmasking vanity in fancied gifts and conceit of vain ones' (1877: 374). *Measure for Measure* is the transition towards tragedy, in which the character of Isabella represents 'a type of a *complete* human nature, rendering it plain that all extreme is but imperfect and fragmentary; that moderation is not weakness and indolence; that far rather it forms in man the true moral centre of gravity, which holds him secure from all waverings and errors' (1877: 504).

As the Victorian period advanced, such commentaries on Shakespeare multiplied, and the task of accounting for and explicating not just individual plays but their progress and place in the author's career became more pressing. Following Gervinus's commentaries, a number of book-length studies of Shakespeare's work appeared, of which Edward Dowden's influential *Shakspere: A Critical Study of his Mind and Art* (1875) was pre-eminent. Eschewing the scientific methodologies advocated by Furnivall and later by Moulton, Dowden states his intention: 'To approach Shakspere on the human side is the object of this book' (Dowden, 1875: vi). The human side is that of Shakespeare himself, as the study is concerned 'to connect the study of Shakspere's works with an inquiry after the personality of the writer, and to observe, as far as is possible, in its several stages the growth of his intellect and character from youth to full maturity' (1875: v), and also of his characters. 'Full maturity' seems to equate to the tragedies: Dowden has little to say about the comedies of the 1590s, and rather than considering comedy as a genre, he touches on it in a chapter 'The Humour of Shakespeare'. Dowden argued that 'the humour of Shakspere like his total genius is many-sided', but that 'mere laughter wearies him' (1875: 341–2). Both tragedy and comedy work through incongruity:

> the tragic incongruity arises from the disproportion between the world and the
> soul of man; life is too small to satisfy the soul; the desires of man are infinite;

and all possible attainment exists under strictest limitation. The comic incongruity is the reverse of this. It arises from the disproportion between certain souls of men, and even this very ordinary world of ours. When a man's wits are so unjointed and so ill-trained that, if put into motion, they forthwith get at cross purposes with themselves, while the happy imbecile remains supremely unconscious of his incapacity, we are in the presence of an example of the comic incongruity. (Dowden, 1875: 351)

According to Dowden's account of Shakespeare's literary biography, he moves from the enjoyment of 'fun pure and simple, comic surprises and grotesque incidents' (1875: 358) to a 'tentative period' in which 'the comic and the serious, tender or sentimental elements of the drama exist side by side' (1875: 360). By the time of *As You Like It*, *Much Ado About Nothing* and *Twelfth Night*, Shakespeare 'had entered into vital union with the real life of the world, but . . . he had not started upon any profound enquiry concerning the deeper and more terrible problems of existence' (1875: 369). Dowden's most significant contribution to the understanding of Shakespeare's comedies was his lengthy discussion of the last plays, 'his period of large, serene wisdom'. These plays are connected by something 'spiritual', 'romantic': all are written in 'a spirit of deep or exquisite recreation' (1875: 403). Following on from the tragedies, these plays still consider 'the graver trials and tests which life applies to human character . . . the wrongs which man inflicts on man; but his present temper demanded not a tragic issue, – it rather demanded an issue into joy or peace' (1875: 406). The word which interprets the plays is 'reconciliation', rather than, as in the earlier comedies, 'dénouement'. The resolution of discord is 'not a mere stage necessity . . . Its significance here is ethical and spiritual; it is a moral necessity' (1875: 407). The last of these plays, *The Tempest*, has 'possessed this quality, of soliciting men to attempt the explanation of it, as of an enigma, and at the same time of baffling their enquiry' (1875: 425). Dowden concludes:

> Let us not attenuate Shakspere to a theory . . . Shakspere does not supply us with a doctrine, with an interpretation, with a revelation. What he brings to us, is this – to each one, courage, and energy, and strength, to dedicate himself and his work to that, – whatever it be, – which life has revealed to him as best, and highest, and most real. (1875: 430)

Something of the popularity of Dowden's account can be traced in its frequent reissuing, going through a dozen editions by the end of the nineteenth century.

Dowden's rival for this market was the poet A. C. Swinburne, whose *A Study of Shakespeare* was first published in 1880. Swinburne had his own division of Shakespeare's writing, into a first period, 'lyric and fantastic', a second period, 'comic and historic' and a third, 'tragic and romantic'. Swinburne elaborates that 'it is not, so to speak, the literal but the spiritual order which I have studied to observe and to indicate: the periods which I seek to define belong not to chronology but to art' (Swinburne, 1880: 16). He argued against the New Shakspere Society's preferred scientific metrical analysis as the approach of the 'horny eye and the callous finger of a pedant (1880: 7). Swinburne's criticism was concerned with the change of Shakespeare's language, the growth and development of his verse and tone, but these were modulations that 'can only be traced by ear and not by finger' (1880: 16). Like Coleridge, Swinburne sees traces of Shakespeare's boyhood experience in the evocation of provincial life, this time in *The Merry Wives of Windsor* (1880: 118). Shakespeare's highest achievement in comedy is described:

> There is but just enough of evil or even of passion admitted into their sweet spheres of life to proclaim them living: and all that does find entrance is so tempered by the radiance of the rest that we retain softened and lightened recollections even of Shylock and Don John when we think of the *Merchant of Venice* and *Much Ado About Nothing*; we hardly feel in *As You Like It* the presence or the existence of Oliver and Duke Frederick; and in *Twelfth Night*, for all its name of the midwinter, we find nothing to remember that might jar with the loveliness of love and the summer light of life.

Against this delightful view of comedy, *Measure for Measure* appears in 'its very inmost essence a tragedy' (1880: 203). The late plays are 'Shakespeare's culminant and crowning constellation', and queen of this stellar world is Imogen, 'half glorified already the immortal godhead of womanhood' (1880: 227), the divine name on which Swinburne ends his study.

Walter Pater included essays on *Love's Labour's Lost* and *Measure for Measure* among his *Appreciations* (1889). Pater connects the wordplay and themes of the earlier comedy with Shakespeare's sonnets, and argues that 'play is often that about which people are most serious' (1889: 170). On *Measure for Measure* he speculates that 'the play might well pass for the central expression of [Shakespeare's] moral judgments'. The play combines tragedy and comedy in a 'real example of that sort of writing which is sometimes called *suggestive*, and which by the help of certain subtly calculated hints only, brings into distinct shape the reader's own half-developed imaginings' (1889: 179). Pater suggests that the main interest of the play is not that of its source, Whetstone's *Promos and Cassandra*, in which the central relationship is that of Isabella and Angelo. Rather it is Claudio and Isabella who dominate: Isabella's 'cold, chastened personality' is subjected to 'two sharp, shameful trials' which 'ring out of her a fiery, revealing eloquence' (1889: 184). Claudio is likened to Hamlet, 'with perhaps the most eloquent of all Shakspere's words upon his lips' (1889: 188). Pater's view of the play sees it presenting:

the moral judgments of an observer, of one who sits as a spectator, and knows how the threads in the design before him hold together under the surface: they are the judgments of the humourist also, who follows with a half-amused but always pitiful sympathy, the various ways of human disposition, and sees less distance than ordinary men between what are called respectively great and little things. (1889: 190–1)

The play becomes the exemplar of a moral view of literature: 'true justice is dependent on just those finer appreciations which poetry cultivates in us the power of making' (1889: 191).

Swinburne's untroubled view of the comedies of the 1590s and Pater's particular interest in *Measure for Measure* have their logical development in F. S. Boas's *Shakspere and his Predecessors* (1896). Boas divides the comedies into four sections: early works, a group of plays called 'The Golden Prime of Comedy' (*The Merry Wives of Windsor, Much Ado About Nothing, Twelfth Night* and *As You Like It*), the group of late plays now familiar as 'dramatic romances', and, distinctively, a separate group consisting of *All's Well that Ends Well, Measure for Measure, Troilus and Cressida* and *Hamlet*. The influential name, derived from contemporary categorizations of dramatists such as Ibsen, given to this group was 'problem plays'. Boas characterized the problem plays as the bridge between 'comedies of matchless charm and radiance' before 1601, and plays 'in which comedy for the most part takes the grim form of dramatic satire' (1896: 344):

All these dramas introduce us into highly artificial societies, whose civilization is ripe unto rottenness. Amidst such media abnormal conditions of brain and emotion are generated, and intricate cases of conscience demand a solution by unprecedented methods. Thus throughout these plays we move along dim and untrodden paths, and at the close our feeling is neither of simple joy nor pain; we are excited, fascinated, perplexed, for the issues raised preclude a completely satisfactory outcome, even when, as in *All's Well* and *Measure for Measure*, the complications are outwardly adjusted in the fifth act. (Boas, 1896: 345)

This categorization is echoed by George Bernard Shaw: 'Shakspeare's bitter play with a bitter title, *All's Well that Ends Well*, anticipates Ibsen: the happy ending at which the title sneers is less comforting than the end of *Romeo and Juliet*. And Ibsen was the dramatic poet who firmly established tragic-comedy as a much deeper and grimmer entertainment than tragedy' (Wilson, 1969: 260). Shaw's championing of these problem plays was reiterated: in a summary of his views on Shakespeare printed in a newspaper in 1905, he preferred the 'real studies of life and character in – for instance – *Measure for Measure* and *All's Well that Ends Well*', but 'the public would not have them, and remains of the same mind still, preferring a fantastic sugar doll, like Rosalind, to such serious and dignified studies of women as Isabella and Helena' (Wilson, 1969: 26), and later he identified these same 'unpopular plays' with a Shakespeare 'ready and willing to start at the twentieth century if the seventeenth would only let him' (1969: 266). By contrast, he argues that Shakespeare 'had no idea of comedy', and gives as his example the failure of the characterization of Claudio in *Much Ado About Nothing*: 'Shakespear, for want of comedic faculty, gets no dramatic value out of him whatever, and fails to convey to the audience anything except a disagreeable impression of a conventional hero who is driven by the mere letter of the plot' (1969: 165–6).

A companion to this volume, the *Blackwell Guide to Criticism, Shakespeare's Tragedies*, ends the section on pre-twentieth-century criticism with A. C. Bradley's monumental *Shakespearean Tragedy* (1904). There is no such statement in criticism of the comedies, which, by the end of the nineteenth century, were repeatedly subdivided with implicit reference to some ideal, unarticulated form of comedy. Following Boas's taxonomy of early, golden, problem and late plays, individual plays are variously idealized or pathologized: no theory of comedy as capacious as that embedded in the catalogue of the First Folio exists. All of these internal categories of comedy tend to be described in relation to the tragedies which are the teleological focus of most critics' attention. Perhaps Umberto Eco's conceit, in his medieval whodunit *The Name of the Rose* (1984), which centres on a crucially lost treatise on comedy by Aristotle, points to one reason for its relative neglect among classically trained readers and scholars: the absence of ancient critical precedent. With a few scattered exceptions, it was not until the twentieth century that the critical structures of myth, of social history and gender relations, and of psychoanalytic theories of comedy were to offer a vocabulary and a framework in which Shakespeare's comedies, severally and as a genre, could be more fully and sustainedly appreciated.

References and Further Reading

Bate, Jonathan (1989) *Shakespearean Constitutions: Politics, Theatre, Criticism 1730–1830*. Oxford: Clarendon Press.
——(1992) *The Romantics on Shakespeare*. New Penguin Shakespeare Library. London: Penguin.
Bell, John (1969) *Bell's Edition of Shakespeare's Plays* (1774), 8 vols. London: Cornmarket Press.
Boas, Frederick Samuel (1896) *Shakspere and his Predecessors*. London.
Bradley, A. C. (1904) *Shakespearean Tragedy: Lectures on Hamlet, Othello, King Lear, Macbeth*. London: Macmillan.
Carlyle, Thomas (1993) *On Heroes, Hero-worship, and the Heroic in History* (1840). Berkeley, CA: University of California Press.

Clark, Sandra (1997) *Shakespeare Made Fit: Restoration Adaptations of Shakespeare.* London: Dent.

Dennis, John (1712) *An Essay on the Genius and Writings of Shakespear.* London.

Dobson, Michael (1992) *The Making of the National Poet: Shakespeare, Adaptation and Authorship, 1660–1769.* Oxford: Clarendon Press.

Donaldson, Ian (ed.) (1985) *Ben Jonson.* Oxford: Oxford University Press.

Dowden, Edward (1875) *Shakspere: A Critical Study of his Mind and Art.* London.

Dryden, John (1969) *Of Dramatic Poesie* (1668). Menston: Scolar Press.

Fuller, Thomas (1662) *The History of the Worthies of England.* London.

Furnivall, F. J. (1874) 'New Shakspere Society prospectus', *Transactions of the New Shakspere Society*, 1.

Gervinus, G. G. (1877) *Shakespeare Commentaries*, trans. F. E. Bunnett, new rev. edn. London.

Gildon, Charles (1718) *The Complete Art of Poetry*, 2 vols. London.

Griffith, Elizabeth (1971) *The Morality of Shakespeare's Drama Illustrated* (1775). London: Frank Cass.

Hawkes, Terence (ed.) (1969) *Coleridge on Shakespeare.* Harmondsworth: Penguin.

Hazlitt, William (1998) *The Selected Writings of William Hazlitt*, 9 vols, ed. Duncan Wu. London: Pickering and Chatto.

Hogan, Charles Beecher (1952) *Shakespeare in the Theatre, 1701–1800.* Oxford: Clarendon Press.

Jameson, Anna Brownell (1832) *Characteristics of Women, Moral, Poetical, and Historical*, 2 vols. London.

Johnson, Samuel (ed.) (1765) *The Plays of William Shakespeare*, 10 vols. London.

LeWinter, Oswald (1970) *Shakespeare in Europe.* Harmondsworth: Penguin.

Meres, Francis (1598) *Palladis Tamia. Wits Treasury: The Second Part of Wits Commonwealth.* London.

Montagu, Elizabeth Robinson (1970) *An Essay on the Writings and Genius of Shakespear* (1769). London: Frank Cass.

Moulton, Richard Green (1885) *Shakespeare as a Dramatic Artist: A Popular Illustration of the Principles of Scientific Criticism.* Oxford: Clarendon Press.

Pater, Walter (1889) *Appreciations, with an Essay on Style.* London.

Pope, Alexander and Rowe, Nicholas (1725) *The Works of Shakespear: In Six Volumes.* London.

Rowe, Nicholas (1709–10) *The Works of Mr William Shakespear: Revis'd and Corrected, with an Account of the Life and Writings of the Author, by N. Rowe*, 7 vols. London.

Schlegel, August Wilhelm von (1846) *A Course of Lectures on Dramatic Art and Literature*, ed. John Black and A. J. W. Morrison. London.

Schoenbaum, Samuel (1975) *William Shakespeare: A Documentary Life.* Oxford: Clarendon Press in association with Scolar Press.

Swinburne, Algernon Charles (1880) *A Study of Shakespeare.* London: Chatto and Windus.

Taylor, Gary (1991) *Reinventing Shakespeare: A Cultural History from the Restoration to the Present.* London: Viking.

Theobald, Lewis (1726) *Shakespeare Restored: or, a Specimen of Many Errors, as well Committed, and Unamended, by Mr Pope in his Late Edition of this Poet. London.*
——(1733) *The Works of Shakespeare: in Seven Volumes.* London.
Thompson, Ann and Roberts, Sasha (1997) *Women Reading Shakespeare, 1660–1900: An Anthology of Criticism.* Manchester: Manchester University Press.
Vickers, Brian (1974) *Shakespeare: The Critical Heritage*, 6 vols. London: Routledge and Kegan Paul.
Wells, Stanley W. and Taylor, Gary (1986) *William Shakespeare: The Complete Works.* Oxford: Clarendon Press.
Whiter, Walter (1972) *A Specimen of a Commentary on Shakespeare* (1794). Menston: Scolar Press.
Wilson, Edwin (1969) *Shaw on Shakespeare.* Harmondsworth: Penguin.
Woudhuysen, H. R. (1989) *Samuel Johnson on Shakespeare.* New Penguin Shakespeare Library. London: Penguin.

2

Genre

The group of plays listed by the First Folio catalogue as comedies has been the one most susceptible to redefinition and subdivision by subsequent critics. Following nineteenth-century divisions of the plays by date and tone, much mid-twentieth-century criticism was concerned either to reify these distinctions or to account for the development of Shakespeare's use of comedy through his career.

Developing Boas's description 'problem plays' (see p. 25), W. W. Lawrence was concerned with *Shakespeare's Problem Comedies* (1931) – *Measure for Measure*, *All's Well that Ends Well* and *Troilus and Cressida* – which he saw as distinct from the plays which had gone before: 'Instead of gay pictures of cheerful scenes, to be accepted with a smile and a jest, we are frequently offered unpleasant and sometimes even repulsive episodes, and characters whose conduct gives rise to sustained questioning of action and motive' (Lawrence, 1960: 3). This description of the particular characteristics of the 'problem comedies' shows how the definition was often based on suppressing any possible dark elements in the non-problem comedies. E. M. W. Tillyard's *Shakespeare's Problem Plays* (1950) reintroduced discussion of *Hamlet* alongside the others as a group 'powerfully united by a serious tone amounting at times to sombreness; they show a strong awareness of evil, without being predominantly pessimistic' (1950: 13). Tillyard argued that the two distinctive interests of the problem plays 'in speculative thought and in the working of the human mind' were both strength and weakness: 'they create a peculiar sense of real life but they prevent the sharp clarity of intention we are apt to demand of very great art' (1950: 14). A. P. Rossiter, in his lectures published as *Angel with Horns* (1961), preferred the term 'tragi-comedy' to 'problem plays', arguing succinctly that 'tragi-comedy is an art of inversion, deflation and paradox', and that the plays are characterized by 'scepticism' rather than cynicism (1961: 117, 116). In *The Myth of Deliverance* (1938), Northrop Frye considers the problem plays,

Measure for Measure, All's Well that Ends Well and *Troilus and Cressida. Measure for Measure* he describes as 'a comedy about comedy' (1938: 25) and draws structural and thematic parallels with the romances; the bed-tricks in *Measure* and *All's Well* function as 'an image of passage through death to new life, a passion-motivated descent into an illusion that reverses itself and turns to reality and renewed energy' (1938: 53). *Troilus and Cressida* is included as an ironic comedy, which, rather than dramatizing Frye's central theme of the 'myth of deliverance', shows 'human beings getting into the kind of mess that requires deliverance, a secular counterpart of what Christianity calls the fall of man' (1938: 62). Richard Wheeler's *Shakespeare's Development and the Problem Comedies* (1981) discusses the problem plays' incorporation of elements from earlier and later comedies, and the ways in which 'the marriages that conclude *All's Well* and *Measure for Measure* seem only superficially to resolve antagonisms that have developed between degraded sexual desire and the moralized social orders of these two plays' (1981: 3). Wheeler's analysis of genre within a psychological model of conflict and development stresses individual, sexual and social identities as part of the problematic of the problem plays.

Developing Dowden's categorization of 'romance' (see p. 23), numerous critics have considered Shakespeare's last plays, often including *Cymbeline* and *King Henry VIII*, as a separate generic group. G. Wilson Knight's *The Crown of Life* (1947) interpreted these late plays as 'the inevitable development of the questioning, the pain, the profundity and the grandeur of the plays they succeed' – the 'sequence from tragedy to myth' (1947: 9, 27). 'The Final Plays of Shakespeare must be read as myths of immortality' (1947: 30): they are an organic part of a thematically and temperamentally unified Shakespearian world. In his *Shakespeare and the Romance Tradition* (1949), E. C. Pettet argues that Shakespeare's movement from romantic comedy to tragedy to romance is partly motivated from within and partly by the influence of popular romances by Beaumont and Fletcher. Frances A. Yates, in her *Shakespeare's Last Plays: A New Approach* (1975), argues for the importance of the Elizabethan revival of the Jacobean period to the ideas of religion and politics discussed in the plays (see also chapter 5 for works which develop this approach). Howard Felperin's *Shakespearean Romance* (1972) discusses the category 'romance' within Shakespeare's work and elsewhere. He suggests that Shakespeare's romances 'are on one level a stern reprimand of romance (while remaining romance) and test to the breaking point not only the characters they contain but the mode they employ. The moral and mimetic dimension of Shakespearean romance comes into being through its stubborn refusal to accept and repeat the conventions of romance without revaluating them' (Felperin, 1972: 54). Felperin includes a final section on the history of criticism of the romances: this supplements Philip Edwards's analysis of twentieth-century views in 'Shakespeare's Romances: 1900–1957' (1958).

Simon Palfrey's *Late Shakespeare: A New World of Words* (1997) discusses the plays in the category of romance and as political documents: 'the romances explore what it means to be a subject: an agent of the self, within the state, seeking for satisfaction. And so the epitomic figures are the ones denied their place at the centre: not only the rogues, slaves, fishers, and vagabonds, but the itinerant princes and, crucially, the exiled women' (1997: 265). Ruth Nevo's *Shakespeare's Other Language* (1987) sees the late plays as 'beyond genre', but also considers the relationship between 'the mode of tragicomedy and the state, or work, of mourning' (1987: 5) within a Freudian psychoanalytic framework. Anthologies of essays on the late plays include *Later Shakespeare*, edited by John Russell Brown and Bernard Harris (1966) and Carol Kay and Henry Jacobs's *Shakespeare's Romances Reconsidered* (1978); more recently, two collections of essays, Kiernan Ryan's *Shakespeare: The Last Plays* (1999) and Jennifer Richards and James Knowles's *Shakespeare's Late Plays: New Readings* (1999), present studies of individual plays as well as considering the interconnections between them.

The idea of myth as a key to comedy has been extensively discussed. In *Shakespeare's Festive Comedy: A Study of Dramatic Form and its Relation to Social Custom* (1959) C. L. Barber deals with the comedies of the 1590s, in which 'the saturnalian pattern appears in many variations, all of which involve inversion, statement and counterstatement, and a basic movement which can be summarised in the formula, through release to clarification' (1959: 4). He relates the drama to Elizabethan holiday observances and behaviours, including the traditions of the Lord of Misrule and other rituals of inversion and carnival. Thus *A Midsummer Night's Dream* is seen in the context of May games and *The Merchant of Venice* becomes a ritual of scapegoating in which the outsider is ridiculed and expelled. The problem plays offer 'vicious or perverse release [which] leads to developments of absorbing interest' and tend to dwell on 'situation and motives where the energies of life lead to degradation or destruction' (1959: 259). The ritual experience of festival customs suggested by Barber is discussed more extensively and with more emphasis on documentary historical evidence in François Laroque's *Shakespeare's Festive World: Elizabethan Seasonal Entertainment and the Professional Stage* (1991). Northrop Frye's *A Natural Perspective: The Development of Shakespearean Comedy and Romance* (1965) also associates comedy with the popular, the conventional and the mythic. His discussion of the idea of the happy ending in relation to Claudio in *Much Ado* makes clear the importance of structure rather than mood:

> The real critical question involved here is: Does anything that exhibits the structure of a comedy have to be taken as a comedy, regardless of its content or of our attitude to that content? The answer is clearly yes. A comedy is not a play

which ends happily: it is a play in which a certain structure is present and works through to its own logical end, whether we or the cast or the author feel happy about it or not. (Frye, 1965: 46).

By using romance, folklore and classical forms, Shakespeare attempts 'to establish contact with a universal and worldwide dramatic tradition' (1965: 58): 'an anticomic society, a social organization blocking and opposed to the comic drive, which the action of the comedy evades or overcomes' (1965: 73). Comic endings, according to Frye, are a fantasy of wish-fulfilment:

> the irrational society represents social reality, the obstacles to our desires that we recognise in the world around us, whereas the society of the conclusion is the realising of what we want but seldom expect to see. The drive toward a festive conclusion, then, is the creation of a new reality out of something impossible but desirable. The action of comedy is intensely Freudian in shape: the erotic pleasure principle explodes underneath the social anxieties sitting on top of it and blows them sky-high. But in comedy we see a victory of the pleasure principle that Freud warns us not to look for in ordinary life. (Frye, 1965: 75–6)

Other critics have attempted to find unifying themes across the genre. H. B. Charlton's *Shakespearian Comedy* (1938) sees a progress from early romantic comedy to its consummation in the *Much Ado, Twelfth Night, As You Like It* group, in which Shakespeare's 'vision of the reach of human happiness in this world of men and women is richer, deeper, more sustained, and more satisfying than in any other of his plays' (Charlton, 1938: 266). Charlton includes the problem plays and challenges the idea that they are dark in tone; rather, they dramatize 'an intense impulse to discover the true sources of nobility in man and of joy in life' (1938: 211). 'Shakespearian comedy is not finally satiric; it is poetic. It is not conservative; it is creative. The way of it is that of the imagination rather than that of pure reason' (1938: 278). The plays reveal that 'love is the one way to supreme happiness on this earth' (1938: 297). Alexander Leggatt's *Shakespeare's Comedy of Love* (1974) discusses the interplay between convention and variety in the comedies up to *Twelfth Night*, arguing that a disordered world is increasingly shown beyond the ordered comic conclusion and that this scepticism about artificial control in comic form gains its fullest expression in the problem plays. The romances return to the image of character subservient to a total vision of order after the tragedies have explored the primacy of the individual. John Russell Brown, writing *Shakespeare and his Comedies* in 1957, reproached earlier critics for their implicit denigration of the comedies, and argued that the appreciation of these plays, in the theatre and the study, lagged behind the tragedies and histories. His identification of the themes of 'love's wealth', 'love's truth' and 'love's order' saw the playwright presenting 'a comprehensive and developing view of love and personal relationships, and of life itself as experienced through such relationships' (Brown, 1962: 201). John Dover Wilson's significantly titled *Shakespeare's Happy Comedies* (1962) and Ruth Nevo's *Comic Transformations in Shakespeare* (1980) also end with *Twelfth Night*: Nevo sees Shakespeare's increasing mastery of the genre from his initial dependence on New Comedy models. She argues that Shakespearian comedy offers a different type of catharsis, as the plays present remedies for emotional excitement in a manner analogous to that of Aristotelian theories of tragedy.

Kenneth Muir divides the plays into 'Experiment', 'Maturity', 'Problem Comedies' and 'Tragicomedies' for his *Shakespeare's Comic Sequence* (1979), although he prefaces the study with the remark that 'there is no Shakespearian Comedy; there are only Shakespearian comedies' (1979: 1). Robert Ornstein's study *Shakespeare's Comedies* is subtitled 'From Roman Farce to Romantic Mystery' (1986), but sees an essential congruity in the plays and in responses to them 'that testifies to the essential clarity and wholeness of Shakespeare's artistic vision' (1986: 248). Ornstein stresses, however, the willed discomfort of some aspects of the comedies and argues that these elements cannot and should not be explained away: 'we should be able to accept the note of sadness and awareness of human limitations that make the laughter of the comedies so much more precious and meaningful' (1986: 250).

In his *Love and Society in Shakespearean Comedy* (1985), Richard Levin confines himself to discussion of *Merchant*, *Much Ado* and *Twelfth Night* as expressions 'of a single theory of comedy' (1985: 13): the depiction of individuals within social settings. By contrast, Ralph Berry's *Shakespeare's Comedies: Explorations in Form* (1972) stresses multiplicity rather than generic uniformity or progression. Berry argues against Barber and others who stress 'festive' as the governing mood of Shakespearian comedy, suggesting instead that the plays 'permit a distance between our impulse to participate in the feast, and our awareness of the undercurrents and reservations present in the final situation' (Berry, 1972: 15). Berry remarks that 'one comes, then, to see the comedies as a means of preparation for the tragedies. That is the effect, if not the purpose, of the dramas that I discern. The tragedies were always going to be written. The conclusions implied, but not stated in the comedies, were one day to be pursued' (1972: 23). J. Dennis Huston's *Shakespeare's Comedies of Play* (1981) encourages us to reassess and revalue the early comedies for 'their creative energy, their exuberant experimentation with dramatic convention and, ultimately, their joy in the theatrical medium and in the act of play-making itself' (1981: 2). Pamela Mason's collection of essays on *Shakespeare's Early Comedies* (1995) includes a range of critical material on *Two Gentlemen*, *Taming*, *Comedy* and *Love's Labour's Lost*. Other anthologies include D. J. Palmer's *Shakespeare's*

Later Comedies (1971), and Gary Waller's excellent selection of recent criticism across a range of approaches in *Shakespeare's Comedies* (1991).

Robert Miola's *Shakespeare and Classical Comedy* (1994) discusses the influence of Plautus and Terence, and the ways in which Shakespeare interrogates and reformulates the legacy of Roman New Comedy. Plautine influences are also extensively discussed in Wolfgang Riehle's *Shakespeare, Plautus and the Humanist Tradition* (1990). In *Shakespeare and the Traditions of Comedy* (1974), Leo Salingar discusses a range of influences, from medieval, classical and Italianate sources, which shape Shakespeare's deployment of the comedic genre. Salingar argues that Shakespeare's comedies are 'essentially celebrations of marriage, of the approach to marriage, which he presents in a social as well as a personal aspect': 'by the end of the comedy marriage appears as the resolution of the broader tensions, as the type or focus of harmony in society as a whole' (1974: 17). Marriages as definitive of comedy are discussed by Lisa Hopkins in the following reading.

References and Further Reading

Barber, C. L. (1959) *Shakespeare's Festive Comedy: A Study of Dramatic Form and its Relation to Social Custom*. Princeton, NJ: Princeton University Press.

Berry, Ralph (1972) *Shakespeare's Comedies: Explorations in Form*. Princeton, NJ: Princeton University Press.

Brown, John Russell (1957) *Shakespeare and his Comedies*. London: Methuen, 2nd edn, 1962.

——and Harris, Bernard (eds) (1966) *Later Shakespeare*. Stratford-upon-Avon Studies 8. London: Edward Arnold.

Charlton, H. B. (1938) *Shakespearian Comedy*. London: Methuen.

Edwards, Philip (1958) 'Shakespeare's romances: 1900–1957', *Shakespeare Survey*, 11: 1–18.

Felperin, Howard (1972) *Shakespearean Romance*. Princeton, NJ: Princeton University Press.

Frye, Northrop (1938) *The Myth of Deliverance: Reflections on Shakespeare's Problem Comedies*. Brighton: Harvester.

——(1965) *A Natural Perspective: The Development of Shakespearean Comedy and Romance*. New York: Harcourt Brace and World.

Hopkins, Lisa (1998) *The Shakespearean Marriage: Merry Wives and Heavy Husbands*. Basingstoke: Macmillan.

Huston, J. Dennis (1981) *Shakespeare's Comedies of Play*. London: Macmillan.

Kay, Carol McGinnis and Jacobs, Henry E. (eds) (1978) *Shakespeare's Romances Reconsidered*. Lincoln, NB: University of Nebraska Press.

Knight, George Wilson (1947) *The Crown of Life: Essays in Interpretation of Shakespeare's Final Plays*. London: Oxford University Press.

Laroque, François (1991) *Shakespeare's Festive World: Elizabethan Seasonal Entertainment and the Professional Stage.* Cambridge: Cambridge University Press.

Lawrence, William Witherle (1931) *Shakespeare's Problem Comedies.* New York: F. Ungar, 2nd edn, 1960.

Leggatt, Alexander (1974) *Shakespeare's Comedy of Love.* London: Methuen.

——(2001) *The Cambridge Companion to Shakespearian Comedy.* Cambridge: Cambridge University Press.

Levin, Richard (1985) *Love and Society in Shakespearean Comedy: A Study of Dramatic Form and Content.* Newark: University of Delaware Press.

Mason, Pamela (ed.) (1995) *Shakespeare's Early Comedies.* Basingstoke: Macmillan.

Miola, Robert S. (1994) *Shakespeare and Classical Comedy: The Influence of Plautus and Terence.* Oxford: Clarendon Press.

Muir, Kenneth (1979) *Shakespeare's Comic Sequence.* Liverpool: Liverpool University Press.

Nevo, Ruth (1980) *Comic Transformations in Shakespeare.* London: Methuen.

——(1987) *Shakespeare's Other Language.* London: Methuen.

Ornstein, Robert (1986) *Shakespeare's Comedies: From Roman Farce to Romantic Mystery.* Newark: University of Delaware Press.

Palfrey, Simon (1997) *Late Shakespeare: A New World of Words.* Oxford English Monographs. Oxford: Clarendon Press.

Palmer, D. J. (ed.) (1971) *Shakespeare's Later Comedies: An Anthology of Modern Criticism.* Penguin Shakespeare Library. Harmondsworth: Penguin.

Pettet, E. C. (1949) *Shakespeare and the Romance Tradition.* London: Staples Press.

Richards, Jennifer and Knowles, James (eds) (1999) *Shakespeare's Late Plays: New Readings.* Edinburgh: Edinburgh University Press.

Riehle, Wolfgang (1990) *Shakespeare, Plautus and the Humanist Tradition.* Cambridge: D. S. Brewer.

Rossiter, A. P. (1961) *Angels with Horns: Fifteen Lectures on Shakespeare.* London: Longman.

Ryan, Kiernan (ed.) (1999) *Shakespeare: The Last Plays.* Longman Critical Readers. London: Longman.

Salingar, Leo (1974) *Shakespeare and the Traditions of Comedy.* London: Cambridge University Press.

Tillyard, E. M. W. (1950) *Shakespeare's Problem Plays.* London: Chatto and Windus.

Uphaus, Robert W. (1981) *Beyond Tragedy: Structure and Experience in Shakespeare's Romances.* Lexington, KY: University Press of Kentucky.

Waller, Gary (ed.) (1991) *Shakespeare's Comedies.* London: Longman.

Wheeler, Richard P. (1981) *Shakespeare's Development and the Problem Comedies: Turn and Counter-turn.* Berkeley, CA: University of California Press.

Wilson, John Dover (1962) *Shakespeare's Happy Comedies.* London: Faber and Faber.

Yates, Frances Amelia (1975) *Shakespeare's Last Plays: A New Approach.* London: Routledge and Kegan Paul.

Marriage as Comic Closure

Lisa Hopkins

Hopkins's account of Shakespearian comedy's 'pervading obsession with marriage' discusses the ways in which the genre continually disrupts the expectation of conclusive marriage. By questioning the plays' nod towards generic closure and interrogating the particular relationships solemnized in final marriages, Hopkins stresses their disquiet and discontinuities rather than their harmonious resolution. Marriage emerges as a tool of generic – and, by implication, societal – regulation rather than its unproblematic finale. Elsewhere in Hopkins's book she discusses the role of marriage in other Shakespearian genres.

Lisa Hopkins, 'Marriage as Comic Closure', in *The Shakespearean Marriage: Merry Wives and Heavy Husbands* (Basingstoke: Macmillan, 1998), pp. 16–33.

The most outstanding feature of Shakespearean comedy is its pervading obsession with marriage. In many instances single or multiple marriages are used to provide comic closure, as in *As You Like It* and *Love's Labour's Lost*, in which four couples marry or are expected to marry, *A Midsummer Night's Dream* and *Twelfth Night*, in each of which three couples marry, and *Much Ado About Nothing* and *Two Gentlemen of Verona*, in each of which two couples marry. In other examples the very fact of marriage is used as the mainspring of the comedy, as in *The Merry Wives of Windsor*, where the very title of the play indicates the importance of marriage, or, to a lesser extent, *The Comedy of Errors*, *The Merchant of Venice* and *The Taming of the Shrew*, in each of which a marital relationship plays a central part. Indeed, marriage is so central a topic in Shakespearean comedy that it is the presence of marriages in their plots which has problematised the genre classifications of both the late romances and the two 'dark' comedies, *Measure for Measure* and *All's Well that Ends Well*, and which provides the main justification for whatever claim they are accorded to be treated as comedies.[1] We know, moreover, that many of Shakespeare's comedies bear clear marks of having been written expressly for performance as part of the celebrations surrounding the solemnisation of actual marriages, so that the connection would have been still more obvious to their original audiences.

But for all that the plays can indeed be grouped together with reasonable accuracy into these broad classifications, to do so obscures both some significant and some interesting differences between them, and also the problematic ways in which marriage is generally treated in these plays. For one thing, despite the traditional view that marriage provides comic closure, this is, in fact, very rarely achieved.[2] The idea is of course drawn on – the audience is repeatedly encouraged to expect that the proceedings will be appropriately closed with a wedding – but these expectations are then either disappointed, or gratified in such a way that the spectator will be forced to question both the meaning of the events he or she has witnessed and also the assumptions underlying his or her response to the events.

Marriage is appropriate as a provider of closure for comedy because it focuses primarily on the experience of the group, as opposed to the individualist, isolationist emphasis of tragedy. The tragic hero lives and dies a fundamentally lonely figure, traumatically separated from his God, his society and his surroundings. Marriage both counters this element of separation by showing humans in a relationship which is, in theory at least, one of indissoluble bonding, and also holds out the promise of renewed life in the birth of offspring (referred to both in the words of the marriage ceremony and in Elizabethan wedding customs, and assumed to be the inevitable product of all heterosexual intercourse).[3] The ultimate polar opposite of the tragic closure provided by death would of course be birth itself, which is indeed sometimes used in this symbolic sense (*All's Well that Ends Well* may be taken as an example of this); but birth, too, places primacy on the experience of the isolated individual, and the social ritual of marriage, with its stress on continuity and group survival, therefore provides a more effective counterbalance to the finality implied in the death of the tragic individual.

Such an emphasis on continuity is undoubtedly present in much of Shakespeare's work. It can be traced explicitly through the first 18 of his sonnets, and it can also be detected in Oberon's blessing of the bridal bed in *A Midsummer Night's Dream*, and in Rosalind's reference to Orlando, almost as soon as she sees him, as 'my child's father'.[4] It is also possible to discern in Shakespeare's comedies clear signs of the conservatism which is so often felt to flourish in comedy: the lovers in *A Midsummer Night's Dream* may flee from Athens at the outset of the play in rebellion against the patriarchal order articulated by Theseus and Egeus, but they do so only to find themselves in a wood ruled by a patriarch just as powerful (a point neatly made by the theatrical tradition of using the actor who plays Theseus to double Oberon), and at the end of the play the two couples willingly return to the society from which they had fled to take their allotted parts as leading members of it and, no doubt, to assist in its perpetuation. In similar fashion, Rosalind, Celia, Oliver and Orlando return from the Forest of Arden, where they had so briefly glimpsed a world in which traditional gender roles could be reversed and the patriarchal system of property division overturned by Oliver's renunciation of his patrimony in favour of Orlando, to take their places in the hierarchy of the court;

and in *The Two Gentlemen of Verona* the excursion into the forest of Valentine, Proteus, Silvia and Julia merely enables them to return to the city properly established as clearly defined couples. In *Hamlet* and *King Lear*, *Othello* and *Macbeth*, worlds may be broken and assumptions overturned; in the comic universe, however, the world not only remains fundamentally the same, but is indeed reinforced by the reaffirmation of that most basic of all props of social and patriarchal order, marriage.

Although these elements of conservatism may doubtless be traced, other factors, far more radical, are also at work. It is noteworthy that although single or multiple marriages are almost invariably the obvious goal of Shakespearean comedy and are clearly signalled from the outset, either by such transparent devices as the King of Navarre's misogyny,[5] which is clearly riding for a fall, or by the even more obvious sign of a crucially placed, slow-paced meeting between the hero and heroine such as that between Rosalind and Orlando, this expected telos is only very rarely attained within the confines of the play itself. The truism that Shakespeare's comedies all end with marriages is not true. There was of course no theoretical prescription that all comedies should end thus – indeed, comedy in general lacked a theory such as that supplied by Aristotle for tragedy – but there was nevertheless a growing tradition which established marriage as the goal at least of romantic comedy. That tradition Shakespeare habitually disrupts.

As You Like It

As You Like It may appear to contradict this assertion immediately, since it closes with not one but four weddings: those of Rosalind and Orlando, Celia and Oliver, Silvius and Phebe and Touchstone and Audrey.[6] But although the audience certainly perceives these couples as having been finally united and receives the appropriate sense of comic closure, the weddings do not take place on stage, or indeed within the timescale of the play at all. Rosalind and Celia are brought on to the stage by what the New Penguin editor terms 'a masquer representing Hymen'.[7] In the theatre this part is usually taken by the actor who plays Corin, one of the few named characters who does not have to appear on stage at this time; but there is some residual ambiguity about whether we are to perceive this as a metatheatrical doubling or one operating and acknowledged within the fictional world of the play – whether we are to see it as one actor doubling two parts which have no necessary connection between them other than the fact that they never appear on stage at the same time, or whether we are to assume that Rosalind and Celia, having no one else to whom they can turn, have taken Corin into their confidence and asked him to represent Hymen in the masque that they wish to stage.[8] Trivial though this point may seem, it may nevertheless be of some interest; if the masquer is obviously Corin in disguise, and is visibly perceived as such by the other characters on stage, then the whole affair is going to seem very much less mysterious than it might otherwise do. The supernatural elements which Rosalind has earlier tried to invoke with her claim to be the nephew of a magician will be at once debunked, and it will even be apparent to the quick-witted where Rosalind has been hiding all this time, and how the whole scene has been stage-managed. (That this *is* apparent to the characters seems clearly suggested by the fact that nobody ever troubles to explain it, and by Phebe's immediate exclamation 'If sight and shape be true, / Why then, my love adieu!') However, to have Corin taking part in a masque will provide a visual blending of country character with courtly form, offering an image of that utopian mingling of classes which Arden may initially have seemed to promise but which it has never, until now, achieved, so that a sense of magic lost in one area may perhaps be miraculously regained in another.

Whoever plays Hymen, however, one thing is certain: he is not competent to perform a marriage. Indeed he explicitly admits as much in his words to the Duke:

> Good Duke receive thy daughter,
> Hymen from heaven brought her,
>   Yea brought her hither,
> That thou mightst join her hand with his
> Whose heart within his bosom is.
>   (V. iv. 110–14)

The god of marriage, then, seems to be transferring his responsibilities to the Duke; but the Duke is no more able than he to conduct the ceremony. It would, of course, be normally expected that he would have to give his consent, but even that seems to be pre-empted when, immediately after Hymen's speech, Rosalind intervenes:

> Rosalind: [*To the Duke*] To you I give myself, for I am yours.
> [*To Orl.*] To you I give myself, for I am yours.
>   (V. iv. 115–16)

At the same time as she reinscribes herself within the patriarchal order by investing her rights in herself in her father, she also challenges it by asserting her desire for Orlando; Diane Elizabeth Dreher comments of this moment that 'discovering her animus or inner authority, she performs what has traditionally been the father's function, arranging her marriage and those of the other couples'.[9] Fortunately, the Duke is unlikely to prove a demanding father; he will accede happily to her wish to marry the son of his own old friend, and neither he nor the audience is liable to pick up on any potentially disturbing undercurrents in Rosalind's words. Unlike the story of Cordelia, where the divided selfhood which must attempt to please both father and husband becomes a source of anxiety, the emphasis here is less on the division implied by Rosalind's phrasing than on the reintegration and reconstitution of the family. The potential disharmony of the double promise is left unexplored. But it is there.

More obviously an issue, though, is that no one has come forward who has the authority to sanction and legitimate the weddings. As Celia says when Rosalind entreats her to conduct the mock marriage, 'I cannot say the words' (IV. i. 121) – or rather, she can utter them, but in her mouth they have no performative validity. Diane Elizabeth Dreher feels that this exchange 'not only assures Rosalind of Orlando's love, but also approximates a legal marriage';[10] but this seems an odd view to take of it given Celia's own disclaimer of competence in the matter. Only a priest can speak the words of the marriage service, and priests in the forest are few and far between. Indeed clerics in general prove elusive in the play: there is the 'old religious man' who converts Duke Frederick, but his whereabouts are unknown, and there is Sir Oliver Martext, whom Richard Wilson sees as the outlaws' Friar Tuck,[11] but he, as Touchstone and Jaques agree, 'is not like to marry . . . well' (III. iii. 82–3). Just as in the mock marriage performed by Celia – which can indeed be read as foreshadowing this difficulty – so here at the time of the real marriage there is no one who can say the words. Hymen's declaration that ''Tis I must make conclusion / Of these most strange events' (V. iv. 125–6) has its claim to finality undercut when 170 lines later the Duke pronounces the end of the play proper with a rhyming couplet of his own: 'Proceed, proceed. We will begin these rites, / As we do trust they'll end, in true delights' (V. iv. 196–7). Here, closure deconstructs itself with its emphasis on proceeding and beginning; and even this sense of beginning is in turn eroded by Rosalind's immediately following remark that 'It is not the fashion to see the lady the epilogue' (V. iv. 198). Into this slippage of time, paradoxically caught between conclusions, beginnings and epilogues, the weddings themselves disappear. They have not been performed by the end of the play; and when Rosalind with her epilogue returns the audience to the real world of time, the play no longer has any future in which they could still take place. So although the marriages may be promised, implicit and assumed, they can never happen.

Moreover, the whole idea of marriage itself becomes an issue in the play. Touchstone has earlier attempted to disrupt the traditional pattern of comedy by having his marriage to Audrey performed in the very middle of the play (III. iii) but in fact his aim in attempting to arrange such a marriage is paradoxically not to achieve closure, but to leave open in his life possibilities which marriage is seen as precluding: Jaques exhorts him not to have his marriage performed by Sir Oliver Martext because 'This fellow will but join you together as they join wainscot; then one of you will prove a shrunk panel, and like green timber, warp, warp' (III. iii. 77–80). If marriage is traditionally used to achieve closure, then Touchstone's sentiments call into question the very possibility of such closure by his insinuation that marriages are prone to dissolution, and not just by the hand of God removing one of the partners.

Nor is Touchstone's an isolated perspective on his situation: Hymen sings ironically that he and Audrey are 'sure together / As the winter to foul weather' (V. iv. 134–5), while Jaques tells him 'thy loving voyage / Is but for two months victuall'd' (V. iv. 190–1). Granted that what is envisaged here is not so much divorce as squabbling within marriage (as Rosalind in more playful mood also forecasts for herself and Orlando [IV. i. 135–54]), even so Touchstone's earlier resolution to be married by Sir Oliver has explicitly addressed the question of termination of marriages, and it is even possible to see it hinted at when Orlando agrees to go through the mock-wedding ceremony with Ganymede 'now, as fast she can marry us' (IV. i. 127), where 'fast' can be taken to refer not only to the speed but also to the validity of the ceremony. And of course another form of the dissolution of marriages is figured in the plot not only of this play alone but of virtually all Shakespeare's comedies: while both Rosalind and Celia have living fathers and Orlando has one who was alive recently enough for his memory to be green, no one in the play has a living mother.[12] The male partner, it seems, may survive after marriage, but the female partner has borne her children and then disappeared, her identity so utterly effaced that we do not even know what happened to her.[13] The implication may well be that within their marriages a similar fate may lurk to obliterate the vivacity even of a Rosalind or a Celia. Certainly, it would be possible to cast a sceptical eye over the likely effects on Phebe's health and life expectancy of the perpetual pregnancy and parturition forecast for her in Jaques' valediction to Silvius, 'You to a long and well-deserved bed' (V. iv. 189).

But if a constant and life-threatening involvement in the processes of pregnancy and childbirth is the inevitable destiny of the married woman, the married man too has an unpleasant fate which he cannot avoid and which is repeatedly foreshadowed for him in the course of the play: cuckoldry. It forms the standard theme of Rosalind's teasing of Orlando: the snail, she tells him, brings its destiny with it, and when he inquires what that is she replies 'Why horns – which such as you are fain to be beholding to your wives for; but he comes armed in his fortune, and prevents the slander of his wife' (IV. i. 56–9) – with perhaps an implication that even where cuckoldry itself is not present in a marriage, the rumour of it is bound to be. It is seen by Touchstone as not only unavoidable, but in some sense even acceptable:

As horns are odious, they are necessary. It is said, many a man knows no end of his goods. Right. Many a man has good horns and knows no end of them. Well, that is the dowry of his wife, 'tis none of his own getting. Horns? Even so. Poor men alone? No, no. The noblest deer hath them as huge as the rascal. Is the single man therefore blessed? No. As a walled town is more worthier than a village, so is the forehead of a married man more honourable than the bare brow of a bachelor; and by how much defence is better than no skill, by so much is a horn more precious than to want. (III. iii. 45–57)

Indeed, as Touchstone has earlier pointed out, the very environment of the forest is full of reminders of cuckoldry: contemplating his imminent marriage, he remarks, 'A man may, if he were of a fearful heart, stagger in this attempt; for here we have no temple but the wood, no assembly but horn-beasts' (III. iii. 42–4).

This is a point raised again in the short and bizarre scene in which Jaques and the Lords celebrate the deer-killer with a song:

> *What shall he have that kill'd the deer?*
> *His leather skin and horns to wear.*
> *Then sing him home. The rest shall bear*
> *This burden.*
> *Take thou no scorn to wear the horn,*
> *It was a crest ere thou wast born.*
>   *Thy father's father wore it,*
>   *And thy father bore it.*
> *The horn, the horn, the lusty horn,*
> *Is not a thing to laugh to scorn.*
> (IV. iii. 10–19)

The scene seems to be introduced solely to allow for the singing of this lyric, which, like Jaques' speech, both affirms and defuses the inevitability of cuckoldry by representing it as natural, figured even in the idyll of the pastoral by the horns of the deer, which become a badge of potency – the sign of the deer-killer – simultaneously with their more normal role as signifiers of shame. This song also, though, addresses one of the most fundamental of all aspects of cuckoldry, the threat it poses to the transmission of land and property from undoubted father to undoubted son. The spectre is raised in the sixth line ('it was a crest ere thou wast born') simultaneously evokes the pride of ancestry symbolised by heraldry, and casts doubt on the line of descent by associating birth and cuckoldry so intimately. However, the threat has no sooner been raised than it is triumphantly defused: the fear of not being able to identify the father is countered with the assurance that in this matter all fathers are alike – all are cuckolds. A kind of collective identity is thus asserted which can take precedence over the ultimately unknowable individual identity of any one father. Male bonding has triumphed over the apparent threat to patriarchal and class power posed by women's sexual infidelity.[14]

As You Like It does, indeed, then, take marriage as a central theme; but just as the structural patterning of the play resists closure, so does the apparent ideological fixity of the meaning of marriage itself break down under the pressure of the meanings imposed on it by the play. Even the play's Edenic overtones work ultimately to undermine the stability of the marital ideal that is apparently held up at its end: for all the return to a prelapsarian state in the duchy (a theme obviously signalled by Adam's name), this is an Eden with a snake, and, moreover, a lioness (interestingly changed from a lion in Shakespeare's source);[15] and if the couples at the end in any sense figure Adam and Eve, they must equally image the collapse of the pastoral ideal and of marital harmony which was to occur in that first of all marriages. Rather than a device to close the play securely, to ensure female subordination to patriarchal power and to secure the transmission of property between members of the elite, marriage is revealed as allowing interference with all three elements. But while the male characters of the play seem able to accept and even to embrace these contradictions within marriage, for the female characters the absence of mothers – the fact that the previous generation of married women have apparently vanished without trace – postulates a less hopeful future.

A Midsummer Night's Dream

In *A Midsummer Night's Dream* the difference in the nature of the experiences offered by marriage to men and to women is signalled right at the outset, in the opening dialogue between Theseus and Hippolyta. The couple seem to be united in their eagerness for the approach of their ensuing wedding:

> *Theseus:* Now, fair Hippolyta, our nuptial hour
> Draws on apace; four happy days bring in
> Another moon: but O, methinks, how slow
> This old moon wanes! She lingers my desires,
> Like to a step-dame or a dowager
> Long withering out a young man's revenue.
> *Hippolyta:* Four days will quickly steep themselves in night;
> Four nights will quickly dream away the time;
> And then the moon, like to a silver bow
> New bent in heaven, shall behold the night
> Of our solemnities.[16]

In fact, Hippolyta's lines are susceptible of a very different interpretation, as was shown by the way that Penny Downie played the role at Stratford-upon-

Avon in 1982. Her Hippolyta was a deeply reluctant, indeed sullen, bride: her statements that the time would pass quickly were motivated not by joy but by a disempowered acceptance of the inevitable, and her flat future tenses, without any use of the optative, reflected this sense of despairing entrapment.

Such a reading also serves to highlight the fact that Theseus insistently perceives all the blocking figures to their marriage as female. He alludes, in turn, to the moon (most usually figured in Elizabethan discourse in her classical personae as Cynthia, Diana, Dictynna or Artemis, and as such associated with the Virgin Queen herself), a step-dame and a dowager.[17] Hippolyta, in marked contrast, concurs in imaging the moon as female, but views it as a symbol of empowerment, a representation of the 'bow' (I. i. 9) which was once her weapon. Theseus' assumptions are even more remarkable in a play where the blocking figures are in fact uniformly male – Egeus, who objects to his daughter's marriage, and, arguably, Oberon, though, like Theseus, he himself constructs the cause of the quarrel between the fairies as the opposition of Titania – and where the women tend to be unusually powerless for representatives of the comic feminine.[18] But if the plot of the play minimises the power of women, its imagery maximises it, and concomitantly figures men as weakened, clearly suggesting a deep-rooted fear, as in Titania's elegiac comment that 'the green corn / Hath rotted ere his youth attained a beard' (II. i. 94–5). Even the play-within-the-play may encode a fearful female. 'Ninny's tomb' may be funny, but it also memorialises Ninus, King of Assyria, whose wife, as Sir David Lindsay of the Mount recorded in his attack on female rulers, was the 'proude and presumptious' Semiramis,[19] who is one of the examples Lindsay cites to prove the innate unfitness of women to occupy posts of power.

The idea briefly indicated in Hippolyta's speech that women may be unwilling to marry recurs throughout the play.[20] In many of Shakespeare's romantic comedies, the women are seen as being very actively in search of a husband: Viola has barely landed in Illyria before she is enquiring about Orsino's marital status, Olivia rapidly proposes marriage to the supposed Cesario, and Feste is able to tease Maria by alluding to the possibility of Sir Toby marrying her; both Julia and Silvia in *The Two Gentlemen of Verona* actively seek their lovers out, and Rosalind in *As You Like It* effectively engineers her own marriage when Orlando, blinded by her male disguise, does not take the initiative. In *A Midsummer Night's Dream*, Helena does indeed actively pursue Demetrius, but whereas the other heroines who do this are presented as spirited and determined, and invariably preserve their dignity and their self-respect, she is seen as merely ridiculous:

> I am your spaniel; and, Demetrius,
> The more you beat me, I will fawn on you.
> Use me but as your spaniel, spurn me, strike me,

> Neglect me, lose me; only give me leave,
> Unworthy as I am, to follow you.
> What worser place can I beg in your love –
> And yet a place of high respect with me –
> Than to be used as you use your dog?
>
> (II. i. 203–10)

Titania, who (although for very different reasons) similarly pays court to the man of her choice, is equally seen as a butt of jokes. Far more popular, both with the men of the play and generally with audiences and critics, is Hermia, who, unlike the majority of Shakespeare's heroines, shows a distinct concern for propriety – 'Nay, good Lysander; for my sake, my dear, / Lie further off yet; do not lie so near' (II. ii. 42–3). In fact, if Hermia and Lysander had decided to perform a contract of *per verba de futuro* in front of a witness such as Helena and had then consummated their marriage in the woods, it would have become immediately legal; but that is never suggested, and Hermia's behaviour is presented instead as the polar opposite to Helena's. When attitudes such as this are highlighted, the decision to set the opening scene of the 1982 Stratford-upon-Avon production in the Victorian period becomes a highly suitable one.

Hermia's concern to protect her virginity had previously gone even further, when, unamazed by the choice she is offered between enforced marriage, execution, and the cloister, she unhesitatingly chooses the lifelong chastity of sisterhood rather than marriage with Demetrius.[21] Here, of course, her decision is perfectly understandable, since the partner offered her is one she has no liking for; but taken along with other instances of women not wishing to marry or to live within marital relationships in the play, it may nevertheless be seen as significant. Titania may be eager enough for Bottom, but she is undergoing what seems to be an effective separation from her 'lord' Oberon; and whatever Hippolyta's feelings for Theseus may be now, we are told clearly enough what they must have been initially when Theseus reminds her 'Hippolyta, I woo'd thee with my sword, / And won thy love doing thee injuries' (I. i. 16–17). Moreover, the play even includes more or less direct reference to that ultimate refuser of marriage, 'the imperial votress' (II. i. 163) herself, Elizabeth I, whose decision to remain single had given rise to the cult of the Virgin Queen.[22]

As if this were not enough, the play clearly warns of the possible dangers of marriage: a wife risks quarrels and the curbing of her will, such as occurs in the relationship of Titania and Oberon, and death in childbirth, as happens to the mother of the changeling boy; or her children may be deformed – although the fairies promise that this will not happen to any of the couples in the play, their mere mention of deformity nevertheless serves to confirm it as a real possibility.[23] This last is an issue that would affect the husband too, and the death of both Pyramus and Thisbe in the mechanicals' playlet could perhaps serve as a reminder that love offers perils for both sexes. Nevertheless, neither Demetrius nor Lysander is threatened with anything like the dreadful choice that is offered to Hermia, and both Theseus and Oberon end the play with very much the upper hand in their relationships: Titania has been thoroughly humiliated by the discovery of her love for an ass (an ironic and radically reductive rewriting of Theseus' much more heroic adventures with the Minotaur), and Theseus at the banquet firmly overrules Hippolyta's distaste for the mechanicals' play with her first lesson in theatre criticism and public behaviour (V. i. 89–105).

Moreover, in this play too the marriages do not provide closure by occurring at the end of the play.[24] Almost all the plot material has been used up by the opening of Act V: Titania and Oberon are reconciled, the lovers have come together in mutually agreeable couples, returned to the city and been reconciled with Theseus and Egeus, Bottom has been transformed back to his normal shape, and all that remains is for the mechanicals to perform their play. We may perhaps wonder to what extent the fairies Titania and Oberon can be considered bound by the human rite of marriage at all – especially since each accuses the other of having effectively conducted an open relationship. As for the marriages of the mortals, they appear to have taken place between Act IV, scene 1 and Act V, scene 1: in the first of these scenes Theseus announces that 'in the temple by and by with us / These couples shall eternally be knit', and in the second all are looking forward to the advent of the evening which will allow them to consummate the marriages. It would in fact be perfectly possible in narrative terms to end the play after Act IV, scene 1.

What comes after that point is obviously important in terms of providing a suitably celebratory finale, but it offers too a comment on what has occurred. The tragic story of Pyramus and Thisbe may serve to remind us how very easily the events of the play could have developed along the lines of *Romeo and Juliet*; the fairies' final benediction can be seen as indicating how much such a blessing may be needed. Marriage then is not seen as some sort of transcendental signifier which automatically confers meaning on events: its own meaning is open to probing and exploration. Even when closure does finally occur, its meaning is unmade even as it is made:

> If we shadows have offended,
> Think but this, and all is mended,
> That you have but slumber'd here
> While these visions did appear.
> And this weak and idle theme,

> No more yielding but a dream,
> Gentles, do not reprehend:
> If you pardon, we will mend.
> And, as I am an honest Puck,
> If we have unearned luck
> Now to 'scape the serpent's tongue,
> We will make amends ere long;
> Else the Puck a liar call.
> So, goodnight unto you all.
> Give me your hands, if we be friends,
> And Robin shall restore amends.
> (V. i. 409–24)

Puck's paradoxes both return the play to the real world and, at the same time as they offer a final comment on the play, they deny the possibility of making any such comment at all, since the making of meaning must finally be in our hands. In offering itself for approval the play finally abdicates control over its own authority; and thus, although it has been careful to present itself as an ostensible celebration of marriage, the diametrical antithesis of the 'some satire, keen and critical, / Not sorting with a nuptial ceremony' (V. i. 54–5) which Theseus fears, it ultimately acknowledges that the meaning-making audience is equally free to construct out of it as potentially subversive a critique as it wishes of contemporary marriage, and, above all, of the role of women within it. As Christopher Brooke, in his history of marriage, observes of the idea that *A Midsummer Night's Dream* was an occasional play feting an actual wedding, 'I am glad it was not my wedding it celebrated, for it proceeds by showing us the lowest view of human marriage we have so far encountered.'[25]

If both *As You Like It* and *A Midsummer Night's Dream* seem to offer sympathy for the position of women within marriage, it must not be forgotten that the issue of men's role within marriage has, even if only marginally, also been addressed in them.[26] In *The Two Gentlemen of Verona*, as later in *The Merry Wives of Windsor* where Herne the Hunter functions as a recuperative figure in exactly the same way as the horn song does, this becomes of far greater importance.

The Two Gentlemen of Verona

In *The Two Gentlemen of Verona*, the character who in many ways appears the most vulnerable is not Valentine, whose good faith leads him into banishment, nor Silvia, distressed and frightened though she undoubtedly is by the attempted rape, nor even Julia, forced to witness the faithlessness and villainy of her lover, but Proteus himself, the man who causes the suffering of all of them. Proteus says of himself, 'I do as truly suffer, / As e'er I did commit'.[27] These lines, and Proteus' part in general in this scene, have often been considered badly underwritten, but Barry Lynch's moving delivery in the 1991 Swan Theatre production by David Thacker at Stratford-upon-Avon showed that they can in fact be seen as more than adequate to the situation, since what they suggest is that Proteus' own suffering is directly proportional to that experienced by all the other three lovers in combination. Indeed, it could even be argued that he has undergone more than they have had to do: for whereas they have throughout the play been firmly locked into stable, unshakeable identities, Proteus has undergone a most violent and radical attack on his very sense of selfhood, bordering almost on what might now be termed a form of schizophrenia.

This is seen clearly in Act II, scene 6, where, like Richard III before Bosworth, Proteus effectively falls apart. Given, in modern editions, the whole scene to himself, he soliloquises:

> I cannot leave to love; and yet I do;
> But there I leave to love, where I should love.
> Julia I lose, and Valentine I lose;
> If I keep them, I needs must lose myself;
> If I lose them, thus find I by their loss:
> For Valentine, myself; for Julia, Silvia.
> I to myself am dearer than a friend,
> For love is still most precious in itself,
> And Silvia (witness heaven, that made her fair)
> Shows Julia but a swarthy Ethiope.
> (II. vi. 17–26)

Underlying the apparent arrival at a decision here is a terrifying sense of the dizzying relativity of all available senses of identity. The first line sets up a logical impossibility which the balanced syntax can do no more than leave as paradox. It may be glossed over by the sophistry of the second, but that also introduces another, equally worrying, idea: 'I' is no longer absolute, standing unbounded as subject of the sentence, but modified and compromised by its physical location – 'there', 'where'.

'I' finds itself even further destabilised in the third line when both Julia and Valentine successively usurp the apparent subject position of their respective phrases, and in the fourth line the issue is explicitly addressed when Proteus admits to himself the awful possibility that he may 'lose myself'. This is hastily dismissed when a swift change of object alters the situation to losing not himself but 'them' – a safely demonised, externalised group which leaves his own sense of identity apparently unthreatened and intact. But Proteus, as his Protean name suggests, has exposed a far more radical possibility than that of

simple self-loss: lurking behind the exchange of persons which he now proposes is the spectre that he may have no self to lose. If Julia can replace Silvia
and Proteus Valentine, and if Julia's former self is indeed modified and deval-
ued by the mere existence of Silvia, as suggested in the two closing lines, then
in what sense can any of these people be presented as a 'self'? In this sense
Proteus' 'I do as truly suffer / As e'er I did commit' is a statement which is
both admirably expressive and a profound psychological restorative, for in it
he has finally achieved an assertion of the coherence of the two parts of his
previously shattered self: what 'I' has done, 'I' is also paying for, and the
payment is small price for the reintegration of self which the language enables
him to assert. Looked at in this light, the 'marriage' which seals the end of the
play is less one between Proteus and Julia than between Proteus and his
estranged selfhood, or perhaps with Julia as a manifestation of that former,
regretted state of psychological unity.

The play does end with the promise of other, more conventional marriages.
Valentine assures his regained friend:

> Come, Proteus, 'tis your penance but to hear
> The story of your loves discovered.
> That done, our day of marriage shall be yours,
> One feast, one house, one mutual happiness.
> (V. iv. 168–71)

All is apparently well that ends well, and Valentine's extraordinary offer of his
own interest in Silvia to Proteus could also be read as indicating that the
friendship of the two gentlemen will, despite all the strains to which it has
been subject, survive and even prosper. Nevertheless the darker notes are there.
The ring which Julia produces as a token both of her own identity and of
Proteus' former affection for her may serve to remind us that bonds sealed by
rings have been broken before and could be again. Moreover, while the two
women have shown themselves eager for marriage throughout the play, the
behaviour of both Proteus and Valentine can be seen as registering a rather
more ambivalent attitude. When we first meet them, in Act I, scene 1, love is
already a force which threatens to pull their friendship apart: Proteus will stay
at home because of it, losing the chance of adventures and finding himself separated from his friend. And it remains throughout the play the single greatest
threat to male bonding, not only disrupting the relationship of Proteus and
Valentine but also falsifying and eventually undermining their interactions
with the male authority figure, the Duke.

It would be plausible to see Proteus' sudden switch to Silvia as operating
effectively as a continuation of that movement away from love which has
already been inaugurated by his decision to leave Julia: subconsciously, he has

chosen the most inaccessible of all possible females, the beloved of his friend. It is a move guaranteed to precipitate the crisis which has until now been only latent, to force a radical choice between the two parts of his fissured identity. As in *The Two Noble Kinsmen*, so much later in Shakespeare's career, what we see here is the crippling psychological cost in terms of the loss of personal and social selfhood which men may fear will be the price of marriage.[28]

Another fear, too, can be seen as lying behind both this play and others of Shakespeare's apparently 'happy' comedies. Finding himself unable to persuade Silvia to yield to his advances, Proteus decides to rape her. This is not only his own lowest psychological point; it is also devastatingly revealing about his attitude to marriage. Obviously no modern feminist can admit any sort of defence of his act, but it may be possible to look at in a light rather different from that in which it is customarily considered. If Proteus himself regards marriage as a threatening, dangerous state, he might well project such feelings of reluctance onto his female partner – and this could lead him to regard not only Silvia but *all* women as quite simply needing to be raped in order to make marriage possible at all. We can read his action less as an individual, isolated act of violation than as the emblem of his views of all relationships, in which either others or the self must always be lost; in one sense, it is himself that he tries to rape. The idea of female reluctance to marry, which had figured so threateningly in *A Midsummer Night's Dream*, thus recurs here, raising the question of whether it could be that the universal assumption of women's desire to cuckold their husbands by incessant sex actually masks in general the repression of a deeper fear too threatening even to voice – that female participation in sex is reluctant.

Frigid women, who are at the same time impossible to keep chaste; fragmented men in danger of losing their selves, their honour and their friends; incompetent or unavailable priests and defective ceremonies; savage uncivilised settings in which wild beasts roam as the fitting emblem of the human condition – the makings of marriage in Shakespearean comedy are not promising ones. But it is, of course, precisely the innate instability of its personnel and character that make the institution such a vital one. The radical fissuring that splits selves and societies can be kept from cracking only by the constant repetition and reduplication of social and ideological bonds that marriage alone is seen as capable of providing, forming as it does the one framework in which the behaviour of each partner is constantly visible, constantly subject to policing by the other. The Shakespearean 'happy' comedies do not celebrate marriage: they reveal its crucial functioning in the maintenance of society and also the internal stresses and contradictions to which it is constantly subject – an instability instanced by the repeated structural decentring of marriage from its supposed position of comic closure. And contrary to so much of the misogyny and the marital ideology of the time, they powerfully reveal that outside the institution of marriage both men and women are adrift, while inside it both must pay a high price for their security.

Notes

1   See Ejner J. Jensen, *Shakespeare and the Ends of Comedy* (Bloomington, IN: Indiana University Press, 1991), p. 2, on the importance attached by the critical tradition to the ends of comedies.

2   This is noted by Nigel Wood ('Endpiece', in *Theory in Practice: Hamlet*, ed. Peter J. Smith and Nigel Wood [Buckingham: Open University Press, 1996], pp. 124–54, p. 137), in response to Brian Vickers' assertion to the contrary.

3   For the Elizabethan expectation that the birth of a child would inevitably result from sex, see Lisa Jardine, *Still Harping on Daughters: Women and Drama in the Age of Shakespeare* (Brighton: Harvester, 1983), p. 130.

4   William Shakespeare, *As You Like It*, ed. Agnes Latham [1957] (London: Routledge, 1987), I. iii. 11. All future quotations from the play will be taken from this edition and reference will be given in the text.

5   Katharine Eisaman Maus, in 'Transfer of title in *Love's Labor's Lost*: language, individualism, gender', in *Shakespeare Left and Right*, ed. Ivo Kamps (London: Routledge, 1991), pp. 205–23, sees Navarre's academy as an attempt to repress 'the involvement of women in the process of title transfer' (p. 215).

6   The extent to which *As You Like It* is generally perceived as a play riddled with marriages is interestingly indicated by the Oxford and Cambridge 'O' level board question on the play cited by Alan Sinfield, 'Write an editorial for the *Arden Gazette* on the recent outbreak of marriage in the district' ('Give an account of Shakespeare and Education, showing why you think they are effective and what you have appreciated about them. Support your comments with precise references', in *Political Shakespeare*, ed. Jonathan Dollimore and Alan Sinfield [Manchester: Manchester University Press, 1985], pp. 134–57, p. 150).

7   William Shakespeare, *As You Like It*, ed. H. J. Oliver (Harmondsworth: Penguin, 1968), V. iv. 104 s.d.

8   That there is a genuine ambiguity here is something that has become very clear to me when teaching this text, and an assumption either way can produce very different readings, as in Malcolm Evans' discussion of the play in *Signifying Nothing: Truth's True Contents in Shakespeare's Texts*, 2nd edn (Hemel Hempstead: Harvester Wheatsheaf, 1989), where it is taken for granted that it is indisputably the god Hymen who appears. (Evans does not discuss the performance aspect.)

9   Diane Elizabeth Dreher, *Domination and Defiance: Fathers and Daughters in Shakespeare* (Lexington, KY: University of Kentucky Press, 1986), p. 123.

10   Dreher, *Domination and Defiance*, p. 122.

11   See Richard Wilson, *Will Power: Essays on Shakespearean Authority* (Hemel Hempstead: Harvester Wheatsheaf, 1993), p. 75.

12   See Janet Adelman, *Suffocating Mothers: Fantasies of Maternal Origin in Shakespeare's Plays, 'Hamlet' to 'The Tempest'* (New York: Routledge, 1992), pp. 13–14.

13 Barbara J. Bono points out, however, that the forest of Arden echoes the maiden name of Shakespeare's mother Mary Arden, and that the play encodes a recognition of human origin in a maternal body which precludes knowledge of the father ('Mixed gender, mixed genre in Shakespeare's *As You Like It*', in *Renaissance Genres: Essays on Theory, History, and Interpretation*, ed. Barbara Kiefer Lewalski [Cambridge, MA: Harvard University Press, 1986], pp. 189–212, pp. 194 and 211). On absent mothers in Shakespearean drama generally, see most particularly Mary Beth Rose, 'Where are the mothers in Shakespeare? Options for gender representation in the English Renaissance', *Shakespeare Quarterly*, 42: 3 (Fall 1991), pp. 291–314.

14 See Wilson, *Will Power*, p. 76, on the patriarchal values encoded in 'thy father's father'.

15 See Louis Adrian Montrose, '"The place of a brother" in *As You Like It*: social process and comic form', *Shakespeare Quarterly*, 32 (1981), pp. 28–54, p. 50. Montrose also offers a brilliant analysis of the workings of male bonding mechanisms in the play in general and in the horn song scene in particular, which he terms a 'charivari' (p. 49). He sees the play as a whole as working to diminish the power of women. For additional comment on the snake and lioness, see Valerie Traub, 'Desire and the differences it makes', in *The Matter of Difference*, ed. Valerie Wayne (Hemel Hempstead: Harvester Wheatsheaf, 1991), pp. 81–114, p. 105.

16 William Shakespeare, *A Midsummer Night's Dream*, ed. Harold F. Brooks (London: Methuen, 1979), I. i. 1–11. All further quotations from the play will be taken from this edition and reference will be given in the text.

17 For the argument that Shakespeare might be alluding here to the presence of actual dowagers in the audience, see Steven May, '*A Midsummer Night's Dream* and the Carey–Berkeley wedding', *Renaissance Papers* (1983), pp. 43–52, pp. 46–7.

18 For an ingenious reading of *A Midsummer Night's Dream* as structured around the fear and avoidance of older women, see Terence Hawkes, 'Or', in *Meaning by Shakespeare* (London: Routledge, 1992). On the absence of mothers in Shakespeare's plays, see Carol Thomas Neely, *Broken Nuptials in Shakespeare's Plays*, 2nd edn (Urbana, IL: Illini Books, 1993), p. 171.

19 See Paula Louise Scalingi, 'The scepter or the distaff: the question of female sovereignty, 1516–1607', *The Historian*, 41: 1 (1975), pp. 59–75, p. 64. Semiramis is referred to twice in *Titus Andronicus* (II. i. 22 and II. iii. 118), and so is Pyramus (II. iii. 231), which increases the probability of an allusion to her in *Dream*.

20 On lesbian desire in the play, see Valerie Traub, 'The (in)significance of "lesbian" desire in early modern England', in *Erotic Politics: Desire on the Renaissance Stage*, ed. Susan Zimmerman (New York: Routledge, 1992), pp. 150–69, p. 157. For an argument that all Shakespearean comedy is fundamentally informed by homoeroticism, see Jardine, *Still Harping on Daughters*, pp. 20–9.

21 For discussions of the difficulties of ascertaining whether, in this and similar situations, the sympathies of the audience would be engaged on behalf of the unruly lovers or of the patriarchal order which they challenge, see Michael Hattaway, 'Drama and society', in *The Cambridge Companion to English Renaissance Drama*,

ed. A. R. Braunmuller and Michael Hattaway (Cambridge: Cambridge University Press, 1990), p. 110, and Richard Levin, *New Readings vs Old Plays* (Chicago: University of Chicago Press, 1979), pp. 151–3.

22   For an account of some pertinent aspects of the cult, see Roy Strong, *The Cult of Elizabeth* (London: Thames and Hudson, 1977); Susan Bassnett, *Elizabeth I: A Feminist Perspective* (Oxford: Berg, 1988); and my own *Elizabeth I and her Court* (London: Vision Press, 1990). On its potential implications for the play, see particularly Louis Adrian Montrose, '*A Midsummer Night's Dream* and the shaping fantasies of Elizabethan culture: gender, power, form', reproduced most conveniently in *New Historicism and Renaissance Drama*, ed. Richard Wilson and Richard Dutton (Harlow: Longman, 1992), pp. 109–30. For discussion of the relationship between the cult of Elizabeth and comic closure in general, see Peter Erickson, 'The Order of the Garter, the cult of Elizabeth, and class-gender tension in *The Merry Wives of Windsor*', in *Shakespeare Reproduced: The Text in History and Ideology*, ed. Jean E. Howard and Marion F. O'Connor (London: Methuen, 1987), pp. 116–40, p. 130. Philippa Berry comments on the tension between the strong emphasis on marriage in Protestant ideology and Elizabeth's refusal of it, and offers a reading of *A Midsummer Night's Dream* as attempting to restore Elizabeth to 'the control of the patriarchy' (*Of Chastity and Power: Elizabethan Literature and the Unmarried Queen* [London: Routledge, 1989], p. 143) and as mounting a 'challenge [to] the Platonism of Elizabeth's cult by its emphasis upon female heterosexuality and the subordination of woman in marriage' (pp. 143–4). My own reading would agree that women are shown to be subordinated in marriage but would suggest that the implications of this fact may be a possible locus for debate, and hence that it is not being uncritically endorsed.

23   Hawkes (*Meaning by Shakespeare*, p. 20) comments that 'a motif of disfiguring, translating change is all-pervasive'.

24   Though Stephen Greenblatt suggests that the Fairies' use of field-dew at the end of the play is indeed evocative of the marriage blessing ('Resonance and wonder', *Bulletin of the American Academy of Arts and Sciences*, 43 [1990], pp. 11–34; reprinted in Stephen J. Greenblatt, *Learning to Curse: Essays in Early Modern Culture* [London: Routledge, 1990], p. 163).

25   Christopher Brooke, *The Medieval Idea of Marriage* (Oxford: Oxford University Press, 1991), p. 231.

26   The importance of directing critical attention to the male characters as well as the female ones, even and perhaps especially for a feminist reading, has been stressed by, amongst others, Walter Cohen, who characterises as one of the achievements of American feminist criticism 'a psychoanalytically inspired sensitivity to the costs repeatedly exacted in the course of the plots not only from women but, given the constricting norms of male identity, from men as well' ('Political criticism of Shakespeare', in *Shakespeare Reproduced*, ed. Howard and O'Connor, p. 23). He goes on to question Linda Bamber's division into comic women, tragic men (p. 24).

27   William Shakespeare, *The Two Gentlemen of Verona*, ed. Clifford Leech (London: Methuen, 1969), V. iv. 76–7. All further quotations from the play will be taken from this edition and reference will be given in the text.

28   For a discussion of this as a central concern in *The Two Noble Kinsmen*, see Kathleen McLuskie, *Renaissance Dramatists* (Atlantic Highlands, NJ: Humanities Press International, 1989), p. 13, and Bruce P. Smith, *Homosexual Desire in Shakespeare's England: A Cultural Poetics* (Chicago: University of Chicago Press, 1991), p. 72.

False Immortality in *Measure for Measure*

Robert N. Watson

Robert Watson investigates how divergent generic elements in Measure for Measure, *together with the play's insistence on sex leading to pregnancy/marriage, develop a sceptical stance towards religious concepts of immortality. While the comic mode of the play – that society requires a combination of licence and repression – is seen as essentially conservative, Watson argues that the play's depiction of supposed deaths denies them tragic ascendancy and thus presents a view of death simply, terribly, as individual annihilation. The argument draws in many other aspects of the play – connections between the Duke and James I, for example – and offers a corrective to arguments that* Measure for Measure *is a religious allegory of a Christlike Duke being merciful to his lustful subjects. Rather, Watson's play is a challenge to such consolations, encoded in the uneasy generic form of tragi-comedy. These ideas are developed in relation to a wide range of poetic and dramatic texts in Watson's* The Rest is Silence: Death as Annihilation in the English Renaissance *(1994).*

Robert N. Watson, 'False Immortality in *Measure for Measure:* Comic Means, Tragic Ends', *Shakespeare Quarterly*, 41: 4 (1990), pp. 411–32.

> All tragedies are finished by a death,
> All comedies are ended by a marriage;
> The future states of both are left to faith,
> For authors fear description might disparage
> The worlds to come of both. . . .
> *Don Juan*, Canto 3, stanza 9

Ending with marriage emphasizes the survival of the type through procreation; ending with death emphasizes the extinction of the individual creature. In *Measure for Measure* Shakespeare stops short of explicitly disparaging both 'worlds to come', but the abrupt and formulaic comic ending encourages a suspicion that the aftermath of marriage and death alike is merely a biological process with no regard for human consciousness. To expand on Horace Walpole's aphoristic version of the genre distinction, 'the world is a comedy to those that think' about the persistent traits of their species, 'a tragedy to those that feel' their own mortality and that of the individual things they love. *Measure for Measure* is, from this perspective, a tragicomedy.[1] The play certainly portrays and extols the orderly perpetuation of human life, human society, and human virtue. Yet it also takes the three figurations of immortality to which people most commonly cling – the hope for genetic and spiritual heirs, the hope for divine salvation, and the hope for undying fame and honor – and undermines our faith in each of them, even as it undermines our faith in the comic formula as a whole by the unsatisfying impositions of marriage that conclude this death-filled play. Which is the means, and which the end, between the perpetuation of the species and the experience of individual life? Of these comic and tragic concerns, which one comprises sufficient meaning to expose its counterpart as merely an arbitrary ending? The first part of this essay will offer an abbreviated summary of the play's implicit comic argument for the systematic reproduction of the human race. A longer second part will argue, less conventionally, that the play persistently subverts the comic promises of immortality, encouraging instead a suspicion that we are each tragically betrayed by the supposedly benevolent biological and political systems to which God has abandoned His human offspring.

Comedy: The Moral and Morals of *Measure for Measure*

Measure for Measure comes closer than any other Shakespeare play to having a schematic, articulable moral. Its primary topic is sexuality, and its primary argument is that neither individuals nor societies can thrive unless license and repression keep each other in balance. Naturally critics are reluctant to admit that sexual morality is what the play is about, because that is what it *seems* to be about.[2] But in this case it may pay to surrender our ingenuity in the face of the obvious. The polar outposts of this play are brothels and convents, its characters are most vivid for their prudery and lechery, and its two crucial actions are bouts of sexual intercourse, one a premarital impregnation, the other a form of attempted rape. From beginning to end, the dominant motive is the need to convert lustful fornication into fruitful married sexuality. Vienna's Sigmund Freud defined as perversion any sexual activity not primarily directed toward heterosexual genital intercourse; Shakespeare's Vienna defines as treason any such intercourse not directed toward legitimate procreation. For the individual, marriage becomes – as in the patristic commonplaces – a way of reconciling unruly sexual desire with necessary sexual restraint; for the state, it becomes a way of maintaining the substance and order of the social fabric. Though *Measure for Measure* is notorious for its strayings from comic sentiment, it thus builds toward the typical comic conclusion far more forcefully and logically than most comedies: by the end, marriage becomes an overdetermined resolution.

Through a series of variations, the thematic argument remains remarkably consistent. The Duke of Vienna – evidently believing that fornication, which creates life, however unlawfully, must be preferable to execution, which destroys life, however lawfully – has allowed sexual license to corrupt his city. This is an understandable error in a humane ruler, all the more understandable to Shakespeare's audience, who, in 1604, were watching the play in a theatre that had again been closed by epidemic plague the previous year, in a city that had lost close to a quarter of its population to the plague over the preceding decade. So, despite some bad harvests in the 1590s and some complaints about the tendency of young people to procreate before they were ready to support a family,[3] population explosion was hardly to be feared; on the contrary, a common measure of a state's health was the growth of its population. Moreover, as the opening of the second scene reminds us, city-states such as Vienna were perpetually on the brink of war, with its voracious appetite for what Falstaff calls 'food for powder, mortal men'. So there would have been some sociological force to Lucio's warning that Angelo's more severe policy might 'unpeople the province', an inverted reminder of the biblical injunction to 'Be fruitful and multiply' that Renaissance preachers so often emphasized. Even Puritan figures such as Phillip Stubbes – who laments that 'untill every one hath two or three Bastardes a peece, they esteeme him no man' and furiously condemns anyone who argues that 'Otherwyse the World wold become barren' – stresses the obligation to multiply *within* marriage and concludes (like Duke Vincentio), 'let all men that have put away their honest wyves be forced to take them again, and abandon all whores, or els to taste of the law.'[4]

The Duke's problem is that, though his former course may have been understandable, it has not been understood. Lucio says that before the Duke 'would have hanged a man for the getting a hundred bastards, he would have paid for the nursing a thousand. He had some feeling of the sport; he knew the service; and that instructed him to mercy' (III. ii. 113–17). This is intolerable for the Duke, for both the motives and the numbers it claims to reveal. It presents the problem as a disease spreading outward from the Duke's unruly body to his entire body politic, rather than as an enlightened choice for healthy growth. It also suggests the threatening multiplication of the problem in a world where even one bastard child is one too many: the villains of Jacobean tragedy are often illegitimate children who necessarily attack the social order that excludes them. So the Duke stages a play for his city, as Shakespeare does for his, an averted tragedy in which all aberrations from married procreation become collaborations with death.

Angelo applies a simplistic system of accounting to this political com-modity, the legitimate son; the Duke's calculations are more complex and seemingly humane, but perhaps ultimately more cynical as well. According to Angelo, the making of a counterfeit dollar, the forging of that aspect of the state's wealth, is a theft equivalent to the stealing of a real dollar:

> It were as good
> To pardon him that hath from nature stolen
> A man already made, as to remit
> Their saucy sweetness that do coin heaven's image
> In stamps that are forbid. 'Tis all as easy
> Falsely to take away a life true made,
> As to put mettle in restrained means
> To make a false one.
>
> (II. iv. 42–9)[5]

The comparison is typical of Angelo in being too cold and abstract to be wholly convincing, but given the trends Lucio's speech reveals (however slanderously and hyperbolically), the exchange rate has shifted disastrously, devaluing legit-imacy against desire. The Duke is thus obliged to intervene with a temporary didactic choice of order over passion, a morally instructive bit of tragicomic theatre. The laxity of the Duke's own reign leads directly to the excessive restraint promised by Angelo. When Lucio asks the manacled Claudio, 'Whence comes this restraint', Claudio replies, 'From too much liberty, my Lucio. Liberty, / As surfeit, is the father of much fast; / So every scope by the immoderate use / Turns to restraint' (I. ii. 116–20). His individual experience is significantly parallel to that of the state, not just the result of it.

Angelo argues that Isabella should be willing to commit fornication in order to save Claudio's life, since she has implicitly asserted that Claudio's fornica-tion was not enough of an evil to merit death: measure for measure. This conundrum allows Shakespeare to offer further proof that unlimited fornica-tion is not the right cure for mortality, because this supposed antidote for Claudio turns out to be poison instead. When Angelo believes he has enjoyed Isabella's body, he orders that the execution be expedited by a few hours. In terms of the moral argument of the play, her supposed yielding only replicates Claudio's crime and therefore can only accelerate his punishment. The real cure, the Duke and his creator seem to suggest, is marriage, and the substitu-tion of Mariana in the bed allows the Duke to achieve the maximum possi-ble number of living and legitimate Viennese.

Sex and death were conventionally associated in the Renaissance, of course, but (as in its emphasis on venereal disease) *Measure for Measure* uses that association in a particularly tendentious way. Lucio's final words – 'Marrying a punk, my lord, is pressing to death, / Whipping, and hanging' (V. i. 520–1) – are merely the perverse final echo of a thematic association sounded throughout the play. The unholy alliance between these supposed mighty opposites – fornication and repression, conception and execution – surfaces again when the Duke assigns Pompey the bawd to work for Abhorson the executioner. The resulting series of puns and arguments alerts us to the fundamental compatibility of these two professions, even to their moral equivalence. Both men object to the partnership, but Pompey soon concedes, 'I have been an unlawful bawd time out of mind, but yet I will be content to be a lawful hangman. I would be glad to receive some instruction from my fellow-partner' (IV. ii. 14–17). The Provost insists that they 'weigh equally' in any ethical scale, they promise mutual professional courtesy, and Pompey eventually discovers 'many of [his] old customers' from the brothel require his new services at the jail (IV. iii. 1–4). The pun lurking in Abhorson's elided name neatly encapsulates the pattern: the executioner is evidently an abhorred whoreson. Promiscuity again appears to generate its own punishment; the executioner has been created by the fornicator.

If excessive liberty leads to excessive restraint, as the appointment of Angelo demonstrates, then excessive restraint leads to excessive liberty, as the corruption of Angelo demonstrates. The case of Isabella reinforces the same ideas more subtly: that discipline can lead to perversion, that severe rectitude reflects a battle against dangerously powerful appetites and provokes repressed sensuality into a guerrilla war against outward propriety. Angelo insists that Isabella's virgin modesty is what paradoxically inspires his lust; again, extraordinary self-restraint – hers as well as his own – becomes the provocation to an extraordinary self-indulgence. The erotics of Isabella's renunciation could hardly be more lurid:

> . . . were I under the terms of death,
> Th'impression of keen whips I'd wear as rubies,
> And strip myself to death as to a bed
> That longing have been sick for, ere I'd yield
> My body up to shame.
>   (II. iv. 100–4)

The erotic undertones of religious flagellation throughout *Measure for Measure*, the ways mortification of the flesh becomes gratification instead, have been thoroughly documented.[6] Furthermore, the death wish Isabella here expresses becomes extended by her, as by Angelo, to virtually everyone: 'What a merit were it in death to take this poor maid [Mariana] from the world! What corruption in this life, that it will let this man [Angelo] live!' (III. i. 231–3). Her advice to the lovelorn is invariably execution, Robespierre ghostwriting for

Ann Landers. The powerful and persistent death wish Angelo and Isabella express, towards themselves and towards others, is almost indistinguishable from their peculiar sexual appetites.

The fate of Isabella and Claudio as a family further emphasizes the deadly alliance of the two extremes, as the sister faces genetic extinction through her implied sexual repression, and the brother faces execution for an excess of sexual liberty. The ascetic and libertine tendencies (though each rather sympathetically represented in this pair) appear as a two-edged sword cutting down a family tree. So *Measure for Measure* is a tragicomedy not only because a convincing threat of barrenness or death appears before sexual desire resolves itself into marriage but also because the play exposes the potentially deadly attributes of sexuality itself. Both fornication and its extreme repression are wastrel expenditures of the bodies natural and politic.

Tragedy: Denying the Denial of Death

Within this rather commonplace moral admonition about physical, social, and psychological decadence, Shakespeare develops a potentially heretical, even blasphemous, meditation about the fate of the human individual. *Measure for Measure* evokes a tragic resistance to comic solutions, not only by emphasizing the destructive potential of sexuality but also by widening our perspective on its creative potential. Valuing procreation as a contribution to demographics and the ecological balance, rather than as individual assertion and gratification, may not sound especially sinister. But the anti-Malthusian conclusion that all is well because the population of Vienna keeps growing does not really answer the fears roused by the various threats of execution and particularly by Claudio's own confused but eloquent terror of death. Claudio evidently finds no consolation in the disguised Duke's argument that, from the standpoint of atomistic philosophy, he really has no self to lose (III. i. 19–21); nor is he reconciled to his fate by the idea that he has fathered a child to take his place, which should be thoroughly consoling if genetic survival were truly felt to be an adequate compensation for individual death. As in the more vivid instance of Macbeth, a resolution that is satisfactory for the purposes of the state may not eradicate our terrifying vision of the individual will and consciousness obliterated by nature and mortality.

The comic triumph here belongs not to love or to the hero but instead to a version of what Michel Foucault called 'bio-power': specifically, the need of the state, under the guise of personalized benevolence, simply to keep the procreative machine running. Indeed, *Measure for Measure* refutes Foucault's claim that this concern was an invention of the eighteenth century, since the ending of this Jacobean play could be trenchantly described in exactly the terms

Foucault used to describe a supposedly post-Enlightenment mode of government: 'It is no longer a matter of bringing death into play in the field of sovereignty, but of distributing the living in the domain of value and utility.'[7] In *Measure for Measure* domestic bliss is exposed as a euphemism for the domestication of the human animal; it is not only bawds (as Elbow supposes) who 'buy and sell men and women like beasts' (III. ii. 2). Men have commonly blamed women for such Circean transformations, but that is hardly surprising, since (through the figure of Eve) men have long blamed women (who issue mortal bodies and rouse decadent lusts) for death itself. But even Angelo recognizes that Isabella is not really a 'tempter' culpable for his own descent into 'carrion'; that process is merely the dark side of biology (II. ii. 162–8). The comic dance of marriage is, measure for measure, also a Dance of Death, and the disguised ruler in the black cowl may carry a sickle as well as a pardon. The state has reached an accommodation with the jealous god Death, and as we play out our biological roles, each of us becomes a propitiary sacrifice. No wonder statecraft is so oddly associated with pregnancy in Vienna (e.g. I. i. 11, IV. iv. 18). Against the ongoing decimations of the Grim Reaper, *Measure for Measure* pits a Duke who might be called the Grim Breeder, hardly more appealing in his ways of creating people than the Reaper is in destroying them. Vienna is left without eternals, with only maternals and paternals to take their place.

While thus questioning the adequacy of procreation as a response to human mortality, *Measure for Measure* also subjects honor and piety to similarly cynical psychological and political perspectives. These virtues, and the hopes commonly attached to them, stand exposed in Freudian and Machiavellian ways as merely illusory forms of personal redemption. This devastating interrogation of all the 'heroic' modes in which individuals attempt to perpetuate their individuality brings me, at last, to my declared main topic: false immortality. *Measure for Measure* resists its genre by undermining the three modes in which comedy usually promises immortality – fame, salvation and procreation – and by replacing them with an emphasis on the destruction of the individual, an emphasis that is typical of tragedy. Whether or not we accept the pseudo-biographical impression that Shakespeare here vandalizes his own comic form in deference to the great tragedies he had recently begun to write, we can hardly deny the inadequacies of the comic resolution of *Measure for Measure*, the darkness it fails to dispel. It is tragicomic not only because death is strongly present prior to the resolution but, more crucially, because mortality remains imperfectly refuted at the center of that resolution.

'One can see *Measure for Measure* as a play that opens with the law being invoked to punish fornication by death and that closes with the law being utilized to punish fornication by marriage.'[8] This witty observation cuts deep; it opens for inspection the common discomfort with the 'comic resolution' of *Measure for Measure*: two marriages tainted by unwilling and unenviable bridegrooms, the other two compromised by their peculiar brides, one arguably reluctant and still in a nun's habit, the other newly out of jail and barely back on her feet after childbirth. Given the fact that even the most promising marriages in Shakespeare's plays often teeter on the brink of tragic collapse, we can hardly foresee great good coming of all these awkward alliances, except in tidying up the bookkeeping of the Viennese bureaucracy.

And yet it is not so cynical or unreasonable for a government to treat marriage as merely another, preferable instrument for controlling desire – which is one plausible definition of punishment. From the normal perspective of the romantic individual or of romantic comedy, the absence of choice and love in such matchmaking may be disturbing, but from the perspective of the state, choice and love are subordinate values. The state cannot finally concern itself with the motivation behind marriage any more than it can condemn citizens for unacted evil desires: 'Thoughts are no subjects,' Isabella tells the Duke, 'Intents, but merely thoughts' (V. i. 451–2). The opening lines of the play invite us to recognize what follows as a dramatized treatise on the properties of government, and that is largely what we get. But by presenting that treatise in the form of an impassioned human story, Shakespeare creates a peculiar disturbance in our fantasies of personal significance. Amid the threats of death to characters in this play, which fit it to most definitions of tragicomedy, lurks a threat to the spectators' strategies of immortality, a threat to reveal supposedly transcendent values as mere instruments of state, to reveal the hope for individual survival as a hollow fantasy subserving the survival instincts of the body politic.

The solution is thus achieved only in sociological terms. The resurrection of Claudio and the pardons for Angelo and Barnardine are political tricks that only defer the question of mortality. Claudio was told that Angelo's ill-won pardon would gain him merely 'six or seven winters' of sickly life; will the Duke's nobler pardon gain him more? The one gesture toward a truly eternal solution – Isabella's religious vocation – apparently yields to the demands of dynastic survival, and the play does not audibly mourn for it. The essence of the Duke's final triumph (and Shakespeare's comic solution) is marriage – not as individual fulfillment but as a practical, worldly, even legalistic solution to the problem of maintaining the size of the Viennese population, and to the no-more-romantic problem of controlling illegitimacy and veneral disease among the city's many wayward citizens. The question of personal annihilation might thus be neatly avoided – except that the play raises it, indirectly but repeatedly. The focus on government appears to offer some respite from the question of individual death, but that anxiety nonetheless finds ways to break through to the surface.

Measure for Measure starts with the Duke fashioning Angelo into a son and heir to the throne. The diction is relentlessly suggestive:

> I say, bid come before us Angelo.
> What figure of us, think you, he will bear?
> For you must know, we have with special soul
> Elected him our absence to supply;
> Lent him our terror, drest him with our love,
> And given his deputation all the organs
> Of our own power.
>
> (I. i. 15–21)

The Duke intends thus to make Angelo 'at full ourself.' Angelo responds to the suggestion that he is to 'bear a figure' of his predecessor when, later in the scene, he expresses his anxiety about having 'so great a figure . . . stamp'd upon' him (I. i. 49–50); in the second act of the play, he will use the same coining metaphor to refer to procreation (II. iv. 45). The Duke's implicit fantasy of parthenogenesis is common in the struggle of Shakespeare's tragically mis-guided men (such as Coriolanus and Leontes) against their own mortality.[9] For them to acknowledge either the means or the need to procreate would be to confess the mortally fallen nature of their bodies. Yet to be mere coins in some usurious biological economy can hardly satisfy the desire for transcen-dent personal significance. The Duke's introductory remarks make the prac-tices of heaven in this regard seem suspiciously congruent with those of nature:

> Heaven doth with us as we with torches do,
> Not light them for themselves; for if our virtues
> Did not go forth of us, 'twere all alike
> As if we had them not. Spirits are not finely touch'd
> But to fine issues; nor nature never lends
> The smallest scruple of her excellence
> But, like a thrifty goddess, she determines
> Herself the glory of a creditor,
> Both thanks and use.
>
> (I. i. 32–40)

'Thanks but no thanks' might be the reply of the heroic actor cast as a mere torchbearer. Great creating nature demands back ashes for ashes and dust for dust, and a few pounds more than what we started with. Ben Jonson's epitaph 'On My First Son' demonstrates that this loan-shark aspect of God could elicit bitterness, despite all the standard gestures of submission to divine will. When Gertrude remarries so hastily, Hamlet remarks no less bitterly on the way 'thrift' has been valued over grief for his dead father. Death tenaciously shadows the procreative process, and the efficiency of the biological economy is an insult to the human spirit, especially when a Ben Jonson is asked to accept the loss of a Ben Jonson, a Hamlet the loss of a Hamlet.[10]

By staging his own miraculous return, in the manner of the disguised-ruler plot so popular on the early Jacobean stage, the Duke fulfills another fantasy familiar from Elizabethan drama: namely, the return of a father from death (or at least from a great distance or great poverty) to remedy the wrongs of the prodigal son who has forgotten him and his ways. King Hamlet and King Lear are grim variations on this theme. The persistent appeal of such stories may reside in their implicit denial of death, in the fantastic defeat of the implacable process whereby children replace rather than reproduce their parents. In the case of *Measure for Measure*, the Duke's purpose in this arrangement is twofold and will be served only to the extent that Angelo stumbles in the footsteps of his paternalistic patron. First, the Duke must show his citizens the dangers of provoking excessive restraint by their false equation of life with mere sensual indulgence. Second, he must prove that even an apparently pure embodiment of his moral law makes a very poor substitute for the Duke's own wit and kindness, for the individual humanity that shines redeemingly even through his disguise. The Duke thus entangles himself in a contradiction: trying to prove to his citizens that replacing oneself procreatively is more important than indulging selfish desires, yet aspiring to do so in a way that will prove himself irreplaceable. Furthermore, the Duke's effort to end illegitimacy in Vienna involves making Angelo, in one sense, the Duke's own bastard son. Angelo's failure as a dynastic heir, precisely by the way it bolsters the Duke's claim to lasting political glory, ruins the Duke's figurative claim to procreative survival.

His lack of a true heir is what the Duke must therefore repair at the end by marrying Isabella. He has evidently viewed his entire citizenry as his figurative children, himself as 'the father of their idle dream' (IV. i. 64) – a complaint about the vulnerability of his fame that links it suggestively to his other immortalizing ploys as a figurative father, a kind of playwright, and a feigned holy 'father' (as he is repeatedly called in his disguise). The ending of the play suggests, however, that neither this paternalistic stratagem with Angelo, nor the growth of Vienna's population, nor even his fame-winning masterstrokes in the theatricalized arts of state can adequately substitute for a fruitful marriage. In steering his subjects toward matrimony, the Duke discovers not only a worthy spouse but also the fact of his own mortality that obliges him, too, to marry. If there is any validity to the argument that *Measure for Measure* was written partly in tribute to the accession of King James, it would make sense for the play to contain some endorsement of a monarch who could offer a lineal successor (such as Prince Henry) rather than merely an appointive one, some transformation of the literary legacy that had worshipped a Virgin Queen (though of course Shakespeare would hardly wish to suggest that James's rather indirect accession resembled Angelo's). This is the same promise held out by the mirror portent in *Macbeth*: that James's royal identity will 'stretch out to th' crack of doom' (IV. i. 117), will survive lineally until the Last Judgment revives James himself. Power was intimately bound up with paternity for James,[11] and his legacy to his son Henry was the *Basilikon Doron*, a text on the proper management of a kingdom. The Duke's obsessively paternalistic play, from its very first lines, presents itself as this sort of mixed representation of authority; but power, fatherhood, and authorship all fall short of assuring personal immortality.

The Duke pursues another well-worn path toward immortality in his quest for fame, a category in which I include the putative immortalities of honor and of art. He spreads news of his death (IV. ii. 200) and returns (like Tom Sawyer) to study the reactions, but what he discovers is hardly the canonization he had hoped for. Of course, the Duke claims to be indifferent to fame, even to dislike it:

> I'll privily away. I love the people,
> But do not like to stage me to their eyes:
> Though it do well, I do not relish well
> Their loud applause and *Aves* vehement;
> Nor do I think the man of safe discretion
> That does affect it.
>
>   (I. i. 67–72)

He doth protest too much, methinks. His nagging resentment of Lucio's casual slanders suggests he cares very much about his audience and about his reviews (the excellent BBC-TV 'Shakespeare Plays' production emphasizes this trait when the Duke triumphantly stages himself to the people's eyes in the final scene). He is vainly determined to convince Lucio what a splendid man the Duke actually is, he soliloquizes bitterly about the injuries that await even the most carefully built public reputation, and he promptly begins fishing shamelessly for compliments from Escalus (III. ii. 137–45, 179–82, 254–75, 224–31). Though it might be something King James would be pleased to hear,[12] the Duke's assertion that 'slandering a prince' deserves 'pressing to death, / Whipping, and hanging' (V. i. 520–21) seems revealingly severe.

When he reappears as himself at the start of the fifth act, the Duke seems to mock his own quest for a glorious place in future Mirrors for Magistrates. He extols Angelo's reign, which he intends soon to expose as mortally corrupt, with the same equivocal puns on 'character' and uneasy suggestions of coining used earlier to conflate the immortalities of honor, art, and progeny: Angelo's conduct in office 'deserves with characters of brass / A forted residence 'gainst the tooth of time / And razure of oblivion' (V. i. 12–14). The Duke's irony presses uncomfortably on Shakespeare's earlier explorations of the quest for immortality in *Love's Labor's Lost* and the sonnets. The facts of fallen flesh and blood have already overthrown this immortalizing project before time and nature can even begin to erode gilded monuments.

The Duke's disguise and return also keeps the doctrine of the monarch's two bodies active in the minds of the audience: 'The Duke's in us,' Escalus announces authoritatively to his disguised and unrecognized sovereign (V. i. 293). In a play so concerned with the paradoxical quest for personal immortality, this doctrinal echo (like Hamlet's 'the body is with the King . . .' at IV. ii. 27–30) invites our attention but finally offers no reassurance. When Angelo's corruption of the law renders him instant 'carrion' (II. ii. 167), it may serve to warn the Duke against relying on his official role to immortalize him in any meaningful way. The royal self is hardly the metal stamp of divine justice envisioned earlier; it becomes indistinguishable from the sinful flesh. Angelo describes Isabella as 'deflower'd . . . by an eminent body, that enforc'd / The law against it!' (IV. iv. 19–21). This phallic body politic becomes a source of corruption and death, rather than symbolic immortality, to its citizens.

The Duke's immortal longings also lead him to experiment with piety, with the abjuration of the things of this world in hope of a place in the next. There are repeated suggestions that the Duke is so inclined, ranging from his claim to have always 'lov'd the life remov'd' (I. iii. 8), to his request for reassurance of his reputation for preferring contemplation over pleasure (III. ii. 224–31), to the peculiar evidence that he has long served as a holy confessor to Mariana (IV. i. 8–9, V. i. 524). But he uses his monkish traits finally as a ploy to effect the civil education and earthly salvation of Claudio and to lure Isabella away from her own such choice, away from her betrothal to Christ and into his own earthly marital embrace. Furthermore, the essentially hollow tone and ulterior motivation of his monkish lessons to Claudio serve to undermine the entire belief-system – both onstage and off – that views death as a blessing. Within the play-world these all prove to be ploys of state, designed to foster stability or at least dynamic equilibrium.

The Duke's speech to Claudio at the start of the third act is essentially a compilation of *contemptus mundi* and *ars moriendi* commonplaces. These commonplaces are marked as clichés by their role in a theatrical performance (Duke as monk) that aims at civic reform through pietistic deception, rather than at any pious conversion that would mitigate the state's punitive power. It is clear that the Duke is not, in reality, scornful of this world and this life; his whole mission in the play is the augmentation of both those things, and here he sedulously avoids any mention of the afterlife that might lead Claudio to value it above his imminent fatherhood.[13] It is also clear that Claudio accepts these formulaic assurances only formally, only superficially. Such pragmatic, even hypocritical, uses of the consolation ritual – making Last Things the means to a worldly end – place the audience in a similarly skeptical position toward the standard assurances of immortality offered by the church, and not only by the church.[14] The pious function of the Last Confessor becomes merely one more strategic role in a game of practical survival, reminiscent of the pious fraud Edgar perpetrates on Gloucester at the cliffs of Dover. Hearing it done so well by these dissemblers only heightens our awareness that the most compelling consolatory arguments might prove to be fraudulent if we could see the real faces and motives behind them. *Measure for Measure* thus accords with the views reportedly held by the boldest of Jacobean blasphemers: centuries before Karl Marx criticized religion as the opiate of an oppressed populace, these radicals suggested that priest and preacher were merely dummies for the Machiavellian ventriloquists who held material power.[15]

In comforting Isabella for the supposed death of her brother, the unveiled Duke reverts to some of his monkish commonplaces, in a form that again suggests their hollowness:

> That life is better life, past fearing death,
> Than that which lives to fear. Make it your comfort,
> So happy is your brother.
> (V. i. 395–7)

Editors do their best with this, but the statement verges on mere double-talk. If Claudio has overcome his fear of dying, it is only by no longer having any life to lose; he has become (supposedly) a corpse, not a philosopher. The Duke's remark can be taken as a simple endorsement of the afterlife, but (absurdly) the sole virtue it identifies in that consoling afterlife is that it lacks the fear of death; immortality consists only of non-mortality. In its brittle piety the Duke's consolation for Claudio's supposed death echoes the pregnant Juliet's bitter complaint about Claudio's scheduled execution:

> Must die to-morrow! O injurious love,
> That respites me a life, whose very comfort
> Is still a dying horror!
> (II. iii. 40–2)

''Tis pity of him,' the Provost replies, but it is also pity of all consciously mortal beings enlisted in the Sisyphean struggle of procreation to defeat death. The soon-to-be-born child will likely someday voice the same complaint, even if it is not so soon to be fatherless.

Arguably the Duke is mimicking good Christian practice by encouraging penance through mortification in Claudio, his sister, and his fiancée; and one reward of pious daily dying is the seeming daily demonstration of Resurrection. But the theatre of God's judgments begins to look like an ordinary stage fiction. Claudio's supposed demise is made acceptable to the tragicomic form because we learn that the death, no less than the consolation, is merely a piece of play-acting; but that evasion prepares us very poorly for the instances where the death of those we love is real and the offered consolations sound all too similar, where (like Lear over the body of Cordelia) we wait bewildered for the comic resurrection that never comes.

The standard complaint against the marriages of *Measure for Measure* – that the comic solution seems a forced, unconvincing, insufficient answer or counterweight to the tragic elements and atmosphere of the story – applies to the threatened deaths as well. Death is not refuted any more wholeheartedly than marriage is affirmed. Furthermore, death is assigned rather arbitrarily (in Claudio's condemnation and Ragozine's illness) and avoided the same way (in the pardons of Barnardine and Angelo); we are given no compelling justification for these deaths, any more than for the marriages, beyond the mere mechanisms of biology and statecraft. (Indeed, the use of Ragozine invites us to ask a question that our culture, abetted by its newscasts, fiercely resists: is death by disease any less arbitrary or important than death by accident or execution?) Perhaps it is not merely marriage that is undermined as a comic resolution in this play: all the strategies of secular immortality, all the fantasies (religious, artistic, familial) of resurrection (by miracle or statue or progeny), all the ordinary lines of comic consolation for the central and implacably tragic fact of individual annihilation lie mortally wounded amid the formulaic resurrections of the final scene.

Terrible deaths have been averted, but in a way that provokes a modern suspicion that ordinary deaths are the most terrible of all. As Phoebe Spinrad writes, 'Death, far from being the glorious martyrdom of Isabella's dreams, the comfortable sleep of the Duke's dreams, the nuisance of Barnardine's, the punishment of Angelo's, or the horror of Claudio's, is in fact simply a part of life, to be accepted on its own terms, and neither fled from nor sought after.'[16] Not everyone will agree that this is good news; otherwise we would all agree that *Measure for Measure* is an exemplary comedy and would never turn from it to revenge tragedies, detective novels, war stories, or religious texts for assurances that death is an unnatural event and an ideal occasion for heroism.

Faced with a city that was becoming infamous, impious, and sexually diseased, Duke Vincentio has experimentally revived the three main modes of secular immortality, using his disguise to increase his worldly fame, to appropriate the redemptive mysteries of the clergy, and to establish himself in the genetic future. But even at the end the Duke's fame is under attack from Lucio's slanders, those nagging interruptions from the lower stratum of body and body politic that mar Shakespeare's artistic resolution as well as the Duke's conclusive statecraft. If the Duke's glorious return from supposed death echoes the story of Christ's Resurrection, it does so parodically: it is an illusion manipulated by a fake holy man for his own aggrandizement. Furthermore, this reappearance compromises the principal Christian arguments (which the Duke stressed to Claudio) for the willing surrender of earthly life: that death is certain and that true happiness and justice exist only beyond it. The play alludes to the commonplace that the entire world is a prison from which death is the only true escape, yet several characters are eventually released from death row into worldly pleasures. The pardons constitute a happy ending, but one which (precisely because it *is* happy) subverts a crucial metaphor frequently employed in the Renaissance, within and beyond this play, to reconcile human beings to mortality. Furthermore, the two pleas we hear for bail from this prison are hardly reassuring models of redemptive prayer: Claudio's becomes a solicitation of his sister to fornication – a striking perversion of the prayer to the Virgin for salvation – and Pompey's is met only by diabolical jeering (III. ii. 40ff). We cannot know whether such veiled but persistent blasphemies were the reason, but it is interesting to note that when an English Jesuit censored Shakespeare's works for the Inquisition in the mid-seventeenth century, *Measure for Measure* was the only play he cut out entirely.[17]

The Duke's complex plot serves to remind us that the procreative impulse can be seen as essentially a mechanism of biology manipulated as a ploy of the state, a way of preserving social structures rather than individual consciousness. The state is merely doing its best to harness, rationalize, even sentimentalize, the relentless directionless march of nature. With Isabella apparently about to surrender her virginity, Mariana (by the convention of such stories) probably newly impregnated, Juliet newly delivered, and Lucio's whore the mother of his young child, the self-perpetuating natural system seems to be far more in control than the vagaries of individual human will. Angelo presses Isabella to show that she is a woman 'By putting on the destin'd livery' (II. iv. 137); this equation of her identity as a woman with her sexual submission earns Angelo the jeers of even the most mildly feminist audience, yet the very play that thus makes him the villain suggests that the procreative sheets – and the swaddling clothes, and the burial shroud – are indeed the destined livery of each human being, for all our protestations of free will. One feminist critic rightly complains about the lack in *Measure for Measure* 'of women's personal autonomy – her right to control her body,'[18] but men hardly seem to fare better in that category, whether in bed or in prison. It is not only social hierarchy, as some political critics assume, that the state must mystify to sustain itself: reproductive biology seems to demand and receive a similar disguise.

Isabella, in her determination to abjure the procreative mode of immortality, provides an occasion for inspecting the promises of salvation in a seemingly more authentic instance. Yet from the very start her dedication as a spiritual Bride of Christ is subverted and even parodied by her conversion into a procreative bride for the body politic. Isabella's name proclaims her devoted to God, but Vienna, through an ingenious translation of that devotion, enforces its claim on her womb. For fifteen lines she is allowed to profess asceticism; then Lucio rings the bell at the convent and says, 'Hail virgin, if you be' (I. iv. 1–16). The might be an unremarkable greeting under the circumstances, except that it awakens some truly remarkable echoes. Lucio's salutation translates the beginning of the primary prayer to the Virgin Mary, and then questions whether Isabella is actually suited to the role.[19] Furthermore, that hailing of the Virgin (in a Roman Catholic society such as the play depicts) immediately follows the ringing of a bell, a bell that (even under Elizabethan Protestantism) was known as the Angelus bell. Lucio arrives to lure her out of the convent, and arrives as both an agent of Angelo (who wants to turn her into a sexual object) and of the Duke (who then wants to turn her into a procreative agent). Furthermore, '*Ave virgo*' recurs as the opening of the Annunciation, which is precisely what the Angelus prayer celebrates: the summoning of the Virgin into the task of bearing the son of the Lord as a means of redeeming human mortality. Theologians of course stressed that the Annunciation was by no means an angelic rape but instead the occasion of the Virgin's free consent to the patriarchal Lord of whom the angel was merely a deputy (and Angelo is called Vincentio's 'deputy' a dozen times in the play). The process of Isabella's seduction reduces the decorum of the Annunciation to a 'good cop, bad cop' tactic employed by the interrogating figures of Angelo and the Duke.

The setting Angelo chooses for his tryst with Isabella is heavily marked as a version of the *hortus conclusus* that is the iconographic home of the Virgin Mary. Isabella reports that Angelo

> . . . hath a garden circummur'd with brick,
> Whose western side is with a vineyard back'd;
> And to that vineyard is a planched gate,
> That makes his opening with this bigger key.
> This other doth command a little door
> Which from the vineyard to the garden leads;
> There have I made my promise
> Upon the heavy middle of the night
> To call upon him.
>
> (IV. i. 28–36)

Medieval depictions of the Annunciation often place Mary in front of a garden surrounded by walls and vineyards; sometimes the descended angel holds the key to its portal.[20] But Angelo's markedly virginal garden – nowhere evident in Shakespeare's sources – is also strikingly similar to the trysting places of the Elizabethan fornicators whom Phillip Stubbes reviles:

they have gardens, either polled or walled round about very high, with their harbers and bowers fit for the purpose. . . . And for that their gardens are locked, some of them have three or four keyes a peece, whereof one they keepe for themselves, the other their paramours have to goe in before them . . . to receive the guerdon of their paines. . . .[21]

Isabella is positioned as a holy virgin only to be displaced into an object of sexual and reproductive desire, her symbols degradingly recontextualized.

So the course of Isabella's enlistment into the reproductive economy is marked from the start as a queasy burlesque of her religious mission. When Lucio tells Isabella in this initial exchange, 'I hold you as a thing enskied and sainted / By your renouncement, an immortal spirit,' she replies, 'You do blaspheme the good, in mocking me' (I. iv. 34–5, 38). It is not clear whether Lucio is indeed mocking Isabella as he here calls her back to the earthly business of the body; but it does seem clear that Shakespeare is making a mockery of the pious notion that virginity is a plausible or even permissible way to pursue immortality. Isabella turns the immediate task of bearing Angelo's burden over to Mariana – another refraction of Mary, with a moated grange for her *hortus conclusus* – but soon enough the bells will ring for Isabella as well. Presumably she surrenders her quest for immortalizing chastity by taking the Duke's hand in the final silence of the play, much as Coriolanus surrenders his own heroic immortality strategy to the silent generational panorama by taking the hand of his mother. In silence, and by the body, our shared mortal natures reassert themselves.

The condemnation of Claudio forces Isabella to confront the conflict between (on the one hand) the instincts that resist physical death and (on the other) the daily death at the heart of her religious vocation, with its strident rejection of this world and its confident anticipation of another. In her first confrontation with Angelo, Isabella interprets her brother's threatened execution as a sacrificial preparation for heaven. The proprieties of slaughter seem quite clear to her: as other animals become merely food after death, so human beings become purely souls (II. ii. 85–8). The fact that she can offer so comfortably this grotesque analogy demonstrates her facile confidence in the scheme of salvation (it may also remind us how deeply Western culture depends, for its spiritual complacency as well as its food supply, on the same absolute distinction). Death to her is merely the tiny unpleasant fraction of human experience shared with a crushed beetle; understandably, she cannot imagine sacrificing 'a perpetual honor' for 'six or seven winters' of 'feverous life' (III. i. 73–80).[22] Members of the audience may wince at this reminder of the corrupt bargains they have made with fallen angels for those few extra years of survival. But is honor necessarily any more perpetual than bodies are, than souls might be? When Isabella tells Angelo that she would 'rather give my body than my soul' to save her brother, Angelo replies curtly, 'I talk not of your soul' (II. iv. 56–7). Throughout the play, Isabella is thus steadily drawn into the marketplace of the physical, into a mentality that thinks more about desire than about religion; more about the threat of death than about the hope of immortality; more about bodily confinement (a jail or a grave) than about spiritual injury (disgrace or damnation), about the wounded honor that would be a 'restraint / Though all the world's vastidity you had' (III. i. 68). Both siblings are worried about the 'pollution' of their bodies, but they have virtually opposite definitions of the term, Isabella associating it with sexual reproduction and Claudio with mortal decay. When Claudio thinks the alternative to instant death is 'perpetual durance,' he means imprisonment of his body for the duration of its life – a characteristic misreading of the word 'perpetual' as Isabella understands it. By disallowing her orthodox reference to eternals that would easily resolve the dilemma, the play disables the same simplifying reflex in the audience. No wonder critics alternately condemn her declaration that 'More than our brother is our chastity' (II. iv. 184) as mean-spirited hysteria and defend it as correct Renaissance theology. This stubbornly sociobiological play is as subversive to more recent humanistic pietisms as it is to medieval Christian ones, and there seems to be no defensible middle ground.

Claudio finally tells his sister that 'If I must die, / I will encounter darkness as a bride / And hug it in my arms' (III. i. 83–5). This is an otherworldly resolution with some symptoms of weakness. He is making the afterworld into an image of his earthly desires and deeds – this death sounds like another imperfect marriage prematurely embraced – and equating that afterworld with pure darkness, a plausible symptom of annihilationism. Isabella nonetheless congratulates him – not surprisingly if we remember that she herself had conceived of death as an erotic spouse (II. iv. 102). The peculiar terms of her congratulation show how the various strategies of immortality mingle together in the desperately denying minds of these characters. To salvation and honor she now adds a ghost of procreation. 'There spake my brother: there my father's grave / Did utter forth a voice. Yes, thou must die' (III. i. 85–6). The last three words are a standard and starkly unconsoling message from the grave, but the first sentence implies more subtly that by dying properly (and in defense of his sister's procreative purity) Claudio will become eligible for this kind of procreative, not to say paganish, resurrection.[23] The likeness of a son, he is reminded, means that the father does not really die into a rest of silence. When Claudio weakens again some fifty lines later, she turns the same set of assumptions against him. 'Is't not a kind of incest, to take life / From thine own sister's shame?' (III. i. 138–9), she asks accusingly, as if the life he would save by escaping execution were virtually indistinguishable from the life he would make by procreating within his own genetic field.

When the revenant Duke suggests that Isabella accuses Angelo 'in th'infirmity of sense,' she replies,

> O Prince, I conjure thee, as thou believ'st
> There is another comfort than this world,
> That thou neglect me not with that opinion
> That I am touch'd with madness.
>
> (V. i. 51–4)

This conjuration makes it all the more interesting that her sanity – and thereby, implicitly, all faith in that otherworldly comfort – is repeatedly called into question as the scene goes on, not only by Angelo but by the Duke as well: her complaint against Angelo is 'somewhat madly spoken' (V. i. 92), and her plea to spare his worldly life runs 'against all sense' (V. i. 431). The connection between her faith and her possible psychological infirmities may strike the audience as far less casual than she seems to intend it, especially given the lurid symptomology of her sexual repression. Hers is therefore no random oath of affirmation. It reminds us that belief in an afterlife can be interrogated precisely because it is so necessary a comfort, just as romantic sentiment and the institution of marriage can be analyzed as by-products of biological and political imperatives. To vary Voltaire's famous dictum about God, if there were not conjugal desire, it would be necessary to invent it. Indeed, the Duke seems desperate to simulate both marital love and divine justice precisely because his city seems to have lost track of the original models. As soon as one begins to look behind these necessities, to doubt these comforts – as *Measure for Measure* subtly but persistently invites us to do – the immortality strategies of Isabella and the others may indeed appear insane. A culture of religious faith (such as the Renaissance) commonly diagnoses atheism as a form of insanity;[24] an atheistic culture will doubtless (following Freud) interpret faith as a neurotic symptom. *Measure for Measure* hovers uneasily between those two worlds, leaving Isabella to make a bewildering shift from a religious to a procreative model of immortality.

Angelo studiously rejects the allure of procreation (I. iv. 57–61) in favor of an immortality strategy based on fame, honor, and purity. The willingness to die for these things by war, duel, or suicide is no less rational an answer to mortality than our modern determination to delay death briefly by health care; but if the denial of death is indeed fundamental to the psychic viability of a society, we will necessarily again diagnose a kind of insanity in any conflicting version. *Measure for Measure* seems determined to reduce Angelo's motives, as well as Isabella's, to psychopathological symptoms. Lucio claims that 'Angelo was not made by man and woman, after this downright way of creation' and is therefore 'a motion ungenerative' (III. ii. 100-8). In his sensual restraint and his reluctance to consummate the marriage to Mariana, Angelo refuses to become merely another link in the long chain of mortal human flesh, which transmitted Original Sin (and therefore mortality) through the concupiscence of the generative act. He seeks to be otherworldly here on earth; the coining metaphors suggest that he is ready to be stamped into an 'angel,' a suggestion that again conflates his official stature with holy transcendence. But – like Coriolanus in search of a similar transcendence[25] – Angelo cannot finally redeem the coining metaphor from its conventional reference to procreation; the Duke converts him back into a marker of the fleshly aspect of the state's usuriously breeding wealth.

As soon as Angelo is forced to face the collapse of his immortality strategy (what the psychological philosopher Ernest Becker would call the denial of death by heroic purity),[26] he compares his moral failure to the rotting of dead flesh in the sun (II. ii. 167). This is the same macabre view of mortality, the emphasis on the merely decaying body, that haunts Claudio and (as Philippe Ariès has shown in his histories of death)[27] apparently haunted Western Europe through the late Middle Ages. At the start of the play, Escalus describes Angelo as worthy of the 'ample grace' for which he has been 'elected' (I. i. 18–24); the vocabulary makes public reputation (what Cassio calls 'the immortal part of myself' in *Othello* [II. iii. 263]) an alternative model of eternal salvation. But when the truth about his fleshly failings becomes public as well as private knowledge, Angelo says he feels that 'your Grace, like power divine, / Hath looked upon my passes . . . and sequent death / Is all the grace I beg' (V. i. 367–72). Equating earthly judges with divine ones, he expects a sentence of death – mortality as annihilation – and reaffirms the association by imagining that oblivion is the best to be hoped for from this visitation of grace. Furthermore, the fact that Angelo presumably knows himself to be hypocritical in his pursuit of moral excellence (since he has already mistreated Mariana) only reinforces our uneasy awareness that, upon closer inspection, we might find we did not really believe in the claims to immortality with which we nonetheless console ourselves.

Angelo is fooled by the substitution of Mariana's maidenhead for Isabella's, and again by the substitution of Ragozine's head for Claudio's. The Duke is doubtless right that 'death's a great disguiser' (IV. ii. 174) and that the head of Barnardine might be thereby mistaken for Claudio's. But that reassurance to the Provost must be a disturbance to the audience: however indirectly, it invokes the *transi* figure of medieval tomb sculpture, the stark reminder that in decay all human bodies reveal their horrible sameness. This is the dirty secret that *Measure for Measure* half-reveals in half-concealing it: just as these two women's bodies (even at the moment they are supposedly expressing their most intimate qualities) may be virtually indistinguishable, so are all the rest of us when we fall into the clutches of the omnivorous Angel of Death. More subtly disturbing is the renewed recognition that, from the perspective of nature or the state, in the function of biology or politics, indifference makes perfect sense. Any body will do. The widely expressed critical discomfort with these two substitutions – the bed-trick as immoral, the head-trick as implausible – may cover a symptomatic resistance to this recognition of indifference. Comedies often encourage that recognition but in a far more pleasant manner, on behalf of communal life; tragedies often exhort us to protest against it, but they do so by offering a prospect of heroic transcendence that *Measure for Measure* stubbornly refuses us. The eagerness of commentators to dismiss these juxtaposed substitutions as merely two proximate moments of inferior dramaturgy may partly reflect an unwillingness to see the play's darker purpose – its tragicomic thrust – which is to challenge the sentimental notion of our individual significance.

While humiliating the transcendent strategies of honor and piety that characterize Angelo and Isabella, the play seems, perversely, to reward and endorse the utter negligence of immortality that characterizes Barnardine. He is a kind of reverse synecdoche, a whole man symbolizing an autonomic nervous system. As Claudio hovers, at 'dead midnight,' on the brink of the death that will make him 'immortal,' Barnardine is described as sleeping too soundly to be put to death (IV. ii. 61–6) and as 'A man that apprehends death no more dreadfully but as a drunken sleep; careless, reckless, and fearless of what's past, present, or to come: insensible of mortality, and desperately mortal' (IV. ii. 140–3). Aside from making it difficult to distinguish Barnardine's moral idiocy from the ideal posture of Renaissance Stoicism, this description disturbingly elides a comic failing with perhaps the most central consolatory metaphor for death. This elision recurs twice in Pompey's urgings – only half comic, I think, or at least not casually comic – that the slumbering Barnardine 'awake till you are executed, and sleep afterwards,' and that 'he that drinks all night and is hanged betimes in the morning may sleep the sounder all the next day' (IV. iii. 31–46).[28] The absurdity – or is it absurd propriety? – of this suggestion exposes the weakness of the conventional assurance that death is merely another sleep (an assurance repeatedly offered to the unwilling Claudio, who fears that if dreams come at all, they will be nightmares).

Barnardine is pardoned because the state can much better tolerate an unregenerate soul than an unregenerating body, but again the Duke feels obliged to obscure the distinction with his rhetoric:

> Sirrah, thou art said to have a stubborn soul
> That apprehends no further than this world,
> And squar'st thy life according. Thou'rt condemn'd;

> But, for those earthly faults, I quit them all,
> And pray thee take this mercy to provide
> For better times to come.
>
> (V. i. 478–83)

Barnardine is spared on earth because there is so little hope for him beyond. Perhaps the same worldly assumption underlies – and therefore undermines – the 'resurrection' of Claudio and the pardon of Angelo that follow so quickly. Again – as with Gloucester on Dover Beach – salvation seems to be a fraud engineered by earthly leaders in vague imitation of a myth of grace, because human civilization is really only a confused crowd huddled together on that beach (as Matthew Arnold's poem suggests) against a vast, cold, dark, relentless sea.

The Duke's performance of a Last Judgment at the gates of his city, rather than the gates of heaven, is a culminating instance of the way *Measure for Measure* parodies pious archetypes in asserting the priority of earthly order and human survival. The critics who assert that (for example) 'The Duke's ethical attitude is exactly correspondent with Jesus'[29] fall victim to the same manipulation of pious reflexes by which the Duke controls his citizens. They overlook the fact that the Duke prepares his redemptive intervention by its opposite: this lord turns judgment over to a bad son who insists on the punitive letter of the law rather than the established principle of mercy. The Duke strategically regresses Vienna from the New Testament to the Old so that he can claim credit, as head of state, for reinventing Christian forgiveness. This version of redemption serves to defend, not faith or moral purity, but the public procreative order of Vienna.

Perhaps *Measure for Measure* is a product of the plague year 1603 not only in its emphasis on the replenishment of the population but also in its portrayal of a city abandoned by its benevolent but exasperated Lord to an agency of deadly retribution. The sermons and literature of 1603 predominantly characterize the plague as God's scourge visited on an increasingly immoral nation. At times the Vienna of *Measure for Measure* must seem to its citizens much as the world seems to those who feel (as Reformation theology led many to feel) that God has mysteriously absconded and left his children in a pointless (or at least inscrutable) universe, and in the cold hands of Death:

> The Duke is very strangely gone from hence;
> Bore many gentlemen – myself being one –
> In hand, and hope of action: but we do learn,
> By those that know the very nerves of state,
> His giving out were of an infinite distance
> From his true-meant design. Upon his place,
> And with full line of his authority,

> Governs Lord Angelo; a man whose blood
> Is very snow-broth; one who never feels
> The wanton stings and motions of the sense . . .
>   All hope is gone,
> Unless you have the grace by your fair prayer
> To soften Angelo.
>
> (I. iv. 50–70)

The resemblance to Prospero's 'And my ending is despair, / Unless I be reliev'd by prayer' (Epilogue. 15–16) indicates how strongly Lucio's speech partakes of more eschatological pleas for forgiveness, for relief from the condemnation common to fallen flesh. Lucio is hardly a Job or a Christ, but in this speech he might as well be asking why He has forsaken us, why He has given us thus to the dark fallen angel, the common enemy of man (as Macbeth calls his ultimate foe). Isabella's warning to Angelo about the Last Judgment (II. ii, 73–9) sounds plausibly like a warning about the promised Death of Death after its temporary merciless reign of terror over humankind. When Claudio complains that a seemingly capricious Authority, armed with a deadly blade, makes a few pay for a widely shared sin, he sounds as if he might be talking as much about mortality punishing Original Sin as about execution punishing fornication. Indeed, from the perspective of biological theory that describes death as a necessary by-product of the invention of reproduction, each of us endures Claudio's sentence. Angelo tells Isabella that though Claudio must die under his sentence, 'Yet may he live a while; and, it may be, / As long as you or I' (II. iv. 35–6).

Let me therefore propose one more imperfect but evocative allegory lurking in a play that has perhaps already been allegorized too often and too ingeniously:[30] the Duke, not simply as *imitatio dei*,[31] but as *imitatio dei absconditi*, Angelo as the Angel of Death, Claudio as Everyman, and Isabella as Faith. In this system, Barnardine may represent the body, the stupid force of heartbeat, survival instinct, physical appetite, that is unwilling to die in the condemned Everyman and is (here) finally spared. Lucio, finally, embodies doubt, baffling every path to immortality in mocking Isabella's pious virginity, the Duke's reputation, and the entire procreative process. The state can order that nagging cynical voice to be pressed to death, whipped, hanged, and married to shame, but it cannot be silenced. Even in the triumphant final scene it persists, ruining any hopes – the Duke's, Shakespeare's, ours – that the tragic facts of life can be dispelled (not just disguised) by the warm glow and consoling figurations of comedy. If life goes on, then so does death. 'This news is old enough, yet it is every day's news' (III. ii. 223–4).

Notes

1 In *Measure for Measure, the Law, and the Convent* (Princeton, NJ: Princeton University Press, 1979, pp. 15–60), Darryl J. Gless attempts to locate the genre of the play; see also Mary Lascelles, *Shakespeare's Measure for Measure* (London: Athlone, 1953), which classifies the play as a tragicomedy on a more traditional basis; Gregory W. Lanier, 'Physic that's bitter to sweet end', *Essays in Literature*, 14 (1987), pp. 15–36; and Arthur C. Kirsch, 'The integrity of *Measure for Measure*', *Shakespeare Survey*, 28 (1975), pp. 89–105.

2 For example, Paul Hammond's 'The argument of *Measure for Measure*', *English Literary Renaissance*, 16 (1986), pp. 496–519, resists its own title by asserting that there is finally no moral argument discernible in the play.

3 See, for example, Phillip Stubbes, *The Anatomie of Abuses* (London, 1583), sigs. G8^v–H8^r.

4 Ibid., sig. H4^r.

5 All references to *Measure for Measure* are based on the Arden edition, ed. J. W. Lever (London: Methuen, 1965). References to other plays are based on *The Riverside Shakespeare*, ed. G. Blakemore Evans et al. (Boston: Houghton Mifflin, 1974), with Evans's square brackets removed to avoid confusion with my own interpolations.

6 Carolyn E. Brown, 'Erotic religious flagellation and Shakespeare's *Measure for Measure*', *English Literary Renaissance*, 16 (1986), pp. 139–65.

7 Michel Foucault, *The History of Sexuality*, 3 vols, trans. Robert Hurley (New York: Pantheon, 1978–86), vol. 1, p. 144. Foucault maintains that 'In the eighteenth century, sex became a "police" matter – in the full and strict sense given the term at the time: not the repression of disorder, but an ordered maximization of collective and individual forces . . . One of the great innovations in the techniques of power in the eighteenth century was the emergence of "population" as an economic and political problem: population as wealth, population as manpower or labor capacity . . . At the heart of this economic and political problem of population was sex: it was necessary to analyze the birthrate, the age of marriage, the legitimate and illegitimate births, the precocity and frequency of sexual relations, the ways of making them fertile or sterile, the effects of unmarried life or of the prohibitions . . . This was the first time that a society had affirmed, in a constant way that its future and its fortune were tied . . . to the manner in which each individual made use of his sex' (vol. 1, pp. 25–6). Surely this description fits the governmental work that propels *Measure for Measure*. Perhaps Shakespeare is once again being prescient – or perhaps Foucault is once again exaggerating the disjunctions in recent human history. On 'bio-power' as an eighteenth-century invention, see vol. 1, pp. 138–45; on its strained relation to the death-penalty – again anticipated by *Measure for Measure* – see vol. 1, p. 138.

8 Philip C. McGuire, *Speechless Dialect: Shakespeare's Open Silences* (Berkeley, CA: University of California Press, 1985), p. 71. Victoria Hayne, in her forthcoming UCLA dissertation, will argue against this perspective by demonstrating that the

reluctant grooms are merely forced to honor the marital commitments they have already made by word or deed.

9   Robert N. Watson, *Shakespeare and the Hazards of Ambition* (Cambridge, MA: Harvard University Press, 1984), passim.

10   The argument that Angelo's 'virtues' (a word with seminal implications) must go forth in 'issues' (I. i. 27–43) echoes the commonplace arguments for procreation in Shakespeare's sonnets and in fact throughout Renaissance literature, exhortations not to waste nature's finest models by failing to reproduce them in a new generation. In the same passage, the Duke talks about Angelo's life-story as if it were a stable and legible text to be read, and such writing (again with a pun on 'character') becomes another metaphor for procreation at I. ii. 144. This further interweaves the procreative and artistic aspects of the Duke's immortality strategy – the same pair of projects linked so persistently in Jonson's epitaph and in Shakespeare's sonnets. Yet as those sonnets demonstrate, Shakespeare remains painfully aware that these modes of immortality are merely figurative and highly vulnerable; see Gillian M. Kendall, 'The quest for secular immortality in Shakespeare's romances,' unpublished dissertation, Harvard University, 1987, which insightfully explores Shakespeare's highly equivocal endorsement of these answers to death. For discussion of the procreative theme in the sonnets, see the essay by Robert Crosman in *Shakespeare Quarterly*, 41: 4 (1990).

11   Jonathan Goldberg argues that the paternal metaphor permeates James's assertions of authority ('The politics of patriarchy' in *Rewriting the Renaissance: The Discourses of Sexual Difference in Early Modern Europe*, ed. Margaret Ferguson, Maureen Quilligan and Nancy Vickers [Chicago: University of Chicago Press, 1986], pp. 3–32).

12   Gless compares the Duke's complaints about slander with those of King James (*Measure for Measure, the Law, and the Convent*, pp. 161–2); others, notably Josephine Waters Bennett in *Measure for Measure as Royal Entertainment* (New York: Columbia University Press, 1966), pursue the connection more extensively. However, Richard Levin forcefully refutes this instance of 'occasionalist' interpretation in *New Readings vs. Old Plays* (Chicago: University of Chicago Press, 1979), pp. 167–93.

13   Brown, summarizing an observation several critics have made, comments that the consolations the disguised Duke offers are 'conspicuously devoid of the promise of a Christian afterlife' ('Erotic religious flagellation', p. 151). Lever characterizes the Duke's argument as 'essentially materialist' (*Measure for Measure*, p. lxxxvii).

14   Stephen Greenblatt skilfully explores the notion that in improvising cynically on the belief systems of Native Americans, English colonists might have compromised their own Christian confidence ('Invisible bullets' in *Shakespeare's 'Rough Magic': Renaissance Essays in Honor of C. L. Barber*, ed. Peter Erickson and Coppélia Kahn [Newark: University of Delaware Press, 1985], pp. 276–302).

15   This Marxist/Machiavellian perspective on religion is most obvious in the writings of the radical Reformers, though traces of it may be found in canonical figures such as Marlowe, Montaigne, and Hobbes as well.

16 Phoebe Spinrad, '*Measure for Measure* and the art of not dying', *Texas Studies in Literature and Language*, 26 (1984), pp. 74–94, esp. p. 91. She also analyzes Claudio as an anticipation of the modern 'quasi-solipsist who in his own demise sees the disappearance of the universe' (p. 82).

17 Roland M. Frye records this censorship in *Shakespeare and Christian Doctrine* (Princeton, NJ: Princeton University Press, 1963), pp. 291–2.

18 Irene G. Dash, *Wooing, Wedding, and Power: Women in Shakespeare's Plays* (New York: Columbia University Press, 1981), p. 251.

19 Gless notes the echo by which Lucio's 'salutation mocks Catholic devotion to the Blessed Virgin' (*Measure for Measure, the Law, and the Convent*, p. 103) but overlooks the further resonances of the Annunciation, which make it much harder safely to isolate the blasphemy as merely anti-monasticism in the mouth of a profane scoundrel. Virtually the entire Annunciation text, which the Book of Common Prayer takes directly from Luke 1: 28–35, offers suggestive parallels to Isabella's experience, from the initial novitiate's unease at Lucio's apparently mocking greeting, and embarrassment at the sexual implications of his message, to the submission to shadowy powers that will make her the prospective mother of her lord's son: 'And the Angel went in vnto her, & said, Haile . . . And when she sawe *him*, she was troubled at his saying, & thoght what maner of salutacion that shulde be . . . [Her child] shalbe great, & shalbe called the Sonne of the moste High . . . Then said Marie vnto the Angel, How shal this be, seing, I know no man? And the Angel answered, and said vnto her, The holie Gost shal come vpon thee, & the power of the most High shal ouershadowe thee . . .' (quoted from the Geneva Bible). An eerie futurist echo of Shakespeare's twist on the Annunciation story occurs in Margaret Atwood's recently filmed novel, *The Handmaid's Tale* (New York: Random House, 1985), in which the few women still fertile are dressed in red nuns' habits and forced to bear the children of the ruling men to perpetuate the society.

20 Stanley Stewart, *The Enclosed Garden: The Tradition and the Image in Seventeenth-century Poetry* (Madison: University of Wisconsin Press, 1966), pp. 40–1.

21 Stubbes, in the version of *The Anatomie of Abuses* edited by William B. D. D. Turnbull (Edinburgh: W. and D. Laing, 1836), pp. 87–8; this passage does not appear in the 1583 first edition but was included well before the time of *Measure for Measure*.

22 This effort to turn the bodily discomforts of both wintry cold and feverous heat against Claudio's prospective nostalgia for the earthly life of the senses backfires when both extremes reappear less than fifty lines later as part of his terror of death.

23 Later the Duke similarly warns that Claudio's 'ghost his paved bed would break, / And take her hence in horror' if Isabella were to forgive Angelo (V. i. 433–4). Again the prospect of a posthumous voice is used to extort an earthly response, demanding sacrifices (as sociobiology would predict) in defense of close genetic kin.

24 G. E. Aylmer, 'Unbelief in seventeenth-century England' in *Puritans and Revolutionaries*, ed. Donald Pennington and Keith Thomas (Oxford: Clarendon Press, 1978), pp. 22–46, esp. pp. 33–4.

25   In my *Shakespeare and the Hazards of Ambition*, I have argued that Coriolanus' effort to extricate himself from the mortal flesh he shares with his fellow Romans obliges him to define his 'coining' as a mechanical rather than a procreative process; see pp. 145–61, 169–70, 178, 183, 188.

26   Ernest Becker, *The Denial of Death* (New York: Free Press, 1973).

27   Philippe Ariès, *The Hour of our Death*, trans. Helen Weaver (New York: Random House, 1982).

28   Compare Angelo's assertion at II. ii. 91 that 'The law hath not been dead, though it hath slept.' He is resurrecting, by a standard consolatory metaphor, the moral laws by which he has defined his own immortality.

29   G. Wilson Knight, *The Wheel of Fire* (1930; rev. edn, London: Methuen, 1949), p. 82.

30   Lever cites the various Christian allegories that have been applied (*Measure for Measure*, p. lvii). Gless also comments on the oversupply of 'personification allegory' concerning *Measure for Measure*, then offers a different way of allegorizing the play (*Measure for Measure, the Law, and the Convent*, pp. 4–5 and 53–60). On pages 247–50, Gless discusses the possibility of identifying the Duke with the Christian God. See also Knight, *The Wheel of Fire*, p. 74; Roy W. Battenhouse, '*Measure for Measure* and Christian doctrine of the atonement,' *Proceedings of the Modern Languages Association*, 61 (1946), pp. 1029–59; and Robert G. Hunter, *Shakespeare and the Comedy of Forgiveness* (New York: Columbia University Press, 1965), pp. 204–26.

31   Louise Schleiner, 'Providential improvisation in *Measure for Measure*,' *Proceedings of the Modern Languages Association*, 97 (1982), pp. 227–36, characterizes the Duke's actions as an *imitatio dei*.

3

Language

Shakespeare's plays are, first, words on the page. D. H. Lawrence's poem 'When I Read Shakespeare' opens: 'When I read Shakespeare I am struck with wonder / that such trivial people should muse and thunder / in such lovely language.' The different approaches to this 'lovely language', through the varied lenses of historical linguistics, studies of imagery, and post-structuralism, have produced extremely varied criticism over the past century, and some of the key movements in this critical history are described in this chapter.

There have been many studies of early modern English and Shakespeare's plays. Margreta de Grazia's overview 'Shakespeare and the Craft of Language' in de Grazia and Wells (2001) provides an introduction to rhetoric, punning and historical linguistics. Joseph (1947), Hulme (1962), Blake (1983), Salmon and Burness (1987) and Hussey (1992) all offer more detailed studies or collections of essays on Shakespeare's language. The historical context of Shakespeare's language is discussed by Barber (1997) and Hope (1999), and Cercignani (1981) writes about Elizabethan pronunciation. Houston (1988) and Wright (1988) discuss Shakespeare's metre and syntax; Ness (1941) catalogues Shakespeare's use of rhyme. Lanham (1969/1991) is the standard work on rhetorical terms. There are interesting approaches to Shakespeare's language from the point of view of actors speaking the verse in Barton (1984), Berry (1993) and Rodenburg (2002).

Literary studies of Shakespeare's language have made a major contribution to criticism over the past century. L. C. Knights's argument that 'the only profitable approach to Shakespeare is a consideration of his plays as dramatic poems' (Knights, 1946: 6), Wilson Knight's attempt 'to see each play as an expanded metaphor' (Knight, 1930: 16), and C. S. Lewis's injunction 'to surrender oneself to the poetry and the situation' (Lewis, 1964: 208) are all instances of a critical reaction against the stress on character promoted by A. C. Bradley (1904) and his Romantic antecedents. In her study *Shakespeare's*

Imagery and What it Tells Us (1935), however, Caroline Spurgeon is less concerned with individual characters than with the overall linguistic mood of a play. She offers 'suggestions as to the light thrown by the imagery (1) on Shakespeare's personality, temperament and thought, (2) on the themes and characters of the plays' (Spurgeon, 1935: ix). The book groups image clusters together by theme and also identifies dominant strains of imagery in specific plays. Spurgeon takes comedies and romances as distinct genres. In the comedies, *Midsummer Night's Dream* makes repeated use of lunar imagery, *Much Ado About Nothing* takes much of its lexicon from country pursuits and concerns, and *Twelfth Night* has an unexpectedly high number of topical images which add to its sophistication. In *Measure for Measure* 'Shakespeare seems to be torn . . . between deeply stirred idealistic thought and reflection and a tendency to cynical bitterness and grim realism which delights in a certain violence and even distortion of speech and figure' (1935: 289), and, in this, Boas's sense of the intrinsic connection to *Hamlet* is upheld (see p. 25). Spurgeon sees the romances' imagery as 'more subtle and less concrete than in the earlier plays' (1935: 299), and gives as an example the structuring importance of the 'sense of *sound*' in *The Tempest* and 'the common flow of life in all things' in *The Winter's Tale* (1935: 300, 305). Wolfgang Clemen, in his *The Development of Shakespeare's Imagery* (1951/1977), focuses on the tragedies, and argues that 'characteristic of the imagery in the early comedies is the pleasure taken in the phenomenon itself, in its technical, rhetorical aspect': 'we cannot speak of a true organic relationship of the images to the individual characters who employ them, nor to the whole of the play' (1977: 38–9). Clemen seems to agree with Spurgeon's sense of a subtler, less explicit imagistic patterning in the late plays. Clemen analyses the references to sea and storm in *The Tempest*, and identifies how the first three acts in *The Winter's Tale* utilize tragic imagery, as distinct from the romance vocabulary and symbolism of the second half.

Frank Kermode's *Shakespeare's Language* (2000) also argues that there is a significant shift in Shakespeare's deployment of language for individual characterization around the time of *Hamlet*. Thus he gives comparatively little attention to the comedies of the 1590s, except to the extent that they anticipate the works to come. *Love's Labour's Lost*, for example, is seen as 'a witty, teasing investigation of language, with hints, but no more than hints, of the sort of intense brooding over words that becomes so important in the later plays' (Kermode, 2000: 64). A chapter on *All's Well that Ends Well* and *Measure for Measure* finds 'a wilful obscurity' (2000: 144) in *All's Well* and discusses different interpretations of the word 'prone' in *Measure for Measure* (I. ii. 171). For Kermode, the poetry of the play 'is all in the tragedy' (2000: 164). Writing of *The Winter's Tale*, Kermode argues that 'Shakespeare's associative late style is peculiarly well-suited to disturbed mental states' (2000: 278), and he develops this point in a careful reading of Prospero's exposition of events leading to their arrival on the island in Act I, scene 2, where awkwardnesses of syntax, metaphor and rhythm are 'a tribute more to Prospero's agitated state of mind than to any kind of expository clarity' (2000: 288). Also on the language of the late plays is Anne Barton's often-anthologized essay 'Leontes and the Spider: Language and Speaker in Shakespeare's Late Plays', first published in a book of essays on *Shakespeare's Styles* (Edwards et al., 1980), and reprinted in Ryan (1999).

Brian Vickers's analysis of *The Artistry of Shakespeare's Prose* (1968) discusses its particular use in comedies. Often prose scenes or speeches are seen in juxtaposition to verse ones, as a structural device in which themes or situations are echoes in plot and subplot, or among the higher social strata and the lower. Vickers's account shows how Shakespeare develops his prose styles from comedy into tragedy, from engaging wit into bitter slander. The only comedy to be given extensive treatment in M. M. Mahood's *Shakespeare's Wordplay* (1957) is *The Winter's Tale*. Mahood stresses the economy of the play's expression, its use of theological language such as the reiterated 'grace', and the highly wrought and pressured explosion of Leontes' jealousy. Puns are also discussed by Michel Grivelet in his essay 'Shakespeare as "Corrupter of Words"' (1963), which argues that puns in tragedies 'place darkness at the heart of bright vision' (Grivelet, 1963: 73), whereas in comedies they aid the plot movement towards enlightenment and resolution.

Bawdy innuendo can be excavated with reference to Partridge's *Shakespeare's Bawdy*, an essay and an extensive glossary first published in 1947 with revised editions in 1958 and 2001. R. A. Foakes's 'Suggestions for a New Approach to Shakespeare's Imagery' (1952) tackles a lack of methodological sophistication in the work on Shakespeare's imagery. He argues that there has been little assessment of the difference between 'poetic' and 'dramatic' imagery (Foakes, 1952: 81–2), and that a definition of imagery derived from drama is needed:

> While it is possible for a poem to be a metaphor, to exist only in an image or images, this cannot properly be said of a Shakespearian play. The poetic image in a play is set in a context not of words alone, but of words, dramatic situation, interplay of character, stage-effect, and it is also placed in a time sequence. (1952: 85–6)

Thus, a

> discussion of dramatic imagery then would include reference to the subject-matter and object-matter of poetic imagery, to visual and auditory effects, iterative words, historical and geographical placing, and to both the general and particular uses of these things. Dramatic imagery would be examined primarily

in relation to context, to dramatic context, and to the time-sequence of a play; the general or overall patterns of word and image would be examined in relation to other effects as well as for their own value. (1952: 90)

Also on methodological questions is Robert Weimann's essay 'Shakespeare and the Study of Metaphor' (1974) which reminds us that 'The essence of metaphor is to connect' (Weimann, 1974: 150) and that the study of metaphor cannot therefore be separated from these points of reference. Weimann suggests that the formalist study of Shakespeare's language has 'not considered the theatrical functions of dramatic speech and the way it is correlated to non-verbal means of expression. To read the figures in the carpet is to see them in their two-dimensional extension, not as part of a process in time, and on the stage' (1974: 158–9). He argues for the interrelation of metaphor in 'the total meaning of Shakespeare's poetry in the theater' (1974: 167).

Attention to the language of plays in performance is offered by Philip C. McGuire in his book *Speechless Dialect: Shakespeare's Open Silences* (1985). Of particular interest to his thesis are *Twelfth Night* – in which the final silence of Antonio and Sir Andrew is described in relation to performances – and *Measure for Measure*. A number of different productions of Act V are analysed to activate the range of meanings and effects generated by the silence of many of the characters at the end of the play. A chapter on *Measure for Measure* in Kenneth Gross's *Shakespeare's Noise* (2001) discusses what is, and is not, heard by the Duke, who moves through the play 'as an isolated, occulted ear, in flight both from public praise and slander' (2001: 69). For Terry Eagleton (1986) Shakespeare's puns are a radical challenge to the ostensible conservatism of the drama:

> Even those who know very little about Shakespeare might be vaguely aware that his plays value social order and stability, and that they are written with extraordinary eloquence, one metaphor breeding another in an apparently unstaunchable flow of what modern theorists might call 'textual productivity'. The problem is that these two aspects of Shakespeare are in potential conflict with one another. For a stability of signs – each word securely in its place, each signifier (mark or sound) corresponding to its signified, (or meaning) – is an integral part of any social order: settled meanings, shared definitions and regularities of grammar both reflect, and help to constitute, a well-ordered political state. Yet it is all this which Shakespeare's flamboyant punning, troping and riddling threaten to put into question. His belief in social stability is jeopardized by the very language in which it is articulated. It would seem, then, that the very act of writing implies for Shakespeare an epistemology (or theory of knowledge) at odds with his political ideology. This is a deeply embarrassing dilemma, and it is not surprising that much of Shakespeare's drama is devoted to figuring out strategies for resolving it. (Eagleton, 1986: 1)

Connecting linguistic approaches to politicized and theoretical methodologies has produced some exciting work. In *Shakespeare from the Margins* (1996) Patricia Parker returns to Shakespeare's wordplay with a more theoretically informed attention to punning, metaphor and the subterranean connections within and between plays which can be revealed by close, historically aware reading. She is particularly concerned with the status of homophone puns in an era before standardized orthographic and printing conventions. Her discussion of biblical echoes in *The Comedy of Errors*, the imagery of artisanship around the 'rude mechanicals' in *A Midsummer Night's Dream*, interlinking attitudes to translation, legitimacy and adultery in *The Merry Wives of Windsor*, and the language of increase, both sexual and monetary, which dominates *All's Well that Ends Well*, offers a densely argued and stimulating reevaluation of the practice of close reading, not as an activity which divorces literature from its culture but which can imbricate it more closely in social and cultural linguistics. In *Poetic Will: Shakespeare and the Play of Language* (1997), David Willbern discusses Malvolio's reading of Olivia's supposed letter in *Twelfth Night* as a 'dramatic paradigm of the risks of unconscious projection as a style of reading' (1997: 32). William Carroll's 'The Virgin Not: Language and Sexuality in Shakespeare' (1993) discusses the paradox of the 'virgin (k)not' as an image for the ultimate occlusion and unrepresentability of virginity. A number of essays in *Shakespeare and the Question of Theory*, edited by Parker and Hartman (1985), apply post-structuralist and psychoanalytic ideas about language to the plays. Howard Felperin discovers 'the deconstruction of presence' in the language of *The Winter's Tale*; Geoffrey Hartman discusses 'Shakespeare's poetical character in *Twelfth Night*' and Joel Fineman reads *The Taming of the Shrew*. Essays taking a similarly theoretical approach are collected by Atkins and Bergeron in *Shakespeare and Deconstruction* (1988).

References and Further Reading

Atkins, G. Douglas and Bergeron, David M. (1988) *Shakespeare and Deconstruction*. New York: Lang.

Barber, Charles Laurence (1997) *Early Modern English*. Edinburgh: Edinburgh University Press.

Barton, John (1984) *Playing Shakespeare*. London: Methuen.

Berry, Cicely (1993) *The Actor and the Text*, rev. edn. London: Virgin.

Blake, N. F. (1983) *Shakespeare's Language: An Introduction*. London: Macmillan.

Bradley, A. C. (1904) *Shakespearean Tragedy: Lectures on Hamlet, Othello, King Lear, Macbeth*. London: Macmillan.

Carroll, William C. (1976) *The Great Feast of Language in Love's Labour's Lost*. Princeton, NJ: Princeton University Press.

——(1993) 'The virgin not: language and sexuality in Shakespeare', *Shakespeare Survey*, 46: 107–19.

Cercignani, Fausto (1981) *Shakespeare's Works and Elizabethan Pronunciation*. Oxford: Clarendon Press.

Clemen, Wolfgang (1951) *The Development of Shakespeare's Imagery*. London: Methuen, 2nd edn, 1977.

de Grazia, Margreta and Wells, Stanley W. (eds) (2001) *The Cambridge Companion to Shakespeare*. Cambridge: Cambridge University Press.

Eagleton, Terry (1986) *William Shakespeare: Rereading Literature*. Oxford: Blackwell.

Edwards, Philip, et al. (eds) (1980) *Shakespeare's Styles: Essays in Honour of Kenneth Muir*. Cambridge: Cambridge University Press.

Elam, Keir (1984) *Shakespeare's Universe of Discourse: Language-games in the Comedies*. Cambridge: Cambridge University Press.

Foakes, R. A. (1952) 'Suggestions for a new approach to Shakespeare's imagery', *Shakespeare Survey*, 5: 81–92.

Grivelet, Michel (1963) 'Shakespeare as "corrupter of words"', *Shakespeare Survey*, 16: 70–6.

Gross, Kenneth (2001) *Shakespeare's Noise*. Chicago: University of Chicago Press.

Hope, Jonathan (1999) 'Shakespeare's "Native English"', in *A Companion to Shakespeare*, ed. David Scott Kastan, pp. 239–55. Oxford: Blackwell.

Houston, John Porter (1988) *Shakespearean Sentences: A Study in Style and Syntax*. Baton Rouge: Louisiana State University Press.

Hulme, Hilda M. (1962) *Explorations in Shakespeare's Language: Some Problems of Lexical Meaning in the Dramatic Text*. London: Longman.

Hussey, S. S. (1992) *The Literary Language of Shakespeare*, 2nd edn. London: Longman.

Joseph, Miriam (1947) *Shakespeare's Use of the Arts of Language*. New York: Columbia University Press.

Kermode, Frank (2000) *Shakespeare's Language*. London: Allen Lane.

Knight, George Wilson (1930) *The Wheel of Fire: Essays in Interpretation of Shakespeare's Sombre Tragedies*. London: Oxford University Press.

Knights, L. C. (1946) *Explorations: Essays in Criticism, Mainly on the Literature of the Seventeenth Century*. London: Chatto and Windus.

Lanham, Richard A. (1969) *A Handlist of Rhetorical Terms: A Guide for Students of English Literature*. Berkeley, CA: University of California Press, 2nd edn, 1991.

Lewis, C. S. (1964) Hamlet: the prince or the poem, in *Studies in Shakespeare: British Academy Lectures*, ed. Peter Alexander, pp. 201–18. London: The British Academy.

McGuire, Philip C. (1985) *Speechless Dialect: Shakespeare's Open Silences*. Berkeley, CA: University of California Press.

Mahood, M. M. (1957) *Shakespeare's Wordplay*. London: Methuen.

Ness, Frederic W. (1941) *The Use of Rhyme in Shakespeare's Plays*. New Haven, CT: Yale University Press.

Parker, Patricia (1987) *Literary Fat Ladies: Rhetoric, Gender, Property*. London: Methuen.

——(1996) *Shakespeare from the Margins: Language, Culture, Context*. Chicago: University of Chicago Press.

——and Hartman, Geoffrey H. (1985) *Shakespeare and the Question of Theory*. London: Methuen.

Partridge, Eric (1947) *Shakespeare's Bawdy: A Literary and Psychological Essay, and a Comprehensive Glossary*. London: Routledge.

Rodenburg, Patsy (2002) *Speaking Shakespeare*. London: Methuen.

Ryan, Kiernan (ed.) (1999) *Shakespeare: The Last Plays*. Longman Critical Readers. London: Longman.

Salmon, Vivian and Burness, Edwina (1987) *A Reader in the Language of Shakespearean Drama*. Amsterdam: John Benjamins.

Spurgeon, C. F. E. (1935) *Shakespeare's Imagery and What it Tells Us*. Cambridge: Cambridge University Press.

Vickers, Brian (1968) *The Artistry of Shakespeare's Prose*. London: Methuen.

Weimann, Robert (1974) 'Shakespeare and the study of metaphor', *New Literary History*, 6: 149–67.

Willbern, David (1997) *Poetic Will: Shakespeare and the Play of Language*. Philadelphia, PA: University of Pennsylvania Press.

Wright, George T. (1988) *Shakespeare's Metrical Art*. Berkeley, CA: University of California Press.

Here Follows Prose

Russ McDonald

Russ McDonald's concise book Shakespeare and the Arts of Language *includes the following chapter on prose. While prose is by no means synonymous with comedy – McDonald investigates that common association – his analysis of Shakespearian prose across a range of genres is of particular interest in considering the language of the comedies. McDonald gives the background to Shakespearian prose in the Euphuistic phrasing and diction popular in the 1580s, and proposes a number of technical frameworks for the discussion and appreciation of prose both as a foil to verse and as an aesthetic vehicle in its own right.*

Russ McDonald, 'Here Follows Prose', in *Shakespeare and the Arts of Language* (Oxford: Oxford University Press, 2001), pp. 108–36. Reprinted by permission of Oxford University Press.

In the garden scene of *Twelfth Night*, as Malvolio reads aloud and tries to decipher a mysterious love letter found on the walkway, he pauses to register a change in the style of the anonymous author: 'Soft, here follows prose.' His notice of the stylistic shift is telling. The movement from verse to prose denotes a change in mood, a formal relaxation that sets the remainder of the letter apart from its poetic beginning. Especially significant is the fact that Malvolio comments on the change. Since he is reading, his eye immediately notes a difference in lineation. Likewise, in the case of oral discourse, the Elizabethan ear was apparently alert to the change from one form to another. In *As You Like It*, as Jaques and Rosalind converse informally in prose, the love-struck Orlando enters speaking verse, a single line of iambic pentameter: 'Good day and happiness, dear Rosalind.' The wooer's formality is too much for Jaques, who leaves the stage with 'Nay then, God b'wi'you an you talk in blank verse.'

These two episodes constitute historical proof of a major difference between the early modern and the modern ear, specifically that Shakespeare's first audiences seem to have been more sensitive to verbal structures than their modern counterparts. The distinction may also have to do with changes in performance style. Little is known for certain about the style of Elizabethan acting, but some scholars believe that dramatic verse was declaimed in an oratorical and perhaps sing-song manner, thus differentiating it immediately from less rigidly structured prose.[1] Whether this is so or not, we can be sure that Shakespeare counted on his listeners to hear the difference between the structured rhythms of verse and the comparative informality of prose, and that he exploited those differences for theatrical effect.

The most useful definition of prose is that it is not poetry, and the cardinal difference between verse and prose is one of rhythm, or, more specifically, the kind of rhythm. Though Shakespeare uses a variety of verse measures, by far the commonest is blank verse. As indicated in [chapter 5 of *Shakespeare and the Arts of Language*], blank verse normally consists of lines of ten syllables organized into five beats, each beat constituting an iamb, one unaccented followed by one accented syllable ('Tŏ bé'). Thus, on the printed page, the verse line ends after the tenth syllable (the fifth beat), with a new line beginning at the left-hand margin and signified by a capital letter. Metrical variations often disturb such lines, and many lines consist of more than ten syllables, especially in the later plays, but in general the regular beat is audible and, once we are alert to it, familiar and pleasing. Since prose lacks the regular rhythms of verse, it is printed without such breaks, its lines extending all the way to the right-hand margin and with capital letters used mainly to mark the beginning of a new sentence. But to say that prose is without the uniform beat of verse is not to say that it lacks cadence or harmony. Every competent writer or speaker develops some kind of rhythm in individual sentences and in their combination: several long sentences may be abruptly followed by a short one, for example, or a number of similarly constructed sentences may unfold in sequence. A talented stylist will manipulate these variations so as to affect the ear and guide the mind of the listener. Often the rhythms of prose are situational, developed according to the topic of the speech and the particular impulses or style of the speaker. But superficially speaking, prose is less strictly organized than poetry, less formal and intense. And therein lies its principal dramatic value for Shakespeare. In order to consider that value, I have divided the topic into four main parts: (1) the historical contexts of Elizabethan prose, (2) the established conventions for using dramatic prose and Shakespeare's modification of them over the course of his career, (3) a description of the major syntactical structures and verbal flourishes that the dramatist employs, and (4) a brief survey of some of the most brilliant uses of prose in the mature work. The chapter ends with a coda describing the indescribability of certain memorable passages.

Prose Models *circa* 1590

Shakespeare's skill at writing dramatic prose should be seen in light of the philosophical and pedagogical debates over language occurring at the end of the sixteenth century. The conventions of prose style were much discussed by Tudor rhetoricians, who usually took their arguments and examples from their Latin predecessors, and a non-dramatic writer's stylistic choices were thought to be charged with meaning. Indeed the kind of English prose a writer chose to employ carried intellectual and even moral significance. It is worth reiterating not only that the English language was coming into its own in the early modern age, but that thinkers in the period seem very much aware that it was doing so. The fierce debate over whether the Bible should be translated into the vernacular, one of the major issues of Reformation politics in England and on the Continent, indicates that language itself was a topic of grave concern for many British people. Recognizing the emergence of England as an international force, scholars and courtiers felt the need for a vernacular appropriate to the dignity of a world power. Moreover, since education was a growing concern of the Elizabethans, proper composition was then, as it is today, a central component of the pedagogical conversation.

Familiarity with the prose models Shakespeare inherited will clarify his own practice, particularly the ways in which he took up and varied the prevailing forms of expression. The prevalent view at the middle of the sixteenth century favoured intricate sentences based on parallel clauses, other elaborate rhetorical patterns, and stylistic decoration for its own sake: the Ciceronian style. The competing opinion, which eventually supplanted the older view, regarded style strictly as a means of conveying thought and consequently disapproved of obvious rhetorical patterns: this has come to be known as Senecan prose. Such easy categories are easy to dismiss, and the simplification involved in such division has provoked objection, but the distinctions are nevertheless useful for the writing of the period. The great monuments of late sixteenth- and early seventeenth-century English prose can be divided more or less neatly, according to the stylistic sympathies of their creators, into two main categories: the formal, scrupulously patterned, 'rhetorical' style of John Lyly's *Euphues* (1578) or Richard Hooker's *Laws of Ecclesiastical Polity* (1594) which more or less followed the Ciceronian model; and the loose, asymmetrical, more 'natural' style of Thomas Nashe's *Unfortunate Traveller* (1594) or Francis Bacon's *Essays* (1597–1625), works which conformed to the Senecan model. In practice, of course, the results were never as tidy as the dicta of the rule-givers would imply. Nashe began writing a kind of Ciceronian prose that he eventually transformed into its opposite, and a work like Sidney's *Arcadia* resists classification in such terms.

Nevertheless, such categories help to reveal the controversies about the forms and functions of prose and, what is more, the basis for those differences. The following sentences from *Euphues: The Anatomy of Wit* make for a useful starting point:

> The sun shineth upon the dunghill and is not corrupted, the diamond lieth in the fire and is not consumed, the crystal toucheth the toad and is not poisoned, the bird Trochilus liveth by the mouth of the crocodile and is not spoiled, a perfect wit is never bewitched with lewdness, neither enticed with lasciviousness. Is it not common that the holm tree springeth amidst the beech? That the ivy spreadeth upon the hard stones? That the soft featherbed breaketh the hard blade? If experience have not taught you this you have lived long and learned little; or if your moist brain have forgot it you have learned much and profited nothing. But it may be that you measure my affections by your own fancies, and knowing yourself either too simple to raise the siege by policy or too weak to resist the assault by prowess, you deem me of as little wit as yourself or of less force, either of small capacity or of no courage.[2]

Our sense of the symmetrical balances of Lyly's prose may be illuminated and sharpened by a comparison with a passage from one of Bacon's essays.

> To pass from theological and philosophical truth to the truth of civil business, it will be acknowledged even by those that practise it not that clear and round dealing is the honour of man's nature; and that mixture of falsehood is like allay in coin of gold and silver, which may make the metal work the better, but it embaseth it. For these winding and crooked courses are the goings of the serpent, which goeth basely upon the belly and not upon the feet. There is no vice that doth so cover a man with shame as to be found false and perfidious. And therefore Montaigne saith prettily, when he enquired the reason why the word of the lie should be such a disgrace and such an odious charge – saith he, 'If it be well weighed, to say that a man lieth is as much to say as that he is brave towards God and a coward towards men'. For a lie faces God and shrinks from man.[3]

These excerpts point the distinction between Ciceronian and anti-Ciceronian prose with particular clarity because Lyly and Bacon rely on many common elements, notably an argumentative thrust and a liberal use of metaphor. The resemblances are overshadowed, however, by the contrasting form of the sentences. Whereas Lyly's words and phrases come in patterns ('is not corrupted ... is not consumed ... is not poisoned ... is not spoiled') and pairs ('*rai*se the *s*iege by *p*olicy ... *r*es*i*st the *a*ssault by *p*rowess'), and even exhibit alliteration and assonance within those structural patterns, Bacon resolutely avoids any such arrangement. Even though many of his sentences are long and intricately structured, they lack the ornamentation and stylistic self-regard of the older type.

An analytic description of Shakespeare's prose in relation to contemporary practice requires a multitude of qualifications and caveats. First, Shakespeare's prose is a theatrical instrument, speech written for dramatic characters, and that function makes it qualitatively different from the foregoing models. Second, every major character is given a more or less distinctive voice, and naturally some speakers lean more towards the patterned style than others. Certain gifted speakers, a Hamlet or an Iago, for example, move nimbly from style to style depending on the moment. The most self-conscious may themselves parody a distinctive style, as Falstaff does when he uses Lylyan Euphuism to impersonate the King in the tavern scene of *1 Henry IV*: 'If then thou be son to me, here lies the point: why, being son to me, art thou so pointed at?' (II. v. 409–11). Third, the playwright alters and varies his prose speech as his career proceeds, a development that makes critical generalizations about twenty years' worth of 'Shakespearian prose' especially hazardous. Still, the benefits of historical contextualization finally outweigh the risks, and we should probably say that the playwright's prose more nearly resembles the old-fashioned, Lylyan style than it does the Baconian.

The requisite modification to this blunt statement is that Shakespeare transforms the fundamental patterns of Euphuism into a more apparently natural style. Still, the skeleton of Lyly's balanced sentences and his fondness for lexical repetition are never entirely effaced. They are clearly audible in Falstaff's mocking threat to Prince Hal: 'An old lord of the Council rated me the other day in the street about you, sir, but I marked him not; and yet he talked very wisely, but I regarded him not; and yet he talked wisely, and in the street too' (*1 Henry IV*, I. ii. 83–7). Falstaff's pride in his verbal invention might lead us to expect such echoing, but even when a speaker is not so playful, the equivalent syntactical shape makes itself felt: 'I cannot be a man with wishing, therefore I will die a woman with grieving' (*Much Ado*, IV. i. 323–4). One hears it even in parts of sentences, as in Portia's 'If I live to be as old as Sibylla I will die as chaste as Diana' (*The Merchant of Venice*, I. ii. 103–4). Jonas Barish identifies nicely the particular nature of Shakespeare's debt to his Ciceronian predecessors:

> Shakespeare starts with the highly specialized set of expressive devices worked out by Lyly, inflects them variously, fills them with nuance, widens their range, and so finally transcends them, but without departing from the structural principles on which they are based. One tends not to notice the logicality of Shakespeare's prose because it is managed with such virtuosity as to seem as natural as breathing. But by his constant invention of fresh logical formulas, his endless improvising of new patterns, Shakespeare, if anything, carries logical syntax even further than Lyly.[4]

Rarely do Shakespeare's symmetries seem as bald or self-promoting as Lyly's, but as Barish's last clause implies, they are more efficacious in the sense that they are calculated to elucidate contrarieties of meaning. Recognition of the Lylyan precedent leads to the discovery that its traces are everywhere, and having established this lineage, we discover further that Shakespeare's transformation of the model is even more significant than his dependence on it.

Prose, Comic and Tragic

For Shakespeare, verse is the dominant form and prose the subordinate, a relationship consistent with the practice of most early modern dramatists. When Elizabethan playwrights did write dialogue in prose, they tended to employ it for comic scenes, and indeed some playwrights wrote comedies entirely or mainly in prose: George Gascoigne in *Supposes* (1576), his translation of an Italian comedy, John Lyly in his court comedies of the 1580s, and Ben Jonson in his comical satires at the turn of the seventeenth century. Tragedies or chronicle plays, on the other hand, were normally written in verse. This division reflects the persons and milieux considered appropriate for each mode: put in the simplest terms, Elizabethan tragedy dealt with kings, comedy with clowns, or at least with ordinary people. Since the representation of common folk would seem to require the equivalent of everyday language, the characters of comedy were more apt than high-born persons to speak prose. As a beginner, Shakespeare tends to observe this social distinction fairly strictly. His first history plays are composed almost entirely in verse, as is his first tragedy, *Titus Andronicus* (except for one prose exchange between Titus and a rustic messenger); the early comedies offer both verse and prose, with the lords and ladies speaking blank verse and the secondary figures prose. Even in the early plays there are exceptions to these guidelines, but in general Shakespeare's practice as a dramatic apprentice is thoroughly conventional.

In the earliest comedies the stylistic distinctions are socially determined. Upper-class characters tend to speak verse, servants and lower-class figures prose. Love stories, usually involving the high born, are conducted in verse, whereas the more farcical scenes ask for the informality of prose. Thus these first comedies contain much more verse than prose: in *Two Gentlemen of Verona*, *The Taming of the Shrew*, *The Comedy of Errors*, *Love's Labour's Lost*, and *A Midsummer Night's Dream*, the proportion of prose lines is never more than 30 per cent (*Errors* has less than 15 per cent). The connection between rank and speech appears plainly in *A Midsummer Night's Dream*: the members of the Athenian court (not only Theseus and Hippolyta but also the young lovers) and the denizens of the spirit world, including Puck and the attendant fairies, speak verse, whereas the amateur actors, the 'rude mechanicals', speak prose, except in their theatrical performance at court, a tragedy written in execrable rhyme. Although Bottom addresses Titania in prose, she speaks verse to him, a separation which comically sustains the distinction of rank between them. Even in *A Midsummer Night's Dream*, however, exceptions occur, as in the last act, when the courtly figures punctuate the labourers' performance with informal commentary in prose.

From about 1595 the percentages change as Shakespeare begins to devise his own rules for appropriate speech. Although prose is still given to servants and clowns, exceptions become more numerous and more extensive. In the great romantic comedies, the apogee of his work in this mode, the earlier proportion of verse to prose is reversed: over 70 per cent of *Much Ado About Nothing* is written in prose, and the percentages for *As You Like It* and *Twelfth Night* are almost as great. In these plays the alternation between verse and prose is so frequent, so unschematic, and so skilful that it is risky to generalize. The undeniable fact, however, is that theatrical demands tend to overrule the conventions of social class. In *Twelfth Night*, for example, Sir Toby Belch and Sir Andrew Aguecheek are both knights, but as agents of low comedy they speak only prose.

A similar flexibility marks the dramatist's movement from the earlier to the later histories. The first tetralogy (*1*, *2*, *3 Henry VI* and *Richard III*), consisting of plays which are more conventional than those that will follow, contains mostly verse. In the later cycle (*Richard II*, *1* and *2 Henry IV*, and *Henry V*), however, a great deal of prose is spoken, mostly in the tavern and on the battlefield among non-ranking soldiers.[5] Royal characters often use prose to answer prose-speaking servants or messengers, and sometimes kings in private moments will descend to prose, as Henry V does in wooing Princess Catherine. Sir John Falstaff, although he can speak verse and does so in the company of the King, speaks mostly prose. His inventive locutions are supplemented by various forms of prose: the confused speech of Mistress Quickly, the nattering of Justice Shallow, and the sober lectures administered to

Falstaff by the Lord Chief Justice (who addresses the new King in verse, of course). A full 40 per cent of *Henry V* is written in prose, not only the royal wooing but the frivolous chat of the French courtier-soldiers and the variously inflected speech of the English, Welsh, Irish, and Scottish soldiers who make up the British force at Agincourt.

One of the mature comedies, *The Merry Wives of Windsor* (*c.* 1597), is written almost entirely in prose, and in this respect it stands as a notable exception in the Shakespearian canon. It differs from the norm in other ways as well. The relative emphasis of the two plots inverts Shakespeare's normal practice: typically he foregrounds the romantic plot and subordinates the farcical or satiric story, emotionally, if not statistically. Here, however, he focuses on Falstaff's ludicrous seduction schemes, glancing only briefly at young Fenton's attempts to marry Anne Page against the wishes of her father and mother. Consequently, the verse of the two lovers, the only verse speakers in the play, accounts for only 5 per cent of the lines. A legend first recorded in the eighteenth century holds that the playwright concocted *The Merry Wives* because Queen Elizabeth desired to see Falstaff in love, and such a theory of origin might help to account for the local setting: this is the only Shakespearian comedy set in England. Whether the legend is true or not, it seems clear that the bourgeois nature of the setting – no kings or princesses here – dictated the choice of medium.

When Shakespeare turned to tragedy around 1599–1600, he began to create some of the most memorable blank verse in the canon, but the contribution of prose to plays such as *Hamlet* and *Othello* is hardly negligible. The most productive way of thinking about its role in Shakespearian tragedy is to revert to the simple negative definition: prose is not poetry. Since verse is the dominant form, he employs prose precisely because it is not poetry, because it makes a change. In other words, the introduction of a speech or scene in prose signals an alteration of mood, a relaxation of tension, a tonal variation that influences the audience whether or not they are conscious of the shift. Prose can also signal reversals in character, indicating for example the onset of madness or a loss of control: familiar instances include Ophelia's mad scenes in the second half of *Hamlet*; Othello's psychological disintegration, represented by his epileptic seizure, in Act IV; and Lady Macbeth's sleepwalking scene.

Usually, however, the shift into prose is less obvious, its effect primarily tonal. The transition may occur in the midst of a scene, and only for a moment. A compelling example is the conversation between Lady Macduff and her son, in the scene which ends with their murder (*Macbeth*, IV. ii). The episode divides into three parts: Ross's justification of Macduff's flight to England; the Lady's falsely telling her son that his father is dead and was a traitor; and the murder itself. The first and third sections are in verse. The second divides stylistically into two parts: it begins in verse, but as the conversation becomes more intimate and even comic – e.g. the boy's claim that if her husband were dead Lady Macduff would be looking for a new one – mother and son relax into the private form of prose banter. This stylistic informality ironically prepares for the entrance of the murderers. Sometimes the shift from verse to prose is more pointed. In the third scene of *Othello*, after the formal and public defence of his marriage, Othello and Desdemona exit the stage with the Venetian grandees, leaving Iago and Roderigo to converse privately and lengthily in the more informal style. Here the privacy of the encounter and the malignity of Iago's words emphasize the sinister strain that will later infect and destroy the hero. In the fourth act prose works differently: the touching nocturnal conversation as Emilia helps Desdemona prepare for bed is mostly in verse, but it dips briefly into prose when Emilia playfully confesses her casual views of female adultery. Again, what is most important about many of these moments is the shift itself from one medium to another, and most of the remainder of this chapter will be concerned with the theatrical effect of such transitions. First, however, it will be worthwhile to examine the shapes and colours of some typical sentences.

Logic and the Shape of the Sentence

When the young Shakespeare began to write dramatic prose, he found in the Ciceronian stylists a syntactical shape hospitable to his most profound habit of mind. This way of looking at the world, noticed by everyone from critics to actors to acute listeners, may be described as an unfailing passion for antithesis. The taste for opposition, for comparison and contrast, for juxtaposition, helps to explain the forms adopted by his prose speakers, but it accounts for considerably more than that. It determines the word choices that fill those forms, the construction of his verse sentences, the pairing of characters, the alternation of scenes, the blending of modes (as in tragicomedy), the complementarity of ideas. We might expect, given such an antithetical approach to experience, that Shakespeare's prose would conform to the pattern known as parataxis, a term connoting the equal disposition of clauses and phrases. And to some extent this is true. In the paratactic style, elements are linked with conjunctions, 'and' or 'but' or 'neither . . . nor', and compound sentences tend to predominate, frequently with clauses of relatively equal length. Hypotaxis, its opposite number, lends itself more readily to a hierarchical arrangement of ideas and entails a high quotient of complex sentences, introductory clauses, and other such subordinated elements. In light of the complex demands of dramatic context, it is probably vain to try to designate Shakespeare's style as predominantly paratactic or hypotactic, as can be done with those of his non-dramatic predecessors and contemporaries. The prevailing effect is more apt to be paratactic than hypotactic since prose is often used for informal conversation rather than for carefully structured argument, and since hypotaxis tends to require extended speech and lengthy sentences. For the most part, however, Shakespeare combines the two kinds of syntactical arrangement.

To describe the structure of Shakespearian prose, I return briefly to Barish's identification of the insistent logicality of the Shakespearian prose sentence: its argumentative movement, its division into constitutive parts, its accentuation of that division, its dependence on 'if . . . then' clauses, its fondness for syllogism, its symmetrical comparisons and demarcation of segments, its intricate but palpable counterbalances. A few examples will reveal the outlines of the formal structures that Shakespeare favours. In *The Taming of the Shrew*, Petruccio's servant describes the journey of his master and Katherine to his country home:

> *Grumio*: But hadst thou not crossed me thou shouldst have heard how her horse fell and she under her horse; thou shouldst have heard in how miry a place, how she was bemoiled, how he left her with the horse upon her, how he beat me because her horse stumbled, how she waded through the dirt to pluck him off me, how he swore, how she prayed that never prayed before, how I cried, how the horses ran away, how her bridle was burst, how I lost my crupper, with many things of worthy memory which now shall die in oblivion, and thou return unexperienced to thy grave.   (IV. i. 64–75)

Here, Henry V woos the French princess:

> *King Henry*: What! A speaker is but a prater, a rhyme is but a ballad; a good leg will fall, a straight back will stoop, a black beard will turn white, a curled pate will grow bald, a fair face will wither, a full eye will wax hollow, but a good heart, Kate, is the sun and the moon – or rather the sun and not the moon, for it shines bright and never changes, but keeps his course truly. If thou would have such a one, take me; and take me, take a soldier; take a soldier, take a king. And what sayst thou then to my love? Speak, my fair – and fairly, I pray thee.   (*Henry V*, V. ii. 158–68)

In *Twelfth Night*, the Clown displays his mental agility for the Duke, Orsino:

> *Feste*: Now my foes tell me plainly I am an ass, so that by my foes, sir, I profit in the knowledge of myself, and by my friends I am abused; so that, conclusions to be as kisses, if your four negatives make your two affirmatives, why then the worse for my friends and the better for my foes.   (V. i. 16–21)

In *Othello*, Iago begins his scheme against his master by enlisting the aid of Roderigo, love-sick for Desdemona:

Iago: I have told thee often, and I re-tell thee again and again, I hate the Moor.
My cause is hearted, thine hath no less reason. Let us be conjunctive in our
revenge against him. If thou canst cuckold him, thou dost thyself a pleasure,
me a sport.   (I. iii. 363–8)

It might be objected that some of these passages represent special cases, King
Henry's a persuasive brief for marriage, Feste's a virtuoso analysis of a paradox.
Even so, in their logical connectives and balanced phrases ('thyself a pleasure,
me a sport'), they are only slightly magnified versions of the syntactical shapes
audible in almost every prose passage. Syllogistic organization is especially
serviceable because Shakespeare often employs prose as a vehicle for comic
interplay, and such dialogue often depends on specious logic and rhetorical
pretension. Yet even in the most serious passages, the same framework can be
discerned beneath the embellishments, permitting 'the utmost freedom and
flexibility, like a ground bass on which an infinite number of variations may
be played'.[6]

Shakespeare fleshes out the syntactical bones of his prose with an array of
verbal flourishes to individuate his various speakers. Such effects, which might
be grouped under the category of 'coloration', include malapropism, eccentric
pronunciation, extravagant repetition, peculiar diction, and other linguistic
idiosyncrasies. Perhaps the informality of the medium encourages the development of peculiarities not so often found or so extravagantly set forth in verse:
this is not to say that such effects are unavailable to the poetic speaker, but
they seem to be more frequent in prose. And since prose is frequently spoken
in comic situations, verbal tics and extravagant stylistic turns seem much more
prominent.

Certain characters, for example, seem uncommonly devoted to the making
of lists. This serializing impulse represents a specific manifestation of the generally paratactic structure of Shakespearian prose, with clauses strung together
by means of conjunctions or linked by nothing more than parallel structure.
Pompey in *Measure for Measure*, former pimp and now assistant to the
Viennese executioner, describes various customers from the brothel he encounters in the prison: 'young Dizzy, and young Master Deepvow, and Master
Copperspur and Master Starve-lackey the rapier and dagger man, and young
Drop-hair that killed lusty Pudding, and Master Forthright the tilter, and
brave Master Shoe-tie the great traveller, and wild Half-can that stabbed Pots,
and I think forty more' (IV. iii. 12–17). This familiar comic turn also animates
Biondello's recitation of Petruccio's wedding costume and his pitiful horse in
The Taming of the Shrew:

hipped, with an old mothy saddle and stirrups of no kindred, besides, possessed
with the glanders and like to mose in the chine, troubled with the lampass,

infected with the fashions, full of windgalls, sped with spavins, rayed with the yellows, past cure of the fives, stark spoiled with the staggers, begnawn with the bots, weighed in the back and shoulder-shotten, near-legged before and with a half-cheeked bit and a headstall of sheep's leather which, being restrained to keep him from stumbling, hath been often burst and now repaired with knots, one girth six times pieced, and a woman's crupper of velour which hath two letters for her name fairly set down in studs, and here and there pieced with packthread. (III. ii. 48–61)

Many other instances of such series might be cited, such as Edgar's (Mad Tom's) list of demons (*King Lear*, III. iv), or the Clown's grocery list in *The Winter's Tale* (IV. iii). And occasionally the series is inflated into sentences and paragraphs, as in Falstaff's description of Justice Shallow as a youth at the end of the Gloucestershire visit in *2 Henry IV* (III. ii. 297–323). The sequence is not entirely unknown in verse passages: Hamlet's 'For who would bear the whips and scorns of time, / Th'oppressor's wrong . . .' (III. i. 72–8) is a well-known example. Still, it seems more common and useful in prose.

Enumeration of this kind is a subspecies of another consistently productive verbal strategy – repetition. George Puttenham and the other cataloguers prescribe several repetitive poetic schemes, such as *epizeuxis* and *ploce* (the repetition of words and phrases with little or no break), and many of these are heard in Shakespeare's verse. But comic, colloquial prose affords him the liberty for the prodigal doubling and tripling of words and phrases. In fact, sometimes he indulges in precisely the kind of excessive repetition that Puttenham specifically condemns.[7] The touchstone for such excess is the voluble Robert Shallow, the country justice of the peace in *2 Henry IV*, who never says anything once.

> Come on, come on, come on! Give me your hand, sir, give me your hand, sir.
> (III. ii. 1–2)

> Where's the roll, where's the roll, where's the roll? Let me see, let me see, let me see; so, so, so, so, so. Yea, marry, sir. 'Ralph Mouldy'. [*To Silence*] Let them appear as I call, let them do so, let them do so. Let me see, (*calls*) where is Mouldy?
> (III. ii. 95–9)

> *Sir John*: You must excuse me, Master Robert Shallow.
> *Shallow*: I will not excuse you; you shall not be excused; excuses shall not be admitted; there is no excuse shall serve; you shall not be excused. – Why, Davy!
> *Enter Davy*
> *Davy*: Here, sir.
> *Shallow*: Davy, Davy, Davy; let me see, Davy, let me see, Davy; let me see.
> (V. i. 3–9)

This is *epizeuxis* if there ever was *epizeuxis*, and the incessant repetition is a brilliant trick of characterization: it identifies a new character, confers immediate theatrical authority, and distinguishes him from his partner, Justice Silence, who, until he gets drunk, does not say anything, even once. It does considerably more than characterize, however, raising important questions about the truth of historical re-creation. Shallow spends virtually all his stage time talking about the past, repeating for us and his companions his glory days at the Inns of Court five and a half decades before, reminiscing – in another list – about friends and foes such as Jane Nightwork, Francis Pickbone, Samson Stockfish, John of Gaunt, and, most notably, the now deceased Old Double.[8] The dramatist, by associating a recalling of the past with the re-calling of words and phrases, is beginning to generate meaning out of the homeliest stylistic materials.

Verbal duplication makes Shallow one of Shakespeare's most memorable and endearing prose speakers. Misnomer, or what would later come to be called malapropism (after Sheridan's Mrs Malaprop), does the same for Dogberry: 'O villain! Thou wilt be condemned into everlasting redemption for this' (*Much Ado About Nothing*, IV. ii. 54–5). Here as elsewhere the Constable's errors offer a brilliant comic turn and simultaneously promote Shakespeare's themes. A play in which the innocent heroine is a victim of slander, and in which Beatrice and Benedick protect their vulnerable hearts with sharp and witty words, *Much Ado* explores the human damage that language can do. As Hero says in pretending to censure Beatrice's acidic tongue, 'One doth not know / How much an ill word may empoison liking' (III. i. 85–6). Dogberry's words are 'ill' in another sense, and his confusion supplies an additional and important strand in the web of ideas about the connection between words and things. His struggles with vocabulary give him a distinctive voice that makes him one of Shakespeare's most popular verbal buffoons.

One of his near relations is the 'fantastical' Spaniard from *Love's Labour's Lost*, Don Adriano de Armado. Armado specializes in fancy diction, driven as he is by the irrepressible need to call a spade anything but a spade. Elaborate, pleonastic, and ridiculous, his astonishing style of speech is captured in the love letter he sends to Jaquenetta, the country girl with whom he is besotted. When the letter is misdelivered, Boyet reads it aloud to the Princess of France and her ladies.

> 'By heaven, that thou art fair is most infallible, true that thou art beauteous, truth itself that thou art lovely. More fairer than fair, beautiful than beauteous, truer than truth itself, have commiseration on thy heroical vassal. The magnanimous and most illustrate King Cophetua set's eye upon the penurious and indubitate beggar Zenelophon, and he it was that might rightly say "*Veni, vidi, vici*", which to annothanize in the vulgar – O base and obscure vulgar! – *videlicet* "He came, see, and overcame." He came, one; see, two; overcame, three. Who came? The

King. Why did he come? To see. Why did he see? To overcome. To whom came he? To the beggar. What saw he? The beggar. Who overcame he? The beggar. The conclusion is victory. On whose side? The King's. The captive is enriched. On whose side? The beggar's. The catastrophe is a nuptial. On whose side? The King's – no, on both in one, or one in both. I am the King – for so stands the comparison – thou the beggar, for so witnesseth thy lowliness. Shall I command thy love? I may. Shall I enforce thy love? I could. Shall I entreat thy love? I will. What shalt thou exhange for rags? Robes. For tittles? Titles. For thyself? Me.

Thus, expecting thy reply, I profane my lips on thy foot, my eyes on thy picture, and my heart on thy every part.

Thine in the dearest design of industry,

Don Adriano de Armado.'

(IV. i. 60–86)

A thorough analysis of the comic felicities displayed here practically warrants its own chapter, but a brief analysis will have to suffice instead.

The letter represents one of the most tempting dishes in this 'great feast of languages', to borrow an ironic phrase from one of the play's clowns, offering the most concentrated example of Armado's self-absorption and pretension. Since one of the general concerns of the play is the discrepancy between pretence and truth, particularly in the linguistic register, the posturing Spaniard's affected phrases and overwrought locutions radiate into other corners of the play-world. Moreover, Armado's prose supplies an early look at Shakespeare's own discovery of what he could do with language, particularly his command of prose rhythm, aural patterning, syntactical contrast, and rhetorical schematization. The basis of the plea to Jaquenetta is the antithesis between high and low – King Cophetua and the beggar maid – and that opposition shapes much of the speaker's rhetoric: 'heroical vassal', 'magnanimous and illustrate King . . . penurious and indubitate beggar', 'For rags? Robes. For tittles? Titles. For thyself? Me.' Shakespeare tickles the listener's ear with the extravagance and variety of the many syntactical structures, and he dramatizes that variety by emphasizing the shift from one to another. The long and graceful sentences at the beginning, for example, are supplanted by the choppy rhythms of the questions and answers near the end of the letter. That interrogative pattern even gives an aural dimension to the high–low antithesis, with the speaker's voice rising in the question and falling in the reply.

Armado's prose is also culturally determined, in that much of it is specifically parodic. The elaborate ornamentation may refer mockingly to the celebrated splendour of the Spanish Armada, the defeat of which (1588) still occupied the English imagination. More specifically, however, his mannerisms seem to burlesque the elaborate styles of a number of well-known Elizabethan writers. To mention only the most obvious cases, the ostentatious wordplay at the beginning ('More fairer than fair, beautiful than beauteous . . .') mimics a favourite trick of Sir Philip Sidney in the *Arcadia*; the conspicuously balanced and stylized clauses sound like imitations of John Lyly's Euphuistic sentences; and the articulated series of questions and answers mocks the well-known style of the Cambridge don Gabriel Harvey. The coining of words ('annothanize') and the contrast between Latin and the vernacular ('O base and obscure vulgar') allude to the linguistic controversies over English and Latin discussed in [chapter 1 of *Shakespeare and the Arts of Language*].[9] Other speakers approach Armado's heights of linguistic folly, notably the pedantic Holofernes, who describes Armado as 'too picked, too spruce, too affected, too odd, as it were, too peregrinate, as I may call it' (V. i. 12–14). But Armado is the greatest comic speaker in this early play, mostly because his prose stimulates in the audience the kind of mixed response – comic delight and melancholy together – that will distinguish some of Shakespeare's greatest creations.

Another form of coloration is the use of accents and other tricks of speech. These also constitute a form of repetition, a technique of coherence by which the playwright marks a character, often a minor figure whose special characteristic separates him or her from the rest of the cast. Here the pertinent text is the other play in which Justice Shallow appears, *The Merry Wives of Windsor*. In this comedy Shallow's repetitions are still a part of his manner, but they seem less blatant than in *2 Henry IV*, partly because they are surrounded by the idiosyncrasies of other secondary figures, particularly Doctor Caius, Parson Evans, the Host of the Garter Inn, and Mistress Quickly. As in *Much Ado About Nothing*, their different verbal profiles contribute to a symbolic study of the positive and negative possibilities of language. And the potential monotony of a nearly all-prose play is variegated by foreign accents (French and Welsh), manic repetitions of a single phrase, outrageous malapropisms, and many other such deviations. Doctor Caius, the most obvious deformer of standard English, specializes in obvious but amusing errors:

> *Evans*: If there is one, I shall make two in the company.
> *Caius*: If there be one or two, I shall make-a the turd.
> (III. iii. 224–5)

Parson Evans speaks the Welsh equivalent of Caius's stage Franglais, substituting 'p' for 'b', 't' for 'd', often dropping initial consonants (*'oman*), adding an erroneous 's' to singular terms, arranging his thoughts into a simplified, childlike pattern, and often correcting the verbal errors of others. As Master Page puts it, the Parson 'makes fritters of English'. Quickly's speciality, carried over from her speech in the *Henry* plays, is malapropism: 'rushling' for 'rustling', 'infection' for 'affection', 'Ginny's case' for 'genitive case' (a bawdy joke, since 'case' could mean 'vagina'), and, funniest of all, describing the 'virtuous' Mrs Ford as 'fartuous'. Since prose is designed to seem more 'natural', it is not surprising that it often seems connected with the body, both in its subjects and in its relatively loose construction.

Shakespeare does more with prose than cultivate speakers' tics, however, and one benefit of its informality is that prose permits a quick tempo. In conversations requiring rapidity, such as the banter of Petruccio's household servants in *The Taming of the Shrew* (IV. i), prose permits quick exchanges without the stiffness sometimes attendant on verse. This scene in particular offers a moment of release, placed as it is immediately after the comic tension of the wedding scene:

> *Grumio*: Call them forth.
> *Curtis*: (*calling*) Do you hear, ho? You must meet my
> master to countenance my mistress.
> *Grumio*: Why, she hath a face of her own.
> *Curtis*: Who knows not that?
> *Grumio*: Thou, it seems, that calls for company to
> countenance her.
> *Curtis*: I call them forth to credit her.
>
> (IV. i. 86–93)

Prose not only sets this episode apart from those involving the principal characters but also provides a 'natural' atmosphere for the trading of silly witticisms. Were it spoken in verse – we might compare the matching tri-metre lines of Richard III and Lady Anne in *Richard III*, I. ii – the feeling of the dialogue would be considerably different.

So it is with two interludes in *The Comedy of Errors*, those scenes in which the pair of foreigners, Antipholus and Dromio of Syracuse, forsake their usual verse and relax into lengthy comic dialogue in prose. Frustrated and confused at being mistaken for their Ephesian twins, all this taking place in the street in a strange city, master and servant take temporary comfort in the security of each other's presence and delight in the exercise of verbal contests. The first (II. ii. 35–111) turns on a lengthy series of jokes about time and hair (the mock-disputation ends with 'a bald conclusion'), while the second (III. i. 71–152) prompts Dromio of Syracuse to an elaborate figurative description of the fat serving maid who pursues him ('She is spherical, like a globe. I could find out countries in her'). The more relaxed medium of prose underwrites the digressive, self-generating quality of these conversations, setting them apart from the more intense and comically manic exchanges of verse. Shakespeare replays this distinctive effect when in mid-career he moves into the tragic mode: the quicksilver repartee between Hamlet and the Gravedigger, for example, depends upon the relative freedom that prose affords.

Most of the properties illustrated so far cohere in the language of Shakespeare's greatest prose speaker, Sir John Falstaff. That a knight of the realm should be the most accomplished speaker of low-life language is an essential element of Shakespeare's design in the two *Henry IV* plays. Prose scenes often, especially in history plays, specifically burlesque the serious topics set forth in the verse of the court, and Falstaff is the mouthpiece for such mockery. His keen ear serves him most obviously in the play-within-the-play of the great tavern scene (*1 Henry IV*, II. v), in his prose parodies of both Prince Hal and King Henry. These are party-pieces, but even in his less theatrical moments Falstaff's speech beguiles the audience with the familiar elements of Shakespearian prose: logical structure, repetitive patterns, rhythms both familiar and surprising, a distinctive vocabulary including biblical allusions and striking similes, and, perhaps above all, the unfailing knack for surprise. What is more, all these components are overlaid with a heavy coating of irony, for no one takes as much pleasure in Falstaff's verbal gifts as Falstaff himself.

Any of his virtuoso speeches might serve as illustration, the disquisition on honour (*1 Henry IV*, V. i. 127–40), or the defence of sherry-sack (*2 Henry IV*, IV. iii. 83–121): in both he addresses the audience in soliloquy. A less familiar excerpt, however, catches him in a less obviously performative mode.

> *Doll Tearsheet*: They say Poins has a good wit.
> *Sir John*: He a good wit? Hang him, baboon! His wit's as thick as Tewkesbury mustard; there's no more conceit in him than is in a mallet.
> *Doll Tearsheet*: Why does the Prince love him so, then?
> *Sir John*: Because their legs are both of a bigness, and a plays at quoits well, and eats conger and fennel, and drinks off candles' ends for flap-dragons [i.e. a bar trick], and rides the wild mare with the boys, and jumps upon joint-stools, and swears with a good grace, and wears his boot very smooth like unto the sign of the leg, and breeds no bate with telling of discreet stories, and such other gambol faculties a has that show a weak mind and an able body.
>
> (II. iv. 241–54)

Even when not delivering one of his star turns, Falstaff is always performing, as the exorbitant parataxis implies. Such histrionic, self-conscious rhetoric bespeaks an imaginative impulse. Falstaff has just explicitly turned the conversation away from mortality, and his sketch of Poins thus constitutes an assertion of vigour and a strategy for chasing away the blues.

The Making of Meaning

The brief treatment of Falstaffian eloquence having edged the discussion into the realm of character, I want now to consider the extraordinary utility of Shakespeare's prose. It would be easy to study various instances of characterization by means of prose, but a more efficient way of demonstrating Shakespeare's craft is to subordinate dramatic portraiture to the larger rubric of juxtaposition. Falstaff, for example, owes much of his eloquence to the contrary voices of King Henry and Hotspur. Quite early in his career Shakespeare discovered the value of prose as an alternative medium, specifically the expressive power of its simplicity relative to verse. Usually it is this relation that matters. And it is worth restating the rule established earlier, that many of Shakespeare's most startling effects derive from his productive breaking of rules, particularly the introduction of prose in unexpected places. Such artistic independence helps to account for the semantic possibilities of everyday language.

Even in its title, *Romeo and Juliet* is built on opposition, a principle that manifests itself in the alternation between verse and prose. The street scene (II. iii), after the nocturnal meeting of the two lovers and before the deadly swordfight, produces a palpable decrease in tension, although the feeling of relaxation is still ominous and deceptive, given the tragic context. Romeo enters to the mockery of his fellows and responds playfully to their jests:

> *Mercutio*: . . . I am the very pink of courtesy.
> *Romeo*: Pink for flower.
> *Mercutio*: Right.
> *Romeo*: Why, then is my pump well flowered.
> *Mercutio*: Sure wit, follow me this jest now till thou hast worn out thy pump, that when the single sole of it is worn, the jest may remain, after the wearing, solely singular.
> *Romeo*: O single-soled jest, solely singular for the singleness!
> *Mercutio*: Come between us, good Benvolio. My wits faints.
> *Romeo*: Switch and spurs, switch and spurs, or I'll cry a match.
>
> (II. iii. 54–65)

Such byplay diverts the audience from the suspenseful intensity of the love story, and Mercutio even comments on this distraction:

> Why, is this not better now than groaning for love? Now art thou sociable, now art thou Romeo, now art thou what thou art by art as well as by nature, for this drivelling love is like a great natural [idiot] that runs lolling up and down to hide his bauble in a hole. (III. ii. 81–5)

Elsewhere such verbal games are conducted in verse, but at this crucial point in the action, with the audience conscious of Romeo's emotional transformation and anxious about the progress of the lovers' clandestine plans, prose helps to ensure an altered mood, briefly slackening the tension and thereby, paradoxically, helping to magnify the tragic anxiety.

Shakespeare's gift for such formal alternation is especially apparent in *Much Ado About Nothing*, a play which fairly represents the prose of the mature comedies. To begin with, the distinction between verse and prose sometimes reflects social difference and sometimes does not. The highest ranking characters, Don Pedro, Don John, and Claudio, speak both verse and prose; the division sometimes corresponds to amatory scenes and sometimes not. In these cases Shakespeare delicately adjusts the language according to the tone he seeks to achieve, and as indicated earlier, tone is often determined by the need for contrast with what comes before or after. The romantic intrigue in *Much Ado* involves two parallel overhearing scenes (II. iii and III. i): in the first, the male characters promulgate a fiction contrived to make the eavesdropping Benedick think that Beatrice loves him; in the second, the females put a similar trick over on Beatrice. The first of these juxtaposed scenes is in prose, the second in verse. Evidently Shakespeare has altered the language for the purpose of variety, to keep the analogous actions from becoming too repetitious and formulaic.

The climactic church scene, in which Claudio sarcastically rejects his innocent bride, begins in genial prose, although its jocular informality is overshadowed by the audience's ironic awareness of impending disaster. As Claudio announces his 'discovery' of Hero's infidelity, he shifts into the formal register of verse, and the characters continue to speak verse for over 200 lines while a plot is hatched to restore Hero's honour. The scene concludes, however, with the private conversation of Benedick and Beatrice, a kind of coda in which, as he attempts to comfort her for her cousin's misfortune, they finally confess their affection for each other. Here prose seems the appropriate medium: the two wits have resisted and sparred with each other in prose from the opening scene, and their attraction and self-revelations are thus made to seem 'natural' and clear-sighted. Such a tonal relaxation is especially meaningful following the formality of Claudio's ugly charge, an artificial (i.e. false) accusation delivered in a relatively artificial form. This devotion to multiplicity also governs the distribution of verbal forms in *Twelfth Night*: since Shakespeare's dominant consideration is the tonal mixture of high and low comedy, he mingles verse and prose to heighten the dramatic effect of each.

Shakespeare subtly exploits the perceived differences between verse and prose to deepen the audience's engagement with his comic stories and thus to magnify their delight in shift and reversal, both narrative and linguistic. *As You Like It*, composed between *Much Ado* and *Twelfth Night*, owes much of its comic sparkle to such differences. As in *Much Ado*, the integration of the two forms subtly enriches the meaning of the action. While Shakespeare might have chosen simply to link the artificiality of the court with the structure of verse and allow prose to dominate the simple world of the forest of Arden, his actual practice is much more complex, chiefly because one of the foundational themes of the comedy is that the difference between court and country is by no means as clear as we might believe. The complexity of the linguistic palette is further enriched, as in the other romantic comedies, by the extraordinary number of songs and poems and outbreaks of rhyme. Here, however, we can discern with unusual clarity Shakespeare's availing himself of the *ordinariness* of prose. By this point in his career language itself has become one of his chief preoccupations. He seems particularly fascinated with the human propensity to deceive ourselves with fancy speech, especially in matters of the heart.

Prose thus becomes an instrument for exposing such perilous illusions. In the great wooing scene (IV. i), Rosalind, disguised as the experienced shepherd Ganymede, agrees to enact 'Rosalind' so that Orlando can rehearse his love-making. Their discourse is conducted, at the teacher's insistence, entirely in prose. Her aim is to deconstruct Orlando's conventional and derived efforts at courtship, to reveal to him that genuine love consists of more than mooning over the image of a distant female and pinning poems on trees. Consequently their flirtation often reverts to a concern with words, what a lover should say.

> *Rosalind*: . . . Am I not your Rosalind?
> *Orlando*: I take some joy to say you are because I would be talking of her.
> *Rosalind*: Well, in her person I say I will not have you.
> *Orlando*: Then in mine own person I die.
> *Rosalind*: No, faith; die by attorney. The poor world is almost six thousand years old, and in all this time there was not any man died in his own person, videlicet, in a love-cause. Troilus had his brains dashed out with a Grecian club, yet he did what he could to die before, and he is one of the patterns of love. Leander, he would have lived many a fair year though Hero had turned nun if it had not been for a hot midsummer night, for, good youth, he went but forth to wash him in the Hellespont and, being taken with the cramp, was drowned; and the foolish chroniclers of that age found it was Hero of Sestos. But these are all lies. Men have died from time to time, and worms have eaten them, but not for love.
>
> (IV. i. 83–101)

Orlando and Rosalind both play roles, she consciously, he consciously (in wooing a stand-in) and unconsciously (as the naive courtly lover). 'Ganymede' is the proxy for Rosalind; Orlando is urged to 'die by attorney'. The scraps of legal discourse that creep into the dialogue ('videlicet', 'love-cause') remind us of the logical foundations of Shakespeare's prose. Speaking disputatiously, Rosalind moves rationally through a list of mythical lovers and debunks the romance of each legend.

This passage illustrates Shakespeare's ability to make the prose part of the meaning. Rosalind's last two sentences – at once flat, rhythmic, ironic, affectionate, sardonic – conclude her proof, clinching the argument for clear-sighted, genuine affection. A further irony attends this dismantling of the clichés and illusions of conventional romantic love, however. Rosalind's role as instructor is a pose, an artificial performance that paradoxically leads her pupil to truth and simulates his genuine affection for him/her. By the same token, she presses the case for 'authentic' affection in prose that, while putatively more 'genuine' and 'natural' than the rhymes and ornaments of poetry, is itself highly artificial and structured. The language sounds ordinary only because Shakespeare has carefully counterposed it against its opposite. And so the medium in which Rosalind tells the story, a roster of reversals and false appearances and paradoxical discoveries, becomes part of the story.

The worth of prose as a foil to verse is evident in these comedies, but this complementary function is also essential to the effect of the tragedies. The shattering effect of the opening scene of *King Lear* owes much to Shakespeare's instinct for surrounding verse with prose to enhance dramatic tension. Over the course of 300 lines the dramatic intensity takes the shape of a pyramid: (1) a quiet prelude, the conversation among Gloucester, Kent, and Edmund, (2) a heightening of anxiety, as the love test unfolds and Cordelia objects, (3) an outburst of royal anger ending in banishment, (4) a degree of relaxation as Kent exits and Cordelia's marriage to France is arranged, and (5) a quiet coda, in which Goneril and Regan confidentially look to the future. This pattern of heightening and diminishing is underscored by the outbreak of couplets, spoken mostly by Kent, in the central panel (part 3). Sections (2) and (4) are mostly in blank verse, while the opening and closing movements are both in prose. The intimacy and informality of the opening lines communicate a deceptive sense of calm soon displaced by the formality of the ceremony, which is then exploded by the failure of Lear's scheme for dividing the kingdom. Likewise, the closing *tête-à-tête* between Goneril and Regan (5) is quiet and ominous, a moment of sinister calm after the tempestuous events preceding it. At this stage of artistic maturity, Shakespeare is able to manipulate the contrasting verbal forms with extraordinary subtlety and so to control the audience's responses in ways that they may not consciously recognize.

Occasionally the dramatist seems to place prose in competition with verse and to make it obvious that he does so. Such stylistic self-consciousness serves the larger thematic contest between form and substance. To some extent Rosalind's puncturing of Orlando's illusions exemplifies this practice, and the tragic counterpart of that treatment of prose is found in *Julius Caesar*, written probably in the same year as *As You Like It*. One of the most famous passages in the play is Brutus' lament over the body of Caesar, in which 'public reasons' are offered as justification for the conspiracy. Only about 6 per cent of *Caesar* is in prose, most of it spoken by the plebeians; except for a handful of brief prose replies (and these could be regarded as short verse lines), Brutus adheres stoutly to verse, even when those around him are speaking prose. His reversion to prose for the oration is ideological, expressive of his idealistic commitment to undecorated truth. His absolute belief in the sacrificial nature of the assassination dictates his prohibition of oaths for the conspirators (II. i). And over Caesar's body, before the citizens, he insists that the deed be judged dispassionately, that it be described rationally and straightforwardly, without poetic flourish.

> Romans, countrymen, and lovers, hear me for my cause, and be silent that you may hear. Believe me for mine honour, and have respect to mine honour, that you may believe. Censure me in your wisdom, and awake your senses, that you may the better judge. If there be any in this assembly, any dear friend of Caesar's, to him I say that Brutus' love to Caesar was no less than his. If then that friend demand why Brutus rose against Caesar, this is my answer: not that I loved Caesar less, but that I loved Rome more. Had you rather Caesar were living, and die all slaves, than that Caesar were dead, to live all free men? As Caesar loved me, I weep for him. As he was fortunate, I rejoice at it. As he was valiant, I honour him. But as he was ambitious, I slew him. There is tears for his love, joy for his fortune, honour for his valour, and death for his ambition. (III. i. 13–29)

It is surely meaningful that the plea lacks imagery.[10] The powerful irony at work here is that while the speech is not poetic, it is nevertheless manifestly rhetorical, so intricately organized and so thoroughly dependent on schemes of equivalence and repetition that it seems calculated and even manipulative. It offers perhaps the clearest demonstration in the canon that prose is never artless, that in the mouths of certain speakers it can be as highly structured, if by different means, as verse is. Famously, of course, Shakespeare juxtaposes Brutus' defence with Antony's emotional and poetic condemnation of the murder. Brutus speaks in prose because he wishes to seem sincere; Antony *is* sincere, and his poetic passion exposes the aridity and speciousness of Brutus' calculated prose.

Rarely are prose and poetry so starkly opposed as in *Measure for Measure*, a dark comedy written during the tragic phase and a play vitally concerned with the meretriciousness of surfaces. Here the conflict between control and disorder in both the body politic and the body personal is expressed in the juxtaposition – we might even say the competition – between poetry and prose. The most passionate verse speaker in the play is the self-deluding Angelo, whose false commitment to 'seeming' leads first to his self-discovery (in his soliloquy, II. iv. 1–17) and ultimately to his comic exposure. The conventional and rarely examined axiom that the difference between prose and verse is socially determined is indeed applicable in this play, but Shakespeare uses that contrast in subtle and meaningful ways and asks the audience to be sensitive to the differences. The realm of the court, of which Angelo is the representative – Shakespeare makes much of his status as 'deputy' – is placed in direct competition with the world of the street, the brothel, and the prison. In fact, the main problem of this problem comedy, that the boisterous underworld is in danger of fatally contaminating the entire civic structure of Vienna, is aurally suggested by the tendency of verse to yield to the more urgent and earthy claims of prose. In the very centre of the play (III. i), when the action reaches what looks like an impasse – Claudio is to be executed because Isabella refuses to save him by submitting to Angelo's sexual demands – the play notoriously shifts into prose as the Duke scrambles to salvage his plot to test Angelo and remedy the corruption of the city.

Throughout the fourth act, most pointedly in the prison scene with the Provost, the Duke's attempts to maintain the dignity of verse are thwarted by the unpredictable and uncontrollable impulses of disorderly humanity, such as Barnadine's refusal to be executed as a substitute for Claudio. At one point the Duke, in what seems like a desperate effort to encapsulate and emphasize the ironic justice of his scheme, even ventures into rhymed couplets: 'This is his pardon, purchased by such sin / For which the pardoner himself is in' (IV. ii. 110–11). But of course the message – delivered in cold and unmistakable prose – does not bring the pardon and forces the Duke to new shifts. The lengthy prose trial scene (II. i), in which Escalus patiently attempts to decipher Elbow's errors and Pompey's evasions, helps to clarify the difference between the two realms; Angelo can hold out (and speak their language) only so long, shortly leaving the stage in disgust. Of all the colourful speakers in this play, it is Lucio who, from his entrance in I. ii until his numerous prose intrusions in the final scene, stands for the undeniability of the physical, the everyday, the prosaic.

Many other functions might be described and examples summoned to illustrate the range and utility of Shakespeare's prose. For example, prose is usually the medium for letters (although they sometimes contain poems). Lady Macbeth makes a memorable entrance reading a prose letter from her husband describing his 'day of success'. *The Winter's Tale*, one of his last plays, contains some brilliantly inventive prose. The long and wrenching trial of the innocent Hermione is conducted almost entirely in passionate verse, but it is resolved instantaneously by the flat prose of an oracular pronouncement: 'Hermione is chaste, Polixenes blameless, Camillo a true subject, Leontes a jealous tyrant, his innocent babe truly begotten, and the King shall live without an heir if that which is lost be not found' (III. ii. 132–5). The play's penultimate scene is one of the most original Shakespeare wrote. Expecting to see the resolution of the action – the tender reunion of the King and his daughter – we are confronted instead with a long prose discussion in which three unknown gentle-men *narrate* the climax that we have been hoping for. The prosaic quality of this episode is a foil, a preparation for the moving and poetic surprise ending that Shakespeare has in store.

Ineffable Power

I have postponed until last a difficult topic, one that might be called the inde-finable affective power of prose. Although it lacks the patterned sound of poetry, prose can be arranged into musical schemes, and since the writer is not confined to the framework of iambic pentameter, words and phrases can be employed in more various and sometimes more intricate combinations. It is also possible that the absence of the poetic beat invites the writer to seek out other forms of rhythm in composing crucial lines. Such rhythmic distinction is audible in the moving phrases Hamlet uses to confide to Horatio his altered attitude about death and his belief in the 'special providence' that determines human events: 'If it be now, 'tis not to come. If it be not to come, it will be now. If it be not now, yet it will come. The readiness is all' (V. ii. 166–8). These lines can virtually be scanned, although exactly where the emphases fall is up to the actor. I believe that the accent ought probably to fall on the last word of each clause 'now', 'come', 'come', 'now', 'now', 'come'. Alternatively, an actor might do much with the repeated 'not' in each sentence. However the lines are spoken, the repeated 'now' at the end of the first, fourth, and fifth clauses offers speaker and listener ominous confirmation of what we suspect awaits Hamlet at the hands of Claudius and Laertes. And the triply repeated and subtly varied phrases prepare for the moving conclusion, the iambic phrase, 'The readiness is all.' Some of Shakespeare's most memorable lines are written in prose, and as in this case, it is often the rhythmic pattern, especially when based on one of the rhetorical schemes of repetition, that accounts for the incantatory power of the passage.

Readers can readily supply their favourite excerpts: Shylock's 'Hath not a Jew eyes?'; Lance's narrative about his dog Crab in *The Two Gentlemen of Verona*; the Porter's drunken bit in *Macbeth*; several of Falstaff's virtuoso pieces; Iago's 'Put money in thy purse'; some of Autolycus' clever self-justifications. Dogberry's great defence of himself against Conrad's insult ('Away, you are an ass, you are an ass') makes use of most of the rhythmic effects and tonal com-plexity that the mature Shakespeare is able to achieve with 'ordinary' speech.

> Dost thou not suspect my place? Dost thou not suspect my years? O that he were here to write me down an ass. But masters, remember that I am an ass. Though it be not writtten down, yet forget not that I am an ass. No, thou villain, thou art full of piety, as shall be proved upon thee by good witness. I am a wise

fellow, and which is more, an officer, and which is more, a householder, and which is more, as pretty a piece of flesh as any is in Messina, and one that knows the law, go to, and a rich fellow enough, go to, and a fellow that hath had losses, and one that hath two gowns, and everything handsome about him. Bring him away. O that I had been writ down an ass! (IV. ii. 72–84)

This outburst displays the familiar technical tricks: malapropism, reiterated words and phrases, clauses linked paratactically, contrasts in sentence length, the speaker's unsuccessful efforts at irony set against the playwright's skill at it. The lines also benefit from their location, at the end of a comic episode immediately following the wedding scene; thus they lighten the tonal gloom that the shaming of Hero has generated. Thanks also to its comic specificity, the speech is a triumph of tonal complexity. Of course Dogberry's proud self-assessment is ludicrous, and yet Shakespeare has managed by the judicious introduction of detail ('and one that hath had losses') to complicate our feelings of scornful delight, revealing briefly the vulnerable human beneath the foolish exterior and then swiftly pulling back to the boastful surface ('and one that hath two gowns'). And it is also helpful to remember that this passage, like virtually all the others examined in this chapter and many that perhaps should have been included, benefits from what Brian Vickers refers to as 'Shakespeare's gift of phrasing which defies analysis'.[11]

Notes

1   See R. W. David, 'Shakespeare and the players', *Proceedings of the British Academy*, 47 (1961), pp. 139–59.

2   John Lyly, *Euphues: The Anatomy of Wit*, in Paul Salzman, *An Anthology of Elizabethan Prose Fiction* (New York: Oxford University Press, 1987), p. 98.

3   Francis Bacon, 'Of truth', in *The Essayes or Counsels, Civill and Morall*, ed. Michael Kiernan (Cambridge, MA: Harvard University Press, 1985), pp. 8–9. I have modernized the spelling.

4   Jonas Barish, *Ben Jonson and the Language of Prose Comedy* (New York: Norton, 1970), p. 23.

5   *Richard II* is an exception, and its relatively early date (*c*.1595) separates it from the rest of the tetralogy: most of its characters are associated with the court, and even the extended scene with the gardeners is spoken in verse.

6   Barish, *Ben Jonson and the Language of Prose Comedy*, p. 31.

7   George Puttenham, *The Arte of English Poesie*, ed. Gladys Doidge Willcocks and Alice Walker (Cambridge: Cambridge University Press, 1936), pp. 201–2.

8   For a fascinating analysis of the rhetorical implications of Shallow's language, see Patricia Parker, *Literary Fat Ladies* (London: Methuen, 1987), pp. 70–2.

9   For more specific commentary on the particulars of Shakespeare's parodic style, see the notes to the Arden edition of *Love's Labour's Lost* by Richard David

(London: Methuen, 1951), and the more recent Arden edition by H. R. Woud-huysen (London: Thomas Nelson, 1998).

10   See Brian Vickers, *The Artistry of Shakespeare's Prose* (London: Methuen, 1968), pp. 241–5, for a thorough analysis of the complexities of this speech.

11   Ibid., p. 61.

Transfer of Title in *Love's Labour's Lost*

Katharine Eisaman Maus

Revisiting a comedy long associated with some kind of linguistic self-consciousness, Katharine Maus discusses Love's Labour's Lost *from the standpoint of feminist criticism. This enables her to open out questions of naming, identity and gender through a close analysis of the play's rhetorical strategies, and brings gender politics to the heart of its linguistic concerns. The play's deferral of a conclusion in marriage is viewed as the logical consequence of its problem of and with signification, and of unresolved differences between the language of the sexes.*

Katharine Eisaman Maus, 'Transfer of Title in *Love's Labor's Lost*: Language, Individualism, Gender', in *Shakespeare Left and Right*, ed. Ivo Kamps (New York: Routledge, 1991), pp. 205–23.

Influential feminist critics of Shakespeare have rarely dealt with Shakespeare's early, linguistically extravagant work.[1] Most have confined themselves to discussing Kate's capitulation scene in *The Taming of the Shrew*, or to tracing in the first years of Shakespeare's career basic plot or image patterns that recur in what is often considered the 'mature' *oeuvre*. Understandably, feminists have preferred to concentrate upon the later comedies, the histories, the tragedies, and some of the romances. Proponents of a new critical discourse can most efficiently demonstrate the power of their approach by influencing the ways the most impeccably canonical Shakespearean texts are discussed in professional publications and conferences, and taught in the undergraduate and graduate classroom. Moreover, the perennially fascinating characterological complexity of Shakespeare's later work has proven congenial to feminist critics, allowing them an ample field upon which to display the insights that become available when gender becomes a primary analytical category.

Nonetheless, these critical predilections have some unfortunate consequences. Suspicion of a depoliticized formalism, whether New Critical or deconstructive, has sometimes encouraged feminists to imply dubious distinctions between the language of the plays and poems and their politics. In 'The Rape in Shakespeare's *Lucrece*' Coppélia Kahn (1976), for instance, complains that its 'rhetorical display-pieces invite critical attention for their own sake, offering readers a happy escape from the poem's insistent concern with the relationship between sex and power' (1976: 45). In Kahn's formulation the feminist critic must resist such temptations, must look beneath the linguistically ornate surface to discern the social and characterological realities which make the work interesting and important.

In this repudiation of 'mere rhetoric' Kahn follows, intentionally or not, a host of earlier critics who find themselves apologizing for the early Shakespeare's unseemly linguistic superfluity. In Harley Granville-Barker's (1927) account, *Love's Labor's Lost* seems the symptom of a Shakespearean artistic pubescence: 'To many young poets of the time their language was a new-found wonder; its very handling gave them pleasure. The amazing things it could be made to do!' (1927: 9). For James Calderwood, *Love's Labor's Lost* shows the young Shakespeare 'passing from a sensuous enchantment with language, a wantoning with words, to a serious consideration of his medium, his art, and their relation to the social order' (Calderwood, 1965: 318). Calderwood sees *Love's Labor's Lost* as a rite of passage after which Shakespeare, having sown his verbal wild oats, shakes off such adolescent temptations to indulgence, settles down to become the artistic equivalent of a responsible husband, and begins to write the history plays and romantic comedies we value today. Feminist criticism might well question the assumptions about manly adulthood upon which such a critical practice relies, but by and large it has not bothered to do so.

Meanwhile critics who do not concern themselves with gender, but who do confront directly the remarkable linguistic elaborateness of *Love's Labor's Lost*, have developed an interesting critical perspective upon the play. William Carroll (1976) and Keir Elam (1984) discuss *Love's Labor's Lost* in terms of sixteenth-century Neoplatonic linguistic philosophy, popularized in Elizabethan England as part of a new self-consciousness about the expressiveness and literary potential of the vernacular. An essentialist theory of language derived from Plato's *Cratylus* proved particularly influential: a theory, that is, that 'there is an inherent rightness in names, that names are not arbitrary signs but are in some sense themselves the essence of what is named' (Carroll, 1976: 12).[2] Carroll and Elam maintain that *Love's Labor's Lost* is both deeply invested in, and deeply critical of, a Cratylanism they associate with Navarre's Academy. In the course of the play, both critics argue, the inadequacy of this linguistic theory becomes increasingly obvious. Its plausibility is hopelessly undermined by elaborate puns, daring tropes, novel epithets, multilingual malapropisms, ambiguities intended and unintended by the characters: all the verbal exorbitance for which *Love's Labor's Lost* has long been condemned.

By demonstrating that important sixteenth-century philosophical debates about words and meaning inform the play's linguistic self-consciousness,

Carroll and Elam are able to make impressive sense of features of *Love's Labor's Lost* previously considered trivial. In their account, the play is not just a display of linguistic possibilities; it is *about* linguistic possibility. My own focus upon issues of naming and reference in the pages that follow bespeak my indebtedness to their arguments. Nonetheless, their thesis has its limitations. Both critics abstract the linguistic issues in *Love's Labor's Lost* from the sexual politics of its comic plot, ignoring the misogynist assumptions upon which Navarre's failed Academy is founded, the affinities insisted upon in the play between verbal invention and erotic energy, and the tense sexual dynamics of the unexpectedly anti-comic conclusion. In consequence their readings seem deracinated from and unenlightened about psychological or generic concerns.

Is it possible for feminist criticism to avoid, on the one hand, treating Shakespearean verbal complexity as a distraction from politics or psychology, and on the other, treating politics or psychology as a distraction from verbal complexity? Perhaps we ought to wonder not merely why Shakespeare writes a play overtly concerned with linguistic problems and with problems of figuration, but why these problems become important in this unusual comedy, in which a group of men and a group of women fail to reconcile their differences. To answer this question, we need to understand how apparently abstract intuitions about linguistic meaning acquire psychological and political urgency in the court of Navarre. For in fact, I shall argue, some of the important linguistic issues in *Love's Labor's Lost* are inseparable from its generic, comic concern with sexual politics and with the construction of a gendered identity in a social context.[3]

As *Love's Labor's Lost* begins, the King of Navarre is completing his plans for an 'Academy' devoted to celibate study and to the mortification of the senses, and requiring his courtiers to sign a document listing the conditions by which they propose to live for the next three years. He explains his rationale in an intricate opening speech, the complexities of which deserve close attention:

> Let fame, that all hunt after in their lives,
> Live register'd upon our brazen tombs,
> And then grace us in the disgrace of death;
> When, spite of cormorant devouring Time,
> Th'endeavor of this present breath may buy
> That honor which shall bate his scythe's keen edge
> And make us heirs of all eternity.
> Therefore, brave conquerors – for so you are,
> That war against your own affections
> And the huge army of the world's desires –
> Our late edict shall strongly stand in force:
> Navarre shall be the wonder of the world;

> Our court shall be a little academe,
> Still and contemplative in living art.
>
> (I. i. 1–14)[4]

What is the appeal of this project? As a way for a king to spend his time, it would have been inconceivable a few generations earlier. In the course of the sixteenth century, however, the humanist emphasis on the education of secular leaders makes intellectual pursuits, previously considered fitting only for churchmen, newly respectable for an aristocrat.[5] Thus while we learn in the second act that Navarre's late father involved himself in military adventures, the son, like the young Hamlet in a later play, turns to scholarship. As a result, the conflicts he anticipates are largely spiritual or internal. The new enemies are one's own affections, the huge army of the world's desires.

Interestingly, however, Navarre assumes that the metaphors of the battle-field remain appropriate, and the anticipated gratification similar. In *The Book of the Courtier* Castiglione writes:

> Where the courtier is at skirmish, or assault, or battle upon the land, or in such other places of enterprise, he ought to work the matter wisely in separating himself from the multitude, and undertake noble and bold feats which he hath to do, with as little company as he can, and in the sight of noble men that be of most estimation in the camp . . . for indeed it is meet to set forth to the shew things well done. (Castiglione, 1974: 95)[6]

Castiglione's courtier neither concerns himself with military discipline, nor sees himself as carrying out part of an overall strategy involving an entire army. Rather he uses the circumstances of conflict to detach himself from the group and cut an unmistakable figure in the eyes of others. In *Love's Labor's Lost*, Navarre wants the same rewards from scholarly asceticism. Traditional forms of contemplation, dissolving the individual in the apprehension of the absolute, are not for him. Rather he imagines himself undergoing the contemplative life as if it were a heroic ordeal, emerging victorious and universally admired. Self-mortification becomes a means to self-exaltation, a way to acquire the traditional aristocratic *desiderata*, honor and fame.[7] The potential absurdities of such a combination will be suggested later in the play in the figures of Armado, the bombastic soldier, and Holofernes, the militant pedant, who burlesque from opposite directions, so to speak, Navarre's idealized conflation of martial valor with learning and eloquence.

Navarre's opening speech, as well as the scene that follows it, connects his particular kind of identity-formation with a particular rhetorical anxiety. *Love's Labor's Lost* begins with edicts proclaimed, contracts endorsed, and promises extracted – a flurry of what J. L. Austin (1975) calls 'performative utterances'.

This kind of language is not referential; it performs actions rather than describe or point to an extralinguistic reality. As such, performative utterances seem to close the gap between signifier and signified, *verba* and *res*, word and world. Closing that gap is something Navarre seems to find highly desirable. In his opening speech he suggests that the fame he expects for his ascetic heroism will take the form of a stable description, a name permanently 'registered' on a tomb. 'Navarre shall be the wonder of the world!' In the meantime he demands another sort of stabilization of and through the name, asking his courtiers to ratify their promises with their signatures.

Navarre's desire for the permanence of his own name and those of his friends is quite comprehensible, because proper nouns seem to attach uniquely and immutably to their referents as other identifying features might not. They are, as Hobbes (1962) puts it, 'singular to only one thing.'[8] If, moreover, William Carroll is right that Navarre would like to believe that names 'are not arbitrary signs but are in some sense the essence of what is named', if *verba* and *res* are really inseparable, then ensuring the permanence of the name becomes a magical way of ensuring the permanence of the self. Thus the King sees an inscription upon the tomb as a way of overcoming death. If his logic seems specious here, it is no more so than that of many Renaissance writers of love poetry, Shakespeare included, who assert that their words grant the beloved a kind of immortality.[9]

Navarre's opening speech suggests, however, that the permanence he desires is not merely an automatic consequence of the usual relationship between names and things. Rather, it is a hard-won achievement. He describes a kind of transaction: hardships in the present 'buy' an honor that mitigates the effects of mortality. In this passage he seems less the Cratylan essentialist than the prudent investor who has learned how to make a profit from 'cormorant devouring Time', contractually assenting to deprivation in the short term in order to realize a long term gain. This long term gain is represented as an inheritance: the King expects that he and his friends will become 'heirs of all eternity'.

What are the implications of these metaphors? Why should the problem of stabilizing the name, of making an indissoluble connection between signifier and signified, be formulated in terms of exchange or inheritance? Perhaps an association between naming and inherited property seems 'natural' for the King because the aristocratic male name – Navarre, Berowne, Dumaine, Longaville – is normally an inherited name; moreover, it is the name of *what* is inherited, the piece of property that guarantees its owner income and status.

The close connection in the aristocratic mind between a name and a title to property is adumbrated later in the play, when Longaville catches sight of a lady, immediately falls in love with her, and 'desires her name' of Boyet. Boyet playfully refuses to tell him, so Longaville rephrases his request:

> Pray you, sir, whose daughter?
> *Boyet*: Her mother's, I have heard.
> *Longaville*: God's blessing on your beard!
> *Boyet*: Good sir, be not offended.
> She is an heir of Falconbridge.
> *Longaville*: Nay, my choler is ended.
> She is a most sweet lady.
>
> (II. i. 201–7)

And Longaville exits forthwith, satisfied despite never, apparently, receiving an answer to his question. For it is Maria's place in the network of aristocratic entitlements that matters to Longaville, that constitutes her 'name'.

The inextricability of person and property has important consequences for the way the King is able to formulate his desire for immortal fame. When he declares, in his opening speech, that 'Navarre shall be the wonder of the world!' it is unclear whether he is referring to himself – the founder of the Academy – or rather to the site upon which it will be located. (Likewise, when Boyet tells Longaville that Maria is 'an heir of Falconbridge', there is no way of knowing whether Falconbridge is *what* or *from whom* she will inherit.) A related ambiguity confuses the claim Navarre makes in his opening speech, when he imagines himself and his associates as the 'heirs of all eternity'. Is he thinking of eternity as testator or as bequest?

Perhaps Navarre sees no reason to distinguish the two possibilities because for him they have amounted to the same thing: he has inherited the territory of Navarre from a father named Navarre. But becoming the 'heir of eternity' is more problematic, since inheritance requires the death of the previous possessor, and eternity is precisely what does not die. The dream of a fixed name, called forth by an anxiety about 'the disgrace of death', turns out paradoxically, as the King has formulated it, to need what it wants to resist or avoid.

In other words, the King demands a name that will refer permanently and uniquely to *him*, but he is frustrated by the fact that the aristocratic male name is a doubly transferred name – transferred in space, so to speak, from possession to possessor, and then again in time, down the generations from one possessor to the next. The names the courtiers 'subscribe' to Navarre's document in the first scene are metonymies in both a synchronic and a diachronic sense.[10] And an aristocrat's name seems, as proper names go, an unusually unstable matter, since if his father or older brother dies, then his name changes to reflect the alteration in status and property rights.

Moreover, the Cratylan position is stronger than is required to maintain the aristocratic privilege of Navarre and his courtiers. The landowning class as a group needs not fixity of reference but predictability of reference: regular and orderly methods of managing the necessary transfer of title from father to

child, from debtor to lender, from buyer to seller. The propriety of the aristocratic proper name actually rests not upon an essential, immutable connection
to the individual whom it denotes, but upon the legitimacy of the means
by which that name has been acquired and by which it will be passed along.
Thus when Boyet praises Navarre as 'the sole inheritor / Of all perfections that
a man may owe' (II. i. 5–6), he uses 'owe' here in its common Renaissance
sense, a variant of 'own'. But the language simultaneously invokes the sense
still current today, suggesting not possession but its apparent opposite,
debt – the obligation to relinquish ownership. These two senses are not as
inconsistent as they might seem. The fact of death, which makes possible the
acquisition of property from one's ancestors, also necessitates its eventual
surrender.

For Navarre, however, this is not good enough. To be 'matchless', in his
terms, is to take possession of his proper name once and for all. But this desire
is covertly, illogically linked to an incompatible order of inherited transfer, in
which the possessor of a name is merely the temporary bearer of a title acquired
from the father and passed along to the son. Resisting the inevitability of his
own mortality, Navarre resists at the same time the effect his mortality has
upon the meaning of his name. Without acknowledging it, he asks to be
installed forever in a place that he is only allowed to occupy for the time being.
The imagery of inheritance that comes naturally to him thus seems ill-suited
to the aggressively meritocratic and competitive quality of the sentiments he
uses that imagery to express. Navarre makes, as it were, an excessive demand
upon the very system to which he owes his preeminence.

The linguistic confusion here is structurally identical with an ambiguous
feature of Renaissance aristocratic psychology first discussed by Jacob
Burckhardt (1958) and analyzed more recently by Stephen Greenblatt
(1980). Well-off, educated men in early modern Europe manifest a powerful
desire to distinguish themselves from each other, to demonstrate their freedom
and uniqueness. But because the aristocratic impulse to individuality is the
cultural construction of a particular class, the aristocrat's convictions about
his own independence and originality are themselves inevitably derivative,
part of a group *ethos*. What seems like a meritocratic claim has subterranean
links to a system of inherited entitlement it seems to oppose or subvert. In
Love's Labor's Lost, the meritorious aristocrat desires an identity based upon
his own individual exploits, but in fact derives his prestige not from his
own heroic exertions, but from the transferred glory of accomplished
ancestors.

Given this incoherence, it is not surprising that the intelligent Berowne
finds Navarre's scheme objectionable. He suggests a different way of conceiving of the relation between name and referent:

These earthly godfathers of heaven's lights,
That give a name to every fixed star,
Have no more profit of their shining nights
Than those that walk and wot not what they are.

(I. i. 88–91)

The 'name' for Berowne's purposes is the first or Christian name, bestowed by a godfather who has no proprietary interest in the child, rather than the last or family name, derived from a father whose stake in his own offspring is far more consequential. Berowne suggests that the names of the fixed star have nothing to do with how they originated, whether they shine, or who profits from them. Language is merely arbitrary, unconnected to facts about inheritance and social privilege.

Berowne's separation of naming from paternity has a number of advantages. Not only does his account avoid the contradictions of Navarre's essentialism, but it promotes more radical possibilities for individuation, since if signifiers are no longer strictly aligned with signifieds, then the topic of an utterance no longer determines usage. The idiosyncratic pressures of the speaker's personality and choices – his individual *style* – determines how he speaks and what he says. Not surprisingly, most critics of *Love's Labor's Lost* have seen Berowne as the most 'realistic' or 'fully realized' character in the play, a harbinger of the highly particularized protagonists of the romantic comedies Shakespeare writes a few years later.[11]

Nor is it surprising that despite his expressed doubts, Berowne does agree to participate in Navarre's project, for despite their difference the two men share important common ground. For both of them, the linguistic problem of what and how names mean is inextricably linked to a psychological problem of self-construction. They both want to be 'individuals', though they envision different paths to that goal. As such they are both caught up in what might be called the quintessential humanist problem, that is the relation of original to copy, archetype to type, model to imitation, source to derivation, ancestor to heir.[12] Much of the so-called action in *Love's Labor's Lost*, a virtually plotless play, concerns the manifold ways in which one thing can stand in for another, replacing and displacing it: Dull's representation, or reprehension, as he calls it, of the King's authority; Armado's search for precedents in love; the oddly prolonged discussion about whether Cain can substitute for Adam in an old joke about the moon; the bizarre argument about how many actors are going to 'pursent' (present, personate) the Nine Worthies. On a dramatic level the problem might be seen as intrinsic to the theatrical medium, in which a character is always an impersonation or counterfeit. On the linguistic level the problem is one of the substitutability of one word for another, and finds expression in the play's obsession with figures of synonymy: coelo, the sky, the welkin, the heaven; wench, damsel, virgin, maid; carry-tale, please-man, zany, mumble-news, trencher-knight. The most elaborate and gratuitous example of the anxiety generated by such substitutions is the curiously exaggerated hostility the courtiers displayed at the masque of the Nine Worthies near the end of the play. Their ridicule suggests a discomfort at the way the names and attributes of quintessentially exemplary individuals – Hector, Hercules, Alexander, Judas Maccabeus – are subject to appropriation by incompetent place-holders, degraded even at the moment of memorialization.

> *Costard*: I Pompey am, –
> *Berowne*: You lie, you are not he.
> (V. ii. 541)

While the masque purportedly celebrates the immortal fame of virtuous heroes, it actually conducts a final assault upon the aristocratic fantasy of an absolute heroic identity, unalterable by death or by the passage of time.

The issues about language and meaning that Navarre and his courtiers debate in the first scene of *Love's Labor's Lost*, and which continue to arise in many of the scenes thereafter, are thus profoundly implicated in their own sense of themselves as men of a particular class and generation. In Navarre's case the unacknowledged incoherence of this self-conception is connected with a refusal to acknowledge women, whose role in the production of a new generation involves them indispensably in the process of title transfer. Navarre establishes 'Academe' as an entirely male community, protected from female incursion by a penalty reminiscent of Tereus's abuse of Philomela: any woman who approaches the court will have her tongue cut out. With some help from Longaville, who devises this threat, Navarre wishfully defines language as a wholly male possession, and imagines women as speechless and passive. Their attitude is consistent with that expressed in English Renaissance linguistic and historical writing, which often associates linguistic slippage and transfer with a female sexuality both indispensable for social and familial order and potentially uncontrollable by that order.[13] William Camden, for instance, looking back at the English spoken before the Norman invasion, admires the Anglo-Saxon preference for expressing complex or abstract ideas in compound words derived from native elements, rather than importing words, as sixteenth-century speakers do, from French, Latin, or Greek: 'Our ancestors seemed . . . as jealous of their native language, as those Britons which passed hence into Armorica in France, and marrying strange women there, did cut out their tongues, lest their children should corrupt their language with their mothers' tongues' (Camden, 1984: 32). By means of a violence identical to that contemplated by Navarre and his courtiers in the first scene of *Love's Labor's Lost*, the British fathers maintain the fixity and purity of their language by passing it directly to the next generation, without the intrusion of the women who under ordinary circumstances would introduce their children to language. The accurate transfer of the mother tongue from generation to generation requires the silencing of actual mothers. Like Navarre in *Love's Labor's Lost*, Camden associates originary language, true naming, with the male. By contrast, the openness of modern English to alien influence constitutes a kind of corruption of its bloodline, which perhaps contributes to its hybrid vigor but which also defies regulation and makes purity impossible. Navarre's desire to clarify the relation between names and things thus not surprisingly requires the exclusion of female sexuality, associated as it is with a corruption of the truth. Since Berowne is not so heavily invested in this particular notion of truth – since for him signifiers are arbitrarily applied anyhow – Navarre's interdictions make no sense to him, and he attempts to make a case for a more accommodating attitude toward women.

If Navarre's fantasy of a fixed name represents a kind of excessive attempt to guarantee *aristocratic* privilege, the fantasy of the silent women represents a similarly excessive assertion of *male* privilege. The connections between these two kinds of privilege quickly become clear. The Princess of France arrives to enquire about title to Aquitaine, a title disputed because of a deal made between her father and Navarre's father. As she enters for the first time at the beginning of the second act, her courtier, Boyet, is describing her mission to her:

> Consider who the King your father sends,
> To whom he sends, and what's his embassy:
> Yourself, held precious in the world's esteem,
> To parley with the sole inheritor
> Of all perfections that a man may owe,
> Matchless Navarre; the plea of no less weight
> Than Aquitaine, a dowry for a queen.
> (II. i. 2–8)

In Boyet's account the Princess seems to exemplify woman's place in a strict patriarchal system, an item of exchange among men. While Navarre's position, as we have already seen, is that of an heir ('the sole inheritor / Of all perfections') the Princess is by contrast a valued object, something 'held precious in the world's esteem'. Her task requires her to act as an intermediary between father and potential husband, representing her father's interest in a negotiation for a territory described as a 'dowry'. Nonetheless, her arrival forces 'matchless Navarre' – matchless not only in the sense of being unique, but in the sense of being still unmarried – to confront everything he has tried to repress: the involvement of women in the process of title transfer, the dependence of the present generation upon the actions of its predecessors, and the possibility that the title itself may be ambiguous, subject to conflicting claims.

Moreover, since the paternal source of her authority is remote, offstage, the Princess seems to operate in the world of the play as a power in her own right. Her first action is to command one of her male followers to act as deputy or 'fair solicitor' between herself and the young King. The drama of title transfer, in other words, casts the Princess as both object and subject in a system of exchange. Another way of describing this doubleness is that the women in *Love's Labor's Lost* turn out to talk, as well as to listen to themselves being talked about.[14] Their lovers imagine them attending silently to sonneteering monologues, the topics and recipients of an erotic discourse they themselves are not permitted to speak. But the Princess and her ladies are, in fact, vocal and witty critics of the poems and gifts sent to them by the men. The female tongues the men imagine excising in the first scene turn out to be cutting, not cut: by Act V, scene 2 Boyet is remarking gleefully that 'The tongues of mocking wenches are as keen / As is the razor's edge invisible' (V. ii. 256–7). As the play proceeds the women appropriate many of the postures associated with the subject-position conventionally occupied by an aggressive male lover. In Act IV, scene 1 Rosaline, skillfully launching arrows at a target, indulges simultaneously in a bawdy dialogue with Boyet in which she identifies herself as the shooter/suitor who 'hits' (copulates with) the 'mark' (female genital) with a 'prick'. In the hunting scenes, the Amazonian princess penetrates her deer/dear with a similar phallic efficiency; as Holofernes puts it, 'The preyful Princess pierc'd and prick'd a pretty pleasing pricket' (IV. ii. 55–6). Helpless at last, Berowne presents himself to Rosaline as a target:

> Here stand I, lady; dart thy skill at me;
> Bruise me with scorn, confound me with a flout;
> Thrust thy sharp wit quite through my ignorance;
> Cut me to pieces with thy keen conceit.
>
> (V. ii. 396–9)

The mutilated Philomela of the first scene is here replaced by the male victim Orpheus, dismembered by unruly female Bacchantes.

How are we to understand the kinds of power and prestige the women in the play find it possible to acquire and deploy?[15] In theory, the role of the female in the passing down of titles is merely instrumental. In *Love's Labor's Lost* the women do not have surnames at all, and in Shakespeare's England, woman's property like her surname ordinarily disappears into her husband's when she marries. Aristocratic men are endowed with the goods, power, and equipment they need to become Renaissance self-fashioners and heirs of all eternity, while the female role seems in contrast to be defined as purely ancillary. Thus when Boyet tells the enamored Longaville that Maria is her mother's daughter, Longaville finds it a mere impertinence. He imagines the mother as a necessary but ideally unnoticed conduit between the father who possesses wealth and the child who will inherit it. For ideally, under the rule of primogeniture, the patriarch passes the bulk of his property to his eldest son, who succeeds to his position of power over the resources of the family.

In practice, however, things do not always work this way. To function smoothly, primogeniture requires a son who survives to manhood. When there is no surviving son, inheritance customs diverge; in some systems, title to the property goes to the next surviving relative, even if that relative is female, and in others, title passes over the females to the next surviving male, if one can be found. In England, where *Love's Labor's Lost* is written, the first practice was normal; in France, where the play is set, the second prevailed; but in both cases an absence of male heirs could allow women to occupy places in the inheritance system supposedly reserved for men. So even while Longaville belittles the role of the mother he is gratified to learn that the lady he desires is 'the heir of Falconbridge'. Just as the conventions of sonneteering courtship employed by Navarre and his associates deny women a position from which to speak – a position the women nonetheless find it possible to appropriate for themselves – so in some circumstances the conventions of inheritance grant aristocratic women the very power they seem at first glance designed to preclude. But this does not really feminize power, since the woman's possession of it is accidental, perhaps temporary, and most importantly remains defined in male terms. For despite their apparent independence, the Princess and her ladies never have available to them a specifically *feminine* subjectivity, a special claim upon the cultural or material resources available to the men. Camped for the duration of the play in a field just outside the borders of the male domain, they find it possible to insinuate themselves precariously into a subject-position normally defined as male, taking advantage of the absence, naiveté, or inattentiveness of those who are its normal occupants. This is why Rosaline's and the Princess's seizure of initiative is figured by phallic attributes (pricking the picket) and why the men may react by accusing them of a usurpation which, in fact, they have in a way committed.

The possibility of a woman inhabiting such roles, however, does function to cut social facts loose from biological ones and to blur or complicate the significance of gender difference. Moreover, it suggests that the sharp demarcation between men and women Navarre insists upon early in the play involves a significant mystification of the facts of male lives. For it is possible to think of men, too, as conduits through which the family title passes from generation to generation. Unlike their mothers and sisters, male heirs are allowed some control over their property in their lifetimes, but as we have already seen this may not satisfy those to whom the fact of mortality itself seem unacceptable. Perhaps the men exaggerate the passivity and discursive inconsequence of the women in order to displace onto them an anxiety generated by their own inconsistent sense of identity: how are they to reconcile an inherited status, which must eventually be relinquished to the next generation, with an energetic egoism that refuses to give up what it has acquired, defying 'cormorant devouring Time' with a demand for eternity?

And there are further complications. Since a woman can function as a subject rather than a mere object or a conduit, with a mind and a speech of her own, she possesses the power to interrupt or derail the orderly process of transferring names from father to son, from original to likeness. This disruptive potential is the subject of many of the notoriously bawdy *double entendres* in *Love's Labor's Lost*. One class of such jokes implies fantasies of simply bypassing female subjectivity altogether: by rape, in which the woman's desires are overruled, or by homosexuality or onanism, in which they become irrelevant. Another class of jokes recognizes the indispensability of female subjectivity for the functioning of kinship networks and property transfers, but stresses the unreliability built into such a system. The constant witticisms about light women, horns, and cuckoos constitute reminders that although fathers may possess titles, their relationship to the children who will inherit those titles is always open to question.[16]

Many critics have noticed that the aristocratic women in *Love's Labor's Lost* seem more 'serious' than their male counterparts about the ways language can be used – a seriousness evident in the attitudes they express toward language rather than in any plain-style austerity of usage.[17] The Princess, for instance, repeatedly deplores the 'painted flourish' of flattery and professes horror at oath-breaking; Rosaline regrets Berowne's uncontrolled wit. It is hardly surprising that the women are more likely than the men to construe the referentiality and reliability of words as a specifically *moral* issue. They cannot help knowing that the truth of names in patriarchy is the consequence not of some intrinsic connection between names and things but of female sexual fidelity.

While 'truth' for the men, in other words, is an issue of right definitions – a matter of correctly aligning words and things-in-the-world – for the women 'truth' is a behavioral matter, the keeping of a marital vow that demands submission to a patriarchal order. For the women, truth is an exercise not of the intellect but of the will: and not, moreover, of an ambitiously self-assertive will but of a will that disciplines itself, that brings desires into accord with social requirements. For the Princess and her ladies are not revolutionaries. They do not want to undermine or escape from patriarchy, but to find themselves a secure and relatively advantageous position within it. Thus Berowne's skepticism, with its refusal to acknowledge a connection between words and practice, is despite its apparent tolerance at least as threatening to their interests as Navarre's rigid misogynist exclusivism. For the happiness of their lives will depend upon their husbands' scrupulous fulfillment of their contractual obligations in marriage.

The aristocratic women's relatively earnest association of truth with virtuous self-restraint has, however, a flip side – a playful awareness of the way they can, by their own initiative, alter the relationship between sign and referent. When they learn that their lovers, disguised as Muscovites, are coming to woo them, the ladies mask, and exchange among themselves the love-tokens the men have just sent them. They know that the lords will not think of questioning the symbols of male entitlement – that they will be, in the Princess's phrase, 'deceived by these removes' (V. ii. 135). As Berowne laments when he learns of the ruse, 'we / Following the sign, wooed but the sign of she' (V. ii. 469). The ladies in *Love's Labor's Lost* perform the equivalent of a bed-trick on the level of the signifier. The way the Princess describes the deception suggests that the aristocratic concern with property can be as pressing for the women as for the men:

> There's no such sport as sport by sport o'erthrown,
> To make theirs ours and ours none but our own.
> (V. ii. 153–4)

Appropriating male sport and subsuming it under the rubric of a sport 'owned' by the women, she reverses the direction in which property and power ordinarily flow in patriarchal marriage. Although it is never as ambitious, the Princess's desire for self-ownership – 'ours none but our own' – resembles Navarre's competitive individualism in some respects. But while Navarre's strategies of self-assertion involve thinking of the relationship of name and thing as a clear and permanent matter, the Princess's self-assertion involves subverting that clarity and permanence, rupturing the connections between desire and its objects, signifier and signified. These reversals are, however, limited ones, unlike Berowne's more wholesale subversions: a game in which rules and durations are carefully specified.

The significant conceptual differences between the sexes become starkly evident at the end of the play, when Jacquenetta's pregnancy is announced, the death of the King of France is reported, and the aristocratic women refuse to marry the men. The men have sworn to abjure the company of women, but they find themselves in love nonetheless. Berowne satisfies them that their perjury can be overcome by a process of redefinition, that the performative utterances with which the play began do not really matter. In Berowne's account the eyes of women become sources of truth:

> From women's eyes this doctrine I derive:
> They are the grounds, the books, the academes,
> From whence doth spring the true Promethean fire.
>
> . . .
>
> For where is there any author in the world
> Teaches such beauty as a woman's eye?
>
> . . .
>
> Then when ourselves we see in ladies' eyes,
> Do we not likewise see our learning there?
>
> (IV. iii. 298–312)

Berowne reformulates the place of sexual desire in the pursuit of knowledge, repudiating Navarre's original conception of passion as an enemy to the scholar's 'still and contemplative' mind. The truth-seeker comes upon himself not directly, but as a displaced image, reflected in the object of his passion. Berowne rejects Navarre's notion that by some strenuous effort of self-creation the scholar can achieve a perfect autonomy. Nonetheless, like Navarre, Berowne assumes that truth is a *place*, a locus of authority from which originary meaning issues. Although he installs women in that place of privilege, his assumptions are very different from those of the women themselves, whose conception of truth is social and contractual.

Unfortunately for the men, the women insist upon the seriousness of male vacillation far more vigorously than might be expected. The Shakespearean heroine – Julia in *Two Gentlemen of Verona*, Helena in *A Midsummer Night's Dream*, Hero in *Much Ado*, Mariana in *Measure for Measure*, Imogen in *Cymbeline* – typically asks not that her lover has kept faith throughout the play, but that he promise improvement in the future. Comic endings require a certain female charity, or laxness of standards, that the Princess and her entourage refuse to endorse. In *Love's Labor's Lost*, the women's refusal to credit the men's apparently sincere declarations of ardor makes the predictable unions impossible. Instead, in the last lines of the play, the women impose tasks upon the lovers. The Princess insists that Navarre perform a version of his original project, sequestering himself in a hermitage for a year, learning to keep his word. Rosaline sends Berowne away to try jesting with the sick at hospital beds:

> A jest's prosperity lies in the ear
> Of him that hears it, never in the tongue
> Of him that makes it.
>
> (V. ii. 851–3)

These tasks involve a re-education in the nature of truth as the women conceive it: as the faithful submission to the command of another, and as a speech-act completed not when it is uttered but when it is heard and assented to.

The ending of *Love's Labor's Lost* is derailed, then, because the women find it impossible to believe the men. But issues of belief, trust, and faith are implicated in relations of power. The death of fathers – Navarre's before the play begins, the Princess's as it ends – makes the transfer of title possible, indeed necessary, imposing the pleasures and obligations of reproduction upon the next generation. Making these transfers, however, requires the cooperation of women, and *Love's Labor's Lost* calls the inevitability of this cooperation into question. The only union in the play, Armado's and Jacquenetta's, provides a father's name to a child whose paternity is in fact very much in doubt. The aristocratic women disrupt the process of transfer by a different strategy, insisting upon the postponement of their nuptials. 'Our wooing doth not end like an old play', complains Berowne. 'Jack hath not Jill. These ladies courtesy / Might well have made our sport a comedy' (V. ii. 864–6).

Patricia Parker has recently argued that the delay of closure in courtship and in literature is identified with women's interest and women's power, and the pressure towards an ending represents reimposition of a stable patriarchal order in which men can exert their control unchallenged (Parker, 1987: 8–35). Courtship, reversing the normal currents of social authority, grants women a kind of power, a power Berowne casts in philosophical terms when he grants an originary status to women, instead of defining them as secondary, derivative, or ancillary. 'O! I am yours, and all that I possess', he declares to Rosaline (V. ii. 383). This ownership of men by women is a temporary matter, however, and will be reversed in the event of their marriage. For normally, women finally submit to men, finally extend the 'courtesy' that allows courtship to come to an end. But *Love's Labor's Lost* ends without closure, with the women's insistence upon further delay. They sustain the fiction of their power in order, they hope, to be able to dispense with it at last.

A refusal to provide the expected satisfactions of a comic *denouement*, then, is part and parcel with the play's inquiry into problems of signification. The socially prescribed ways the characters conceive of themselves, and the ways they try and fail to interact with each other across the psychic rifts of gender difference, are deeply implicated in anxieties about the naturalness of meaningful language, and with a closely related concern for the elusiveness and displacement of origin. The linguistic pleasures and perplexities of *Love's Labor's Lost* are inseparable from its sexual politics, as the play calls the relations between the sexes and the appropriateness of names into question by the same means and for similar reasons.

Acknowledgements

I would like to thank Fred Maus, Clare Kinney, and the members of the University of Virginia Renaissance Area Discussion Group for their comments on a draft of this essay.

Notes

1   For instance, Carol Neely (1985) gets underway with *Much Ado About Nothing*; Peter Erickson (1985) with *As You Like It*; Marianne Novy (1984) with *The Taming of the Shrew*. Linda Bamber (1982) discusses *Twelfth Night* and *The Merchant of Venice* in the context of the histories and tragedies. The earlier plays addressed by the essays in *The Woman's Part* (Lenz et al., 1980) are *Richard III* and *The Taming of the Shrew*. Coppélia Kahn's *Man's Estate* (1981) contains a chapter on *Venus and Adonis*, but as in her essay on *The Rape of Lucrece* (Kahn, 1976), she downplays Shakespeare's rhetorical self-consciousness in order to pursue other lines of inquiry.

2   Keir Elam (1984: 114–58) makes a somewhat more elaborate philosophical argument with similar consequences for a reading of the play.

3   A fuller reading than I have room to present here would take account of class as well as gender. *Love's Labor's Lost* explicitly frames the interactions among aristocrats, professionals, and peasantry in terms of the possession of a literacy imagined in humanist terms as both the ability to read and write and as access to the classical past.

4   All references are to the Arden edition of *Love's Labor's Lost*, ed. Richard David (Shakespeare, 1951).

5   Numerous historians of education have commented upon the significance of this change in the conception of the aristocrat, and its impact upon educational institutions and curricula. See, e.g., Hexter (1950), Curtis (1959) and Stone (1964).

6   I have modernized the spelling in this and other passages from Renaissance texts.

7   In fact, by the latter part of the sixteenth century changes in military technology have already rendered obsolete the individualistic military strategy Castiglione describes. With the widespread employment of weapons capable of killing at long range (muskets, cannons, etc.), sophisticated group maneuvers become more effective than uncoordinated one-to-one confrontations in the battlefield. For a succinct account of these changes see, e.g., Gilbert (1943). One reason Navarre may be searching for an alternative form of self-display is that older means of acquiring honor in hand-to-hand combat are no longer available, except in the artificial circumstances of the jousting ring.

8   Cf. Elam (1984: 120–1): 'The great paradigm for language at large in *Love's Labor's Lost* is the proper name . . . the appeal, as it were, of appellation is evident first in the obsessive adamic ceremony of nomination as such and in the very range of names for naming drawn upon . . . and then in the carefully cultivated anxiety that

the pedants in particular express over nominal propriety.' Although she does not deal with *Love's Labor's Lost*, or with much other Shakespeare for that matter, Anne Ferry (1988: 69–80) usefully illuminates the privilege given to the proper name in sixteenth-century linguistic theory.

9   It is also a kind of error that Shakespeare elsewhere associates with royalty. What a king says or demands often happens, and the correlation between his words and the real world can present itself to him as an issue about the nature of language rather than about the nature of politics. Thus Sigurd Burckhardt writes about Lear: 'The full, gapless identity of sentence and of power, of word and act, is the essence of Lear's conception of himself and his place' (1968: 276). But of course this is a mystification. The end of the first scene of *Love's Labor's Lost* demonstrates efficiently that the truth of the king's words requires the subject's participation: Costard, arrested in the company of Jacquenetta and asked if he had noticed the decree forbidding him the company of women, admits 'much the hearing of it, but little the marking of it'.

10   The sixteenth-century antiquarian William Camden remarks upon the impulse to suppress the metonymic transfer of the name from places to persons: 'I cannot see why men should think that their ancestors gave names to places, when the places bare those very names, before any men did their surnames. Yea the very terminations of the names are such as are only proper and appliable to places, and not to persons in their significations . . . Who would suppose hill, wood, field, ford, ditch, pole, pond, tower, or ton, and such like terminations to be convenient for men to bear in their names, unless they could also dream hills, woods, fieldes [sic], fords, ponds, pounds, etc. to have been metamorphosed into men by some supernatural transformation' (Camden, 1984: 104).

11   See, among many others, Bobbyann Roesen (1953: 415–18), Alexander Leggatt (1973: 79) and Kenneth Muir (1979: 35).

12   For a discussion of the linguistic issues of origin, copy, and translation in humanist texts from Erasmus to Montaigne, see Cave (1979).

13   For a discussion of the way fears of female uncontrollability are figured in Renaissance rhetorical treatises, see Parker (1987: 103–13).

14   It is perhaps easy to exaggerate what seems to be a validation of female subjectivity in this play; the Princess and her insouciant ladies are, after all, boy-actors speaking lines written for them by a male playwright. Nonetheless love-comedy virtually requires a different and more active fictional role for women than does the sonnet sequence: one needs to put female characters on the stage, and once they are there they must be given something to say.

15   Claude Lévi-Strauss (1963: 60–1) comments on women's ambiguous position both as signifiers in a kinship system that works as 'a kind of language', and as producers of signs in their own right: 'words do not speak, while women do.'

16   A recognition of the mutual dependence of the sexes is, Berowne suggests, one of the differences between falling in love and indulging the rape fantasies that beguile the men in the early scenes; he recommends that the courtiers abandon their original oaths 'for men's sake, the authors of these women / Or women's sake, by whom we men are men' (IV. iii. 356–7).

17   The usual way of interpreting this difference is in terms of the greater 'maturity' of the women: see, e.g., Greene (1971).

References

Austin, J. L. (1975) *How to Do Things with Words*, 2nd edn. Cambridge, MA: Harvard University Press.

Bamber, Linda (1982) *Comic Women, Tragic Men: A Study of Gender and Genre in Shakespeare*. Stanford: Stanford University Press.

Burckhardt, Jacob (1958) *Civilization of the Renaissance in Italy*, trans. S. G. C. Middlemore. New York: Harper.

Burckhardt, Sigurd (1968) *Shakespearean Meanings*. Princeton, NJ: Princeton University Press.

Calderwood, James (1965) '*Love's Labor's Lost*: a wantoning with words', *Studies in English Literature*, 5 (1965), pp. 317–32.

Camden, William (1984) *Remains Concerning Britain*, ed. R. D. Duncan. Toronto: University of Toronto Press.

Carroll, William (1976) *The Great Feast of Language in Love's Labor's Lost*. Princeton, NJ: Princeton University Press.

Castiglione, Baldassare (1974) *The Book of the Courtier*, trans. Sir Thomas Hoby. London: J. M. Dent.

Cave, Terence (1979) *The Cornucopian Text*. Oxford: Clarendon Press.

Curtis, Mark H. (1959) *Oxford and Cambridge in Transition 1558–1642*. Oxford: Clarendon Press.

Elam, Keir (1984) *Shakespeare's Universe of Discourse: Language-games in the Comedies*. Cambridge: Cambridge University Press.

Erickson, Peter (1985) *Patriarchal Structures in Shakespeare's Drama*. Berkeley, CA: University of California Press.

Ferry, Anne (1988) *The Art of Naming*. Chicago: University of Chicago Press.

Gilbert, Felix (1943) 'Machiavelli: the Renaissance of the art of war', in *Makers of Modern Strategy: Military Thought from Machiavelli to Hitler*, ed. Edward Meade Earle, pp. 3–15. Princeton, NJ: Princeton University Press.

Granville-Barker, Harley (1927) *Prefaces to Shakespeare: First Series*. London: Sidgwick.

Greenblatt, Stephen (1980) *Renaissance Self-fashioning*. Chicago: University of Chicago Press.

Greene, Thomas (1971) '*Love's Labor's Lost*: the grace of society', *Shakespeare Quarterly*, 22: 315–28.

Hexter, J. H. (1950) 'The education of the aristocracy in the Renaissance', *Journal of Modern History*, 22: 1–20.

Hobbes, Thomas (1962) *Leviathan*, ed. Michael Oakeshott. New York: Collier.

Kahn, Coppélia (1976) 'The rape in Shakespeare's *Lucrece*', *Shakespeare Studies*, 9: 45–72.

——(1981) *Man's Estate: Masculine Identity in Shakespeare*. Berkeley, CA: University of California Press.

Leggatt, Alexander (1973) *Shakespeare's Comedy of Love.* London: Methuen.

Lenz, Carolyn Ruth, Greene, Gayle and Neely, Carol Thomas (eds) (1980) *The Woman's Part: Feminist Criticism of Shakespeare.* Urbana: University of Illinois Press.

Lévi-Strauss, Claude (1963) *Structural Anthropology.* New York: Basic Books.

Muir, Kenneth (1979) *Shakespeare's Comic Sequence.* Liverpool: Liverpool University Press.

Neely, Carol Thomas (1985) *Broken Nuptials in Shakespeare's Plays.* New Haven, CT: Yale University Press.

Novy, Marianne (1984) *Love's Argument: Gender Relations in Shakespeare.* Chapel Hill, NC: University of North Carolina Press.

Parker, Patricia (1987) *Literary Fat Ladies: Rhetoric, Gender, Property.* New York: Methuen.

Roesen, Bobbyann [Anne Barton] (1953) 'Love's Labor's Lost', *Shakespeare Quarterly*, 4: 411–26.

Shakespeare, William (1951) *Love's Labor's Lost*, ed. Richard David. London: Methuen (The Arden Shakespeare).

Stone, Lawrence (1964) 'The educational revolution in England 1560–1640', *Past and Present*, 28: 41–80.

4

Gender and Sexuality

In her groundbreaking study, *Shakespeare and the Nature of Women* (1975), Juliet Dusinberre proposes that 'the drama from 1590 to 1625 is feminist in sympathy' (Dusinberre, 1975: 5). Chapters on the significance of boy-players, on chastity and virtue and on female authority develop the thesis that the stage reflected changing attitudes to women in contemporary society, and that 'Shakespeare's feminism consists of more than a handful of high-born emancipated heroines: it lies rather in his scepticism about the nature of women' (1975: 305): '[Shakespeare] did not divide human nature into the masculine and the feminine, but observed in the individual woman or man an infinite variety of union between opposing impulses. To talk about Shakespeare's women is to talk about his men, because he refused to separate their worlds physically, intellectually, or spiritually' (1975: 308).

Having established the specificity of her subject, Dusinberre seems here to conclude by erasing it. But this was only the beginning of a burgeoning critical field. Philip Kolin takes *Shakespeare and the Nature of Women* as the starting-point for his bibliography *Shakespeare and Feminist Criticism* (1991), and countless critics cite it in approbation or disagreement. Looking back over the two decades of revisionist literary scholarship since the first edition of her study, Dusinberre cites the book's place in a wider feminist politics, a 'battle about ownership' (Dusinberre, 1996: xii), connecting the debate about Shakespeare with modern gendered struggles for a critical and social position from which to speak. She admits that 'if I were rewriting the book I would have to address the theoretical problems surrounding the relation of history to the play as fiction' (1996: xxi), that 'I wouldn't now use the language of authorial intention' (1996: xxii), and that the need to discuss the plays in performance is now firmly established. This list of additional factors and changing methodologies, as well as Dusinberre's double focus on the historical context of Shakespeare's plays and current feminist debates, make her review of the state of recent feminist scholarship on Shakespeare a good introduction to the lively and wide-ranging field of gender criticism.

Following Dusinberre, Marilyn French's *Shakespeare's Division of Experience* (1981) proposed that the 'gender principle' was of fundamental importance to Shakespeare's drama, arguing for a movement from 'profound suspicion of "feminine"' qualities in his early work towards some 'fear' of the 'masculine principle' and an idealization of the feminine (French, 1981: 17). French describes the tragedies as 'in a masculine mode' (1981: 201), and associates the comedies of the 1590s with the theme of constancy, which she allies to the feminine. The problem plays are dominated by 'sexual disgust' as the ideals of 'female chaste constancy and male legitimacy' (1981: 143, 145), key to Shakespeare's earlier work, are here placed under searching scrutiny. The power struggle between male and female is seen as the structuring principle of the romances, with the feminine principle 'granted a power that is almost magical, almost divine' in order to achieve the ultimate synthesis of the gendered world. In her *Comic Women, Tragic Men: A Study of Gender and Genre in Shakespeare* (1982), Linda Bamber makes it clear that her approach 'locates the feminism in the critic – not in the author or even the work', although her argument proceeds by contrasting a comic Shakespeare 'who seems if not a feminist then at least a man who takes the women's part' with the 'nightmare female figures . . . charged with sexual antagonism' in the tragedies (Bamber, 1982: 2). Central to her thesis is the argument that 'the feminine is the foremost representative in Shakespeare of the challenge by the Other of the Self', and that it is in the comedies only that 'we see the feminine Other face to face' (1982: 107, 109):

> In the tragedies anxiety develops because the feminine Other, like the masculine Self, is forced to make choices, and these choices may go against the hero. In the comedies, however, choice is almost unnecessary. The comic world is frankly controlled and unified by its creator; it is a world of 'both/and' rather than of 'either/or,' as in tragedy. Our confidence in the feminine Other is partly the effect of the world she lives in, a world in which we need not fear her choices because no choices confront her. Consider, for instance, Shakespeare's favorite love triangle, the constellation of father, daughter, and prospective son-in-law. In the tragedies, the women are forced to make a choice between the father and the lover; in the comedies the choice is almost always avoided (Bamber, 1982: 112).

By contrast, Marilyn Williamson argues for *The Patriarchy of Shakespeare's Comedies* (1986).

The most significant form for the development of gender criticism has been the collection of essays rather than the monograph. Lenz, Neely and Greene's *The Woman's Part: Feminist Criticism of Shakespeare* (1980) is an early attempt 'to liberate Shakespeare's women from the stereotypes to which they have too often been confined; [to] examine women's relations to each other; [to] analyze the nature and effects of patriarchal structures; and [to] explore the influence of genre on the portrayal of women' (Lenz et al., 1980: 4). John Bean argues for a reading of *The Taming of the Shrew* where 'Kate is tamed not in the automatic manner of behavioral psychology but in the spontaneous manner of the later romantic comedies where characters lose themselves in chaos and emerge, as if from a dream, liberated into the bonds of love' (Lenz et al., 1980: 66). Clara Claiborne Park engagingly allows that 'as classics go, Shakespeare isn't bad reading for a girl' (Lenz et al., 1980: 101) and discusses Shakespeare's comic heroines as types of female *bildungsroman*. Charles Frey and Lorie Jerrell Leininger each discuss the late plays, and Janice Hays argues that *Much Ado About Nothing* is based on 'the sexual distrust of woman' (Lenz et al., 1980: 79). Valerie Wayne's collection *The Matter of Difference: Materialist Feminist Criticism of Shakespeare* (1991) includes articles on the comedies by Cristina Malcolmson (*Twelfth Night*), Carol Leventen (*The Merchant of Venice*) and Valerie Traub, who discusses 'erotic difference' and its erasure in criticism of the cross-dressed actor.

In her introduction to *A Feminist Companion to Shakespeare* (2000), Dympna Callaghan categorizes the contributors to the volume as 'part of an ever-growing body of scholarship that has set out to discover what the world, and in this instance, quite specifically what a hugely influential body of canonical literature, might look like from the perspective of women, from the margins of hitherto patriarchal knowledge' (Callaghan, 2000: xiii–xiv). Essays in the collection include a number of considerations of comedy: Mihoko Suzuki discusses 'Gender, Class, and the Ideology of Comic Form'; Juliet Dusinberre returns to the subject of 'Women and Boys playing Shakespeare'; Carol Thomas Neely's essay on 'Lovesickness, Gender and Subjectivity: *Twelfth Night* and *As You Like It*' historicizes the questions of subjectivity and desire raised by the plays; Jyotsna Singh and M. Lindsay Kaplan each develop ideas about *The Merchant of Venice* and its economies of exchange; and Ania Loomba brings a post-colonial perspective to the 'Indian boy' of *A Midsummer Night's Dream*.

At the head of the collection of essays *Shakespeare and Sexuality* (2001), edited by Catherine Alexander and Stanley Wells, is a review essay by Ann Thompson (Alexander and Wells, 2001: 1–13). Thompson identifies four key concerns of scholarship in the area of sexuality: 'feminism', 'men in feminism and gay studies', 'the boy actor and performance studies' and 'language'. She offers brief commentary on these areas and makes useful suggestions for further reading. Elsewhere in the volume Subha Mukherji discusses 'Consummation, Custom and Law in *All's Well that Ends Well*' and John Russell Brown considers comedies and tragedies in his investigation of 'Representing

Sexuality in Shakespeare's Plays'. Kate Chedgzoy's collection of important essays representing a range of approaches to *Shakespeare, Feminism and Gender* (2001) also offers a review of the field in its introduction. The methodological range of gender criticism is showcased in diverse contributions from Ania Loomba on 'The Colour of Patriarchy: Critical Difference, Cultural Difference and Renaissance Drama', Lizbeth Goodman on feminist performance in 'Women's Alternative Shakespeares and Women's Alternatives to Shakespeare in Contemporary British Theatre', and Alan Sinfield on 'How to Read *The Merchant of Venice* without being Heterosexist'.

The collection *Shakespeare and Gender: A History*, edited by Deborah Barker and Ivo Kamps (1995) offers a range of feminist scholarship framed by an introduction which emphasizes the move towards history and away from essentializing notions of gender. Carol Cook's essay on *Much Ado About Nothing* discusses the necessity of Hero's blankness as a space for patriarchal fantasy. Catherine Belsey uncovers Shakespeare's Venice as a space for multiple, riddling permutations of desire, and Joseph Pequigney also develops this theme in his analysis of 'The Two Antonios and Same-sex Love in *Twelfth Night* and *The Merchant of Venice*', reprinted from the journal *English Literary Renaissance*, vol. 22 (1992). Pequigney aims 'to *secure* the homoerotic character of the friendship' (Barker and Kamps, 1995: 179) between Antonio and Sebastian in *Twelfth Night*, and analyses the relationship between *The Merchant of Venice*'s melancholic Antonio and Bassanio in the light of this enquiry. His discovery of sexuality inherent in such male bonding is developed at more length in Bruce Smith's careful and thorough *Homosexual Desire in Shakespeare's England* (1991). Smith reads legal, medical and literary texts to establish the relationship between the homosocial and the homosexual. Shakespeare's comedies and sonnets are discussed in a nexus of references, including poems by Donne, Spenser and Barnfield, and plays by Marlowe and Marston. Also in Barker and Kamps's anthology, Leah Marcus discusses how editors of *The Taming of the Shrew* have marginalized the play's 'intertext', the anonymous *The Taming of a Shrew*, and the consequences of this suppression for the play's account of gender relations.

This historicist approach to gender criticism is an important strand. Jardine's aim in her *Still Harping on Daughters: Women and Drama in the Age of Shakespeare* (1983/1989) is to suggest 'possibilities for reading the relationship between real social conditions, and literary representation' (Jardine, 1989: 7), and she brings extensive historical material to bear on her readings of the plays. In 'Female Roles and Elizabethan Eroticism' she reads Shakespeare's heroines against a background of anti-theatrical polemic and suggests cross-dressed women characters 'as sexually enticing *qua* transvestied boys' (1989: 29). Jardine's essay on *Twelfth Night* in a collection entitled *Erotic Politics* and edited by Susan Zimmerman (1992) discusses the erotics of the household, and elsewhere in the volume there are adjacent essays by Jean Howard, Bruce Smith and Catherine Belsey. Stephen Greenblatt also takes a historicist perspective in 'Friction and Fiction' (*Shakespearean Negotiations*, 1988) which discusses Renaissance cultural investment in the so-called 'one-sex' model and the possibilities of slippage between sexes and between genders. Writing in the collection *Alternative Shakespeares* edited by John Drakakis (1985), Catherine Belsey discusses the ways in which cross-dressing disrupts binary ideas of sexual difference. Stephen Orgel's *Impersonations: The Performance of Gender in Shakespeare's England* (1996) discusses the connections between boy-players, cross-dressing within plays, effeminacy, and the fragility of gendered identity in the early modern period. He excavates the significance of Viola's disguise as Cesario and Rosalind's taking of the homoerotically charged name Ganymede. Other accounts of the significance of cross-dressed actors can be found in Howard (1988), Garber (1992) and Levine (1994).

Writing in 1987, however, Lynda Boose defended more psychoanalytical approaches to gender criticism against this historicist orthodoxy, arguing that new historicism tended to marginalize issues of gender, and that the stress on male actors often seemed to imply that 'there are no more women in Shakespeare's plays' (Boose, 1987: 730). Dympna Callaghan's *Shakespeare without Women: Representing Gender and Race on the Renaissance Stage* (1999) discusses the implications for mimetic representation of the simultaneous absence of women and Africans from the early modern theatre. The idea of impersonation, both gendered and racial, emerges as a crucial example of theatrical representation's paradoxical dependence 'on the absence of the thing it represents' (Callaghan, 1999: 9). An investigation of early modern medical and anatomy texts as a background to the young male actors playing women's roles on the stage stresses both the aural and the visual aspects of this gender impersonation. For a vehemently argued account challenging the premise of feminist or gender-based approaches, see Brian Vickers's *Appropriating Shakespeare* (1993), and, in particular, his chapter 'Feminist Stereotypes: Misogyny, Patriarchy, Bombast'.

Gender criticism has also focused on masculinity and on male identity. Coppélia Kahn's *Man's Estate: Masculine Identity in Shakespeare* (1981) argues that Shakespeare's 'male characters are engaged in a continuous struggle, first to form a masculine identity, then to be secure and productive in it' (Kahn, 1981: 1). A chapter on cuckoldry anxieties in the comedies examines the trope as 'a masculine fantasy of feminine betrayal' (1981: 120). Kahn's final chapter locates the struggle for male selfhood in the context of the family and the life-cycle, stressing the male identity crises which dominate *The Comedy of Errors*, *The Winter's Tale*, *The Tempest* and *Pericles*. Ambivalence towards the family, and the suppression of women as an aspect of male identity projection, are conceptualized in Oedipal terms. Janet Adelman's subject in *Suffocating*

Mothers: Fantasises of Maternal Origin in Shakespeare's Plays, 'Hamlet' to 'The Tempest' (1992) is related in its stress on perilous masculinity in relation to the maternal presence. Peter Erickson's account of *Patriarchal Structures in Shakespeare's Drama* (1985) is less concerned with individual masculine identity, and instead engages with the social structure – sometimes benevolent, sometimes tyrannical – of patriarchal power in the plays. Writing on *As You Like It*, Erickson argues that 'patriarchy is not a slogan smuggled in from the twentieth century and imposed on the play but an exact term for the social structure that close reading reveals within the play' (1985: 25): in the end the play 'is primarily a defensive action against female power rather than a celebration of it' (1985: 37). In his *Shakespeare and Masculinity* (2000), Bruce R. Smith derives from feminist criticism an understanding of gender as historical and social construction, and applies this to concepts of masculinity. Robin Headlam Wells's *Shakespeare on Masculinity* (2000) discusses Shakespeare's plays as responses to and interventions in contemporary debates about militant Protestant heroic masculinity. He argues that, through his career, Shakespeare develops a more sceptical relation to this version of masculinity, and studies Prospero as the ultimate embodiment of this shift.

References and Further Reading

Adelman, Janet (1992) *Suffocating Mothers: Fantasies of Maternal Origin in Shakespeare's Plays, 'Hamlet' to 'The Tempest'*. New York: Routledge.
Alexander, Catherine M. S. and Wells, Stanley W. (eds) (2001) *Shakespeare and Sexuality*. Cambridge: Cambridge University Press.
Bamber, Linda (1982) *Comic Women, Tragic Men: A Study of Gender and Genre in Shakespeare*. Stanford, CA: Stanford University Press.
Barker, Deborah and Kamps, Ivo (eds) (1995) *Shakespeare and Gender: A History*. London: Verso.
Boose, Lynda (1987) 'The family in Shakespeare studies; or – studies in the family of Shakespeares; or – the politics of politics', *Renaissance Quarterly*, 40: 707–42.
Callaghan, Dympna (1999) *Shakespeare without Women: Representing Gender and Race on the Renaissance Stage*. London: Routledge.
——(ed.) (2000) *A Feminist Companion to Shakespeare*. Oxford: Blackwell.
Chedgzoy, Kate (ed.) (2001) *Shakespeare, Feminism and Gender*. Basingstoke: Palgrave.
Drakakis, John (ed.) (1985) *Alternative Shakespeares*. London: Methuen.
Dusinberre, Juliet (1975) *Shakespeare and the Nature of Women*. London: Macmillan, 2nd edn, 1996.
Erickson, Peter (1985) *Patriarchal Structures in Shakespeare's Drama*. Berkeley, CA: University of California Press.
French, Marilyn (1981) *Shakespeare's Division of Experience*. New York: Summit Books.

Garber, Marjorie B. (1992) *Vested Interests: Cross Dressing and Cultural Anxiety.* New York: Routledge.

Goldberg, Jonathan (1992) *Sodometries: Renaissance Texts, Modern Sexualities.* Standford, CA: Stanford University Press.

Greenblatt, Stephen J. (1988) *Shakespearean Negotiations: The Circulation of Social Energy in Renaissance England.* Berkeley, CA: University of California Press.

Howard, Jean (1988) 'Cross-dressing, the theater and gender struggle in early modern England', *Shakespeare Quarterly*, 39: 418–40.

Jardine, Lisa (1983) *Still Harping on Daughters: Women and Drama in the Age of Shakespeare.* Brighton: Harvester, 2nd edn, 1989.

Kahn, Coppélia (1981) *Man's Estate: Masculine Identity in Shakespeare.* Berkeley, CA: University of California Press.

Kolin, Philip C. (1991) *Shakespeare and Feminist Criticism: An Annotated Bibliography and Commentary.* New York: Garland.

Lenz, Carolyn Ruth Swift, Neely, Carol Thomas and Greene, Gayle (eds) (1980) *The Woman's Part: Feminist Criticism of Shakespeare.* Urbana: University of Illinois Press.

Levine, Laura (1994) *Men in Women's Clothing: Anti-theatricality and Effeminization, 1579–1642.* Cambridge: Cambridge University Press.

McCandless, David Foley (1997) *Gender and Performance in Shakespeare's Problem Comedies.* Drama and Performance Studies. Bloomington, IN: Indiana University Press.

Newman, Karen (1991) *Fashioning Femininity and English Renaissance Drama.* Chicago: University of Chicago Press.

Orgel, Stephen (1996) *Impersonations: The Performance of Gender in Shakespeare's England.* Cambridge: Cambridge University Press.

Smith, Bruce R. (1991) *Homosexual Desire in Shakespeare's England: A Cultural Poetics.* Chicago: University of Chicago Press.

—— (2000) *Shakespeare and Masculinity.* Oxford: Oxford University Press.

Traub, Valerie (1992) *Desire and Anxiety: Circulations of Sexuality in Shakespearean Drama. Gender, Culture, Difference.* London: Routledge.

Vickers, Brian (1993) *Appropriating Shakespeare: Contemporary Critical Quarrels.* New Haven, CT: Yale University Press.

Wayne, Valerie (ed.) (1991) *The Matter of Difference: Materialist Feminist Criticism of Shakespeare.* London: Harvester Wheatsheaf.

Wells, Robin Headlam (2000) *Shakespeare on Masculinity.* Cambridge: Cambridge University Press.

Williamson, Marilyn (1986) *The Patriarchy of Shakespeare's Comedies.* Detroit: Wayne State University Press.

Zimmerman, Susan (ed.) (1992) *Erotic Politics: Desire on the Renaissance Stage.* New York: Routledge.

Helena's Bed-trick

David McCandless

David McCandless's essay focuses on how the bed-trick, by which All's Well's *Helena presents herself in Bertram's bed in place of Diana, works in the context of the play's 'erotic subtexts'. McCandless uses psychoanalytic theory to bring out the play's curious inscription of folkloric elements, and also draws on performance criticism to locate some of the possibilities for Helena's representation on the stage. His ideas on this play are further developed in his book,* Gender and Performance in Shakespeare's Problem Comedies *(1997).*

David McCandless, 'Helena's Bed-trick: Gender and Performance in *All's Well that Ends Well*', *Shakespeare Quarterly*, 45: 4 (1994), pp. 449–68.

The starting point for this essay is Susan Snyder's recent characterization of *All's Well* as a 'deconstructed fairy tale':[1] lurking beneath the folkloric narrative of the poor physician's daughter who deploys magic and cunning in order to overcome a dashing count's disdainful resistance are the unrepresentable specters of female sexual desire and male sexual dread. Indeed, the play invests the fairy-tale motifs that W. W. Lawrence believes undergird *All's Well* – 'The Healing of the King' and 'The Fulfillment of the Tasks' – with potent erotic subtexts.[2] In adapting 'The Healing of the King', Shakespeare, like his model Boccaccio, departs from tradition in making the King's healer a woman. Lawrence barely mentions this innovation, but it seems to me highly significant, especially since Shakespeare, unlike Boccaccio, makes Helena's gender – more particularly her sexual ardor and allure – indispensable to the cure.

Integral to the narrative of 'The Fulfillment of the Tasks' is the bed-trick, an explicitly sexual event in which a disprized wife wins back her husband by making love to him incognito, taking the place of another woman, in some versions the wife herself in disguise, whom he has wooed. *All's Well* deconstructs this folkloric device by wedding it to genuine sexual perturbation. The bed-trick is not simply the consummation of a marriage, in which Helena cleverly satisfies Bertram's seemingly impossible conditions, but an act of prostitution, in which Helena services Bertram's lust and submits to humiliating anonymous 'use', and a type of rape, in which Helena coerces Bertram into having sex with her against his will.

Yet, as many critics have noted, the play seems to suppress its own erotic subdrama.[3] Certainly Shakespeare idealizes and mystifies the sexual arousal that empowers Helena's cure of the King. He lends Helena magical and hieratic powers, giving her the capacity to effect a supernatural cure. He similarly desexualizes her erotic agency in the bed-trick, allowing Diana to serve as Helena's sexualized double. Diana suffers Bertram's degrading slander in the final scene, thus allowing Helena to reenter the play as a saintly resurrected figure whose visible pregnancy sanctifies her sexuality and who elicits an instantaneous reformation from Bertram. The bed-trick becomes a transcendent event, vastly removed from bodies groping in the dark, from the kind of event imaged as 'defil[ing] the pitchy night' (IV. iv. 24).[4]

In performance the bed-trick is further removed from sexual experience precisely because it is undramatized, not part of the play's visceral theatrical life, a plot mechanism scarcely capable of disconcerting audiences as it has critics. I want to examine how staging the bed-trick can assist in dramatizing the 'deconstructed fairy tale' that lies at the heart of *All's Well*, thus bringing to the surface the erotic subdrama that the play represses, and, in so doing, extend the play's provocative interrogation of gender roles.

I

Helena has been a puzzle and provocation to critics because she occupies the masculine position of desiring subject, even as she apologizes fulsomely for her unfeminine forwardness and works desperately to situate herself within the feminine position of desired object. Bertram, too, poses problems because he occupies the feminine space of the Other, even as he struggles to define himself as a man by becoming a military and sexual conqueror. He is the desired object, the end of the hero's – or in this case heroine's – gendered journey of self-fulfillment.

Helena's opening soliloquy conveys the plight of a woman trapped between active ('masculine') and passive ('feminine') modes of desire. She clearly expresses her desire to consummate a sexual love, calling herself a 'hind' who wishes to be 'mated by the lion' (I. i. 85–92). At the same time, she adopts a 'feminine' posture: she cannot mate but can only be 'mated'. Furthermore, as a hind desiring a lion, she cannot mate at all. Helena thus naturalizes the culturally established distinctions of gender and class that make Bertram a forbidden object. In addition, Helena appropriates the masculine privilege of the gaze, submitting her 'curled darling' to rapturous objectification, only to affirm a 'feminine' helplessness, lamenting the impossibility of eliciting her beloved's look.[5] Her gaze becomes masochistic: it is pleasurable torment – 'pretty, though a plague' – to survey his beauteous, unattainable form 'every hour' (ll. 92–3).

Once galvanized by Parolles's bracing antivirginity jape, however, Helena resolves to 'feed' her desirous gaze, to make the object of worship an object of consumption:

What power is it which mounts my love so high,
That makes me see, and cannot feed mine eye?
The mightiest space in fortune nature brings
To join like likes, and kiss like native things.

(ll. 220–3)

That Helena imagines a sexual feeding here seems plausible, given the imagery
of 'joining' and 'kissing', not to mention the suggestive phraseology of
'mount[ing] my love'. The 'space' separating her and Bertram she portrays as
a product not of nature, which favors their 'join[ing]', but of 'fortune', which
seems here to mean 'standing in life' and thus to represent culture.

The language Helena employs is characteristically elliptical, stemming from
her guarded, coded, sexually charged dialogue with Parolles. The obscurity of
her discourse perhaps reflects the unspeakability of her desire. Her exchange
with Parolles begins as a theatrical turn, with Helena playing straight man for
the swaggering poseur. As straight man Helena channels her unspeakable
desire into the discourse of male bawdry, seeking a kind of release through the
sublimated pleasures of naughty talk, even if her lines serve principally as cues
for Parolles's ribaldry.

At a certain point, however, Helena seems to take seriously Parolles's
aspersion of virginity – or, more specifically, his vision of the naturalness and
regenerativeness of sexuality; she steps outside the scene's theatrical frame and
trades the role of straight man for that of surprised pupil: 'how might one do,
sir', she asks, 'to lose it [her virginity] to her own liking?' (ll. 150–1). She dis-
regards his censure of her wish to choose rather than be chosen ('Off with't
while 'tis vendible; answer the time of request' [ll. 154–5]) and answers his
challenge – 'Will you anything with it?' – decisively if obscurely:

Not my virginity yet;
There shall your master have a thousand loves,
A mother, and a mistress, and a friend,
A phoenix, captain, and an enemy,
A guide, a goddess, and a sovereign,
A counsellor, a traitress, and a dear;
His humble ambition, proud humility;
His jarring concord, and his discord dulcet;
His faith, his sweet disaster; with a world
Of pretty, fond, adoptious christendoms
That blinking Cupid gossips.

(ll. 163–75)

Modern editors have been inclined to assume a missing line between Helena's
terse defense of virginity and her expansive list of lovers' endearments. 'There'

is usually taken to mean 'at the court', and the speech is explained as Helena's anxious contemplation of courtly rivals whose enchantments may well stir Bertram's desire. The speech may perhaps be better understood, however, as a coded disclosure of Helena's own erotic stirrings. That she speaks cryptically and elliptically may simply reflect the difficulty of articulating female desire. If one gives up the idea of a missing line, the sense of Helena's response is captured in G. Wilson Knight's paraphrase: '"I shall not part with my virginity to anyone yet, because therein your master has an infinite love."'[6] Knight, however, backs away from the aggressively sexual connotations of this decoding and asserts, 'I do not think that, at this early stage in her story, it can mean "In giving your master my virginity I shall give him a thousand loves", since she has no good reason at this stage to expect such an event.'[7] Helena's lacking any reason to expect 'such an event' is surely beside the point; she clearly desires to 'mate' with Bertram, and, stoked by Parolles's libidinous exhortations, she presumably builds on the tantalizing possibility of losing her virginity to her own liking, that is, to Bertram. The speech thus becomes the link between this heretofore unthinkable idea and the conception of her bold plan for winning him. Perhaps 'at the court' has seemed the best candidate for Helena's imagined 'there' because virginity – or rather the unpenetrated female territory it predicates – has been perceived, within a phallocentric register of meaning, not as a 'there' but as a 'nowhere', a 'nothing-to-be-seen', in Luce Irigaray's striking phrase.[8]

Thus the key to the speech may lie not in a missing line but in a missing language – one that embodies a woman's 'thereness' and enables the articulation of a distinct female desire. From a Lacanian perspective, female desire is literally unspeakable, inconceivable within a phallocentric linguistic system that makes woman a signifier of man, reducing her difference to opposition, reconfiguring her desire as the desire for his desire.[9] The unspeakability of Helena's passion perhaps compels her to express it evasively and mystically. She thus characterizes her 'virginity' as a kind of philosopher's stone, a 'tinct and multiplying medicine' (V. iii. 102) that blesses Bertram with a supernally expansive love and allows her, for his sake, to assume all the guises of the courtier's beloved, to become a kind of shape-shifting superwoman. Helena, however, continues to believe that she must be 'mated': she cannot unleash this mystical female power – cannot become Bertram's idealized courtly lover – until Bertram 'has' her maidenhead, discovers her wonders 'there'. Once more the play seems to dramatize the contradiction of female subjectivity: Helena expresses an active (masculine) longing to consummate her passion in terms that betray a 'feminine' urge to empower and sustain Bertram, to fit herself to his fantasies – or at least to his received images of femininity. Helena's (feminine) hope that Bertram might find her desirable after 'having' her sexually eventually impels her (masculine) orchestration of the bed-trick.

Helena continues to feminize her desire throughout her campaign to win Bertram, offering compensatory performances of exemplary chastity to atone for the unchaste boldness of her plan.[10] Forced by the Countess to confess her love for Bertram, Helena disclaims the desire to win him that we know she harbors, reviving the self-abasing hopelessness of her first soliloquy, once more portraying Bertram as an unattainable heavenly body that she worships (I. iii. 204–7). In conversation with the King she betrays a similar compulsion to appear normatively chaste, instantly withdrawing her suit when he taints her proffered cure with imputations of prostitution, 'Humbly entreating' a 'modest' thought – requesting the King's belief in her chastity – as she prepares to take her leave (II. i. 127–8). Her willingness to suffer a prostitute's punishment if her cure fails seems designed to dispel any lingering suspicions of unchastity, to distance her holy magic from wanton witchery (ll. 170–3).[11]

In Act II, scene 3, the scene in which Helena is to choose a husband, Helena's status as desiring subject becomes public. The King, parading a contingent of eligible wards, formally confers on her the power of the gaze: 'Fair maid, send forth thine eye . . . Peruse them well' (ll. 52, 61); he also lends her the masculine privilege of choice: 'Thou hast power to choose, and they none to forsake' (l. 56). Her public position as dominant woman is so unprecedented that Lafew mistakenly believes the young lords have rejected her rather than vice versa: as a woman she cannot be the chooser but only the object of choice. Helena's singular ascent requires another compensatory performance of 'femininity'. Though she has, in fact, 'command[ed]' the King to grant the fulfillment of her desire (II. i. 194), she protests her chastity to the assembled suitors and blushingly retires before the King ratifies her authority and compels her to continue. In Susan Snyder's words, 'when [Helena] finally addresses Bertram, she does her best to deny her role as aggressive, desiring subject and to recast herself properly as object'[12] ('I dare not say I take you, but I give / Me and my service, ever whilst I live, / Into your guiding power' [II. iii. 102–4]). Bertram, however, discerns and resists this implicit emasculation, dismissing her protestations of vassalage and demanding the return of masculine looking power: 'I shall beseech your Highness, / In such a business, given me leave to use / The help of mine own eyes' (ll. 106–8).

To call attention to Helena's 'performative' femininity is not to accuse her of hypocrisy or willful deception. To point out that her self-effacements are self-serving is not to rehearse the tired, limited characterization of her as a two-faced, manipulative manhunter.[13] It seems to me more helpful to understand Helena's hyperfemininity as a kind of Lacanian misrecognition that she persistently reenacts. Helena performs femininity so convincingly because she has successfully internalized a culturally imposed image of Woman. When Helena seems to affect femininity for the sake of covering her unfeminine, predatory tracks, she may not be crudely dissembling but rather, like a good method actress who loses herself in the role, truthfully simulating, thereby authenticating the role demanded of her. 'The action of gender', Judith Butler suggests, 'requires a performance that is repeated. This repetition is at once a reenactment and reexperiencing of a set of meanings already socially established.'[14] Butler is not alone in contending that subjectivity entails a subjection to cultural norms, predicating a process by which socialization is mistaken for individuation.[15] Helena challenges a restrictive standard of feminine chastity, but, while doing so, she must answer to the chaste self-image shaped by patriarchal society. As John Berger puts it, a woman is 'almost continually accompanied by her own image of herself'.[16] One reason, no doubt, that critics have so often discerned two Helenas – saintly maiden and cunning vixen – is that Helena so vividly embodies the contradiction that Teresa de Lauretis identifies as essential to female subjectivity: self and cultural mirror, woman and Woman.[17]

In performance one way to call attention to that contradiction would be to assign two actors to the role of Helena: a woman and a man in drag who would step in whenever Helena 'acts feminine'. These two Helenas would then take turns, sometimes within the same scene (Helena's interview with the King in Act II, scene 1, for instance) or even the same speech (for example, the first soliloquy), while at other times a single Helena would dominate (the female for Helena's combative exchanges with Parolles, the crossdressed male for her doleful evasions of the Countess). In a modern-dress production of *All's Well*, costuming could accentuate this duality, with the crossdressed male (as cultural mirror) far more unerringly 'feminine' in appearance than the female, whose attire could be freer and more individualized, even androgynous. The prettified, feminine (male) Helena then becomes kin to the lavishly festooned Parolles, a culturally constructed gender image compelling imitation. Such a choice dramatizes the process of misrecognition, participating in a postmodern fragmenting of subjectivity.[18] A less ostentatious approach might, however, prove even more theatrically potent. Since Helena's essential provocation lies in her capacity for forcing masculine and feminine modes of desire to collide, the director might prefer to capture her doubleness not through double casting but through the concentration of its contradictory effects in a single actor, making her as self-possessed and unself-consciously sensual in her 'masculine' moments as she is self-effacing and studiously chaste in her 'feminine' ones.

Helena's 'masculine' desire is no less subject to cultural construction than her 'feminine' chastity. As Foucault has argued, sexual desire is derived as much from culture as from nature.[19] Accordingly, Helena's desire is directed toward the culturally approved goal of marriage, an institution that, at least according to the 'Protestant doctrine' of Shakespeare's time, confirms a woman in femininity by delivering her to permanent chastity – and subservience.[20] In Act II, scene 5, her only scene with Bertram prior to the play's final moments,

Helena seems to savor 'feminine' subservience as the reward for her 'masculine' boldness. She embraces wifely subjugation with a fervor that mortifies Bertram. 'Come, come, no more of that', he protests when she pronounces herself his 'most obedient servant' (ll. 72–3). From a Freudian perspective, she accepts – even flaunts – a neutered passivity for the sake of eliciting male love.[21] When Bertram annuls the marriage she has taken such pains to effect, she takes the desexualization one step further, embracing a monastical chastity by reconfiguring herself as a penitent whore getting herself to a nunnery, disavowing her desire and receding into iconicity, inspiring the Countess to compare her, I would argue, to the Virgin Mary (III. iv. 25–9).[22]

The sexual renunciation ends when Helena locates another mirror of misrecognition: Diana, the young Italian woman who defines femininity for Helena by virtue of her attractiveness to Bertram. As Catherine MacKinnon asserts, 'socially, femaleness means femininity, which means attractiveness to men, which means sexual attractiveness, which means sexual availability on male terms.'[23] In order to win Bertram, Helena the devoted would-be wife must refashion herself as sexual object. Her goal shifts from the fulfillment of desire to the achievement of desirability. Her desire is no longer simply the desire to wed but the desire to be desired. She thus identifies with, and acts through, the woman whom Bertram covets. In a Lacanian context, Helena says not 'I wish to become a woman' but rather 'I wish to be like her whom I recognize as a woman.'[24] Her deputization of Diana offers an extreme instance of Helena's need to conceal her desire. Only when she secures the services of a surrogate who agrees to embody that desire and risk the 'tax of impudence' that Helena herself carefully dodges does Helena manage to secure Bertram.

II

Perhaps the best demonstration of the distance between Helena and Bertram comes when Parolles, urging Bertram to 'steal away' to the wars in order to avoid the emasculation of marriage, characterizes Helena's 'virginity' in terms radically different from her own:

> He wears his honor in a box unseen,
> That hugs his kicky-wicky here at home,
> Spending his manly marrow in her arms,
> Which should sustain the bound and high curvet
> Of Mars's fiery steed.
>
> (II. iii. 279–83)

The site of Helena's miraculously generative sexual love becomes a 'box unseen', a lack that threatens to contain and consume Bertram's manly essence, an effeminizing, contemptible 'kicky-wicky' that would preclude his purchase of masculine honor. The opportunity to mount Mars's fiery steed in manly combat rescues Bertram from an emasculating stint as 'forehorse to a smock' (II. i. 30) – that is, a woman's beast of burden – a humiliating reversal of the roles of man/woman, rider/horse, master/slave that had become homologous in Shakespeare's England.[25]

Parolles embodies a fiction of masculine grandeur that Bertram attempts to actualize, a mirror of misrecognition in which Bertram insists on seeing himself, a narcissistic reflection of an idealized self that confers an illusion of wholeness. In particular, the supposedly battle-tested, sumptuously plumed Parolles offers Bertram an image of military glamor and promotes participation in the Italian war as a rite of passage into manhood. Thus he praises Bertram's determination to fight as evidence of potency: 'Why, these balls bound, there's noise in it. 'Tis hard!' (II. iii. 297).

Yet the Countess and the King both define manhood for Bertram as the imitation of his father, the true 'perfect courtier' (I. i. 61–2 and 207; I. ii. 19–22 and 36–48). Parolles becomes a rival father-figure whom Bertram's own father, speaking through the King, indirectly disparages with his criticism of meretricious fashionmongers who beget nothing but clothes ('whose judgments are / Mere fathers of their garments' [I. ii. 61–2]). Later, Lafew implies that Parolles was begot *as* clothes, that he was not born but made – by a tailor (II. v. 16–19). These images impute to Parolles and his like both sterility and unmanliness and – through the emphasis on costume – imposture and barren theatricality. Parolles functions as a symptom of the tailoredness of gender, performing a masculinity that seems as much a caricature of the cultural norm as does the performed femininity of Helena. In following this counterfeit soldier–courtier, Bertram appears to be doing what Helena has already done: internalizing and authenticating a culturally inscribed myth of gender, saying not 'I'm a man' but rather 'I'm like him whom I recognize to be a man.'

Despite exhorting Bertram to emulate his father, the King denies him the opportunity to do so by forbidding his soldiership, rendering him unable to prove himself the son of a worthy Frenchman (II. i. 11–12). Rather than being allowed to 'woo' and 'wed' honor (to use the King's language to his departing soldiers), Bertram becomes an object of a woman's wooing and wedding. The King, at Helena's behest, subjects Bertram to the very calamity he urged his soldiers to avoid – bondage to female sexuality:

> Those girls of Italy, take heed of them.
> They say our French lack language to deny
> If they demand. Beware of being captives
> Before you serve.
>
> (II. i. 19–22)

Bertram is captive before he serves, in thrall not to one of those 'girls of Italy' whom the King stigmatizes but to the girl from Rossillion, the girl next door. While he is primed to resent any imposed responsibility that keeps him from going a-soldiering, marriage to Helena is the very worst of fates, taking him even further back into boyhood by returning him to the maternal domination he presumably escaped by ending his constrictive 'marriage' to the Countess. ('In delivering my son from me, I bury a second husband' [I. i. 1–2], she asserts as the play begins.)[26]

Bertram protests that he 'cannot' love Helena. She cannot be an object of his sexual desire, cannot be a 'real girl', in Havelock Ellis's terms.[27] This fact is striking, since she so easily achieves that status with the other men in the play, sexually provoking Parolles, Lafew, and the King alike. Lafew considers Helena so much a 'real girl' that he would like to consign those seemingly standoffish suitors to the fate of castration (II. iii. 86–8). From Lafew's perspective, anyone who would not consider Helena a 'real girl' is not a real man.

From a psychoanalytic perspective, Bertram cannot love Helena because she is a forbidden object. The Count's responsibility for 'breeding' Helena (II. iii. 114) reinforces her status as a sister-figure. The Countess's sponsorship of Helena's matrimonial campaign makes Helena a kind of mother-surrogate as well. The Countess sees in the passionate Helena an image of her younger self (I. iii. 128–31). By colluding in Helena's plot, the Countess aims to help Helena secure her son as husband and thus to revive by proxy the relationship she herself has lost.[28] Helena may also be considered a maternal figure by virtue of her status as partner to Bertram's surrogate father, the King. In a reversal of a Freudian plot, in which the son sacrifices the mother as the price of masculine autonomy, the King blocks Bertram's achievement of manhood by forcing on him the woman whom Bertram sees as the object of the King's own sexual interest: 'follows it, my lord', Bertram protests, 'to bring me down / Must answer for your raising?' (II. iii. 112–13).[29]

In addition, the first of the identities Helena hopes to derive from marriage to Bertram is the one conspicuously removed from the realm of courtly love that engenders them: 'mother' ('There shall your master have a thousand loves, / A mother, a mistress, and a friend').[30] On one level, of course, Helena simply invokes a biological fact: she may become pregnant as a consequence of intercourse with Bertram. On another, she explicitly identifies with the very maternal image that repels Bertram and, by raising the specter of castration, drives him to the wars. In one sense, then, Bertram's military campaign represents a retreat: like Parolles, he runs away for advantage when fear – in this case fear of Helena's sexuality – proposes the safety (I. i. 201–3). Lavatch later characterizes Bertram's campaign in precisely the same terms: Bertram will not be 'killed' – his manhood will not be lost – because he runs away from Helena:

'The danger is in standing to't; that's the loss of men, though it be the getting of children' (III. ii. 37–42, esp. 41–2).

III

In appointing Helena her impossible tasks, Bertram sets up a fairy-tale frame-work only for the sake of demolishing it. While the tasks themselves present a fairy-tale challenge – do these things and 'then call me husband' – his decod-ing of them precludes a fairy-tale solution: 'but in such a "then" I write a "never"' (III. ii. 57–60). Helena, however, insists on the fairy-tale framework, reading his metaphor of rejection as a scenario of acceptance and orchestrat-ing the bed-trick, a folkloric convention, in order to secure him as husband. Helena, however, describes the actual event in anything but fantastical terms:

> . . . O, strange men,
> That can such sweet use make of what they hate,
> When saucy trusting of the cozen'd thoughts
> Defiles the pitchy night; so lust doth play
> With what it loathes for that which is away.
>   (IV. iv. 21–5)

Helena here configures Bertram as male Other, as personification of differ-ence, as a creature from whom she is estranged. In addition to the folkloric narratives that Lawrence identifies, *All's Well* also discloses affinities with other 'old tales' that more directly address this problem of difference. I am thinking, in particular, of 'The Loathly Lady', which deals with male fear of female sexuality, and 'Beauty and the Beast', which dramatizes the female's struggle with male sexuality. In each tale, the protagonist's love – acceptance of the loathliness or beastliness (that is, sexual difference) of their opposite – con-verts ugliness into beauty. 'Beauty and the Beast' depicts a young woman's transference of love from father to Beast, the sexually menacing male Other. According to Bruno Bettelheim, 'only after Beauty decides to leave her father's house to be reunited with the Beast – that is, after she has resolved her oedipal ties to her father – does sex, which before was repugnant, become beautiful.'[31] At the start of the play, Helena has already made this transference. 'What was . . . [my father] like?' Helena muses. 'I have forgot him. My imagination / Carries no favor in't but Bertram's' (I. i. 81–3). Moreover, far from fearing male sexuality, Helena embraces Bertram's beastliness as the play begins, portraying him as a lion with whom she wishes to mate. Indeed, by portraying herself as a hind, Helena both affirms her own sexuality and evokes a fundamental dif-ference in 'kind' that divides them. The bed-trick forces Helena to confront the un-kind Beast within Bertram and to undertake his taming. Bertram, by contrast, recoils from Helena's loathliness, her menacing sexual difference ('what [he] hate[s]'), seeing in her an image of the old crone or castrating mother.

Helena's story – and by implication *All's Well* itself – also contains intriguing parallels to what Jane Yolen identifies as the common features of the traditional 'Cinderella' tale: 'an ill-treated though rich and worthy heroine in Cinders-disguise; the aid of a magical gift or advice by a beast/bird/mother; the dance/festival/church scene where the heroine comes in radiant display; recognition through a token.'[32] Helena fits this profile to a significant degree: a worthy yet socially undesirable young woman who finds herself, thanks to a magical gift, miraculously conveyed to and radiantly displayed at a royal public ceremony ('*Mort du vinaigre!*' exclaims Parolles, apparently stunned by her glamorous appearance, 'is not this Helen?' [II. iii. 44]). Indeed, it is surely no accident that both Tyrone Guthrie and Trevor Nunn, directors of two celebrated modern productions of *All's Well*, staged this scene as a lavish ball and costumed the poor physician's daughter in an elegant gown, effectively portraying her as Cinderella-turned-Princess. And, while she fails to enchant the Prince at first, she does become the object of his desire at another clandestine encounter, which she later proves publicly by means of a token that seals their marriage. The token in this instance is a ring, as it is in several versions of the traditional tale.[33]

In a psychoanalytic context, the Cinderella tale presents a heroine coming to terms with her own sexuality. Her cinders-guise externalizes her dread of the dirtiness of her own sexual drives. Her awareness of the underlying dirtiness impels her to exit the dance prematurely three times, unable to yield to her sexual longing for the reciprocally desirous Prince. (The midnight deadline that prompts her departure is not part of the traditional tale but rather the invention of Charles Perrault, whose seventeenth-century version provides the source for the well-known Disney movie.) In the climactic scene she affirms her sexuality by meeting the Prince in her cinders-guise and, in an overtly phallic gesture, triumphantly inserting her foot into the slipper.[34] In *All's Well*, by contrast, the Prince runs from the heroine, whose active sexuality begrimes her chaste feminine persona. She wins the Prince by catching him and taking him into the cinders with her.

Traces of 'Beauty and the Beast' and 'Cinderella' may be found in the twentieth-century romance novel, a kind of fairy tale that also sports parallels to *All's Well*. The 'new heroine' of those novels 'is no longer split between two archetypal female characters: the plain-naive-domestic-selfless-passive-chaste heroine and the beautiful-sophisticated-worldly-selfish-assertive-sexually active Other Woman. Instead, the New Heroine is both good and sexual.'[35] Helena holds in unresolved tension the roles of good girl and sexual adventuress that the new heroine has apparently successfully assimilated. A motif of 'taming the beast' figures prominently in these modern tales: a seemingly beastly – that is, hard and unyielding – man loses his heart to the worthy heroine and becomes a sensitive lover. As though ruled by this fantasy, Helena endeavors, through the power of her love, to transform the beastly Bertram into the Prince Charming of her fantasy. Helena's own narrative of self-fulfillment – and a narrative pressure of the play itself – resembles a romance novel in which the cruel hero's callous disregard of the desirous heroine masks a depth of adoration he ultimately avows.[36] The romance novel – and possibly *All's Well* – predicates a retributive fantasy of benign dominance-and-submission. As Tania Modleski puts it:

> A great deal of our satisfaction in reading these novels comes, I am convinced, from the elements of a revenge fantasy, from our conviction that the woman is bringing the man to his knees and that all the while he is being so hateful, he is internally groveling, groveling, groveling.[37]

It may be said that Helena seeks to transform Bertram's fantasy by enabling it, replacing the pornographic narrative of violating an idealized virgin with the romance-novel plot of eliciting a redemptive kindness from an unyielding male.[38]

Indeed, if the bed-trick were dramatized, it would literally dislocate the narrative of Bertram's debauchery: 'I will tell you a thing', the Second Lord confides to his brother, 'but you shall let it dwell darkly with you' (IV. iii. 10–11). This report of female victimization would then give way to the dramatization of female desire. 'The place and time of feminine desire', says de Lauretis, are 'nowhere' and 'now', which are representable only from an 'elsewhere of vision' and within 'a different narrative temporality'.[39] In virtually all performances of *All's Well*, the place of the bed-trick is precisely 'nowhere' or 'elsewhere'. Its narrative temporality is other than the play's – parallel but not precisely coincident with that of the French captains' gossip. Indeed, the literal death they ascribe to Helena (IV. iii. 47–59) becomes the only means of registering the metaphorical death she experiences during the bed-trick, the only means of invoking her sexual pleasure.[40] Through the bed-trick Helena deflects Bertram's teleological quest for manhood into the timeless 'now' of her desire, replacing the march of 'masculine' time with the occupation of 'feminine' space. The site of the bed-trick emblematizes female difference, expresses the 'unseen wonders' of the woman's own enclosed space and thus is not only unrepresented but unrepresentable within a phallocentric framework that associates that site with a 'nothing-to-be-seen'. In that sense Helena's reported death – signifying her ultimate absence – becomes symbolic of the 'lack' culturally inscribed on her body.[41] How then does one stage an event whose place is unseen and unseeable ('nowhere') and whose subject – female sexuality – is unrepresentable? Can one theatrically embody or evoke the 'there' to which Helena cryptically alludes?

As Jeanie Forte notes, contemporary feminist performance artists have instinctively searched for the theatrical equivalent of the distinctive female language imagined by Luce Irigaray and Hélène Cixous, a mode of representation that would liberate women from a phallocentric signifying economy.[42] These artists aim to 'perform the body' in much the same spirit that Cixous exhorts feminists to 'write the body', achieving what Forte calls 'erotic agency', either by dramatizing a bodily 'pleasurability' or enacting a resistance to bodily oppression, in the first instance asserting subjectivity, in the second defying objectification.[43] As an example of the former, Forte cites the work of Marianne Goldberg, whose dance texts celebrate 'her subjective pleasure in her own body and its possibilities for movement'; for instance, in 'Hudson Rover' (1987) 'she rolls on the floor, slowly wrapping and then unwrapping her (clothed) body in blue fabric, seemingly oblivious to anything other than the feel of hard and soft surfaces.'[44] As an example of the latter, Forte points to Karen Finley, whose penchant for smearing her body with food, candy, and ashes evokes 'both self-abuse and self-pleasuring' and confounds an objectifying gaze that equates looking with consuming.[45]

While the tactics and techniques of feminist performance art offer fascinating possibilities for deconstructive stagings of Shakespeare, they are not especially well suited to Helena's bed-trick, which unfolds within the very realm of desire that these artists reject and thus precludes exclusive focus on a pansexual, performed female body. By maintaining rather than abandoning the phallocentric system of representation, however, one may stress the singularity of Helena's ascent to the position of desiring subject in order to accentuate her contradictory status within the play's narrative and, in doing so, underline the contradictory position of women within patriarchy's limited signifying economy. This effect seems in accord with de Lauretis's notion that feminism must

> redirect identification toward the two positionalities of desire that define the female's oedipal situation; and if the alternation between them is protracted enough . . . the viewer may come to suspect that such duplicity, such contradiction cannot and perhaps even need not be resolved . . . The most exciting work in cinema and in feminism today is not anti-narrative and anti-oedipal. It is narrative and oedipal with a vengeance for it seeks to stress the duplicity of that scenario and the specific contradiction of the female subject in it.[46]

In staging the bed-trick, one might actually make explicit Helena's dominance, a dominance that the text only hints at. Helena effectively inscribes a condition of lack onto Bertram's body. The restrictions that she imposes – darkness and silence – deprive him of the two patriarchal capacities that define him as (masculine) subject: the gaze and speech. She positions Bertram so that he lacks the language to deny what she commands. The language of bodies now prevails, and Helena, like Diana in Act IV, scene 2, secures control of Bertram partly through manipulation of the lust she elicits.

An often overlooked marker of Helena's control is her curious postcoital detention of Bertram. 'When you have conquer'd my yet maiden bed', Diana says on Helena's behalf, 'Remain there but an hour, nor speak to me' (IV. ii. 57–8). What, one must ask, is the point of this detention? What takes place during that hour? Does the dilation of the trick create a space for the operations of a less propulsively phallic, consumptive sexuality? Does it summon the freer, more resourceful and expansive processes of female desire?[47] Certainly it seems that Bertram is being set up for something – but that something is never explicitly revealed. This ellipsis perhaps offers yet another register of unrepresentable female desire which a staged bed-trick could represent.

The staged bed-trick could, for example, begin with Diana's placing a blindfold on Bertram and yielding her place to Helena. The blindfold would not only provide a realistic explanation for Bertram's inability to distinguish her from Diana but also visually link him with his double, Parolles, who is likewise blindfolded and tricked in the very next scene. The blindfold would both deprive Bertram of the gaze and signify his blindness to the threat of castration that originally drove him away from Helena.

The principal strategy in staging the bed-trick would be to present a kind of suspended foreplay, Helena deflecting Bertram's propulsive, lust-driven energies into more dilatory, sensual rhythms, with Helena positioned as gazing subject and Bertram as gazed-upon object. Helena's masculine gaze, initially frustrated by her feminine powerlessness, would here operate freely and powerfully.[48]

The play provides other possibilities for reinforcing such a gaze. Just as Diana, her mother, and Mariana all positioned themselves as spectators to the triumphal procession of soldiers in Act III, scene 5, with Diana sending forth her eye over the glistening combatants, one could turn Bertram's attempted seduction of Diana into a spectacle by positioning Helena, the Widow, and Mariana as spectators, concretizing the female frame of reference that contains the scene. Within this play-within-a-play, Diana acts the part of sexual tease, defamiliarizing the role of 'the-girl-who-says-no-but-means-yes' by exposing it as performative, presenting herself instead as 'the-girl-who-says-yes-but-means-no'. The concealed female audience also marks Bertram's incipient masculinity as performative: 'My mother told me just how he would woo', exclaims Diana, 'As if she sate in 's heart. She says all men / Have the like oaths' (IV. ii. 69–71). Like Helena in her hyperfeminine mode, Bertram enacts a culturally inscribed script without knowing it, affirming his kinship with 'all men' by venting unctuous oaths and fulsome endearments in order to arrange a one-night stand. Since the play's audience not only watches Bertram's performance but also watches women watching it, the scene parallels that of Parolles's capture, in which concealed pranksters also watch their victim walk into a trap.

Even if the voyeurism and fetishism of this gaze reverse rather than over-turn masculine–feminine polarities, the powerful position of gazing subject afforded Helena by the staged bed-trick would not only empower her desire but perhaps also momentarily free her from a process of representation that enables her consumption as sexual object. There are at least two scenes, in particular, that position Helena, the desiring subject, as desired object: her early skirmish with Parolles and her interview with the King. Performance could make clear the extent to which Parolles not only jests with Helena but also cheekily flirts with her, launching, behind the cover of licentious badi-nage, an assault on her own virginity. In the latter scene, performance could also emphasize the erotic arousal enveloped by magical incantation and miraculous faith healing. Some productions have, in fact, attempted to bring the scene's erotic undercurrents to the surface. In John Barton's 1967 pro-duction Helena was 'a tease of a girl', titillating the King by sitting on his bed and fluffing up his pillows,[49] and in Elijah Moshinsky's BBC version she was a very proper young woman whose provocation of the King – culminating in a lingering, erotic kiss – seemed utterly unintentional. Barry Kyle, in his 1989 RSC production, apparently attempted both to accent the scene's eroticism and to preserve its mysticism: his Helena 'kick[ed] off her shoes to perform a circling, energetic, sexually assertive, slightly fey dance', exuding an aura of 'white witchery'.[50]

In both scenes Helena claims the only kind of female power available in a phallocentric economy by activating and frustrating male desire, 'blow[ing] up' both Parolles and the King, making them swell with desire (I. i. 118–26, esp. 118–19). Helena's active sexuality is discernible throughout the play but, beyond the space of the bed-trick, is constricted not only by internalized notions of normative femininity but also by the external operations of an objectifying gaze.

As befits Helena's status as desiring subject, the ultimate goal of her bed-trick seems to be that of 'taming difference'.[51] In the immediate aftermath of the trick, she recoils from male lust and affirms Bertram's strangeness ('O, strange men, / That can such sweet use make of what they hate'). In the play's final scene, however, she emphasizes his kindness, a word that connotes kin-dredness as well as gentleness or generosity: 'O my good lord, when I was like this maid, / I found you wondrous kind' (V. iii. 309–10).[52] Helena needs to claim Bertram as one of her kind, needs to create him in her own image – the same image she has sought doggedly to impose despite all his obstinate assertions of alienness. In the final scene, Helena tries to confirm Bertram in kind-ness by 'crush[ing]' him 'with a plot'.

Helena avenges her earlier humiliation at Bertram's hands by orchestrating his utter ruin: he is censured, disgraced, and threatened with execution. She enacts a version of the romance-novel retributive fantasy, bringing Bertram to his knees – a posture he has, in fact, assumed in more than one production – abusing him in order to please him, positioning him to savor the bondage he initially abhorred.[53] It appears that Helena schemes to rescue Bertram from the calamity she has herself created in order to elicit feelings of indebtedness conducive to capitulation. She depends on his feeling like the rescued sinner of the medieval morality plays to ensure her reception as savior and wife.[54] Her strategy, which recalls Duke Vincentio's determination to make Isabella 'heavenly comforts of despair' (*Measure for Measure*, IV. iii. 110), appears to work: in penitently promising love and accepting her as wife, Bertram accepts transformation from beast to Prince Charming, at long last consenting to actualize her fantasy (V. iii. 315–16 and 308).

The success of Helena's plot does not, however, guarantee a successful marriage with Bertram, for it validates neither the sincerity of his conversion nor the seemliness of their union. Critics have lamented the paltriness of Bertram's conversion speech, but the problems with the play's final scene run much deeper. Since Bertram has twice before falsely professed admiration for Helena (II. iii. 167–73, V. iii. 52–8), no words of his, no matter how eloquently or torrentially penitential, could ever suffice to confirm his sincerity. Nor, for that matter, could his actions. Even the most extravagant self-abasing gestures may simply be symptoms of feverish gratitude rather than of genuine conversion. Helena may be able to work up feelings in Bertram that simulate and even enable love but do not actually generate it. And of course Bertram may simply cunningly simulate a penitential swoon. In either case, Helena manipulates Bertram into affecting a kind-ness that he may quickly discontinue upon assuming his male prerogatives in marriage. Perhaps Bertram functions here as a male Kate – a seemingly tamed lout who performs the submissive role his dominant spouse has taught him, but who may, after all, only be performing. Since, in the play's second half, Helena's aim seems to shift from wedding Bertram to eliciting his desire, it may be that, for the second time in the play, her goal eludes her even as she appears to achieve it.[55]

Moreover, Helena's success seems mitigated by not only the dubiousness of Bertram's conversion but also the dubiousness of her own objectives, her willingness to deliver herself unequivocally to normative femininity. Her dominance of Bertram ultimately enables her to submit to him in marriage. Ever in thrall to Bertram, she wins him only by putting him temporarily in her thrall so that she may put herself permanently in his. Although Helena's narrative dominates Bertram's and allows her to construct him as the Other out of whom she creates herself, at the same time her fundamental, culturally prescribed desire is to become the object of his desire, the Other out of whom he creates himself:

> The end of the little girl's journey, if successful, will bring her to the place where the boy will find her, like Sleeping Beauty, awaiting him, Prince Charming. For the boy has been promised, by the social contract he has entered into at his Oedipal phase, that he will find woman waiting at the end of his journey.[56]

Indeed, while Bertram may or may not gratify Helena's fantasy, Helena seems prepared to embrace Bertram's. His 'impossible conditions' essentially ask for assurance that Helena can conceive a child without sexually contaminating herself or surrendering maternal purity.[57] Bertram's apparent acceptance of Helena's success in meeting his conditions subjects them to a final reinterpretation: 'I'll be your husband if you can have sex with me without shaming or emasculating me.' Through the bed-trick Helena allows Bertram to fulfill his forbidden desire for her involuntarily, assimilating for his sake the seemingly unassimilable roles of wife and lover, mother and 'real girl'.

The finale of *All's Well* could be said to dramatize the amelioration of castration anxiety. Helena steps forward as the eroticized mother-figure of Bertram's dreams. Her resurrection at the play's end represents the final mystification of her own sexuality, an unthreatening eroticizing of the saintly guise she assumed for the pilgrimage. She replaces her own degraded double, rescuing and retiring the wayward desiring self that the beleaguered Diana personifies. Her pregnancy – that is, her status as mother – purifies the sexuality it affirms. It also ratifies Bertram's manhood, signaling his conquest of her, his success in 'blowing her up'. Moreover, given the belief circulating in Shakespeare's day that a woman could conceive only if she experienced an orgasm,[58] Helena's pregnancy serves as the proof not only of his potency but also of her pleasure, of her satisfaction by him. The bed-trick thus becomes Bertram's initiation into manhood, with Helena serving as his initiator. This fact may simply mean that, in this world of absent fathers, no viable model of manhood exists for Bertram. His father's masculinity, as Bertram confronts it in Act I, scene 2, may be no more authentic than that of Parolles, for it is also derived from a performance, from the King's dramatic, deathbed celebration of the Count. The King constructs an exceptional figure, a hero/courtier of fabulous proportions who seems partly a product of the King's intense nostalgia for a lost youth. Bertram is thus left with a choice between two equally fantastical images of manhood: the inaccessibly legendary and the insidiously fashionable. In marrying Helena, Bertram finds his manhood affirmed through a reassuring maternal presence and gets what he may have wanted all along: a wife/lover/mother who allows him to become a man by remaining a boy.

The play's refusal to dissipate its tensions or substantiate its tentative resolutions leaves its drama of sexual difference suspended, arrested in an unresolved but provocative, even poignant tension. Helena's attempt to tame difference meets with uncertain success, and Bertram seems to reaffirm difference in the play's final moments, confronting a female strangeness that mystifies rather than repels. When he declares, 'if she, my liege, can make me know this clearly' (V. iii. 315), the 'this' he wishes to know surely encompasses a good deal more than the details of Helena's fulfillment of his conditions: it must include the mystery of female otherness. The body Bertram used and discarded returns in the person of a would-be wife, a once and future lover, to claim him like an avenging spirit. Helena brings him, however obscurely, new knowledge of female sexuality, offering tantalizing allusions to their time in bed and visible proof of their mutual gratification. Bertram may wish to know more, to see the unseen wonders to which he was previously blind. Bertram's 'this' becomes homologous with Helena's 'there', suggesting that the performance of sex has possibly solved his problem with sexuality. Yet this solution and the knowledge it assumes are simply intriguing possibilities. As the play ends, Helena and her body remain unknown and perhaps unknowable to Bertram – objects of fascination, further knowledge, perhaps even desire.

Helena remains a mystery to be solved by the reader and spectator – and director and actor – as well. So too does Bertram. Both characters aim to ground themselves in genders that the play suggests are groundless – or at least unstable, fluid, performative. Neither manages to forge a stable identity or secure a clear destiny. Modern performance could underline Helena's and Bertram's status as subjects-in-process, active agents inextricably engaged with subjugating myths of gender. And a staged bed-trick, by fetishizing the male body and empowering a female gaze, could underline the instability of the genders that Helena and Bertram seek to stabilize, taking the play's provocative dramatization of difference to startling and invigorating lengths.

Acknowledgements

This essay was originally prepared for the seminar on *All's Well* that Professor Susan Snyder led at the 1993 SAA conference in Atlanta. I am grateful both to her and to Joan Hutton Landis for their encouragement and support. I would also like to thank Janet Adelman, Barbara Hodgdon, and Charles Lyons for their invaluable criticism of my work on *All's Well*.

Notes

1 This phrase appears in Snyder's description of her *All's Well that Ends Well* research seminar posted in the *Bulletin of the Shakespeare Association of America*, 16 (1992), p. 4.

2 Although Lawrence insists in *Shakespeare's Problem Comedies* (New York, 1931) that these plays should be accepted simply as stories, requiring the same level of unsophisticated reception as the widely known traditional tales from which, by his reckoning, they were derived (1931: 73–7), folklore scholars have been uncovering for some time the potent cultural and psychological dramas that such tales encode. See, for instance, Alan Dundes, 'The psychoanalytic study of folklore', *Parsing Through Customs: Essays by a Freudian Folklorist* (Madison, WI, 1987), pp. 3–46. *All's Well* may be considered a play that pushes the folktale's subterranean psychic drama provocatively close to the narrative surface. Ruth Nevo proposes a method for tracing this covert drama: 'we must attempt to read, as we say, between the lines, and to hear with a third ear. The space between the lines is the psychic space of evocation and resonance shared by both audience and *dramatis personae*. It is the space of precipitation by the text into consciousness of the normally unconscious' ('Motive and meaning in *All's Well that Ends Well*', in *'Fanned and Winnowed Opinions': Shakespearean Essays Presented to Harold Jenkins*, ed. John W. Mahon and Thomas A. Pendleton [London, 1987], pp. 26–51, esp. p. 29). Creating a theatrical space that similarly enables the infiltration of that which the play leaves unsaid or unseen thus seems a particularly apt and exciting directorial choice.

3 See, for example, Janet Adelman, *Suffocating Mothers: Fantasies of Maternal Origin in Shakespeare's Plays, Hamlet to The Tempest* (New York, 1992), pp. 84–6; Barbara Hodgdon, 'The making of virgins and mothers: sexual signs, substitute scenes and doubled presences in *All's Well that Ends Well*', *Philological Quarterly*, 66 (1987), pp. 47–71; Susan Snyder, '"The King's not here": displacement and deferral in *All's Well that Ends Well*', *Shakespeare Quarterly*, 43 (1992), pp. 20–32, and *'All's Well that Ends Well* and Shakespeare's Helens: text and subtext, subject and object', *English Literary Renaissance*, 18 (1988), pp. 66–77.

4 For a provocative discussion of the bed-trick's transmutation into a transcendent event, see Adelman, *Suffocating Mothers*, pp. 84–5. Citations of *All's Well that Ends Well* follow the *Riverside Shakespeare*, ed. G. Blakemore Evans (Boston, 1974). Evans's square brackets have been removed to avoid confusion with my own interpolations.

5 I borrow the resonant phrase 'curled darling' from Robert Ornstein, *Shakespeare's Comedies: From Roman Farce to Romantic Mystery* (Newark, DE, 1986), p. 182. Carolyn Asp in her fascinating psychoanalytic account of the play, also notes Helena's initial embrace of masochistic femininity; see 'Subjectivity, desire and female friendship in *All's Well that Ends Well*', *Literature and Psychology*, 32 (1986), pp. 48–63, esp. p. 52.

6 G. Wilson Knight, *The Sovereign Flower: On Shakespeare as the Poet of Royalism Together with Related Essays and Indexes to Earlier Volumes* (London, 1958), p. 137.

7   Ibid., pp. 137–8. In a sense Knight extends Helena's (or Shakespeare's) mystification of virginity: 'the love is infinite, "a thousand loves"; it is the window to a great insight. It may be related to the state of perfect integration from which poetry is born.'

8   Luce Irigaray, 'Blind spot of an old dream of symmetry', *Speculum of the Other Woman*, trans. Gillian C. Gill (Ithaca, NY, 1985), p. 50.

9   See *Feminine Sexuality: Jacques Lacan and the école freudienne*, ed. Juliet Mitchell and Jacqueline Rose (1982; rpt London, 1985), pp. 144–5.

10   Lisa Jardine perceives a more fundamental split in Helena's behavior: her exemplary passivity in the play's second half atones for her transgressive forwardness in the first: 'the sexually active Helena of the first part of the play [becomes] the virtuously knowing, ideal wife . . .' ('Cultural confusion and Shakespeare's learned heroines', *Shakespeare Quarterly* 38 [1987], pp. 1–18, esp. p. 11). I would contend that Helena is consistent throughout the play in mitigating her audacity with displays of 'femininity,' that her recession in the play's second half simply extends her strategy – or habit – of compensatory self-effacement. Her urge to assume an exemplary femininity reflects Shakespeare's need – or rather a cultural need working through him – to purify and mystify female sexuality in order to neutralize its provocations; hence the possible value of a staged bed-trick that foregrounds and demystifies female desire.

11   As Jardine points out, the infamy that Helena courts, if realized, could 'ostracize [her] from the community, recasting her wisdom as witchcraft' (Jardine, 'Cultural confusion', p. 10).

12   Snyder, '*All's Well that Ends Well* and Shakespeare's Helens', p. 74.

13   While relatively few modern critics have subscribed to such an extremely negative view of Helena (cf. Bertrand Evans, *Shakespeare's Comedies* [Oxford, 1960], pp. 145–66; and Richard A. Levin, '*All's Well that Ends Well* and "All Seems Well"', *Shakespeare Studies*, 13 [1980], pp. 131–44), many have felt compelled, until only very recently, to judge Helena's character in some measure and have often found cause to indict or at least regret the duplicitous and predatory tactics that belie her celebrated virtue. See E. K. Chambers, *Shakespeare: A Survey* (London, 1925), pp. 200–7; Clifford Leech, 'The theme of ambition in *All's Well that Ends Well*', *English Literary History*, 12 (1954), pp. 17–29; Alexander Leggatt, '*All's Well that Ends Well*: the testing of romance', *Modern Language Quarterly*, 32 (1971), pp. 21–41; W. L. Godschalk, '*All's Well that Ends Well* and the morality play', *Shakespeare Quarterly*, 25 (1974), pp. 61–70; David Scott Kastan, '*All's Well that Ends Well* and the limits of comedy', *English Literary History*, 52 (1985), pp. 575–89. Critics have of course also judged in Helena's favor. See my own earlier essay, '"That your Dian / was both herself and Love": Helena's redemptive chastity', *Essays in Literature*, 17 (1990), pp. 160–78. Judgments of Helena perhaps follow inevitably from a formalist focus on the play's 'genre trouble' rather than its 'gender trouble' (to borrow Judith Butler's term).

14   Judith Butler, *Gender Trouble: Feminism and the Subversion of Identity* (New York, 1990), p. 140.

15   Central to the work of Michel Foucault and Jacques Lacan is the notion that sub-

jectivity entails subjection to a culture's dominant mode of signification; see Foucault's 'The subject and power', *Critical Inquiry*, 8 (1982), pp. 777–95, and Lacan's *The Four Fundamental Concepts of Psychoanalysis*, ed. Jacques-Alain Miller, trans. Alan Sheridan (1977; rpt New York, 1981). Teresa de Lauretis summarizes subjectivity as 'a process by which . . . one places oneself or is placed in social reality, and so perceives and comprehends as subjective (referring to, even originating in, oneself) those relations – material, economic, and interpersonal – which are in fact social and, in a larger perspective, historical' (*Alice Doesn't: Feminism, Semiotics, Cinema* [Bloomington, IN, 1984], p. 159). De Lauretis, like many feminists, feels that Foucault's account of power and Lacan's of language preclude consideration of women as historical agents who are engaged in forging subjectivities in opposition to patriarchal structures of meaning (pp. 94–5 and pp. 164–5).

16 John Berger, *Ways of Seeing* (New York, 1973), p. 121.

17 De Lauretis, *Alice Doesn't*, pp. 156–9.

18 In their review of Jill Dolan's 1991 *Midsummer Night's Dream*, Stacy Wolf and Michael Peterson describe Dolan's use of both fragmentation and crossdressing in the presentation of Act II, scene 1: 'when Helena prostrated herself and pleaded with Demetrius to "beat me", Puck halted the action, directing "ACT-UP" fairies to reconfigure Helena's masochistic desires by taking over for her and Demetrius. The male and female actors moved in and out of the Balinese-derived masks which indicated these two roles, suggesting the construction of gender and the representational constraints placed on women' ('Review of *A Midsummer Night's Dream*', *Theatre Journal*, 42 [1992], p. 228). In addition, Dolan underlined the theatricality of gender by cross-dressing Theseus and Hippolyta in the final scene and by 'cross-casting' Oberon and Titania: the fairy king was a mustachioed woman in suit and hat, the queen a man in high heels, leather miniskirt, and rhinestone-studded bra.

19 According to Foucault, 'Sexuality must not be thought of as a kind of natural given which power tries to hold in check, or as an obscure domain which knowledge tries gradually to uncover. It is the name that can be given to a historical construct: not a furtive reality that is difficult to grasp, but a great surface network in which the stimulation of bodies, the intensification of pleasures, the incitement to discourse, the formation of special knowledges, the strengthening of controls and resistances, are linked to one another, in accordance with a few major strategies of knowledge and power' (*The History of Sexuality, Volume I: An Introduction*, trans. Robert Hurley [New York, 1978], pp. 105–6).

20 Though feminist scholars have challenged her estimation of the liberating effects of Elizabethan marriage for women, Juliet Dusinberre gives a good account of the ideal of marital chastity with which Puritan reformers sought to displace a monastic (Catholic) one; see *Shakespeare and the Nature of Women* (London, 1975), pp. 20–63.

21 According to Freud, the little girl surrenders or represses the active part of her libido ('masculine' desire) in return for her father's (i.e., male) love, consenting to a condition of 'lack', of passivity and dependence. See Sigmund Freud, 'Feminin-

ity', *The Standard Edition of the Complete Psychological Works of Sigmund Freud*, ed. and trans. James Strachey and Anna Freud, 24 vols. (London, 1953–74), 22: 112–35.

22   David Bevington also regards these lines as evocative of the Virgin Mary; see *The Complete Works of Shakespeare*, 4th edn (New York, 1984), p. 386n.

23   MacKinnon, 'Feminism, Marxism, method, and the state: an agenda for theory', *Signs*, 7 (1982), pp. 530–1.

24   'The statement, "I'm a man," . . . at most can mean no more than, "I'm like he whom I recognize to be a man, and so recognize myself as being such." In the last resort, these various formulas are to be understood only in reference to the truth of "I is an other"' (Jacques Lacan, 'Aggressivity in psychoanalysis', *Écrits: A Selection*, trans. Alan Sheridan [New York, 1977], p. 23).

25   Lynda E. Boose, 'Scolding brides and bridling scolds: taming the woman's unruly member', *Shakespeare Quarterly*, 42 (1991), pp. 179–213, esp. pp. 199–200; see also Peter Stallybrass, 'Patriarchal territories: the body enclosed' in *Rewriting the Renaissance: The Discourses of Sexual Difference in Early Modern Europe*, ed. Margaret W. Ferguson, Maureen Quilligan, and Nancy J. Vickers (Chicago, 1986), pp. 123–42, esp. p. 126.

26   For a superb psychoanalytic account of Bertram's fear of Helena's engulfing maternalism, see Adelman, *Suffocating Mothers*, pp. 79–86.

27   Ellis wrote: 'But only the girl with whom one has not grown up from childhood, and become accustomed to, can ever be to us in the truly sexual sense, a real girl. That is to say, she alone can possess these powerful stimuli to the sense of sexual desirability, never developed in people one has grown unconsciously used to, which are essential to the making of a real girl' (*Sex and Marriage* [Westport, CT, 1977], p. 42).

28   Nevo contends that the Countess is 'rather more than half in love with her son' and 'since she cannot have a husband in her son, she will identify with the girl who would be his wife, and so transform her love for Bertram into a double maternal solicitude' (Nevo, 'Motive and meaning', pp. 33 and 35). My argument is closer to that of Adelman, who identifies a 'binding maternal power' in the Countess which Helena enacts and extends (Adelman, *Suffocating Mothers*, pp. 79–80).

29   For a brilliant discussion of the oedipal conflict between Bertram and the King, see Richard P. Wheeler, *Shakespeare's Development and the Problem Comedies: Turn and Counter-turn* (Berkeley, CA, 1981), pp. 35–45.

30   Nevo also notes the strangeness of 'mother' within the menu of lovers' epithets ('Motive and meaning', pp. 37–8).

31   Bruno Bettelheim, *The Uses of Enchantment: The Meaning and Importance of Fairy Tales* (New York, 1975), p. 308.

32   Jane Yolen, 'America's Cinderella' in *Cinderella: A Folklore Casebook*, ed. Alan Dundes (New York, 1982), p. 298.

33   Ibid., p. 296.

34   My reading of the traditional tale of 'Cinderella' is indebted to that of Bettelheim (*The Uses of Enchantment*, pp. 267–72), who regards the climactic insertion of foot into slipper as both an affirmation of female sexuality and a palliation of a male

castration anxiety symbolized by the Prince's inability to observe the blood from the amputated parts of the stepsisters' feet. The limits of Bettelheim's reading reflect the limits of its Freudian predicates: to characterize Cinderella as an 'uncastrated woman' whose dangled foot expresses a 'desire for a penis' presupposes the embeddedness of 'penis envy' in the female psyche and the experience of lack as a biological condition rather than a patriarchal construction. The point seems worth stressing because, shorn of its Freudian fatalism, Bettelheim's reading of 'Cinderella' applies most intriguingly to *All's Well:* through the bed-trick Helena both affirms her sexuality and ameliorates Bertram's castration anxiety – the dread of loss and lack that accompanies his aversion to her. Helena not only gives Bertram a taste of the sexuality that Cinderella symbolically evokes but presents herself at the end as uncastrating (rather than uncastrated), one who has already had Bertram sexually without damaging him.

35 Carol Thurston, *The Romance Revolution: Erotic Novels for Women and the Quest for a New Sexual Identity* (Urbana, IL, 1987), p. 8.

36 Thurston points out that the callous male who learns to be sensitive has recently been challenged by a 'new hero' whose sensitivity is manifest from the outset (ibid., p. 72).

37 Tania Modleski, *Loving with a Vengeance: Mass-produced Fantasies for Women* (New York, 1982), p. 45. As a genre of twentieth-century fiction written exclusively by and for women and as a site of recent feminist criticism, the romance novel seems a valuable referent for a male critic/director pondering the narratives – both old and new – that intersect with *All's Well*'s drama of sexual difference. For a spirited and compelling defense of the link between Shakespeare and popular culture, see Harriet Hawkins, *Classics and Trash: Traditions and Taboos in High Literature and Popular Modern Genres* (Toronto, 1990). For a very different critical use of the romance novel, see Linda Charnes, 'What's love got to do with it? Reading the liberal humanist romance in Shakespeare's *Antony and Cleopatra*', *Textual Practice*, 6 (1992), pp. 1–17. Charnes discerns a romance-novel sensibility not in Shakespeare's play but in the 'traditional liberal-humanist' reading of it, in which ' "love" will proleptically revise and make emotional sense of all preceding experience, no matter how violent and disjunctive' (ibid., p. 11).

38 'In both [*All's Well that Ends Well* and *Measure for Measure*], the bedtricks are employed to cure or transform male fantasy through its apparent enactment' (Carol Thomas Neely, *Broken Nuptials in Shakespeare's Plays* [New Haven, CT, 1985], p. 94). Neely's discussion of the bed-trick is extremely helpful and insightful. See also Susan Griffin's discussion of the pornographic narrative, where she observes that 'Over and over again, the pornographer's triumph, the piece de resistance in his fantasy, occurs when he turns the virgin into a whore' (*Pornography and Silence* [New York, 1981], p. 22).

39 De Lauretis, *Alice Doesn't*, pp. 99 and 83.

40 See Neely, *Broken Nuptials*, p. 73, and Hodgdon, 'The making of virgins and mothers', p. 60.

41 See Asp, 'Subjectivity, desire and female friendship', p. 57.

42 Jeanie Forte, 'Focus on the body: pain, praxis, and pleasure in feminist perfor-

mance' in *Critical Theory and Performance*, ed. Janelle G. Reinelt and Joseph P. Roach (Ann Arbor, MI, 1992), pp. 248–62. See Hélène Cixous, 'Sorties' in Hélène Cixous and Catherine Clement, *The Newly Born Woman*, trans. Betsy Wing (Minneapolis, MN, 1986); see also Luce Irigaray, *This Sex Which Is Not One* (Ithaca, NY, 1985). Dissenters from what is often referred to as 'French feminism' object that the notion of a distinctive female pleasure and language presupposes a body free of patriarchal inscriptions. Forte argues that feminist performance artists avoid this essentialist trap by asserting the material body against subjugating modes of representation (Forte, p. 254).

43   Forte, 'Focus on the body', pp. 256–9.

44   Ibid., p. 258.

45   Ibid., p. 257.

46   De Lauretis, *Alice Doesn't*, pp. 153 and 157.

47   Irigaray's account of female sexuality, in *This Sex Which Is Not One*, seems to me persuasive even if one is inclined to view the differentiation it posits as contingent rather than essential.

48   The notion of the gaze has undergone significant revision since Laura Mulvey first posited an active, male, voyeuristic gaze and a passive, female, exhibited object of that gaze, a scopic regime that limited female spectators to the untenable alternatives of masochistic identification with a female object/victim or sadistic identification with the male subject – in other words, denial or erasure of female subjectivity ('Visual pleasure and narrative cinema' in *Feminism and Film Theory*, ed. Constance Penley [New York, 1988]). As Linda Williams observes, feminist film theorists 'have fruitfully shifted to a model of bisexuality of more fluid movements on the part of both male and female spectators that alternate . . . between masculine and feminine identifications' (*Hard Core: Power, Pleasure, and the 'Frenzy of the Visible'* [Berkeley, CA, 1989]). These theorists have also identified bisexual fluidity in representation as well as identification. Carol Clover finds in slasher films examples of female characters assuming a masculine position, and Kaja Silverman explores Werner Fassbinder's films for instances of male figures adopting the feminine; see *Men, Women, and Chainsaws* (Princeton, NJ, 1992), and 'Fassbinder and Lacan: a reconsideration of gaze, look, image', *Male Subjectivity at the Margins* (New York, 1992), pp. 125–56. Recently Silverman has argued that the equation of the gaze with male voyeurism stems from a misreading of Lacan, for whom the gaze is a mechanism of social surveillance rather than of libidinal fixation. Lacan describes the gaze as the all-seeing 'spectacle of the world' that 'determines' us as beings who are looked at (quoted in Silverman, p. 151). The gaze, Silverman suggests, is 'the signifier for that which constitutes the subject as lacking within the field of vision' (p. 407). This gaze is outside desire and utterly inaccessible to any individual viewer. Neither gender can own it or escape it. What film theorists have called the male gaze is really a male look that 'transfers its own lack to the female subject and attempts to pass itself off as the gaze' (p. 144). In deference to Silverman's persuasive analysis, perhaps I should speak not of Helena's masculine gaze but of her desiring look, which during the bed-trick emulates the gaze in making a spectacle of Bertram.

49 See J. L. Styan, *Shakespeare in Performance: All's Well that Ends Well* (Manchester, UK, 1984), pp. 25 and 51.

50 Robert Smallwood, 'Shakespeare at Stratford-upon-Avon, 1989 (part II)', *Shakespeare Quarterly*, 41 (1990), pp. 491–9, esp. p. 494.

51 The phrase *taming difference* heads Barbara Freedman's fascinating essay on *The Taming of the Shrew* in her invaluable book *Staging the Gaze: Postmodernism, Psychoanalysis, and Shakespearean Comedy* (Ithaca, NY, 1991). Though Freedman's definition of 'staging the gaze' is more theoretical and sophisticated than mine, much of her commentary confirms the necessity of destabilizing symbolic (phallocentric) structures of representation: 'Theater enacts the costs of assuming the displacing image returned back by society – the mask that alienates as it procures entry into society . . . feminist theater requires a performance that exposes and stages this taming of the gaze by the symbolic order' (pp. 139–40).

52 For an excellent discussion of the implications of the word *kind* for Shakespeare's audience, see Arthur Kirsch, *Shakespeare and the Experience of Love* (Cambridge, 1981), p. 142.

53 Asp also identifies Helena's veiled sadism: 'I would go so far as to say that lurking behind Helena's apparent psychological masochism of her initial attitude towards Bertram lies its opposite, i.e., anger or rage at having been denied subjectivity by him and a willingness to inflict pain, a psychological form of sadism' ('Subjectivity, desire and female friendship', p. 58).

54 Some critics have contended that the play itself resembles a morality play. See, for instance, Knight, *The Sovereign Flower*, pp. 138–57; Robert Grams Hunter, *Shakespeare and the Comedy of Forgiveness* (New York, 1965), pp. 123–31; and William B. Toole, *Shakespeare's Problem Plays: Studies in Form and Meaning* (The Hague, 1966), pp. 122–57.

55 In Susan Snyder's Lacanian reading of *All's Well*, Helena's goal eludes her because it is essentially illusory: 'the "bright particular star" (I. i. 85) she pursues is her own fantasy, a far cry from the increasingly soiled and compromised actuality of Bertram . . . The whole shape of the story thus enacts desire in Lacanian terms: at best you get a flawed, imperfect substitute for the image that drives you' ('"The King's not here"', p. 30). In Asp's Lacanian account, by contrast, Helena's desire for Bertram 'seems to be displaced by her own maternity and by her return to the mother'. Helena thus moves beyond the Imaginary Order, in which she is initially trapped, to the Symbolic, where through her maternity 'she is inserted into the larger cultural sphere of social and familial engagement' ('Subjectivity, desire and female friendship', pp. 55–6).

56 De Lauretis, *Alice Doesn't*, p. 133.

57 Adelman makes much the same argument in her brilliant discussion of *All's Well* (*Suffocating Mothers*, p. 85). See also Nevo, 'Motive and meaning', p. 44, and Kay Stockholder, *Dream Works: Lovers and Families in Shakespeare's Plays* (Toronto, 1987), pp. 75–6, for corroborative readings of the wish-fulfillment fantasy encoded in Bertram's impossible conditions.

58 Thomas Laqueur, *Making Sex: Body and Gender From the Greeks to Freud* (Cambridge, MA, 1990), pp. 1–9.

The Homoerotics of Shakespearian Comedy

Valerie Traub

The following reading is a chapter from Valerie Traub's book, Desire and Anxiety *(1992), which forms a wide-ranging and sophisticated attempt to locate (homo-)erotic energy in Shakespearian drama not by labelling particular characters or their interactions but by discussing the circulation of erotic energies within the comedies themselves. Here she is concerned to re-examine the 'boy-player' convention in the light of previous critics and then to discuss the different signification of homoerotic desire in* As You Like It *and* Twelfth Night. *Traub is especially revealing about the ways in which previous critics have contained or neutralized homoerotic valences in the texts, and attentive to performative moments of erotic desire as opposed to essentialized inscriptions.*

Valerie Traub, 'The Homoerotics of Shakespearean Comedy', in *Desire and Anxiety: Circulations of Sexuality in Shakespearean Drama* (London: Routledge, 1992), pp. 117–44.

The phenomenon of boy actors playing women's parts in Shakespearean comedy has engendered analyses primarily along three axes. The boy actor: (1) is merely a theatrical convention in the lineage of medieval drama; (2) is a political convention specifically necessitated by the determination to keep women, excepting Elizabeth I, off any public stage or platform; or (3) is an embodiment of the meta-dramatic theme of identity itself: always a charade, a masquerade, other. Certainly it is too much of a caricature to label the first formulation as formalist, the second as feminist, and the third as new historicist. And yet it might be provisionally useful to do so, if only to place these positions in the context of debates about: (1) the relative political import and impact of aesthetic events; (2) the determining power of patriarchal ideology within a general political economy; and (3) the extent to which politics and gender impinge on the problematics of subjectivity. It is as an intervention in these debates that I situate the following [discussion].

I want to argue first that the practice of employing boys to act the parts of women was not merely a dramatic convention, nor was it solely a patriarchal strategy. As Stephen Orgel points out, boy actors were 'a uniquely English solution'; when, in 1599, women were banned from the Spanish stage, 'the spectacle of transvestite boys was found to be even more disturbing than that of theatrical women, and the edict was rescinded four years later.'[1] However much the practice did keep women from too publicly displaying themselves, it continued not merely because of its negative power of constraint, but because it made possible complex desires and fantasies, and mediated cultural anxieties. Those desires and anxieties were not only gendered but erotic in their origination and implication. Secondly, costuming boys as women, who might then impersonate men (and then sometimes women as well), was especially well suited for a drama devoted to exploring the construction and dissolution of identity; however, the relevant concept of identity was not that of a generic, nondifferentiated 'selfhood', but of a complex subjectivity always already imbricated by gender and erotic pressures.

I propose that the boy actor works, in specific Shakespearean comedies, as the basis upon which homoeroticism can be safely explored – working for both actors and audiences as an expression of non-hegemonic desire within the confines of conventional, comedic restraints. The phenomenon of the boy actor is not the by-product or the side-effect of a drama 'really' about identity or illustrative of misogyny, but rather is the basis upon which a specific deployment of erotic desire and anxiety can be played out. In this [discussion] I mean to demonstrate [. . .] that certain Shakespearean texts display a homoerotic circulation of desire, that homoerotic energy is elicited, exchanged, negotiated, and displaced as it confronts the pleasures and anxieties of its meanings in early modern culture. Shakespearean drama not only responded to the ideological matrix [. . .] by which homoerotic desire was understood; it also contributed, in its own ambivalent way, to the early modern signification of homoeroticism. Neither a transparent mirror, mimetically reflecting social reality, nor a literary-historical aberration explainable by the author's sexual preference, the homoerotics of Shakespearean comedy are most accurately perceived as a cultural intervention in a heterosexually overdetermined field. They thus provide us with a useful theoretical analytic, not only of early modern sexualities, but of contemporary erotic concerns.

The circulation of homoerotic desire in *As You Like It* and *Twelfth Night* is what I mean to invoke when I employ the term transvestism over disguise or cross-dressing to describe the consequences of Rosalind's and Viola's adoption of (what was then perceived to be) masculine attire. Although psychoanalytically, transvestism implies the erotic excitement achieved by wearing the clothes of a different gender, and thus is anachronistically and illegitimately applied to the activities of these characters, it is nonetheless because of the specifically erotic valence of the term that I use it. The transvestism in these plays has a more generalized erotic effect, dispersed throughout the entire fabric of the text, rather than located and fixed within one character's desire.

Part of my support for such assertions comes from the anti-theatricalists themselves, who increasingly focused their condemnations of the theater on the figure of the boy actor. In a mimetic theory of sexuality, the anti-theatricalists not only charged that the boy actor dressed as a woman aroused the erotic interest of men in the audience, but that spectators were encouraged to play out their fantasies in off-stage, behind-the-scenes scenes. The specifically erotic images with which Stephen Gosson, John Rainoldes, Phillip Stubbes, and William Prynne denounced theatrical practices demonstrates that they perceived actors in their costumes to cross not only status and gender boundaries, but erotic boundaries as well.[2]

However much we might discredit the anti-theatricalists as 'fanatics' or crude mimeticists, their intuitions about erotic arousal should not be presumed to be incidental to theatrical production. Bodies, in their culture as in ours, were invested with erotic meanings – bodies making a spectacle of themselves on stage even more so. And clothing, as both the anti-theatricalists and the upholders of sumptuary laws made clear, was an important indicator of one's sexual stance, denoting erotic availability or lack thereof. The anti-theatricalist claim that the theater was a site of erotic, specifically homoerotic, arousal is not in itself pathological; as Stephen Greenblatt notes, 'Shakespearean comedy constantly appeals to the body and in particular to sexuality as the heart of its theatrical magic.'[3] What *is* pathological, however, is the anti-theatricalist paranoia about what this circulation of eroticism implies for male subjectivity. At any rate, it is not a paranoia shared with other early modern texts that represent homoeroticism as a legitimate mode of desire; for instance, Spenser's *The Shepherd's Calendar* and Marlowe's *Hero and Leander*.[4]

Psychoanalytic and early feminist readings of the transvestism of *As You Like It* and *Twelfth Night* stress the liberating effect caused by the temporary inversion of hierarchical gender arrangements, 'through release to clarification', to use C. L. Barber's influential phrase.[5] Whereas some early feminist readings also posited gender role inversion as an impulse toward androgyny, later feminist and new historicist critics argued that any subversion of gender is contained by the comic form which mandates marriage in the final act. Recent debates on the relative subversive or containing power of gender in Shakespeare's plays focus on the extent to which women (through transvestite disguise or appropriation of speech) challenge and disrupt gender difference, or are securely repositioned as objects of exchange in a patriarchal economy dependent on 'the traffic in women'.[6]

Clearly, insofar as gender hierarchies seem to be both temporarily transgressed *and* formally reinstated, the question of subversion versus containment can only be resolved by crediting *either* the expense of dramatic energy *or* comedic closure. Yet, to do either is also to reproduce the artificial distinction between content and form – a capitulation to the logic of binarism. One way beyond such fruitless polarization is to historicize the moment in which subversion is thought to occur, to situate *abstract* transgression within a concrete network of overdetermined social pressures and effects.[7] Another way [. . .] is to stress less the fact of foreclosure than the *way* such containment is attained:

the mechanisms and displacements set to work by the anxiety elicited through subversive action. In the following analysis of erotic transgression, I will attempt to do both.

To the extent that the various critics who have recently written about the phenomena of boy actors and female transvestism have recognized the homoeroticism residing in theatrical transvestism, they have initiated the possibility of a homoerotic analytic.[8] For the most part, however, they have focused their attention on *gender* rather than sexuality – even though [. . .] their language confuses the issue by using synonymously such terms as sexual difference and sexual identity, androgyny and bisexuality, femininity (or masculinity) and heterosexuality. After mentioning the erotic complications raised by the boy actor, they more often than not decline to interrogate how homoeroticism works in specific plays, how homoerotic desire is differentiated between plays, and whether homoeroticism is distinguished along gender lines.

Even in those analyses specifically devoted to uncovering the material reality of homoerotic practice, gender remains the dominant lens of analysis, as in Lisa Jardine's suggestion that male homoeroticism animates all of the cross-dressing scenes. The conclusion extrapolated from Jardine's analysis is that in 'playing the woman's part' the boy actor renders unexceptionable and unthreatening female autonomy and erotic power for a predominantly male audience. If young boys are erotically compelling because of their 'femininity', it is in part because they represent all of the attractions and none of the threats of female heterosexuality. More recently, Stephen Orgel concurs with this line of reasoning: 'The dangers of women in erotic situations, whatever they may be, can be disarmed by having the women play men, just as in the theatre the dangers of women on the stage (whatever *they* may be) can be disarmed by having men play the women.'[9] Whatever the objective truth of these conclusions, they ultimately say more about the gender anxieties of early modern patriarchal culture than about the specificity of homoeroticism. Chapter 4 [of *Desire and Anxiety*] demonstrates that although gender and eroticism are deeply connected, they are not isomorphic. Here, reliance on a gender model causes Orgel and Jardine to refer the motivation of male homoeroticism to a single cause: the fantasized dangers posed by women. Despite their anti-homophobic intentions, Orgel and Jardine continue to place homoeroticism within a category requiring ontological explanation and justification, in which traditional psychoanalytic interpretations are surprisingly reinstalled.

It may well be that gender anxiety is a determining factor in the specific ways homoerotic *practice* is manifested and encoded with social meaning within early modern patriarchal culture. I question, however, whether gender anxiety is *the* salient factor in the construction of homoerotic *desire*. Gender anxiety is no more, and no less, constitutive of homoerotic desire than it is of heterosexual desire. A plenitude of desires are available as unconscious erotic modes within every psyche. But whether a particular mode of desire is given expression or repressed – that is, whether it is manifested as desire or anxiety – is a matter of ideological and institutional elicitations, enticements, and disciplines. To take this argument one step further, whether representations of gendered bodies elicit repulsion or attraction, fear or fascination, is in some ways irrelevant; [. . .] anxiety and desire are two sides of the same erotic coin. As Sedgwick suggests, desire itself is less 'a particular affective state or emotion' than 'the affective or social force, the glue, even when its manifestation is hostility or hatred.'[10] Despite the particular affect involved, the psychic investment is, in each case, comparable. Arbitrary divisions of desire into heterosexual and homoerotic are more indicative of socio-political prerogatives than of inherent psychic or biological imperatives.

Whereas formalist critics often ignore the impact of the boy actor on the text's signification, historical critics such as Jardine and Orgel conversely emphasize the extent to which early modern theatrical practice enabled what is increasingly being called a 'transvestite theater'. In this, they follow the lead of the anti-theatricalists in conflating the material reality of the boy actor with the play's action. Indeed, the concept of a 'transvestite theater' *per se* seems to confuse mimetically not only the reality of the play with the world of the theater, but also the phenomena of transvestism and male homoeroticism. In my view, transvestism does not correlate in a simple fashion with any particular erotic mode: theoretically, it could engender heterosexual as well as homoerotic desires. Rather, I would like to suggest that homoerotic activity within Shakespeare's plays is predicated on, but not identical to, the presence of boy actors playing female parts. The material conditions of the early modern theater offered a de facto homoerotic basis upon which to build structures of desire, which were then, through theatrical representation, made available not only to male but to female audience members. This dual-gender availability suggests a problem with another increasingly popular term, 'sodomitical theatrics'; when used to describe the entire constellation of desires criss-crossing such plays as *As You Like It* and *Twelfth Night*, it fails to distinguish between the erotic practices of both genders; as much as it brings to the fore homoerotic desires among men, it neglects the female desires constructed by the playtexts and imagistically available to female play-goers.

The following comparative analysis of *As You Like It* and *Twelfth Night* attempts to demonstrate the differential ways homoeroticism is treated: how it is experienced as pleasure and when it elicits anxiety for both male and female characters. These plays are sites of struggle for the signification of homoeroticism: they demonstrate that within the early modern erotic economy the homoerotic relation to desire could be represented as both celebratory and strained. At the same time, the representations of homoeroticism in these comedies are as much cultural fantasies as is the representation of the maternal body in the *Henriad* – both representations are 'fantasmic' interventions in 'real' cultural practices, and as such signal the dialectical relation between the psychic and the social.

The homoeroticism of *As You Like It* is playful in its ability to transcend binary oppositions, to break into a dual mode, a simultaneity, of desire. Insofar as Rosalind/Ganymede is a multiply sexual object (simultaneously heterosexual and homoerotic), Orlando's effusion of desire toward her/him prevents the stable reinstitution of heterosexuality, upon which the marriage plot depends. By interrupting the arbitrary binarism of the heterosexual contract, male homoeroticism, even as it affirms particular masculine bonds, transgresses the erotic imperative of the Law of the Father. The proceedings of Hymen that conclude the play, once read in terms of the 'mock' marriage which precedes them, enact only an ambivalent closure. The reinstitution of gender role (and Rosalind's political subordination under her husband's rule) is incommensurate with a rigidification of sexuality.

The homoeroticism of *Twelfth Night*, on the other hand, is anxious and strained. This text explores a diversity of desire, proceeding with erotic plurality as far as it can; then, in the face of anxiety generated by this exploration, it fixes the homoerotic interest onto a marginalized figure. The homoerotic energies of Viola, Olivia, and Orsino are displaced onto Antonio, whose relation to Sebastian is finally sacrificed for the maintenance of institutionalized heterosexuality and generational continuity.[11] In other words, *Twelfth Night* closes down the possibility of homoerotic play initiated by the material presence of the transvestized boy actors. The fear expressed, however, is not of homoeroticism *per se*; homoerotic pleasure is explored and sustained *until* it collapses into fear of erotic exclusivity and its corollary: non-reproductive sexuality. The result is a more rigid dedication to the ideology of binarism, wherein gender and status inequalities are all the more forcefully reinscribed.

> Much virtue in If
>
> Touchstone, *As You Like It*

In '"The Place of a Brother" in *As You Like It*: Social Process and Comic Form', Louis Adrian Montrose began the pathbreaking work of placing women's subordination in Shakespearean drama within the context of male homosocial bonds.[12] In a historicization and politicization of C. L. Barber's analysis of Rosalind in *Shakespeare's Festive Comedy*, Montrose argued that 'Rosalind's exhilarating mastery of herself and others has been a compensatory "holiday humor," a temporary, inversionary rite of misrule, whose context is a transfer of authority, property, and title from the Duke to his prospective male heir.'[13] More recently, Jean Howard continues within the Barber–Montrose lineage: 'The representation of Rosalind's holiday humor has the primary effect, I think, of confirming the gender system and perfecting rather than dismantling it by making a space for mutuality within relations of dominance.'[14] However, she complicates the analysis of Rosalind's subordination through reference to the French feminist analytic of female 'masquerade':

> the figure of Rosalind dressed as a boy engages in playful masquerade as, in playing Rosalind for Orlando, she acts out the parts scripted for women by her culture. Doing so does not release Rosalind from patriarchy but reveals the constructed nature of patriarchy's representations of the feminine and shows a woman manipulating those representations in her own interest, theatricalizing for her own purposes what is assumed to be innate, teaching her future mate how to get beyond certain ideologies of gender to more enabling ones.[15]

The distance traversed in the progression from Barber to Montrose to Howard indicates a corresponding movement from an essentialist view of gender, to an emphasis on social structure as determining gender, to an assertion of the limited possibilities of subversive manipulation within dominant cultural codes. The subjective if constrained agency conferred by Howard upon Rosalind as a woman can be extended as well to Rosalind as erotic subject. In excess of the dominant ideology of monogamous heterosexuality, to which Rosalind is symbolically wed at the end of the play, exist desires unsanctioned by institutional favor. By means of her male improvisation, Rosalind leads the play into a mode of desire neither heterosexual nor homoerotic, but both heterosexual *and* homoerotic. As much as she displays her desire for Orlando, she also enjoys her position as male object of Phebe's desire and, more importantly, of Orlando's. S/he thus instigates a deconstruction of the binary system by which desire in subsequent centuries came to be organized, regulated, and disciplined.

That homoerotic significations will play a part in *As You Like It* is first intimated by Rosalind's adoption of the name Ganymede when she imagines donning doublet and hose. Of all the male names available to her, she chooses that of the young lover of Zeus, familiar to educated Britons through Greek and Latin literature and European painting, and to less privileged persons as a colloquial term used to describe the male object of male love. As James Saslow, who traces the artistic representation of Ganymede in Western culture from the fifteenth to the seventeenth centuries, argues, 'the very word *ganymede* was used from medieval times well into the seventeenth century to mean an object of homosexual desire.'[16] Saslow's argument is seconded by Orgel: 'the name Ganymede [could not] be used in the Renaissance without this connotation.'[17]

That Rosalind-cum-Ganymede becomes the object of another woman's desire is obvious. Consciously, of course, Phebe believes Ganymede to be a man, and is thus merely following the dominant heterosexual course. And yet, what attracts Phebe to Ganymede are precisely those qualities that could be termed 'feminine'. Notice the progression of the following speech:

> It is a pretty youth – not very pretty . . .
> He'll make a proper man. The best thing in him
> Is his complexion . . .
> He is not very tall; yet for his years he's tall.
> His leg is but so so; and yet 'tis well.
> There was a pretty redness in his lip,
> A little riper and more lusty red
> Than that mix'd in his cheek; 'twas just the difference
> Betwixt the constant red and mingled damask.
>
> (III. v. 113–23)

During the first half of her recollection, as she measures Ganymede against the standard of common male attributes – height, leg – Phebe fights her attraction, syntactically oscillating between affirmation and denial: he is; he is not. In the last four lines, as she 'feminizes' Ganymede's lip and cheek, she capitulates to her desire altogether.

Many critics acknowledge the underlying homoeroticism of Phebe's attraction; however, they tend to undermine its thematic importance by relegating it to the status of a temporary psychosexual stage. C. L. Barber, for instance, remarks: 'She has, in effect, a girlish crush on the femininity which shows through Rosalind's disguise; the aberrant affection is happily got over when Rosalind reveals her identity and makes it manifest that Phebe has been loving a woman.'[18] When Barber says that Phebe's 'aberrant' affection is 'happily got over' he reveals the extent to which homophobic anxiety structures the developmental logic of his response. But if a 'girlish crush' is outgrown or overcome, what are we to make of Rosalind's desire to 'prove a busy actor' in the 'pageant truly play'd' of Phebe and Silvius? (III. iv. 50–8). Although her ostensible motivation is her belief that 'the sight of lovers feedeth those in love' (l. 56), s/he soon interjects in order to correct the literal-mindedness that feeds Phebe's 'proud disdain' (III. iv. 52). And yet the pleasure Rosalind/Ganymede takes in this task seems in excess of her putative function. Significantly, it is s/he who first mentions the possibility of Phebe's attraction, interpreting and then glorying in Phebe's changed demeanor:

> Why, what means this? Why do you look on me?
> I see no more in you than in the ordinary
> Of nature's sale-work. 'Od's my little life
> I think she means to tangle my eyes too!
>
> (III. v. 41–4)

Is there not a sense in which Rosalind/Ganymede *elicits* Phebe's desire, constructing it even as she refuses it? Indeed, in these lines the conflict between discourses of gender and of sexuality are intensely manifested: at the level of gender, Rosalind restates compulsory heterosexuality; at the level of sexuality, Ganymede elicits a desire for that which falls outside (or on the cusp) of the binarism of gender. At any rate, s/he is represented as delighting in her role of the rejecting male:

> Down on your knees,
> And thank heaven, fasting, for a good man's love;
> For I must tell you friendly in your ear,
> Sell when you can, you are not for all markets.
>
> (III. v. 57–60)

And why does s/he put Silvius through the exquisite torment of hearing Phebe's love letter to Ganymede read aloud, if not to aggrandize her own victorious position as male rival? (IV. iii. 14–64). Indeed, as a male, her sense of power is so complete that s/he presumes to tell Silvius to tell Phebe, 'that if she love *me*, I charge her to love *thee*' (IV. iii. 71–2, my emphasis).

Homoerotic desire in *As You Like It* thus circulates from Phebe's desire for the 'feminine' in Rosalind/Ganymede to Rosalind/Ganymede's desire to be the 'masculine' object of Phebe's desire. Even more suggestive of the text's investment in homoerotic pleasure is Orlando's willingness to engage in love-play with a young shepherd. Throughout his 'courtship' of Ganymede (who is now impersonating Rosalind), Orlando accepts and treats Ganymede as his beloved. To do so requires less his willing suspension of disbelief than the ability to hold in suspension a dual sexuality that feels no compulsion to make arbitrary distinctions between kinds of objects. That Rosalind-cum-Ganymede takes the lead in their courtship has been noted by countless critics; that there is a certain homoerotic irony in that fact has yet to be noted. As a 'ganymede', Rosalind would be expected to play the part of a younger, more receptive partner in an erotic exchange. S/he thus not only inverts gender roles; s/he disrupts alleged homoerotic roles as well.

What began as a game culminates in the 'mock' marriage, when Orlando takes for his wife the boy he believes to be fictionalizing as Rosalind. It is Celia, not Orlando, who hesitates in playing her part in the ceremony – 'I cannot say the words', she responds to Orlando's request that she play the priest (IV. i. 121) – in part because those words possess a ritualistic power to *enact* what is spoken. Insofar as ritual was still popularly believed to be imbued with sacred or magical power, the fact that Orlando does not hesitate, but eagerly responds in the precise form of the Anglican marriage ceremony – 'I take thee, Rosalind, for wife' (IV. i. 129) – suggests the degree to which the play legitimizes the multiple desires it represents. The point is not that Orlando and Ganymede formalize a homosexual marriage, but rather that as the distance between Rosalind and Ganymede collapses, distinctions between homoerotic and heterosexual collapse as well. As the woman and the shepherd boy merge, Orlando's words resound with the conviction that, for the moment, he (as much as Rosalind and the audience) is engaged in the ceremony as if it were real. As both a performative speech act and a theatricalization of desire, the marriage is both true and fictional at once. The subversiveness of this dramatic gesture lies in the dual motion of first, appropriating the meaning of matrimony for deviant desires; and second, exposing the heterosexual imperative of matrimony as a reduction of the plurality of desire into the singularity of monogamy. The 'mock' marriage is not a desecration but a deconstruction – a displacement and subversion of the terms by which desire is encoded – of the ritual by which two are made one.

When Hymen in Act V symbolically reintroduces the logic of heterosexual marriage, the text's devotion to simultaneity would appear to be negated. The terms in which Hymen performs the quartet of marriages make the ideological function of the ritual clear: 'Peace, ho! I bar confusion. / 'Tis I must make conclusion / Of these most strange events' (V. iv. 124–6). 'Hymen's bands' (V. iv. 128) are called forth to 'make conclusion' not only of erotic 'confusion' but of the play. And yet the play does not end with Hymen's bars and bands, but with a renewed attack on the pretensions of erotic certitude. In a repetition of her previous gender and erotic mobility, Rosalind-cum–boy-actor, still wearing female attire, leaps the frame of the play in order to address the audience in a distinctly erotic manner: 'If I were a woman I would kiss as many of you as had beards that pleas'd me, complexions that lik'd me, and breaths that I defied not' (Epilogue 16–19). As Orgel, Howard, Phyllis Rackin, and Catherine Belsey all intimate, the effect of this statement is to highlight the constructedness of gender and the flexibility of erotic attraction at precisely the point when the formal impulse of comedy would be to essentialize and fix both gender and eroticism.

Throughout the play, what makes erotic contingency possible is a simple conjunction: 'if'. Indeed, Touchstone's discourse on the virtues of 'if' can serve as an index of the play's entire erotic strategy: 'If you said so, then I said so' (V. iv. 99–100). The dependence on the conditional structures the possibility of erotic exploration without necessitating a commitment to it. Orlando can woo and even wed Ganymede as '*if* thou wert indeed my Rosalind' and as *if* the marriage were real (IV. i. 189–90, my emphasis). Through the magic of 'if', the boy actor playing Rosalind can offer and elicit erotic attraction to and from each gender in the audience. 'If' not only creates multiple erotic possibilities and positions, it also conditionally resolves the dramatic confusion that the play cannot sustain. As Rosalind says to Silvius, Phebe, and Orlando, respectively: 'I would love you, if I could'; 'I will marry you, if ever I marry a woman, and I'll be married tomorrow'; and, 'I will satisfy you, if ever I satisfied man, and you shall be married tomorrow' (V. ii. 108–12). Even Hymen's mandate is qualified: 'Here's eight that must take hands / To join in Hymen's bands / *If* truth hold true contents' (V. iv. 127–9, my emphasis).

My own reliance on 'if' should make it clear that I am not arguing that Rosalind or Orlando or Phebe 'is' 'a' 'homosexual'. Rather, at various moments in the play, these characters temporarily inhabit a homoerotic position of desire. To insist on a mode of desire as a position taken up also differs from formulating these characters as 'bisexual': as Phyllis Rackin reminds us, bisexuality implicitly defines the desiring subject as divided in order to maintain the ideologically motivated categories of homo- and hetero- as inviolate.[19] The entire logic of *As You Like It* works against such categorization, against fixing upon and reifying any one mode of desire.

Simultaneity and flexibility, however, are not without their costs. Insofar as the text circulates homoerotic desire, it displaces the anxieties so generated in the following tableau described by Oliver, Orlando's brother:

> A wretched ragged man, o'ergrown with hair,
> Lay sleeping on his back. About his neck
> A green and gilded snake had wreath'd itself,
> Who with her head nimble in threats approach'd
> The opening of his mouth . . .
> A lioness, with udders all drawn dry,
> Lay couching, head on ground, with catlike watch,
> When that the sleeping man should stir . . .
> (IV. iii. 107–17)

The dual dangers to which the sleeping Oliver is susceptible are, on the face of it, female: the lioness an aged maternal figure ('with udders all drawn dry'), the female snake seductively encircling Oliver's neck. Let us first give this passage a conventional psychoanalytic reading: the virile and virtuous Orlando banishes the snake and battles with the lion while his evil 'emasculated' brother, unconscious of his position as damsel in distress, sleeps on – their sibling rivalry displaced onto and mediated by gender conflict. Yet at the same time as the snake encircles her prey, she approaches and almost penetrates the vulnerable opening of Oliver's mouth. Rather than posit the snake, in this aspect, as a representation of the 'phallic mother', I want to argue that in the snake's figure are concentrated the anxieties generated by the text's simultaneous commitment to homoeroticism and heterosexuality. If Oliver is endangered by the snake's 'feminine' sexual powers, he is equally threatened by her phallic ones. He becomes both the feminized object of male aggression and the *e*ffeminized object of female desire. The snake thus represents the erotic other of the text, the reservoir of the fears elicited by homoerotic exchanges – fears, I want to insist, that are not inherent in the experience of homoerotic desire, but that are produced by those ideologies that position homoeroticism as unnatural, criminal, and heretical.

Indeed the relations represented in this tableau suggest that no desire, male or female, heterosexual or homoerotic, is free of anxiety. As Touchstone says in a lighter vein, 'as all is mortal in nature, so is all nature in love mortal in folly' (II. iv. 52–3). But what is most interesting is that in this play sexual danger is encoded as feminizing to the object persistently figured as male. Consistently, the text seems less interested in the threat of a particular mode of desire (hetero/homo) than in the dangers desire *as such* poses to men. It is, in this sense, thoroughly patriarchal, positing man as the center of, and vulnerable to, desire. That the text marginalizes this expression of vulnerability by not dramatizing it on stage but reporting it only in retrospect suggests the extent to which the anxiety is repressed in the interests of achieving comic, heterosexual closure, however partially or problematically.

My highlighting of the affirmative possibilities of multiple pleasures is not meant to imply that *As You Like It* represents a paradisiacal erotic economy, a utopian return to a polymorphously perverse body unmediated by cultural restraints. As the penultimate gesture toward the institution of marriage clearly indicates, endless erotic mobility is difficult to sustain. But just as clearly, *As You Like It* registers its lack of commitment to the binary logic that dominates the organization of desire. If *As You Like It* suggests the 'folly' of desire, part of that folly is the discipline to which it is subject.

> My desire / More sharp than filed steel
> Antonio, *Twelfth Night*

The sexual economy of *Twelfth Night* is saturated with multiple erotic investments: Viola/Cesario's dual desire for Olivia and Orsino; Orsino's ambivalent interest in Viola/Cesario; Sebastian's responses to Olivia and Antonio; and finally, Antonio's exclusive erotic wish for Sebastian. Although Viola's initial impulse for adopting male disguise is to serve the duke as a eunuch (I. ii. 56), her status as sexually neutral dissipates as she quickly becomes both erotic object and subject. Critics often mention Viola's passivity, her inclination to commit 'What else may hap to time' (I. ii. 60), but they fail to recognize that as Cesario she woos Olivia with a fervor that exceeds her 'text' (I. v. 227). S/he asks, with no apparent mandate, to see Olivia's face; and upon viewing the 'picture' (I. v. 228), responds, 'if you were the devil, you are fair' (I. v. 246).

Critics also point to Viola/Cesario's anxiety over the predicament caused by the disguise:

> I am the man. If it be so, as 'tis,
> Poor lady, she were better love a dream.
> Disguise, I see, thou art a wickedness
> Wherein the pregnant enemy does much . . .
> How will this fadge? My master loves her dearly;
> And I, poor monster, fond as much on him;
> And she, mistaken, seems to dote on me.
> What will become of this? As I am man,
> My state is desperate for my master's love;
> As I am woman – now alas the day! –
> What thriftless sighs shall poor Olivia breathe!
> O time, thou must untangle this, not I;
> It is too hard a knot for me t' untie.
>
> (II. ii. 25–41)

The image by which Viola/Cesario expresses her plight is far more resonant than many critics have noted. The implied double negative of a *knot* that *cannot* be untied is precisely the figuration of her complex erotic investments: s/he 'fonds' on her master, while simultaneously finding erotic intrigue and excitement as the object of Olivia's desire. The flip side of her anxiety about Olivia's desire is her own desire to be the *object* of Olivia's desire. This desire s/he can *(k)not* untie because of its status as negation. Why this desire is negated in this play I will take up in a moment. For now, what is important is that the play sets up Viola/Cesario's dual erotic investment, not so much to resolve it as to sustain its dramatic possibilities and to elicit the similarly polymorphous desires of the audience, whose spectator pleasure would be at least in part derived from a transgressive glimpse of multiple erotic possibilities.

To substantiate the play's investment in erotic duality, one can compare the language used in Viola/Cesario's two avowals of love: the first as Orsino's wooer of Olivia, and the second as s/he attempts to communicate love to Orsino. In both avowals, Viola/Cesario theatricalizes desire, using a similar language of conditionals toward both erotic objects. Compare the syntactical and semantic structure of Viola/Cesario's comment to Olivia, 'If I did love you in my master's flame, / With such a suff'ring, such a deadly life, / In your denial I would find no sense; / I would not understand it' (I. v. 259–62) to her comment to Orsino: 'My father had a daughter lov'd a man, / As it might be, perhaps, were I a woman, / I should your lordship' (II. iv. 107–9). What predisposes us to credit the second comment as truth but the first as false, a suspect performance, is, I suggest, largely our assumption of universal heterosexuality. Both speeches are equally theatricalizations of desire. As such, both work to undermine the dichotomy between truth and falsehood, fiction and reality, heterosexuality and homoeroticism.

This is not to suggest that Viola/Cesario's position in relation to homo-erotic desire is celebrated in the text: unlike Rosalind, her erotic predicament threatens her with destruction – or at least so s/he believes – at the hands of Sir Andrew, who is manipulated by Sir Toby to challenge his rival to a duel. The weapon of choice is not incidental, as the whole point of the threatened battle is for Viola/Cesario to demonstrate the 'little thing' that 'would make me tell them how much I lack of a man' (III. iv. 302–3). As Toby says: 'There-fore, on, or strip your sword stark naked; for meddle you must, that's certain, or forswear to wear iron about you' (III. iv. 252–4). At this (phallic) point, Viola/Cesario's 'lack' is upheld as the signifier of gender difference. And yet, to the extent that masculinity is embodied in the sword, it depends upon a particular kind of performance rather than any biological equipment. This theatrical moment simultaneously reinscribes a binary code of gender into the action, *and* suggests the extent to which gender is prosthetic.[20] It seems telling that at precisely this point of pressure on the meaning of gender, the play of erotic difference is abandoned. Or, more accurately, deflected, for who should enter to defend Viola/Cesario but Antonio, the figure who is positioned most firmly in a homoerotic relation to desire.

The entire first scene between Antonio and Sebastian is focused on Sebas-tian's denial of the sailor's help, and Antonio's irrepressible desire not only to protect but accompany the man with whom, we later learn, he has spent 'three months . . . / No int'rim, not a minute's vacancy. / Both day and night' (V. i. 90–2). Antonio singlemindedly pursues Sebastian through the (to him) dan-gerous streets of Illyria: 'But come what may, I do adore thee so / That danger shall seem sport, and I will go' (II. i. 44–5). It is not fortuitous that this scene (II. i) intervenes between Viola/Cesario's wooing of Olivia, when s/he exceeds her 'text' (I. v), and her contemplation of the danger inherent in this action: 'It is too hard a knot for me t' untie' (II. ii). For Antonio's words allude to the perils in early modern culture of an exclusively homoerotic passion: in order to remain in the presence of one's beloved, 'danger' must be figuratively, if not literally, transformed into 'sport'. That the danger is not limited to the threat of Orsino's men (the force of law) is revealed in Antonio's plea to Sebastian, 'If you will not murder me for my love, let me be your servant' (II. i. 33–4). The love Antonio extends is somehow capable of inciting the beloved to murder.

An even greater danger is intimated in this scene, which will ultimately have severe repercussions on the fate of Antonio's desire. Sebastian explains to Antonio that his father 'left behind him myself and a sister, both born in an hour. If the heavens had been pleas'd, would we had so ended! But you, sir, alter'd that, for some hour before you took me from the breach of the sea was my sister drown'd' (II. i. 17–22). Sebastian's life is saved when he is pulled from the 'breach of the sea', an image of the surf that invokes the rebirthing we expect from Shakespearean shipwrecks. But this rebirth is coincident with the supposed death of Sebastian's sister; she is 'drown'd already . . . with salt water' and drowned again in Sebastian's tearful 'remembrance' (II. i. 29–30). In other words, Sebastian's rebirth into Antonio's love is implicated in the destruction of the only woman Sebastian has loved: Viola.

As mentioned, Viola/Cesario *is* threatened with destruction. Crucially, it is Antonio who saves her/him, thinking that he is defending his beloved. His entrance at this moment enacts the central displacement of the text: when the ramifications of a simultaneous homoeroticism and heterosexuality become too anxiety-ridden, the homoerotic energy of Viola/Cesario is displaced onto Antonio – the one figure, as Laurie Osborne notes, whose passion for another does not arise from deception or require a woman for its expression.[21]

Just before the swordfight Antonio finds Sebastian, and greets him with these words:

> I could not stay behind you. My desire,
> More sharp than filed steel, did spur me forth;
> And not all love to see you, though so much
> As might have drawn one to a longer voyage,
> But jealousy what might befall your travel,
> Being skilless in these parts . . . My willing love,
> The rather by these arguments of fear,
> Set forth in your pursuit.
>
> (III. iii. 4–12)

Why do editors gloss 'jealousy' as anxiety, when both words were available to Shakespeare, and both scan equally well?[22] Antonio is clearly both anxious about the dangers that might 'befall' his beloved, and jealous of the attractions that might entice him. And not without reason: Sebastian falls rather easily to the 'relish' of Olivia's charms (IV. i. 59).

Antonio's discourse partakes of what I will call a 'rhetoric of penetration'. Male desire in Shakespearean drama is almost always figured in phallic images – which may seem tautological until one remembers the commonly accepted notion that Shakespeare's fops are not only 'effeminate' but 'homosexual'. On the contrary, *Twelfth Night* represents male homoerotic desire as phallic in the most active sense: erect, hard, penetrating. Antonio describes his desire in terms of sharp, filed steel which spurs him on to pursuit, 'spur' working simultaneously to 'prick' him (as object) and urge him on (as subject). To the extent that heterosexual desire in Shakespearean drama is often associated with detumescence (the triumph of Venus over Mars, the pervasive puns on dying), and homoerotic desire is figured as permanently erect, it is the desire of man for man that is coded as the more 'masculine'.[23]

Many critics have noted in addition that in the early modern period excessive heterosexual lust seems to engender in men fears of 'effeminacy'. Romeo, for instance, complains that desire for Juliet 'hath made me effeminate, / And in my temper soft'ned valor's steel.' Similarly, the Romans maintain that Antony's lust for Cleopatra has so compromised his gender identity that he 'is not more manlike / Than Cleopatra, nor the queen of Ptolemy / More womanly than he'. In contrast, extreme virility, manifested in Spartan self-denial and military exploits, is not only depicted as consistent with erotic desire for other men; it also is expressed in it, as when Aufidius says to Coriolanus, 'Let me twine / Mine arms about that body, whereagainst / My grained ash an hundred times hath broke', and goes on to compare the joy he feels at seeing Coriolanus as being greater than that which he felt 'when I first my wedded mistress saw / Bestride my threshold'.[24]

Fops, on the other hand, while commonly perceived as having a 'passive' interest in male homoerotic encounters, are almost always involved in pursuing (if unsuccessfully) a heterosexual alliance.[25] Sir Andrew, for instance, hopes to marry Olivia, if only for her status and money. True, he is manipulated by Sir Toby, and he may therefore be seen to partake of a homoerotic triangular relation, whereby he woos his ostensible object (Olivia) in order to concretize ties with his real object (Toby).[26] However, Sir Andrew seems more accurately represented as void of erotic desire, merely attempting to fulfill the social requirements of heterosexuality. Indeed, he seems a vessel into which others' desires are poured, especially Sir Toby's triangular manipulation for wealth, ease, and power through the exchange of the body of his niece. Rather than being homosexual, fops are figured as always already effeminated by their heterosexual relation to desire.

Orsino, whose languid action and hyper-courtly language situate him as foppish, appears to be more in love with love than with any particular object. As Jean Howard points out, Orsino 'initially poses a threat to the Renaissance sex-gender system by languidly abnegating his active role as masculine wooer and drowning in narcissistic self-love . . . His narcissism and potential effeminacy are displaced, respectively, onto Malvolio and Andrew Aguecheek, who suffer fairly severe humiliations for their follies.'[27] Orsino is narcissistic and 'effeminate', but I would argue that neither his narcissism nor his 'effeminacy' is indicative of desire for males *per se*. Orsino's 'effeminacy', a gender characteristic, accompanies both his heterosexual desire for Olivia and his homoerotic desire for Cesario. What is most interesting, however, is the extent to which Orsino's desire is anxious, or in our modern parlance, homo-*phobic*. In contrast to Orsino's homosocial ease with Cesario – their intimacy is established in three days (I. iv. 3) – the possibility of a homo*erotic* basis to his affection for his servant creates tension: he defers accepting Viola as his betrothed until she has adopted her 'maiden weeds' (V. i. 252). Indeed, he refuses to really 'see' her as a woman, continuing to refer to her as Cesario, 'For so you shall be, while you are a man; / But when in other habits you are seen, / Orsino's mistress and his fancy's queen' (V. i. 383–5). To the extent that his anxiety *is* desire, Orsino figures as the repressed homoerotic analogue to Antonio.

Throughout his canon, Shakespeare associates 'effeminacy' in men with the fawning superciliousness of the perfumed courtier, and with the 'womanish' tears of men no longer in control. Both Hotspur and Hamlet, for example, rail against the 'effeminacy' of courtiers; Laertes and Lear describe their tears as 'womanish'. Hamlet is as disgusted by Osric and Guildenstern as he is by Ophelia and Gertrude; it is this fear of 'effeminacy' that stimulates the homophobic disgust in his charge, "Sblood, do you think I am easier to be play'd on than a pipe?"[28]

There is little in the canon to suggest that Shakespeare linked 'effeminacy' to homoeroticism, unless we look to the 'feminine' qualities of Cesario that ambivalently attract Orsino to his page. Historically, the charge of 'effeminacy' seems to have been limited to such 'boys' as Cesario, or to those adult men who were 'uxoriously' obsessed with women. The unfailing correspondence of adult homoeroticism and 'effeminacy' is a later cultural development, and is imported into Shakespeare's texts by critics responding to a different cultural milieu.[29] In *Twelfth Night*, both Antonio and Sebastian pointedly use their phallic swords, and are implicitly contrasted to Sir Andrew, whom even Viola/Cesario one-ups, despite the 'little thing that would make [her] tell them how much [she] lack[s] as a man'. 'Appropriate' male desire is phallic, whether homoerotic or heterosexual; without that phallic force, men in Shakespearean drama are usually rendered either asexual or nominally heterosexual.

Despite the attractions of homoeroticism, the pleasure *Twelfth Night* takes in it is not sustained. Not only are Viola/Cesario and Sebastian betrothed respectively to Orsino and Olivia, but Antonio is marginalized – in part because he publicly speaks his desire, in part because his desire is exclusive of other bonds. Like *The Merchant of Venice*'s Antonio, this Antonio gives his beloved his 'purse'; shortly thereafter he is seized by the duke's men. As he struggles with the officers, Antonio states to 'Sebastian':

> This comes with seeking you.
> But there's no remedy; I shall answer it.
> What will you do, now my necessity
> Makes me to ask you for my purse? It grieves me
> Much more for what I cannot do for you
> Than what befalls myself.
>
> (III. iv. 333–8)

After Viola/Cesario offers money but denies not only their acquaintance, but knowledge of Antonio's 'purse', the officers attempt to take Antonio away; but he resists:

> Let me speak a little. This youth that you see here
> I snatch'd one half out of the jaws of death,
> Reliev'd him with such sanctity of love,
> And to his image, which methought did promise
> Most venerable worth, did I devotion.
>
> (III. iv. 360–4)

'What's that to us?' reply the officers, and Antonio is compelled to curse:

> But O how vile an idol proves this god!
> Thou hast, Sebastian, done good feature shame.
> In nature there's no blemish but the mind;
> None can be call'd deform'd but the unkind.
>
> (III. iv. 366–9)

To which the officers conclude: 'The man grows mad. Away with him!' (III. iv. 372).

Antonio is labeled mad by the law not only because of the linguistic and class impropriety of his speech, but because his vocalization of desire is caught uncomfortably between the only two discourses available to him: platonic friendship and sodomy. There are literally no early modern terms by which Antonio's desire can be understood.

Antonio's imprisonment, we conventionally expect, will be revoked when Viola/Cesario's problems are resolved. With the entrance of Sebastian not only do brother and sister rediscover each other, but 'nature to her bias', according to most critics, draws Olivia to Sebastian and Orsino to Viola (V. i. 257). This appeal to 'nature' can be seen to dissolve the previous dramatic energy expended in portraying socially illegitimate alliances, the conventional betrothals displacing the fantasy embodied by Viola/Cesario of holding in tension simultaneous objects of desire. Many feminist and psychoanalytic critics read this conclusion as a celebration of psychic androgyny in which Viola/Cesario is fantastically split, 'An apple cleft in two' into Viola and Sebastian (V. i. 221). However pertinent such a reading may be to the gender politics of the play (and I think that it bypasses rather than resolves the question of gender identity posed by transvestism), it ignores the erotic politics. Antonio's final query, 'Which is Sebastian?' is answered by the 'identification' of Sebastian and Viola and the quick, symmetrical pairings. Or is it? Is the Sebastian whose words to Antonio are: 'Antonio, O my dear Antonio! / How have the hours rack'd and torture'd me, / Since I have lost thee!' (V. i. 215–17) the same Sebastian who has just sanctified his love to Olivia? Despite his miraculous betrothal, Sebastian's own desire seems more complicated than the assumption of 'natural' heterosexuality would suggest. In fact, Sebastian's desire, like Viola/Cesario's, seems to obliterate the distinction between homo-erotic and heterosexual – at least until the institution of marriage comes into (the) play. As a reassertion of the essential heterosexuality of desire, Sebastian's allusion to 'nature's bias' seems a bit suspect.

Joseph Pequigney offers an alternative interpretation of 'nature to her bias' which not only reopens the question of the meaning of 'bias', but inverts its relation to 'nature'. He notes that 'bias' derives from

> the game of bowls played with a bowl or ball designed to run obliquely, and 'bias' denotes either the form of the bowl that causes it to swerve or, as in the metaphor, the curved course it takes. Nature then chose an oblique or curved rather than a straight way of operating . . . This homoerotic swerving or lesbian [sic] deviation from the heterosexual straight and narrow is not unnatural, but, to the contrary, a modus operandi of Nature.[30]

Despite its closure, then, *Twelfth Night*'s conclusion seems only ambivalently invested in the 'natural' heterosexuality it imposes.

Comparison of the treatment of homoeroticism in *As You Like It* and *Twelfth Night* suggests that when homoeroticism is not a mutual investment it becomes problematic. This may seem distressingly self-evident, but to say it underscores the point that the anxiety exposed in Shakespearean drama is not so much about a particular mode of desire, as about the psychic exposure entailed by a lack of mutuality. Heterosexual desire is equally troubling when unrequited. Despite *Twelfth Night*'s nod to heterosexual imperatives in the ambiguous allusion to 'nature to her bias', and despite both texts' ultimate movement toward heterosexuality, homoeroticism is constructed throughout as merely one more mode of desire. As Antonio puts it, in the closest thing we have to an antihomophobic statement in an early modern text: 'In nature there's no blemish but the mind; / None can be call'd deform'd but the unkind' (*Twelfth Night*, III. iv. 368–9). Both modes of desire are responsive to social and institutional pressures; both are variously attributed to 'noble' and 'irra-tional' impulses. In other words, Shakespearean drama measures homoerotic and heterosexual impulses on the same scale of moral and philosophical value.

Secondly, the relative ease or dis-ease with homoerotic desire seems to depend on the extent to which such desire is recuperable within a simultane-ous homoeroticism and heterosexuality that will ensure generational repro-duction. Specifically, in these plays the dramatized fantasy of eliding women in erotic exchanges seems to initiate anxiety. When homoerotic exchanges threaten to replace heterosexual bonds, when eroticism is collapsed into anxiety about reproduction, then homoeroticism is exorcized at the same time as the female gender is resecured into the patriarchal order.

The specific anxiety about reproduction I hypothesize as a *structuring* principle for the movement of these comedies is not explicitly voiced in either play. It is, however, a dominant theme in the sonnets, beginning with the first line of the first poem to the young man: 'From fairest creatures we desire increase / That thereby beauty's rose might never die.'[31] As the poet exhorts his beloved to 'Look in thy glass, and tell the face thou viewest / Now is the time that face should form another' – that if he should 'Die single . . . thine image dies with thee' (Sonnet 3) – the failure to reproduce is figured in narcissistic, even masturbatory, terms: 'For having traffic with thyself alone / Thou of thyself thy sweet self dost deceive' (Sonnet 4). The sonnets' psychic strategy is founded on a paradox: the narcissism of taking the self as masturbatory object can only be countered and mastered by the narcissism of reproducing oneself in one's heirs.

That the failure to reproduce signified by this masturbatory fantasy is a veritable death knell is evidenced by Sonnet 3: 'who is he so fond will be the tomb / Of his self-love, to stop posterity?' Indeed, if one notes that the final couplet of six out of the first seven sonnets explicitly offers death as the sole alternative to reproduction, the anxiety animating the exhortation to reproduce becomes quite clear. The sheer repetition of the sentiment (twelve sonnets out of the first sixteen) attests to the presence of a repetition compulsion, indicating unresolved psychic distress.[32] Such distress obviously structures the reproductive madness of Sonnet 6:

> Then let not winter's ragged hand deface
> In thee thy summer, ere thou be distill'd.
> Make sweet some vial; treasure thou some place
> With beauty's treasure, ere it be self-kill'd.
> That use is not forbidden usury
> Which happies those that pay the willing loan;
> That's for thyself to breed another thee,
> Or ten times happier, be it ten for one;
> Ten times thyself were happier than thou art,
> If ten of thine ten times refigur'd thee.

That ten is ten times better than one is self-evidently true only if the one is not the one who carries, labors, and delivers those ten offspring. The misogynistic pun on vial, referring both to the vessel of the womb and its supposedly vile character indicates a structuring ambivalence. The logic of the sequence implies that homoerotic love can only be justified through a heterosexual reproductivity that is always already degraded by its contact with female genitalia – the underlying fantasy being the wish for reproduction magically untainted by the female body.

'Make thee another self, *for love of me*' (Sonnet 10, my emphasis). Surely it is not fortuitous that the homoerotic investment of the sonnets elicits such a strong investment in reproduction. This investment is finally mediated, and the anxiety regarding women's necessary role in reproduction is displaced, as the poet appropriates for himself reproductive powers. From Sonnet 15, in which the poet claims to 'engraft' his beloved 'new', through the subsequent four poems, heterosexual reproduction slowly but surely gives way to the aesthetic immortality 'engrafted' on the beloved by the poet's skill. The power to create life is transformed into the exclusively male power of the poet's invocation to an exclusively male audience: 'So long as men can breathe or eyes can see, / So long lives this and this gives life to thee' (Sonnet 18).

The historical reasons for the reproductive anxiety explicitly rendered in the sonnets, and implied by the structure of the comedies, are obviously complex. In order to unpack them, it may be useful to reinsert gender provisionally as a relevant analytic category, to examine the relation of homoerotic desire to the gender system. Eve Sedgwick argues that male homoeroticism was not perceived as threatening in early modern culture because it was not defined in opposition or as an impediment to heterosexuality; Trumbach and Saslow emphasize that the general pattern of male homoeroticism was 'bisexual'. *Exclusive* male homoeroticism, however, homoeroticism that did not admit the need for women, would disrupt important early modern economic and social imperatives: inheritance of name, entitlement, and property. Each of these imperatives, crucial to the social hierarchies of early modern England, was predominantly conferred through heterosexual marriage. I am suggesting, then, that the salient concern may be less the threat posed by homoerotic desire *per se* than that posed by non-monogamy and non-reproduction.

In addition, despite patriarchal control of female sexuality through the ideology of chastity and laws regulating marriage and illegitimacy, there seems to have been a high cultural investment in female erotic pleasure – not because women's pleasure was perceived as healthy or intrinsically desirable, but because it was thought necessary for successful conception to occur. According to Thomas Laqueur, early modern medical texts (including those of midwives) judged both male and female erotic pleasure as essential to generation.[33] Viewed as structurally inverted men, women were thought to ejaculate 'seed' at the height of their sexual pleasure; conception supposedly began at the meeting of male and female seed. Because they were perceived as naturally cooler than men, women were thought to achieve orgasm only after the proper 'heating' of their genitalia. In light of this social investment, it seems possible that an exclusive male homoeroticism could be seen as leaving female reproductive organs out, as it were, in the cold.

Insofar as *As You Like It* gestures outward toward an eroticism character-ized by a diffuse and fluid simultaneity, it does so because the text never feels compelled to fix, to identify, or to name the desires it expresses. In contrast, *Twelfth Night* closes down erotic possibility precisely to the degree it complies with the social imperative to name desire, to fix it within definitive bound-aries, and to identify it with specific characters. The 'unmooring of desire, the generalizing of the libidinal' that Greenblatt sees as 'the special pleasure of Shakespearean fiction' is, when one gets down to it, more comfortably evi-denced in *As You Like It* than in *Twelfth Night*.[34] In the tensions exposed between the two plays, it may be that we start to move from what we are begin-ning to discern as Renaissance homoeroticism to what we know as modern homosexuality, from an inventive potentiality inherent in each subject to the social identity of a discrete order of being.[35]

It is of more than passing interest that insofar as each play enacts a 'textual body', only *Twelfth Night* depends on a phallic representation of male homo-eroticism. Much recent feminist and film criticism has implicated a phallic mode of representation within the visual economy of the 'gaze', wherein value is ascribed according to what one sees (or fails to see): hence, the psychoana-lytic verities of female 'castration' and 'penis envy'. In those modes of repre-sentation governed by phallocentric prerogatives, argue many feminist film theorists, only two positions seem possible: the subject and the object of the gaze.[36] Although many theorists are now complicating this binary picture, arguing that women, in particular, negotiate as subjects and not merely as objects of the gaze, it might be helpful to distinguish the erotic economies of *Twelfth Night* and *As You Like It* along the following lines: *Twelfth Night* is predominantly phallic and visual; not only is Antonio's desire figured in phallic metaphors, but Orsino's desire waits upon the ocular proof of Viola/Cesario's 'femininity'. The final value is one of boundary setting, of mar-ginalizing others along lines of exclusion. The erotics of *As You Like It*, on the other hand, are diffuse, non-localized, and inclusive, extending to the audi-ence an invitation to 'come play' – as does Rosalind-cum-boy-actor in the Epilogue.[37] Bypassing a purely scopic economy, *As You Like It* possesses provocative affinities with the tactile, contiguous, plural erotics envisioned by Luce Irigaray as more descriptive of female experience. We don't return to such a polymorphous textual body until the cross-gendered erotic play of *Antony and Cleopatra*.

This introduction of a diffuse, fluid erotics, and my analysis of the repro-ductive anxieties engendered by male homoeroticism, provoke the broader question of the relation of male homoeroticism to feminist politics. Contrary to the beliefs of those feminists who conflate male homosociality with homo-eroticism, male homoeroticism has no unitary relationship to the structures and ideologies of male dominance. Patriarchal power is homosocial; but it also has been, at various times including the present, homophobic. As Sedgwick has demonstrated, 'while male homosexuality does not correlate in a trans-historical way with political attitudes toward women, homophobia directed at men by men almost always travels with a retinue of gynephobia and antifeminism.'[38] Male homoeroticism can be manipulated to reinforce and justify misogyny, or it can offer itself up as the means to deconstruct the binary structures upon which the subordination of women depends.

The logic of the sonnet sequence is, I believe, thoroughly misogynistic, and its homoerotics seem utterly entwined with that misogyny: a debased female reproduction is excised, and its creative powers appropriated, by the male lover-poet who thereby celebrates and immortalizes his male beloved. Conversely, the circulation of male homoerotic desire in *As You Like It* and *Twelfth Night* does not seem to depend upon an aversion to women or an ideology of male dominance as its *raison d'être*. The homoeroticism of *As You Like It* is not particularly continuous with the homosociality of the Duke's court (the homoerotic exchanges occur primarily between those excluded from it), nor are Antonio's, Viola/Cesario's, Orsino's, or Olivia's homoerotic interests particularly supportive of the patriarchal impulses of *Twelfth Night*. Indeed, whether the homoeroticism is embodied as male or female does not seem to have much impact on its subversive potential. Viola/Cesario's desire for a dual mode of eroticism is more threatening within the play than is Orlando's similar desire, but it is less dangerous than the exclusivity posed by Antonio.

In fact, the male and female homoeroticism of both plays interrupts the ideology of a 'natural' love based on complementary yet oppositional genders. In so doing, the deviations from the dominant discourse of desire circulating throughout these texts transgress the Law of the Father, the injunction that sexuality will follow gender in lining up according to a 'natural' binary code. By refusing such arbitrary divisions of desire, homoeroticism in *As You Like It* and *Twelfth Night* disrupts the cultural code that keeps both men and women in line, subverting patriarchy from within.

This is not to suggest that Shakespeare's plays do not demonstrate count-less commitments to misogyny. Why homoeroticism would be so thoroughly supportive of the misogyny of the sonnets, and so seemingly independent of misogyny in these plays is an important question raised by my analysis. To what extent does genre influence the expression of erotic desire and anxiety? To begin to answer that question, and to substantiate those claims I have made, the treatment of homoeroticism in Shakespeare's predecessors, contemporaries, and followers must be analyzed. Obvious sites of inquiry would be a comparison of Shakespearean homoeroticism with that of Marlowe, and a study of the use of transvestism in Lyly, Sidney, Spenser, Jonson, Middleton, and Dekker.[39] What is crucial at this point is that the relation between gender and eroticism be carefully teased out, that eroticism be posed as a problematic in its own right – both intimately connected to and rigorously differentiated from gender.

The danger of pursuing this kind of inquiry at this moment is in ignoring gender differentials altogether, in an energetic pursuit of 'sexuality'. But if we remember that the analyses of both gender and eroticism are only part of a larger project of theorizing about and from the multiple subject positions we all live, and if we reflect on the complexity of our own erotic practices, perhaps we can trace the play of our differences without reifying either them or ourselves. Erotic choice is, as Robert Stoller remarks, 'a matter of opinions, taste, aesthetics'; it is also a matter of political theater, in which we all, even now, play a part.[40]

Notes

1 Stephen Orgel, 'Nobody's perfect: or why did the English stage take boys for women?', *South Atlantic Quarterly*, 88: 1 (1989), pp. 7–8.

2 Stephen Gosson, in *The Schoole of Abuse* (1579; London: The Shakespeare Society, 1841) makes no explicit mention of homoeroticism but initiates the gendered and erotic focus of the anti-theatrical attack by mentioning the theater's 'effeminate gesture, to ravish the sense; and wanton speache, to whet desire to inordinate lust'. The next year, an anonymous pamphleteer (probably Anthony Mundy) argued that the taking of women's parts by men was explicitly forbidden by the Law of God, referring to Deuteronomy 23.5. Due to the strength of this biblical authority, denunciation of theatrical cross-dressing became a most effective argument against the stage. In *Playes Confuted in Five Actions* (*Markets of Bawdrie: The Dramatic Criticism of Stephen Gosson*, ed. Arthur Kinney, Salzburg Studies in Literature 4, Salzburg: Institut für Englische Sprache und Literatur, 1974), Gosson takes up the Deuteronomic code and rails against men adopting 'not the apparell onely, but the gate, the gestures, the voyce, the passions of a woman'. In *The Overthrow of Stage Playes*, John Rainoldes writes: 'A woman's garment beeing put on a man doeth vehemently touch and moue him with the remembrance and imagination of a woman; and the imagination of a thing desirable doth stir up the desire' and 'what sparkles of lust to that vice the putting of wemens attire on men may kindle in vncleane affections, as Nero shewed in Sporus, Heliogabalus in himselfe; yea certaine, who grew not to such excesse of impudencie, yet arguing the same in causing their boys to weare long heare like wemen.' With Phillip Stubbes' *The Anatomie of Abuses* (1583; Netherlands: De Capo Press, 1972), explicit anxieties about homoeroticism enter the debate: 'everyone brings another homeward of their way very friendly and in their secret conclaves they play sodomite or worse. And these be the fruites of playes and Interludes for the most part.' The debate culminates in William Prynne's *Histrio-mastix: The Player's Scourge or Actor's Tragedy* (1633; New York: Garland Publishing, 1974), which charges the theaters as being nothing but a pretext for sodomy by listing those who have historically

engaged in unnatural acts, including the Incubi, 'who clothed their Galli, Succubi, Ganymedes and Cynadi in woman's attire, whose virilities they did oft-time dissect [castrate], to make them more effeminate, transforming them as neere might be into women, both in apparell, gesture, speech, behavior . . . And more especially in long, unshorne, womanish, frizled haire and love-lockes.' For debates about street transvestism, see *Hic Mulier; Or the Man Woman* and *Haec-Vir; Or the Womanish Man* (1620) in *Half Humankind: Contexts and Texts of the Controversy about Women in England, 1540–1640*, ed. Katherine Usher Henderson and Barbara F. McManus (Chicago: University of Illinois Press, 1985), pp. 264–89.

3   Stephen Greenblatt, 'Fiction and friction', *Shakespearean Negotiations: The Circulation of Social Energy in Renaissance England* (Oxford: Clarendon Press, 1988), p. 86.

4   See Orgel, 'Nobody's perfect', pp. 22–9 and Lisa Jardine, *Still Harping on Daughters: Women and Drama in the Age of Shakespeare* (Brighton: Harvester Press, 1983), pp. 9–34.

5   C. L. Barber, *Shakespeare's Festive Comedy: A Study of Dramatic Form and its Relation to Social Custom* (New York: Princeton University Press, 1963), p. 6. Barber writes of *Twelfth Night* (and the same presumably would be true of *As You Like It*): 'The most fundamental distinction the play brings home to us is the difference between men and women . . . Just as the saturnalian reversal of social roles need not threaten the social structure, but can serve instead to consolidate it, so a temporary, playful reversal of sexual roles can renew the meaning of the normal relation' (p. 245). For early feminist analyses, see, for instance, Juliet Dusinberre, *Shakespeare and the Nature of Women* (New York: Barnes and Noble, 1975), pp. 231–71, and Robert Kimbrough, 'Androgyny seen through Shakespeare's disguise', *Shakespeare Quarterly*, 33: 1 (1982), pp. 17–33.

6   The phrase 'traffic in women' was first coined by Emma Goldman in her critique of marriage as a form of prostitution. It gained critical prominence through Gayle Rubin's, 'The traffic in women: notes on the "political economy" of sex', *Toward an Anthropology of Women*, ed. Rayna R. Reiter (New York: Monthly Review Press, 1975), pp. 157–210.

7   I have learned much in this regard from Peter Stallybrass and Allon White, who also critique the reliance on such polarizations. They demonstrate the extent to which binary classifications are always imbued with their others, and argue that the relative radicality of any transgression can only be ascertained by placing it in history. Also helpful is Jonathan Dollimore, 'Subjectivity, sexuality, and transgression: the Jacobean connection', *Renaissance Drama*, 17 (1986), pp. 53–81.

8   In addition to Jean Howard, 'Crossdressing, the theatre, and gender struggle in early modern England', *Shakespeare Quarterly*, 39: 4 (1988), Leah Marcus, 'Shakespeare's comic heroines, Elizabeth I, and the political uses of androgyny', *Women in the Middle Ages and the Renaissance: Literary and Historical Perspectives*, ed. Mary Beth Rose (Syracuse: Syracuse University Press, 1986), and Laura Levine, 'Men in women's clothing: anti-theatricality and effeminization from 1579 to 1642', *Criticism*, 28: 2 (Spring 1986), see Catherine Belsey, 'Disrupting sexual difference: meaning and gender in the comedies', *Alternative Shakespeares*,

ed. John Drakakis (London: Methuen, 1985), pp. 166–90; Phyllis Rackin, 'Androgyny, mimesis, and the marriage of the boy heroine on the English Renaissance stage', *Proceedings of the Modern Languages Association*, 102 (1987), pp. 29–41; and Karen Newman, 'Portia's ring: unruly women and structures of exchange in *The Merchant of Venice*', *Shakespeare Quarterly*, 38 (1987), pp. 19–33.

9   Orgel, 'Nobody's perfect', p. 13.

10 Eve Sedgwick, *Between Men: English Literature and Male Homosocial Desire* (New York: Columbia University Press, 1985), p. 2.

11 Antonio's marginalization parallels that of Antonio in *The Merchant of Venice*, whose bond to Bassanio is initially honored and redeemed by Portia, but later displaced by her manipulations of the ring plot which, paradoxically, foster her subordination in a patriarchal heterosexual economy.

12 Louis Adrian Montrose, '"The place of a brother" in *As You Like It*: social process and comic form', *Shakespeare Quarterly*, 32: 1 (1981), pp. 28–54.

13 Ibid., p. 51.

14 Howard, 'Crossdressing', p. 434.

15 Ibid., p. 435. Terms can be confusing here, in part due to translation. In Luce Irigaray's formulation, *la mascarade* is 'An alienated or false version of femininity arising from the woman's awareness of the man's desire for her to be his other, the masquerade permits woman to experience desire not in her own right but as the man's desire situates her.' Masquerade is the role (playing) required by 'femininity'. Thus, Rosalind's improvisation is really closer to *mimetisme* (mimicry) which, in Irigaray's terms, is 'An interim strategy for dealing with the realm of discourse (where the speaking subject is posited as masculine), in which the woman deliberately assumes the feminine style and posture assigned to her within this discourse in order to uncover the mechanisms by which it exploits her' (*This Sex Which Is Not One*, trans. Catherine Porter [Ithaca: Cornell University Press, 1985], p. 220).

16 James Saslow, *Ganymede in the Renaissance: Homosexuality in Art and Society* (New Haven, CT: Yale University Press, 1986), p. 2.

17 Orgel, 'Nobody's perfect', p. 22.

18 Barber, *Shakespeare's Festive Comedy*, p. 231. See also W. Thomas MacCary, *Friends and Lovers: The Phenomenology of Desire in Shakespearean Comedy* (New York: Columbia University Press, 1985).

19 Phyllis Rackin, in her talk 'Historical difference/sexual difference'.

20 Peter Stallybrass helped me with this formulation.

21 Laurie Osborne, 'The texts of *Twelfth Night*', *English Literary History*, 57 (1990), pp. 37–61. Osborne's excellent analysis of the manipulation of the placement of the Antonio scenes in eighteenth- and nineteenth-century performance editions suggests that the playtexts themselves indicate changing significations of homoeroticism.

22 The *Oxford English Dictionary*'s first entry for 'anxiety', as in 'The quality or state of being anxious; uneasiness or trouble of mind about some uncertain event; solicitude, concern', is 1525. The first entry for 'jealous', as in 'Vehement in feeling, as in wrath, desire, or devotion' is 1382; for 'Ardently amorous; covetous of the love

of another, fond, lustful' is 1430; and for 'Zealous or solicitous for the preservation or well-being of something possessed or esteemed; vigilant or careful in guarding; suspiciously careful or watchful' is 1387.

23   I am indebted to Peter Stallybrass for reminding me of the difference between heterosexual and homoerotic phallic imagery.

24   *Romeo and Juliet* III. i. 113–15; *Antony and Cleopatra* I. iv. 5–7; and *Coriolanus* IV. v. 111–23. I am indebted to Phyllis Rackin for reminding me of some of these instances, and her further amplification in her talk 'Historical difference/sexual difference'.

25   Randolph Trumbach's historical analysis bears this out; see 'The birth of the queen: sodomy and the emergence of gender equality in modern culture 1660–1750', *Hidden from History: Reclaiming the Gay and Lesbian Past*, ed. Martin Duberman, Martha Vicinus and George Chauncey Jr (New York: New American Library, 1989), p. 133.

26   For an analysis of triangular desire, see René Girard, *Deceit, Desire, and the Novel: Self and Other in Literary Structure*, trans. Yvonne Freccero (Baltimore, MD: Johns Hopkins University Press, 1965).

27   Howard, 'Crossdressing', p. 432.

28   *Henry IV, part 1*, I. iii. 29–69; *Hamlet*, V. ii. 82–193 and III. ii. 368–9; *King Lear*, II. iv. 271–8.

29   Trumbach, 'Birth of the queen', p. 134.

30   Joseph Pequigney, 'The two Antonios and same-sex love in *Twelfth Night* and *The Merchant of Venice*', unpublished manuscript presented to the Shakespeare Association of America, 1989, p. 11.

31   I am following David Bevington's numbering of the sonnets; he follows Thomas Thorpe, the original publisher of the sequence. In 'Making love out of nothing at all: the issue of story in Shakespeare's procreation sonnets', *Shakespeare Quarterly*, 41: 4 (Winter 1990), pp. 470–88, Robert Crosman takes up the issue of homo-eroticism from a sympathetic if rather uninformed historical perspective. Whereas Pequigney argues that the first seventeen 'procreation' sonnets record a gradual evolution of the poet's feelings for the young man, Crosman argues that Shakespeare first pretended to fall in love with his patron as a strategy of flattery, and then discovered he was no longer pretending.

32   For an explanation of the repetition compulsion, see Sigmund Freud, *Beyond the Pleasure Principle*, trans. James Strachey (New York: Norton, 1961).

33   Thomas Laqueur, *Making Sex: Body and Gender from the Greeks to Freud* (Cambridge, MA: Harvard University Press, 1990).

34   Greenblatt, 'Fiction and friction', p. 89.

35   James Saslow makes a similar point about Michelangelo's status as a transitional figure; see 'Homosexuality in the Renaissance: behaviour, identity, and artistic expression', in *Hidden from History*, ed. Duberman et al., pp. 90–105.

36   See, for instance, Laura Mulvey, 'Visual pleasure and narrative cinema', and 'After-thoughts on "Visual pleasure and narrative cinema" inspired by *Duel in the Sun*', *Feminism and Film Theory*, ed. Constance Penley (London: Routledge, 1988), pp. 57–79; Janet Bergstrom and Mary Ann Doane, 'The female spectator: contexts

and directions', *Camera Obscura: A Journal of Feminism and Film Theory* 20/21 (May/Sept. 1989), pp. 5–27; and Irigaray, *This Sex Which Is Not One*, pp. 23–33.

37 Jean Howard alerted me to the fact that class differences are implicated in these erotic differences: as nostalgic pastoral, *As You Like It*'s class hierarchy is diffused and inclusive; *Twelfth Night*, on the other hand, is thoroughly aristocratic and, with the exception of Maria, marginalizes those figures below the rank of 'gentleman'.

38 Sedgwick, *Between Men*, p. 216.

39 Rackin has initiated such a comparative analysis of transvestism in 'Androgyny, mimesis, and the marriage of the boy heroine on the English Renaissance stage'.

40 Robert Stoller, *Observing the Erotic Imagination* (New Haven, CT: Yale University Press, 1985), p. 15.

5

History and Politics

Walter Cohen's essay on 'Political Criticism of Shakespeare' (1987) discusses the politicization of literary studies in North America during the 1980s. Cohen usefully identifies 'two main strategies in British Marxist studies of Shakespeare: a revisionist historical analysis of the plays in their own time and a radical account of their ideological function in the present' (Cohen, 1987: 27). It is a distinction which animates the broad topic of 'history and politics' in Shakespeare criticism: whose history and whose politics? In 1952, R. W. Babcock could write that 'probably the most important type of modern criticism is historical criticism' (Babcock, 1952: 6): 'Basically, historical criticism enhances the aesthetic value of a piece of early literary art by increasing its intellectual appeal' (1952: 8). Forty years later, Lisa Jardine argued for the importance of *Reading Shakespeare Historically* (1996) as a way of gaining 'a fresh understanding of the rootedness of our present uncertainties, derived by some kind of engaging dialogue with the textual residue of history' (Jardine, 1996: 1). For Babcock, historical criticism of Shakespeare is about the past; for Jardine, it is about the present, and this dual focus can be seen through the historical and political approaches to Shakespeare in the twentieth century. As Peter Brook puts it in his introduction to Polish theatre director Jan Kott's *Shakespeare, our Contemporary*, 'Shakespeare is a contemporary of Kott, Kott is a contemporary of Shakespeare' (Kott, 1967: x).

Kott's own view of the comedies was pessimistic. His chapter on *As You Like It*, entitled 'Shakespeare's Bitter Arcadia', stresses cruelty and the effects of time; in *The Tempest* he saw a 'precarious optimism' as Shakespeare revisited the feudal political contexts of the history plays, where, on the island 'the history of the world has been performed . . . One cannot escape history . . . one has to start again from the beginning; from the very beginning. Prospero agrees to return to Milan' (Kott, 1967: 267–8). Many critics have worked by historicizing Shakespeare's plays in more detail. Blair Worden's essay

'Shakespeare and Politics', in a volume of *Shakespeare Survey* devoted to the theme, argues that if Shakespeare's plays reveal little about their author, 'they leave little doubt about when they were written' (Worden, 1990: 9). The 'new historicism' associated with Stephen Greenblatt is discussed in Dutton and Wilson (1992) and in Veeser (1989, 1994). Greenblatt's own discussion of Shakespeare can be found in his *Renaissance Self-fashioning* (1980) and *Shakespearean Negotiations* (1988), where he argues for a 'study of the collective making of distinct cultural practices and inquiry into the relations among these practices – a poetics of culture' (Greenblatt, 1988: 5). Exemplary of this approach is Louis Montrose's much-anthologized essay '"Shaping Fantasies": Figurations of Gender and Power in Elizabethan Culture', first published in 1983. Montrose's argument incorporates *A Midsummer Night's Dream*, Elizabethan court politics, and a dream described by the magus Simon Forman. He proposes that the play 'meta-dramatizes the relations of power between prince and playwright', translating the 'Cult of Elizabeth' as it creates and is created by cultural fictions or fantasies. Montrose develops this piece into a book-length study, *The Purpose of Playing* (1996); his article on *Love's Labour's Lost* is collected in Waller's anthology, *Shakespeare's Comedies* (1991); and his article on *As You Like It* appears in *Shakespeare Quarterly* (Montrose, 1981).

Other detailed historicist accounts include *Will Power: Essays on Shakespearean Authority* (1993), in which Richard Wilson develops a number of detailed and compelling readings of comedies. Wilson discusses *As You Like It* as a counterpart to enclosure riots in 1596, refocusing the play around the disinherited Orlando, the outlaw court in Arden and the mythic subtext of Robin Hood. His Foucauldian reading of *Measure for Measure* as a parable of coercive power with its analogues in the Tudor Bridewell prison, and the analysis of spectacles of judicial power in Shakespearian comedy from *The Comedy of Errors* to *The Merchant of Venice*, offer politicized accounts of the plays. A further chapter discusses 'Licensing Maternity in Shakespeare's Late Plays': it interweaves the romances' repeated concern with female bodies and childbirth with contemporary medical texts and the case of John Hall, Shakespeare's physician son-in-law. Leah Marcus's historicist project of 'localization' – reading Shakespeare's plays within an immediate nexus of topical meanings – is applied to *Measure for Measure* in her *Puzzling Shakespeare: Local Reading and its Discontents* (1988). Exploring ambivalent parallels between the Duke and James I, Marcus finds new ways to conceptualize the old sense of the play as a problem: rather than the problem of biography or of temper seen by previous commentators, for Marcus this is the problem of the topical, of a playworld at once Vienna and London. Annabel Patterson's *Shakespeare and the Popular Voice* (1989) also tries to recover Shakespeare's intersections with contemporary social and political events. Her chapter on *A Midsummer Night's Dream* is reprinted below.

Leonard Tennenhouse's *Power on Display: The Politics of Shakespeare's Genres* (1986) argues against the assumption that 'simply because [comedy] is about love and courtship, it cannot by definition be political' (1986: 3). His discussion of literary and non-literary texts 'both as agents and as documents of history' (1986: 15) marks out thoroughly new historicist territory, and in the chapter on Elizabethan comedy, Tennenhouse politicizes romantic comedy in the light of the queen's flirtations with marriage, and of courtly fictions such as Sir Philip Sidney's *Arcadia*. This politicized 'cultural logic' of Shakespearian comedy is observed when the conquest of France in *Henry V* is represented through Henry's comic wooing of the French princess Katherine (Tennenhouse, 1986: 69). Tennenhouse uses the theory of carnival and social unruliness as a figure for Shakespearian comedy, which contains its own staged disruptions through generic and social closure. The particularly Elizabethan interest in lineage and descent which is dramatized in the romantic comedies has a Jacobean twist in the late plays, in which the tropes of romance allow Shakespeare 'to revise certain aspects of aristocratic power' (1986: 179) while mythologizing the Stuart royal family. By contrast to Tennenhouse's hegemonic view, Michael Bristol (1985) politicizes the concept of carnival and its transgressive qualities in relation to the comedies, and Kiernan Ryan (1989) suggests that the comedies script their own alternative visions and modes of social organization. Constance Jordan's *Shakespeare's Monarchies: Ruler and Subject in the Romances* (1997) and David M. Bergeron's *Shakespeare's Romances and the Royal Family* (1985) both develop readings of the late plays in the light of contemporary monarchical politics, building on Frances Yates's work in her *Shakespeare's Last Plays: A New Approach* (1975).

Jean Howard begins in her *The Stage and Social Struggle in Early Modern England* (1994) with 'a brief for political criticism' which uncovers 'the ideological work performed' (1994: 3) by the discourses of anti-theatricality in the period. She connects moments of theatrical self-consciousness or reflexivity with an ambivalence towards dramatic illusion, including a discussion of *Much Ado About Nothing* alongside accounts of other plays and texts. Jardine's *Still Harping on Daughters* (1983) also draws on anti-theatrical rhetoric to contextualize issues of gender and sexuality in the drama. Jonathan Hall's *Anxious Pleasures: Shakespearean Comedy and the Nation-state* (1995) suggests that the simultaneous 'decentering and the fantasized restoration' of a ruler in the comedies both 'collude precariously in the subjectivity required by the formation of the nation-state from its earliest mercantilist beginnings' (1995: 257). Hall concludes that 'Shakespearean comedy has more in common with postmodern critical awareness of the power of the sign and the problematic nature of identity than with even the comic writing of the intervening epochs of absolutist and bourgeois hegemony' (1995: 268).

Hall's movement, like that of Kott – from the sixteenth to the twentieth century – is indicative of a range of politicized interpretations of Shakespeare. Terry Eagleton's conclusion to his 1986 book, *William Shakespeare*, delights in breaking the 'bad news' to Shakespeare: the fallibility of a liberal belief in 'a way of harnessing what is most productive about bourgeois transgression to the old polity, grafting upon that settled structure fertile strains of dynamic energy and individual self-development' (Eagleton, 1986: 99). He admits, though, that Shakespeare 'may well have suspected as much himself', as a man who seems, ironically, to have been 'almost certainly familiar with the writings of Hegel, Marx, Nietzsche, Freud, Wittgenstein and Derrida' (1986: ix–x). In their introduction to the volume *Political Shakespeare*, Jonathan Dollimore and Alan Sinfield claim cultural materialism's particular attentiveness to the political and ideological significance of all cultural productions. Rather than trying to mystify this critical dimension, 'it registers its commitment to the transformation of a social order which exploits people on the grounds of race, gender and class' (Dollimore and Sinfield, 1985: viii). Jonathan Dollimore's essay on *Measure for Measure* discusses surveillance and repression in the play; in an afterword published in the second edition of *Political Shakespeare* (1994), Dollimore considers the impact of gay criticism on political readings of the play. Other historicized and Foucauldian readings of the play are represented in Nigel Wood's guide (Wood and Corbin, 1995) and in Kathleen McLuskie's article in *Political Shakespeare*. The volume also includes Paul Brown's essay on *The Tempest* and colonialism: themes developed by Alden Vaughan (1988) and Jerry Brotton (in Loomba and Orkin, 1998). Readings of *The Merchant of Venice* which consider its racial politics include Gross's history of the character of Shylock (*Shylock: Four Hundred Years in the Life of a Legend*, 1992), Shapiro's careful contextual discussion of the play's historical context and the uses to which it has been put (in *Shakespeare and the Jews*, 1996), and Kim Hall's essay reprinted below. For other politicized approaches, see also chapter 4 on 'Gender and Sexuality' and chapter 6 on 'Performance'.

The debates about these kinds of historicist readings were the subject of an issue of the journal *New Literary History* in 1990. Richard Levin's 'Unthinkable Thoughts in the New Historicizing of English Renaissance Drama' develops some of the contentions of his *New Readings vs. Old Plays* (1979). His article indicts new historicist shibboleths about self-conscious theatre, about the constructedness of gender, about changing concepts of selfhood and subjectivity: 'they homogenize Renaissance thought' (Levin, 1990: 437). He also goes on to counter the claims with opposing evidence. A number of scholars replied in the journal. Catherine Belsey's 'Richard Levin and In-different Reading' defends a criticism which 'deliberately seeks out the moments of difference within the text, looks out for the formal breaks and disruptions which draw attention to discontinuities of meaning' (Belsey, 1990: 455). Jonathan

Dollimore's contribution, 'Shakespeare, Cultural Materialism, Feminism and Marxist Humanism' stresses the specificity of materialist criticism through a critique of writing by Lynda E. Boose (1987), Carol Thomas Neely (1989) and Kiernan Ryan (1989). Another collection of essays, Ivo Kamps's *Shakespeare Left and Right* (1991), includes contributions by Levin and his critics, including Gayle Greene and Michael Bristol, and again makes explicit the ground of the debate about political or ideological approaches to Shakespeare. Graham Bradshaw's *Misrepresentations: Shakespeare and the Materialists* (1993) takes sustained issue with new historicism in a critical debate with Greenblatt (1980, 1988), Evans (1986), Hawkes (1986) and Sinfield (1992), among others. Bradshaw accuses his critical adversaries of a 'failure to engage seriously with Shakespeare's irreducibly complex designs' and consequently the failure 'to engage seriously with their professed belief . . . that values are culturally and historically specific' (Bradshaw, 1993: 18). He cites as fallacious the 'new historicist E-effect, or estrangement effect': 'whatever separates "us" from Shakespeare and the Renaissance is more important than what joins us, so that anybody who thinks Shakespeare is our contemporary is showing how little he or she understands' (1993: 28–9). 'As for the argument that there is no Shakespeare, only "Shakespeares", this book presents a lengthy reply', Bradshaw proposes. 'A short answer would be that "Shakespeares" is interesting but Shakespeare are better' (1993: 33).

References and Further Reading

Babcock, R. W. (1952) 'Historical criticism of Shakespeare', *Modern Language Quarterly*, 13: 6–20.

Belsey, Catherine (1990) 'Richard Levin and in-different reading', *New Literary History*, 21: 449–56.

Bergeron, David Moore (1985) *Shakespeare's Romances and the Royal Family*. Lawrence, KS: University Press of Kansas.

Boose, Lynda E. (1987) 'The family in Shakespeare studies; or – studies in the family of Shakespeareans; or – the politics of politics', *Renaissance Quarterly*, 40: 707–42.

Bradshaw, Graham (1993) *Misrepresentations: Shakespeare and the Materialists*. Ithaca, NY: Cornell University Press.

Bristol, Michael D. (1985) *Carnival and Theater: Plebeian Culture and the Structure of Authority in Renaissance England*. London: Methuen.

Cohen, Walter (1987) 'Political criticism of Shakespeare', in Jean E. Howard and Marion F. O'Connor (eds), *Shakespeare Reproduced: The Text in History and Ideology*. London: Methuen.

Dollimore, Jonathan (1990) 'Shakespeare, cultural materialism, feminism and Marxist humanism', *New Literary History*, 21: 471–93.

——and Sinfield, Alan (eds) (1985) *Political Shakespeare: New Essays in Cultural Materialism*. Manchester: Manchester University Press.

—— and ——(eds) (1994) *Political Shakespeare: Essays in Cultural Materialism*, 2nd edn. Manchester: Manchester University Press.

Dutton, Richard and Wilson, Richard (1992) *New Historicism and Renaissance Drama*. Longman Critical Readers. London: Longman.

Eagleton, Terry (1986) *William Shakespeare*. Oxford: Blackwell.

Evans, Malcolm (1986) *Signifying Nothing: Truth's True Contents in Shakespeare's Text*. Brighton: Harvester Press.

Greenblatt, Stephen (1980) *Renaissance Self-fashioning: From More to Shakespeare*. Chicago: University of Chicago Press.

——(1988) *Shakespearean Negotiations: The Circulation of Social Energy in Renaissance England*. Berkeley, CA: University of California Press.

Gross, John (1992) *Shylock: Four Hundred Years in the Life of a Legend*. London: Chatto and Windus.

Hall, Jonathan (1995) *Anxious Pleasures: Shakespearean Comedy and the Nation-state*. Madison: Fairleigh Dickinson University Press.

Hawkes, Terence (1986) *That Shakespearian Rag: Essays on a Critical Process*. London: Methuen.

Howard, Jean E. (1994) *The Stage and Social Struggle in Early Modern England*. London: Routledge.

—— and O'Connor, Marion F. (eds) (1987) *Shakespeare Reproduced: The Text in History and Ideology*. London: Methuen.

Jardine, Lisa (1996) *Reading Shakespeare Historically*. London: Routledge.

——(1983) *Still Harping on Daughters: Women and Drama in the Age of Shakespeare*. Brighton: Harvester.

Jordan, Constance (1997) *Shakespeare's Monarchies: Ruler and Subject in the Romances*. Ithaca, NY: Cornell University Press.

Kamps, Ivo (ed.) (1991) *Shakespeare Left and Right*. London: Routledge.

Kott, Jan (1967) *Shakespeare, our Contemporary*, 2nd edn. London: Routledge.

Levin, Richard L. (1979) *New Readings vs. Old Plays: Recent Trends in the Reinterpretation of English Renaissance Drama*. Chicago: University of Chicago Press.

——(1990) 'Unthinkable thoughts in the new historicizing of English Renaissance drama', *New Literary History*, 21: 433–47.

Loomba, Ania and Orkin, Martin (1998) *Post-colonial Shakespeares: New Accents*. London: Routledge.

Marcus, Leah S. (1988) *Puzzling Shakespeare: Local Reading and its Discontents*. Berkeley, CA: University of California Press.

Montrose, Louis Adrian (1981) '"The place of a brother" in *As You Like It*: social process and comic form', *Shakespeare Quarterly*, 32: 28–54.

——(1983) '"Shaping fantasies": figurations of gender and power in Elizabethan culture', *Representations*, 1: 61–94.

——(1996) *The Purpose of Playing: Shakespeare and the Cultural Politics of the Elizabethan Theatre*. Chicago: University of Chicago Press.

Neely, Carol Thomas (1989) 'Constructing the subject: feminist practice and the new Renaissance discourses', *English Literary Renaissance*, 18: 5–18.

Patterson, Annabel M. (1989) *Shakespeare and the Popular Voice*. Oxford: Blackwell.

Ryan, Kiernan (1989) *Shakespeare*. London: Harvester Wheatsheaf.

Shapiro, James (1996) *Shakespeare and the Jews.* New York: Columbia University Press.

Sinfield, Alan (1992) *Faultlines: Cultural Materialism and the Politics of Dissident Reading.* Oxford: Clarendon Press.

Tennenhouse, Leonard (1986) *Power on Display: The Politics of Shakespeare's Genres.* London: Methuen.

Vaughan, Alden T. (1988) 'Shakespeare's Indian: the Americanization of Caliban', *Shakespeare Quarterly*, 39: 137–53.

Veeser, H. Aram (1989) *The New Historicism.* New York: Routledge.

——(1994) *The New Historicism Reader.* New York: Routledge.

Waller, Gary F. (ed.) (1991) *Shakespeare's Comedies.* Longman Critical Readers. London: Longman.

Wilson, Richard (1993) *Will Power: Essays on Shakespearean Authority.* London: Harvester Wheatsheaf.

Wood, Nigel and Corbin, Peter (1995) *Measure for Measure.* Theory in Practice Series. Buckingham: Open University Press.

Worden, Blair (1990) 'Shakespeare and politics', *Shakespeare Survey*, 44: 1–15.

Yates, Frances Amelia (1975) *Shakespeare's Last Plays: A New Approach.* London: Routledge and Kegan Paul.

Guess Who's Coming to Dinner?

Kim F. Hall

Kim Hall's article uses the lens of post-colonial theory, together with contextual information about travel and colonization in the Renaissance, to re-examine the question of cultural difference at the heart of The Merchant of Venice. *She brings up the case of the 'Moor', impregnated by Launcelot Gobbo (Act III, scene 5) but never otherwise mentioned in the play, as a symbol for the play's repeated fictions of racial differentiation and intermingling. The theme of miscegenation is closely connected to the theme of commerce, as foreign trade – intercourse – becomes sexualized. Capitalism and the pursuit of wealth are thus always and inevitably implicated with the racial and cultural 'other'. Hall's book* Things of Darkness: Economies of Race and Gender in Early Modern England *(1995) develops aspects of this approach in a broader literary context.*

Kim F. Hall, 'Guess Who's Coming to Dinner? Colonization and Miscegenation in *The Merchant of Venice*', in *Renaissance Drama*, new series, vol. 23: *Renaissance Drama in an Age of Colonization*, ed. Mary Beth Rose (Evanston, IL: Northwestern University Press, 1992), pp. 87–111. Copyright © 1992 by Northwestern University Press.

I

Samuel Purchas introduces his popular collection of travel narratives, *Purchas His Pilgrimes* (the 1625 sequel to Richard Hakluyt's *Principal Voyages*), by recounting the virtues of trade. He equates the benefits of navigation with Christian charity and leads his reader into the collection proper by envisioning a world converted to Protestantism:

> and the chiefest charitie is that which is most common; nor is there any more common then this of Navigation, where one man is not good to another man, but so many Nations as so many persons hold commerce and intercourse of amity withall . . . the West with the East, and the remotest parts of the world are joyned in one band of humanitie; and why not also of Christianitie? Sidon and Sion, Jew and Gentile, Christian and Ethnike, as in this typicall storie? that as there is one Lord, one Faith, one Baptisme, one Body, one Spirit, one Inheritance, one God and Father, so there may be thus one Church truly Catholike, One Pastor and one Sheepfold? (Purchas, 1625: 1, 56)

Charity may not begin at home, but it certainly ends up there, as the charitable cause of conversion redounds to the economic benefit of the English world. The initial ideal of 'commerce and intercourse of amity' among many types of men is replaced by a vision of global unity that denies difference just as Purchas's own language does. (The singular construction ['one Lord, one Faith'] subsumes difference when it replaces the 'and' that allows differences to exist simultaneously ['Jew and Gentile'].) English trade, rather than fostering a mixing of cultures, will eradicate religious differences, as well as cultural and gender differences, under one patriarchal God.

Purchas's glorified version of the end of English colonization similarly serves to efface the multivalent anxieties over cross-cultural interaction that permeate English fictions of international trade. In uniting economics and Christian values, Purchas highlights the fact that colonial trade involves not only economic transactions, but cultural and political exchange as well. The anthropologist Gayle Rubin notes in her influential feminist critique of Lévi-Strauss, 'Kinship and marriage are always parts of total social systems, and are always tied into economic and political arrangements' (Rubin, 1975: 207). Likewise, the exchange of goods (or even the circulation of money) across cultural borders always contains the possibility of other forms of exchange between different cultures. Associations between marriage, kinship, property, and economics become increasingly anxiety-ridden as traditional social structures (such as marriage) are extended when England develops commercial ties across the globe. Extolling the homogenizing influence of trade suggests that English trade will turn a world of difference into a world of Protestant similitude. However, it leaves unspoken the more threatening possibility – that English identity will be subsumed under foreign difference.

It is this problem of 'commerce and intercourse', of commercial interaction inevitably fostering social and sexual contact, that underlies representations of miscegenation in the early modern period.[1] In addition to addressing domestic anxieties about the proper organization of male and female (particularly about the uncontrolled desires of women), the appearance of miscegenation in plays responds to growing concerns over English national identity and culture as England develops political and economic ties with foreign (and 'racially' different) nations. This essay will draw on Purchas's dual sense of the all-encompassing nature of trade encounters and colonialism's alleged homogenizing power to suggest the significance of a brief instance of miscegenation in Shakespeare that has been insistently ignored by critics.

Although the most central – and most commented on – problem of difference and trade in *The Merchant of Venice* is between Jew and Christian, more general anxieties about the problem of difference within economic exchange are encapsulated in an instance of miscegenation never staged. In Act III, the audience witnesses a joking interchange between Shylock's servant, Launcelot, and Lorenzo and Jessica about their mixed marriage:

> *Jessica*: Nay, you need not fear us Lorenzo, Launcelot and I are out, – he tells me flatly that there's no mercy for me in heaven, because I am a Jew's daughter: and he says that you are no good member of the commonwealth, for in converting Jews to Christians, you raise the price of pork.
> *Lorenzo*: I shall answer that better to the commonwealth than you can the getting up of the negro's belly: the Moor is with child by you Launcelot!
> *Launcelot*: It is much that the Moor should be more than reason: but if she be less than an honest woman, she is indeed more than I took her for.
>
> (III. v. 28–39)

The Arden edition of *Merchant* helpfully notes that 'this passage has not been explained' and suggests, 'Perhaps it was introduced simply for the sake of the elaborate pun on Moor/more' (Shakespeare, 1959: 99, n35). Their joking conversation no doubt parodically reflects the investment of the commonwealth in sexual practices. Nonetheless, it also begs the question of the difference between Lorenzo's liaison with a Jew and Launcelot's with a Moor. The Renaissance stage abounds with jokes about bastards: if Launcelot's fault was merely the getting of another, there would be no reason to emphasize that this invisible woman is a Moor. In his *Black Face, Maligned Race*, Anthony Barthelemy notes that this exchange reflects ideas of the licentiousness of the black woman typical of the time (1987: 124).[2] However, it may be that this pregnant, unheard, unnamed, and unseen (at least by critics) black woman is a silent symbol for the economic and racial politics of *The Merchant of Venice*. She exposes an intricately wrought nexus of anxieties over gender, race, religion, and economics (fueled by the push of imperial/mercantile expansion) which surrounds the various possibilities of miscegenation raised in the play.

II

Before moving into the play itself, I would like to sketch out some of these anxieties over miscegenation by examining one of the play's possible 'sub-texts' (Jameson, 1981: 81). In 1596, despite her earlier support of English piracy in the slave trade, Queen Elizabeth expressed concern over the presence of blacks in the realm. She issued a proclamation to the Lord Mayor of London which states her 'understanding that there are of late divers blackmoores brought into this realme, of which kinde of people there are allready here to manie' (quoted in Fryer, 1984: 10) and demands that blacks recently brought to the realm be rounded up and returned. This effort was evidently not very successful, as she followed up that proclamation with another order of expulsion:

> whereas the Queen's Majesty, tendering the good and welfare of her own natural subjects greatly distressed in these hard times of dearth, is highly discontented to understand the great numbers of Negars and Blackamoors which (as she is informed) are crept into this realm since the troubles between Her Highness and the King of Spain, who are fostered and relieved here to the great annoyance of her own liege people that want the relief which those people consume; as also for that the most of them are infidels, having no understanding of Christ or his Gospel, hath given especial commandment that the said kind of people should be with all speed avoided and discharged out of this Her Majesty's dominions . . . And if there shall be any person or persons which are possessed of any such Blackamoors that refuse to deliver them in sort as aforesaid, then we require you to call them before you and to advise and persuade them by all good means to satisfy Her Majesty's pleasure therein; which if they shall eftsoons willfully and obstinately refuse, we pray you then to certify their names unto us, to the end Her Majesty may take such further course therein as it shall seem best in her princely wisdom. (quoted in Jones, 1971: 20–1)[3]

While such critical attention as has been paid to this document concentrates on the attempt to discharge Moors from the realm and uses the attempt itself to prove the existence of a viable black presence in England (Newman, 1987a: 148), the terms of the proclamation demand special attention. The image of large numbers of Moors having 'crept into this realm' suggests that they suddenly appeared of their own volition (despite having been 'fostered and relieved' here by unnamed residents).[4] The proclamation then lays the fault of this invasion at the foot of Spain, a country already suspect for its past history of interracial alliance.[5] The rest of the document is concerned to prevent contact between these 'creeping' invaders and 'her own liege' people despite its contradictory contention that Elizabeth's own subjects are the ones 'possessed' of blackamoors to the detriment of the state.

Although chronic food shortages occurred throughout Elizabeth's reign and certainly seemed to be a goad to plantation and exploration, her naming of 'these hard times of dearth' suggests that both of the expulsions occurred in the context of very immediate state concerns. England from 1594 to 1597 saw dramatic declines in grain harvests (the staple of the lower-class diet), culminating in the famine of 1597. Indeed, much of northern Europe (although, interestingly, not Italy) suffered from famine and starvation from 1595 to 1597. Although the famine in England hit hardest in the northwestern parishes, its effects were felt throughout the realm, as Andrew Appleby notes, 'It is abundantly clear, however, that the grain harvest was the heart of the English economy . . . and that its malfunctions were felt, with disastrous results, throughout the kingdom' (1978: 137). Private citizens, the Privy Council, and the general public showed concern over the unavailability of bread even in the earliest of those years. These 'dear years' carried with them a range of other social dislocations: a reduction in baptismal and marriage rates, a rise in mortality and civil unrest, and, significantly, the unemployment of servant classes. Key government measures were issued in proximity to both expulsions and indicate that the famine generated a degree of class conflict. Elizabeth's order to make starch from bran rather than grain needed for food was issued in the same month as the first order of expulsion. Another proclamation, ending price-fixing and compelling the landed classes to remain in the counties because 'her majesty had thus determined for relief of her people to stay all good householders in their countries, there in charitable sort to keep hospitality' (Hughes and Larkin, 1969: 172), was issued a few months later.

Equally important in the expulsion order is the reference to the religion (or lack of religion) of the Moors, which is based on the supposition that they are a logical group to cut off from state resources because they have 'no understanding of Christ or his Gospel'. In this time of crisis Christianity becomes the prerequisite for access to limited resources. Certainly, Elizabeth's evocation of the religious difference of the Moor would seem to support the common view that religion, not race, is the defining mark of difference in early modern England.[6] I would argue, however, that even though religion is given as a compelling reason for excluding Moors, emphasizing religious difference only clouds the political reality that the Moors' visibility in the culture made them a viable target for exclusion. In other words, it is their physical difference *in association with cultural differences* (a combination that is the primary basis for the category 'race') that provokes their exclusion – not just their religion.

In Elizabeth's proclamation we see what may be a source of the threat posed by Launcelot's Moor. In times of economics stress, visible minorities very often become the scapegoat for national problems. The proclamation shares with

Merchant an alarm over unregulated consumption. Launcelot's evocation of the scarcity of food through his jesting over the rising price of pork reveals a similar unease over limited resources. Thus, famine, one of the more specific rationales for English colonial plantation and expansion, becomes here associated with the black woman. Ultimately both texts draw on and reproduce the same racial stereotype. Just as the image of the black female as consumer of state resources in the twentieth-century United States is statistically inaccurate but politically powerful, so may the black presence have been a threat (albeit small) to white European labor, which is magnified by its very visibility.[7] This sense of privation produces an economic imperative in the play, which insists on the exclusion of racial, religious, and cultural difference. With the finite resources of a Venetian (or Elizabethan) society reserved for the wealthy elite, the offspring of Launcelot and the Moor presents a triple threat that in this world is perceived as a crime against the state. Their alliance is perhaps even more suspect than the ominous possibility of a marriage between Portia and the prince of Morocco, since it would produce a half-black, half-Christian child from the already starving lower classes who threatens to upset the desired balance of consumption. The pun on 'Moor/more' further supports the image of the black woman as both consuming and expanding and is particularly striking in a play where the central image is the literal taking of flesh and where Christian males worry throughout about having 'less'.

The acute sense of privation amid plenty is signaled through *Merchant*'s ubiquitous images of starvation that are interwoven with the incessant eating in the play. Walter Cohen sees Launcelot as integral to the play and notes in particular the way he 'systematically and wittily misconstrues Lorenzo's apparently straightforward order that the kitchen staff "prepare for dinner!"' (1985: 210). Launcelot's first move is to remind Lorenzo of the servants' hunger: 'they all have stomachs' (III. v. 44). Earlier, he claims that he is starving in Shylock's employ: 'I am famish'd in his service. You may tell every finger I have with my ribs' (II. ii. 101–3). Shylock's version, 'The patch is kind enough, but a huge feeder' (II. v. 45), may reinforce the idea that these outsiders literally starve rightful citizens, yet it also suggests a Christian appetite out of control. Bassanio, describing his poor finances, suggests bulk without sustenance in saying that he lost wealth, 'By something showing a more swelling port / Than my faint means would grant continuance' (I. i. 124–5). Finally, Antonio, in reminding Solanio of Venice's strict commercial laws, laments, 'These griefs and losses have so bated me / That I shall hardly spare a pound of flesh / Tomorrow, to my bloody creditor' (III. iii. 32–4).

The associations with eating and starvation link outsiders, particularly Shylock, with one of the most compelling tropes of colonialist discourse: the cannibal.[8] Cannibalism was a source of as much anxiety as fascination for the traveler; it seemed to be one of the final lines drawn between the savage Other and the civilized self (Hulme, 1986: 81–3; Kilgour, 1990: 5–7; Cheyfitz, 1991:

42). The reasons given for imperial plunder by Bertoldo in Philip Massinger's *The Maid of Honour* suggest that much of this obsession springs from a sense that the dividing line is not as clear as one might like:

> Nature did
> Designe us to be warriours, and to breake through
> Our ring the sea, by which we are invirond;
> And we by force must fetch in what is wanting,
> Or precious to us. Adde to this, wee are
> A populous nation, and increase so fast,
> That if we by our providence, are not sent
> Abroad in colonies, or fall by the sword,
> Not *Sicilie* (though now, it were more fruitfull,
> Then when 'twas stil'd the granary of great *Rome*)
> Can yeeld our numerous frie bread, we must starve,
> Or eat up one another.
>
> (I. i. 202–13)

In specifically ascribing to the English an aggression and ferocity that are the essence of European definitions of the cannibal (Hulme, 1986: 83), Bertoldo hints at the tentativeness of that division. The movement of the passage also suggests a blurring of boundaries: the opening image of the breach of England's geographic insularity which releases the energies of a warlike nation rapidly moves into an evocation of violent, desperate want which could easily turn in upon itself. Massinger skates a fine line between identity and difference in allowing his character to suggest that imperial expansion is the only thing separating the civilized Englishman from the cannibal and that the dangers of cannibalism lie on either side of England's borders. His metaphor is similar to an earlier and more specific reference to English want in Richard Hakluyt's *Discourse of Western Planting*. In this attempt to persuade Elizabeth to adopt a plantation policy, Hakluyt associates cannibalism with another marginalized group – the unemployed. He warns Elizabeth:

> But wee for all the Statutes that hitherto can be devised, and the sharpe execution of the same in poonishinge idle and lazye persons for wante of sufficient occasion of honest employmente cannot deliver our common wealthe from multitudes of loyterers and idle vagabondes ... [W]e are growen more populous than ever heretofore: So that nowe there are of every arte and science so many, that they can hardly lyve one by another, nay rather they are readie to eate upp one another. (Hakluyt, 1935: 234)

The troping of cannibalism links actual shortages of food with the need to promote colonial trade in a way that also provides a compelling metaphor for the loss of communal identity in such trade. The desire to make contact with and to exploit Others always carries with it the possibility of engulfment. Such fears of erasure are embedded in metaphors of eating, but the figure of the cannibal specifically locates such fears within a framework of colonial trade and religious difference.

The language of eating in *The Merchant of Venice* situates Shylock within this framework by merging images of cannibalism with older accusations of blood libel. He claims, 'But yet I'll go in hate, to feed upon / The prodigal Christian', and Gratiano describes him, 'thy currish spirit / Govern'd a wolf, who hang'd for human slaughter –' (IV. i. 133–5).[9] According to Maggie Kilgour, feeding from (or eating with) the Other is a perilous involvement which carries the risk of being eaten by the Other:[10]

> To eat in a country is potentially to be eaten by it, to enter into a false identification by being absorbed by a foreign culture – what we call 'going native' – and so be prevented from returning to a place of origin in which one is truly at home. The opposite of returning to one's own hearth is ultimately to be subsumed totally by a hostile host. (Kilgour, 1990: 23)

Shylock's reluctance to eat with the Christians displays the fear of 'be[ing] subsumed . . . by a hostile host', but in terms that ratify the reciprocal Christian fear of being consumed by a guest/alien who has been allowed into the home/country. Economic exchanges with an outsider like Shylock open up Venice to sexual and commercial intercourse with strangers; this breach brings with it the threat of economic upheaval and foreign invasion. Social activities such as eating and marriage resonate because of the already permeable borders of the Venetian economy. In defending his insistence on the completion of a legal bond, Shylock comments on the assumed rights of the Venetians to 'bond' and to preserve their racial purity in a speech laden with references to problematic communal activities:

> You have among you many a purchas'd slave,
> Which (like your asses, and your dogs and mules)
> You use in abject and in slavish parts,
> Because you bought them, – shall I say to you,
> Let them be free, *marry them to your heirs?*
> Why sweat they under burthens? let their beds
> Be made as soft as yours, and let their palates
> Be season'd with such viands?
> (IV. i. 90–7; emphasis added)

Rhetorically, Shylock exposes the fears of a chauvinist culture by revealing the Venetians' problematic economic position, suggesting that, in such an open system, the slaves among them may just as well become sons-in-law.[11] The passage may also tie the problem of eating with colonial trade in the reminder ('let their palates / Be season'd with such viands') that the search for spices for aristocratic palates provided much of the momentum for foreign trade. His questions allow for a provocative glance at Queen Elizabeth's dilemma. Producers of labor are also consumers, and the blacks that she wants to exile are a presence precisely because of the increased economic expansion she supported.

As critics have often noted, the language of commerce and trade permeates the Venetian world. This mercantile vocabulary is tied to an erotic vocabulary in much the same way as Titania's description of her Indian votress in *A Midsummer Night's Dream* links the pregnant maid and Indian trade. Like his companion, Bassanio, Antonio begins the play in a melancholy mood; Solanio attributes his sadness not to love, but to the possibility of economic disaster: 'Believe me sir, had I such a venture forth, / The better part of my affections would / Be with my hopes abroad' (I. i. 15–17). Echoing the eroticized discourse of actual merchant adventure, Solanio's discussion of Antonio's afflictions as 'affections' locates the erotic in the economic, particularly as he makes Antonio's fear of losing his ships sound much like the fear of losing a lover:[12]

> should I go to church
> And see the holy edifice of stone
> And not bethink me straight of dangerous rocks,
> Which touching my gentle vessel's side
> Would scatter all her spices on the stream,
> Enrobe the roaring waters with my silks . . .
>
> (I. i. 29–34)

Solanio's displacement is all the more resonant in its religious overtones and its hints at a loss of Christian belief. Foreign adventure proves a dangerous distraction as the stones of the Christian church provoke reminders of the beguiling hazards of trade.

The potential dangers of Antonio's mercantile involvement with foreign Others, read as seductive sexual union, are offset by the rejection of difference in the golden world of Belmont. Bassanio's discussion of his intent to woo Portia suggests an interesting inversion of Antonio's economic adventures. The narrative of his romantic quest is filled with economic metaphors, and his description of Portia makes it obvious that there is an unfavorable balance of trade on the marriage market. Rather than bringing wealth into the country, suitors are coming to Belmont to win away Portia's wealth, as Bassanio notes:

> Nor is the wide world ignorant of her worth,
> For the four winds blow in from every coast

> Renowned suitors, and her sunny locks
> Hang on her temples like a golden fleece,
> Which makes her seat of Belmont Colchos' strond,
> And many Jasons come in quest of her.
> (I. i. 167–72)

While Antonio participates in the expansion of Venice's economic influence, Bassanio insulates the sexual economy of Venice from foreign 'invasion'. In language closely approximating Bassanio's, his competitor, the prince of Morocco, 'a tawny moor' (and, we presume, a Muslim), frames his own courtship as colonial enterprise and religious pilgrimage when he chooses caskets:

> Why that's the lady, all the world desires her.
> From the four corners of the earth they come
> To kiss this shrine, this mortal breathing saint.
> The Hyrcanian deserts, and the vasty wilds
> Of wide Arabia are as throughfares now
> For princes to come view fair Portia.
> The watery kingdom, whose ambitious head
> Spits in the face of heaven, is no bar
> To stop the foreign spirits, but they come
> As o'er a brook to see fair Portia.
> (II. vii. 38–47)

Morocco reveals the peril of such international competition for wealth (and beauty). The test demanded by Portia's father expands the sex/gender system by opening up the romantic quest to foreign competition, as it were, inviting both the possibility of miscegenation and of another race absconding with the country's money and its native beauty. Morocco explicitly raises this idea and associates it with England:

> They have in England
> A coin that bears the figure of an angel
> Stamp'd in gold, but that's insculp'd upon:
> But here an angel in a golden bed
> Lies all within.
> (II. vii. 55–9)

At the very moment in which he loses the game by making the wrong choice, Morocco raises the specter of a monetary and sexual exchange in England with the image of Portia as an angel in a golden bed. Although the metaphor would seem to deny the comparison ('but that's insculp'd upon: / But here . . .'), Portia is imaged here as the literalized coin of the realm. She, as object of an expanded sex/gender system, can like a coin be circulated among strangers.

The boundaries of Portia's island are hardly impregnable: the surrounding water 'is no bar' and no more than a 'brook' to outsiders; Portia herself is the open 'portal' to Venetian wealth. The sexual and the monetary anxieties of a Venetian state that is open to alien trade are displayed and dispelled in the casket plot, which allows Portia to avoid the threat of contact with others. The prince of Morocco is thus able to attempt to woo but ultimately to lose her. He also loses his right to reproduce his own bloodline, a right not explicitly denied the other suitors (Shell, 1979: 72). The momentary threat posed by the prince's wooing is dispelled, as is the larger cultural threat posed by the sexuality of the black male. The denial of his fertility should perhaps be looked at in juxtaposition with the fertility of Launcelot's Moor: the prince's sexuality denied, Launcelot then has license to replace him as the Moor's 'cultural partner' and to appropriate her body.

The Morocco scene is only the most obvious example of the exclusionary values of Belmont. Portia derides all other suitors for their national shortcomings, reserving her praise for her countryman, Bassanio (a man who at first glance seems to have little to recommend him). Interestingly, the joking about the effects of intermarriage is preceded by the prince of Morocco's attempt to win Portia and Portia's deliverance as he chooses the wrong casket. Portia's response to her narrow escape, 'A gentle riddance, – draw the curtains, go, – / Let all of his complexion choose me so' (II. vii. 78–9), is typical of the generally negative attitudes toward blacks prevalent at the time, but, in true Belmont fashion, in no way reveals the political and economic implications of her aversion.[13]

The economic issues which underlie the romantic world of Belmont rise to the surface in Venice, where there appears to be a real cash-flow problem. Most of the Christian men, it seems, are on the verge of bankruptcy. Bassanio reveals his monetary woes in the opening of the play, ''Tis not unknown to you Antonio / How much I have disabled mine estate' (I. i. 122–3). Despite Antonio's denial, his funds are stretched and the possibility of his financial ruin is evoked from the very beginning. Tellingly, Antonio has no hope for a legal remedy from his bargain because strangers in Venice have certain economic privileges:

> The duke cannot deny the course of law:
> For the commodity that strangers have
> With us in Venice, if it be denied,
> Will much impeach the justice of the state,
> Since that the trade and profit of the city
> Consisteth of all nations.
>
> (III. iii. 26–31)

In Antonio's case, the very openness of Venetian trade has negative effects for the city's males. The protection Venetian law should afford its 'own natural subjects' is weakened by the economic imperatives of mercantile trade.

In contrast to the males, the women are associated with an abundance of wealth. As we have seen, Portia comes with a large fortune and Lorenzo 'steals' two thousand ducats along with a jewel-laden Jessica. The comic resolution of the play is not merely the proper pairing of male and female, but the redistribution of wealth from women and other strangers to Venice's Christian males. Portia's wealth goes to Bassanio, Antonio's is magically restored through her agency, and, most importantly, Shylock's is given over to the state through a law unearthed by Portia/Balthazar:

> It is enacted in the laws of Venice,
> If it be proved against an alien,
> That by direct, or indirect attempts
> He seek the life of any citizen,
> The party 'gainst the which he doth contrive,
> Shall seize one half his goods, the other half
> Comes to the privy coffer of the state.
> (IV. i. 344–50)

The law that allegedly gave advantage to aliens is counteracted by a law that repeals that advantage. More than providing an object lesson for Shylock, 'hitting him where it hurts', as it were, the punishment makes sure that the uneven balance of wealth in the economy is righted along racial and gender lines. Antonio's modification of the sentence only highlights this impulse, as he insists that his portion of Shylock's money be passed down 'unto the gentleman / That lately stole his daughter' (IV. i. 380–1). Lorenzo's final expression of gratitude to Portia, 'Fair ladies, you drop manna in the way / Of starved people' (V. i. 294–5), typifies the tonality of the play. Portia does indeed drop manna (which she redistributes from the city's aliens) upon the males of Venice: she is the bearer of fortunes for Bassanio, Antonio, and Lorenzo.

Economic alliances in the play are made with expectation of one-way exchange, which is often troped through conversion. Thus Bassanio and Antonio stress Shylock's 'kindness' when making the deal in order to give Shylock the illusion of a communal interest and identity rooted in Christian values. Antonio takes his leave, claiming, 'The Hebrew will turn Christian, he grows kind' (I. iii. 174), a phrase which only serves to remind Shylock and the audience that his 'kindness' is still contingent. The pun on 'kind' used throughout this scene reminds us that the courtesy and 'kindness' shown in the play's world is only extended to those who are alike and judged of human 'kin' by Christians. Shakespeare also demonstrates how selective such inclusion can be when the duke, in an attempt to make Shylock forgo his bond, invites him into the community, not by imagining a shared humanity, but by creating a cultural hierarchy which stresses Shylock's difference: 'From stubborn Turks, and Tartars never train'd / To offices of tender courtesy' (IV. i. 32–3). Such rhetorical moves only emphasize that the power of exclusion and inclusion rests with what Frank Whigham calls the 'elite circle of community strength' and that the outsider is powerless to determine his status within that group (1979: 106–7).

The imagery associated with Shylock in the play reveals an ongoing link between perceptions of the racial difference of the black, the religious difference of the Jew, and the possible ramifications of sexual and economic contact with both. We can see clearly how the discourses of Otherness coalesce in the language of the play.[14] In claiming that Chus is one of his countrymen, Shylock gives himself a dual genealogy that associates him with blackness, forbidden sexuality, and the unlawful appropriation of property.[15] Obviously, Shylock's recounting of the Jacob parable has its own cultural overtones and serves to highlight his religious difference.[16] However, his incomplete genealogy is further complicated by the fact that Jacob, the progenitor of the Jews, robbed his brother, Esau, of his birthright as eldest brother.[17] Both Jews and blacks become signs for filial disobedience and disinheritance in Renaissance culture. In the two biblical accounts of blackness, Chus (or Cush), the son of Ham, is born black as a sign of the father's sin. A popular explanation of blackness recounted by George Best in his description of the Frobisher voyages shows the problem of disinheritance:

> and [Ham] being persuaded that the first childe borne after the flood (by right and Lawe of nature) should inherite and possesse all the dominions of the earth, hee contrary to his fathers commandement [to abstain from sex] while they were yet in the Arke, used company with his wife, and craftily went about thereby to disinherite the off-spring of his other two brethren: for the which wicked and detestable fact as an example for contempt of Almightie God, and disobedience of parents, God would a sonne should be borne whose name was Chus, who not onely it selfe, but all his posteritie after him should bee so blacke and lothsome, that it might remaine a spectacle of disobedience to all the worlde. (Hakluyt, 1598–1600: 3, 52)[18]

Like Shylock's genealogy, Best's narrative gives disobedience and disinheritance a crucial role in the formation of difference. In reading Jews and blacks as signs for theft from rightful heirs, such genealogies may have supported the notion for the English reader that these 'aliens' usurp the rightful prerogatives of innocent (pre-Christian) victims. (In other words, forcible seizure of their property is excusable because their ownership is suspect.) The Ham story is a bit more problematic because Ham, the originator of the sin, was himself white. Only his offspring, Chus, bears the burden of the original sin, and the blackness thus becomes a reflection of the nether side of a white self. These biblical 'sub-texts' help support the play's central action: a circulation of wealth to an aristocratic, male elite that is predicated on the control of difference. Aliens must be either assimilated into the dominant culture (Shylock's and Jessica's conversions) and/or completely disempowered (Shylock's sentence). Their use as explanations for racial difference allows for the organization of property, kinship, and religion within an emerging national – and imperial – identity.

III

Since the Venetian sex/gender system is constructed along the axis of foreign trade, it is not surprising that female characters play key (if little noted) roles in the circulation of wealth. The successful end of courtship (endogamous marriage) is achieved through the balancing of the problems of conversion, inheritance, and difference. The proper pairing of male and female thus comes to represent the realignment of wealth and the reassertion of control over difference. In their active desire, these outspoken women are often the more conservative agents of the play. Associated with conversion, they assure that wealth is redistributed into the hands of the male elite.

Merchant offers the Jessica–Lorenzo courtship as a successful type of cross-cultural interaction: one like our original model in Purchas, where cultural difference – and property – are controlled under the aegis of a Christian God. Unlike another disobedient daughter, *Othello*'s Desdemona, Jessica's filial disloyalty is lauded by the community largely because her actions constitute submission to the larger, racially motivated values of Belmont and Venice. Ironically, her very disobedience proves her 'faith' to her husband just as it shows her 'fairness'. Lorenzo declares, 'And fair she is, if that mine eyes be true, / And true she is, as she hath prov'd herself' (II. vi. 54–5). In cutting herself off from her father, Jessica also divorces herself from her Jewish ancestry. When she leaves her father's house, Gratiano declaims, 'Now (by my hood) a gentle, and no Jew' (II. vi. 51), punningly connecting her conversion with the race and the class privileges of Belmont.

In fact, the very desire to marry a Christian separates Jessica from her father's alienness. Shylock's claim of consanguinity is resolutely denied throughout the play. Salerio declares, 'There is more difference between thy flesh and hers, than between jet and ivory, more between your bloods, than there is between red wine and Rhenish' (III. i. 34–6). The terms of Salerio's insistence on absolute difference go as far to exclude Shylock from the realm of humanity (so defined by Christian Venetians) as they do to include Jessica. Jessica herself, in a rehearsal of her own conversion, parodically stages herself as the bride of the Song of Songs, saying, 'I am glad 'tis night – you do not look on me' (II. vi. 34), and covering herself with gold, 'I will make fast the doors and gild myself / With some moe ducats' (II. vi. 49–50), as she begins the 'conversion' of money from Shylock to Lorenzo. Jessica's disobedience is acted out as a gender transgression: she escapes from her father's house dressed as a page and is playfully aware of her transgressive behavior, 'For I am much asham'd of my exchange' (II. vi. 35). Of the 'exchanges' Jessica makes (husband for father, male dress for female, Christian identity for Jewish), the change in dress is the one she marks as potentially subversive. However, Jessica's cross-dressing is seemingly less complicated than Portia's, since her transgression, taking place as it does during a carnival and facilitating her assimilation into the community of Belmont, is validated by the rest of the play.

Like Jessica's cross-dressing, which is not only excused but lauded in the play, Portia's actions work mainly to fulfill the larger economic needs of the commonwealth. Portia is the focal point of the Venetian economy and its marriage practices: it is through her that money is recirculated to the Christian males and difference is excluded or disempowered. She describes her betrothal as a conversion, 'Myself, and what is mine, to you and yours / Is now converted' (III. ii. 166–7). Bassanio's 'pilgrimage' results in the 'conversion' of Portia and her possessions as she too fills the coffers of the male Christians. As Balthazar and as Portia she performs a valuable service to the state. Her disguise allows her to become the agent of conversion and, as Frank Whigham (1979) notes, compulsory conversion is associated historically with confiscation of goods by the state. It is she (as Balthazar) who silences the alien. She is the enabling factor that 'converts' cash to its 'rightful owners', not only hers to Bassanio, but Shylock's to the state and to his Christian heirs.

With their cross-dressing and their active pursuit of female desire, both Portia and Jessica break the constraints of gender; nevertheless, in a text dense with cultural, economic, and gender conflict, glorifying these women as the transgressive disrupters of social order may serve only to obscure the very complex nature of difference for a changing society in which racial categories developed along with changing organizations of gender.[19] To look solely at hierarchies of gender defines the issue too narrowly and valorizes gender as the primary category of difference. Reading Portia as the heroic, subversive female proves particularly problematic when we place her actions in relation to other categories of difference. While her 'witty' remarks about her suitors display a verbal acumen and forwardness typical of the unruly woman, her subversiveness is severely limited, for her strongest verbal abilities are only bent toward supporting a status quo which mandates the repulsion of aliens and outsiders. To valorize such cross-dressed figures as liberating Others is to ignore the way their freedom functions to oppress the racial/cultural Others in the play. Portia's originally transgressive act is disarmed and validated by the play's resolution when these 'disorderly' women become pliable wives.

Although I have argued that these women serve in some ways as successful comic and economic agents, the play itself does not allow for the same neat elimination of difference offered by Purchas in the opening of this essay. Unlike other Shakespearean comedies, *The Merchant of Venice* ends not with a wedding or the blessing of the bridal bed, but with the exchange of rings and the evocation of adultery. The only immediately fertile couple presented in the play, Launcelot and the Moor, are excluded from the final scene. Her fecundity exists in threatening contrast to the other Venetians' seeming sterility, particularly as it is created with Launcelot Gobbo, the 'gobbling', prodigal servant whose appetites cannot be controlled. Like Shylock's absence, their exclusion qualifies the expected resolution of the text and reminds us of the ultimate failure to contain difference completely even as the play's aliens are silenced. The Moor, whose presence may be a visible sign for the conflation of economic and erotic union with the Other in the rhetoric of travel, provides a pregnant reminder of the problematic underpinnings of the Venetian economy.

In her *Literary Fat Ladies*, Patricia Parker (1987) charts the appearance of dilated female bodies in Renaissance texts. While they are specifically located within the rhetorical technique of dilation, these 'fat ladies' are figures for the delay and deferral that is a central topos of many important Renaissance subtexts such as the *Odyssey*, the *Aeneid*, and the Bible (texts that are also key in the troping of imperial desires). The chief purpose of dilation (amplification or the production of *copia*) is mired in an anxiety over uncontrolled excess; hence the texts become as preoccupied with mastery and control over expansion as with the expansion itself. Parker argues, 'Dilation, then, is always something to be kept within the horizon of ending, mastery, and control' (1987: 14). Certainly the problem of controlled expansion reverberates within colonial discourses of the Renaissance as travel writers and editors struggle to produce texts which allow expansion but always within the confines of conversion and colonial mastery. In some ways, the figure of the fat lady serves the same purpose as Purchas's introduction: the promise of profitable conversion within the space allowed by deferral of the judgment of the Second Coming.

These fat ladies resonate within a varied field of meanings associated with the judicial, the temporal, the genealogical, and the erotic. Although Parker does not specifically name Launcelot's Moor in her catalogue of fat ladies, she too operates within a similar web of meaning. She appears in the dilated space of the play that postpones both the resolution of Antonio's dilemma and the consummation of Bassanio's and Portia's betrothal. Like Parker's first example (Nell from *The Comedy of Errors*), she is a large presence that is only described.

Not permitted to speak, the Moor still encapsulates ideas of copious fertility and threatening female sexuality.[20] However, unlike the other Shakespearean fat ladies, Launcelot's Moor cannot be regarded as 'a dilative means to a patriarchal end' (Parker, 1987: 19), that is, as a momentary disruption of the text or a deferral that contains the promise of an ordered conclusion. Her pregnancy is a reminder of the dangerous result of uncontrolled crossing of borders, of trade that holds the dual (and irreconcilable) promises of the production of new wealth and of an insupportable excess. The end she promises is a mixed child, whose blackness may not be 'converted' or absorbed within the endogamous, exclusionary values of Belmont.[21] This dusky dark lady is perhaps more like the women of the *Aeneid*, perpetrators 'of delay and even of obstructionism in relation to the master or imperial project of the completion of the text' (Parker, 1987: 13). She interferes with the 'master/imperial' project of *The Merchant of Venice* – the eradication or assimilation of difference. Unlike other fat ladies, her 'promised end' signals not resolution, but the potential disruption of Europe's imperial text, because in *Merchant*'s Venice – and Elizabeth's England – the possibility of wealth only exists within the dangers of cultural exchange.

Notes

1 Even though the word *intercourse* did not come to have its current sexual connotation until the eighteenth century, Purchas's use of 'commerce and intercourse of amity' resonates powerfully in this way for a modern reader, and I would like to retain this anachronistic sense for the purposes of this paper. Indeed, this paper will read anachronistically throughout. *Miscegenation*, too, is an eighteenth-century term which has particular resonances for the modern American reader. Like 'race', the word *miscegenation* is particularly enabled by later scientific discourses; however, the concepts certainly predated the scientific sense. Although there certainly were Renaissance words, such as *mulatto*, for the offspring of certain interracial couples, I prefer to use the term *miscegenation*, just as I play on *intercourse*, to locate an emerging modern dynamic for which there was no adequate language.

2 Eldred Jones sees this moment as the first glimmer of an emerging stereotype of black women (1965: 119). He also seems to agree with the Arden editor. He argues that the Launcelot/Moor liaison is an 'earthy basic relationship' which completes a structural pattern of romantic relationships in *Merchant*, yet he downplays the relationship's significance: 'This cold douche of earthy realism is not unlike the Jaques/Audrey contrast to the Orlando/Rosalind, Silvius/Phebe love types in *As You Like It*. The fact that Launcelot's partner is a Moor only lends emphasis to the contrast' (Jones, 1965: 71).

3 For a more complete discussion, see Peter Fryer's *Staying Power* (1984: 10–12). Fryer provocatively contends that the second order of expulsion was to make up

the payment for the return of eighty-nine English prisoners from Spain and Portugal.

4 The reprintings of this document indicate some confusion. I have used Eldred Jones's transcription of the 1601 draft proclamation in the Cecil papers, which reads 'are crept'. In contrast, James Walvin's version of this same proclamation (1971: 65) reads 'are carried', as does the version in Hughes and Larkin (1969: 220–1). The facsimile included in Jones (1971: plate 5) appears to me to read 'are crept' and I have thus accepted his transcription.

5 English travel writers, not surprisingly, frequently compared their visions of colonial rule with the Spanish model. England saw itself as in part 'correcting' the vexed model of colonial rule in Spain. In his *View of the Present State of Ireland*, Spenser outlines one of the sources of this sense of Spain's mixed heritage, as he suggests that Spain's current riches are the inheritance of a long history of invasion, particularly by Africans: 'ffor the Spaniarde that now is, is come from as rude and salvage nacions, as theare beinge As it maye be gathered by Course of ages and view of theire owne historye (thoughe they thearein labour muche to ennoble themselues) scarse anye dropp of the oulde Spannishe blodd lefte in them: . . . And yeat after all these the mores and Barbarians breakinge over out of Africa did finallye possesse all spaine or the moste parte thereof And treade downe vnder theire foule heathenishe fete what euer litle they founde theare yeat standinge the which thoughe afterwardes they weare beaten out by *fferdinando* of *Arraggon* and Elizabeth his wiffe yeat they weare not so clensed but that thorogh the mariages which they had made and mixture with the people of the lande duringe theire longe Continvance theare they had lefte no pure dropp of Spanishe blodd no nor of Romayne nor Scithian So that of all nacions vnder heaven I suppose the Spaniarde is the most mingled moste vncertaine and most bastardlie . . .' (Spenser, 1949: 90–1).

6 Kwame Anthony Appiah is the most recent purveyor of this view. In the entry 'Race', in *Critical Terms for Literary Study*, he argues, 'in Shakespearean England both Jews and Moors were barely an empirical reality. And even though there were small number of Jews and black people in England in Shakespeare's day, attitudes to "the Moor" and "the Jew" do not seem to have been based on experience of these people. Furthermore, despite the fact that there was an increasing amount of information available about dark-skinned foreigners in this, the first great period of modern Western exploration, actual reports of black or Jewish foreigners did not play an important part in forming these images. Rather, it seems that the stereotypes were based on an essentially theological conception of the status of both Moors and Jews as non-Christians; the former distinguished by their black skin, whose color was associated in Christian iconography with sin and the devil' (Appiah, 1990: 277–8). It seems apparent in Elizabeth's document that there was a black presence that had its own reality for Elizabeth and that religion appears as rationale after the fact.

7 Patricia Hill Collins lucidly outlines the connections between the welfare mother and mammy stereotypes, arguing, 'Each image transmits clear messages about the proper limits among female sexuality, fertility and Black women's roles in the

political economy' (1990: 78). See also Angela Davis's description of specific political manipulations of the welfare mother image (1990: 23–7).

8   My brief discussion of cannibalism owes a great deal to Peter Hulme's materialist critique of the term 'cannibal' (1986: 78–87) as well as to Maggie Kilgour's (1990) exploration of metaphors of incorporation. For an anthropologist's critique of the charge of cannibalism, see Arens (1979).

9   On blood libel, see Poliakov (1974–5: 58) and Kilgour (1990: 5). Hulme also suggests a connection in his sense that the rise in accusations of anthropophagy involved the 'ritual purging of the body of European Christendom just prior to, and in the first steps of, the domination of the rest of the world: the forging of a European identity' (1986: 85–6). Ben Jonson's *Every Man out of his Humour* contains similar links between economics, cannibalism, and anti-Semitism when Carlo Buffone exclaims, 'Marry, I say, nothing resembling man more than a swine, it follows nothing can be more nourishing: for indeed, but that it abhors from our nice nature, if we fed upon one another, we should shoot up a great deal faster, and thrive much better: I refer me to your usurous cannibals, or such like: but since it is so contrary, pork, pork is your only feed' (V. v. 61–6).

10   Eric Cheyfitz (1991) briefly outlines the relationship of cannibalism to kinship structures in his discussion of Montaigne's 'Of Cannibals': 'Cannibalism expresses, or figures forth, a radical idea of kinship that cuts across the frontiers of hostile groups. To eat the other is to eat the self, for the other is quite literally composed of the selves of one's kin, who compose oneself, just as the self, it follows, is composed of the others one has eaten. Cannibalism, like kinship, expresses forthrightly the essentially equivocal relationship that obtains between self and other' (Cheyfitz, 1991: 149). As I have suggested, it is precisely this aspect of cannibalism that appears so upsetting to European notions of social order and control. In *A Report of the Kingdome of Congo* (1597), Abraham Hartwell expresses horror at the idea of cannibals who eat their own kin: 'True it is that many nations there are, that feede upon mans flesh as in the east *Indies*, and in *Bresill*, and in other places: but that is only the flesh of their adversaries and enemies, but to eat the flesh of their own friends and subjectes and kinefolkes, it is without all example in any place of the worlde, saving onely in this nation of the Anzichi' (Hartwell, 1597: 36).

11   I borrow this multivalent use of 'chauvinist' from Susan Griffin (1988: 298–305).

12   For more on the gendering of the discourses of travel and trade, see Parker (1987: 142).

13   In his liberally sympathetic discussion of Morocco's rejection, Frank Whigham acknowledges the racism of courtly ideology by noting that '[t]hroughout the scenes with Morocco the element of complexion provides a measure of the exclusive implications of courtesy in Portia's society' (1979: 98). However, Whigham then blames the Moroccan prince for his own loss because of 'his statement of defiant insecurity regarding his skin color' (1979: 98), which is rhetorically out of sync with courtesy theory. His reading remystifies the color problem by blaming it on the prince. Portia never mentions his 'imagery of martial exploit and confrontation' (1979: 98), only his complexion; so too the tradition of failed suitors indicates to the audience that his unsuitability is not so much a question

of rhetorical decorum as racial 'propriety'. In Morocco's case, 'defiant insecurity' may simply be a sensible response to the racism implicit in Portia's courtly ethic.

14 Shakespeare draws upon a system of associations between the Jew and the black which is as old as Christianity itself. For a brief outline of the association of blackness with the Jew, see Gilman (1985: 30–5).

15 For an excellent discussion of the racial and economic ramifications of the Jacob and Esau parable, see Shell (1979).

16 In his *Pseudodoxia Epidemica*, Sir Thomas Browne uses this same parable to explain one theory of the causes of blackness, replacing the biblical injunctions against disobedience with a lesson about the powers of the imagination: '[I]t may be perpended whether it might not fall out the same way that Jacobs cattell became speckled, spotted and ring-straked, that is, by the power and efficacy of Imagination; which produceth effects in the conception correspondent unto the phancy of the Agents in generation' (1981: 513).

17 Lars Engle argues that this story is purposely incomplete: 'It is this relation between Jacob and Laban, then, that Shylock is attempting to adduce as an explanation of his own place in the Venetian economy, and, more immediately, as a model for his relation to Antonio' (1986: 31).

18 It is in this same narrative that Best includes one of the earliest recorded instances of miscegenation in early modern England, which he uses to refute the climatic theory of the cause of blackness: 'I my selfe have seene an Ethiopian as blacke as a cole brought into England, who taking a faire Englishwoman to wife, begat a sonne in all respects as blacke as the father was, although England was his native countrey, and an English woman his mother: whereby it seemeth this blacknes proceedeth rather of some natural infection of that man, which was so strong, that neither the nature of the Clime, neither the good complexion of the mother concurring, could any thing alter, and therefore wee cannot impute it to the nature of the Clime' (Hakluyt, 1598–1600: 3, 50–1).

19 Among critics of *The Merchant of Venice*, particularly feminists, there is a great deal of debate over the possible feminist implications of Portia's transvestite disguise. Is Portia truly the disorderly, unruly female preached against in tracts against cross-dressing or are such disguises diversions which ultimately serve to restore patriarchal order? Catherine Belsey finds the play less radical than its earlier counterparts: '*The Merchant of Venice* is none the less rather less radical in its treatment of women as subjects . . . [The play] . . . reproduces some of the theoretical hesitation within which it is situated' (Belsey, 1985: 195–6). Lisa Jardine locates Portia within a tradition of 'confused cultural response[s] to the learned woman' (1987: 17) and notes that although Portia possesses many threatening advantages over the males in the play, the play still ends with the sexual subordination of women (1987: 17). In contrast, Karen Newman finds in Portia a necessary threat to social order: 'Portia evokes the ideal of a proper Renaissance lady and then transgresses it; she becomes an unruly woman' (1987b: 29). Lars Engle also notes a split between conservative and radical elements in the play; however, he sees Portia as part of the latter precisely because she is the agent of exchange: 'On the other hand, more than any other Shakespearean play, *The Merchant of Venice* shows a woman triumphing over men and male systems of exchange: the

"male homosocial desire" of Antonio is almost as thoroughly thwarted in the play as is Shylock's vengefulness' (Engle, 1986: 37). Nonetheless, male homosocial desire (which can be a conservative force) is also a force which threatens the sex/gender system.

20 Parker draws on Jardine's connection of the figure of the pregnant woman and her 'grossesse' with fertility and threatening sexuality (Jardine, 1983: 131; Parker, 1987: 18).

21 Black Africans become in the Renaissance signs for the impossible, which often comes to include the impossibility of their being subdued to European order. The emblem for the impossible, 'washing the Ethiop white', suggests a sense of submission to a European order. Richard Crashaw's poem 'On the Baptized Ethiopian' specifically adapts this as a figure for conversion and the Second Coming. For more see Newman (1987a) and Hall (1990: ch. 2).

References

Appiah, Kwame Anthony (1990) 'Race', *Critical Terms for Literary Study*, ed. Frank Lentricchia and Thomas McLaughlin, pp. 274–87. Chicago: University of Chicago Press.

Appleby, Andrew B. (1978) *Famine in Tudor and Stuart England*. Stanford: Stanford University Press.

Arens, W. (1979) *The Man-eating Myth: Anthropology and Anthropophagy*. Oxford: Oxford University Press.

Barthelemy, Anthony Gerard (1987) *Black Face, Maligned Race: The Representation of Blacks in English Drama from Shakespeare to Southerne*. Baton Rouge: Louisiana State University Press.

Belsey, Catherine (1985) *The Subject of Tragedy: Identity and Difference in Renaissance Drama*. London: Methuen.

Browne, Sir Thomas (1981) *Pseudodoxia Epidemica*, 2 vols, ed. Robin Robbins, vol. 1. Oxford: Clarendon Press.

Cheyfitz, Eric (1991) *The Poetics of Imperialism: Translation and Colonization from The Tempest to Tarzan*. Oxford: Oxford University Press.

Cohen, Walter (1985) *Drama of a Nation: Public Theater in Renaissance England and Spain*. Ithaca, NY: Cornell University Press.

Collins, Patricia Hill (1990) *Black Feminist Thought: Knowledge, Consciousness, and the Politics of Empowerment*. Boston: Unwin Hyman.

Davis, Angela (1990) *Women, Culture, and Politics*. New York: Random House.

Engle, Lars (1986) ' "Thrift is blessing": exchange and explanation in *The Merchant of Venice*', *Shakespeare Quarterly*, 37: 20–37.

Fryer, Peter (1984) *Staying Power: The History of Black People in Britain*. Sydney: Pluto Press.

Gilman, Sander L. (1985) *Difference and Pathology: Stereotypes of Sexuality, Race, and Madness*. New York: Cornell University Press.

Griffin, Susan (1988) 'The sacrificial lamb', *Racism and Sexism: An Integrated Study*, ed. Paula S. Rothenberg, pp. 296–305. New York: St Martin's Press.

Hakluyt, Richard (1598–1600) (ed.) *The Principal Navigations, Voyages, Traffiques, and Discoveries of the English Nation*, vol. 3. London, 3 vols.

——(1935) *Discourse of Western Planting: The Original Writings and Correspondence of the Two Richard Hakluyts*, vol. 2, pp. 211–326. Hakluyt Society no. 77, 2 vols. London: Cambridge University Press for the Hakluyt Society.

Hall, Kim F. (1990) 'Acknowledging things of darkness: race, gender and power in early modern England', unpublished dissertation, University of Pennsylvania.

Hartwell, Abraham (trans.) (1597) *A Report of the Kingdome of Congo, a Region of Africa. And of the Countries that border rounde about the same*. STC 16805.

Hughes, Paul F. and Larkin, James F. (eds) (1969) *Tudor Royal Proclamations*, vol. 3. New Haven, CT: Yale University Press.

Hulme, Peter (1986) *Colonial Encounters: Europe and the Native Caribbean, 1492–1797*. London: Methuen.

Jameson, Fredric (1981) *The Political Unconscious: Narrative as a Socially Symbolic Act*. Ithaca: Cornell University Press.

Jardine, Lisa (1983) *Still Harping on Daughters: Women and Drama in the Age of Shakespeare*. New York: Harvester.

——(1987) 'Cultural confusion and Shakespeare's learned heroines: these are old paradoxes', *Shakespeare Quarterly*, 38: 1–18.

Jones, Eldred D. (1965) *Othello's Countrymen: The African in English Renaissance Drama*. London: Oxford University Press.

——(1971) *The Elizabethan Image of Africa*. Charlottesville: University Press of Virginia.

Jonson, Ben (1981) *Every Man out of his Humour: The Complete Plays of Ben Jonson*, 4 vols, ed. G. A. Wilkes, vol. 1, pp. 275–411. Oxford: Clarendon Press.

Kilgour, Maggie (1990) *From Communion to Cannibalism: An Anatomy of Metaphors of Incorporation*. Princeton, NJ: Princeton University Press.

Massinger, Philip (1976) *The Maid of Honour: The Plays and Poems of Philip Massinger*, 5 vols, ed. Philip Edwards and Colin Gibson, vol. 1, pp. 117–97. Oxford: Clarendon Press.

Newman, Karen (1987a) ' "And wash the Ethiop white": femininity and the monstrous in *Othello*', *Shakespeare Reproduced: The Text in History and Ideology*, ed. Jean E. Howard and Marion F. O'Connor, pp. 143–62. New York: Methuen.

——(1987b) 'Portia's ring: unruly women and structures of exchange in *The Merchant of Venice*', *Shakespeare Quarterly*, 38: 18–33.

Parker, Patricia (1987) *Literary Fat Ladies: Rhetoric, Gender, Property*. New York: Methuen.

Poliakov, Leon (1974–5) *The History of Anti-Semitism*, trans. Richard Howard, vol. 1. New York: Vanguard, 3 vols.

Purchas, Samuel (1625) *Hakluytus Posthumus, or Purchas His Pilgrimes: Contayning a History of the World in Sea Voyages and Lande Travells by Englishment and others*. London.

Rubin, Gayle (1975) 'The traffic in women: notes on the "political economy" of sex',

Toward an Anthropology of Women, ed. Rayna Reiter, pp. 157–210. New York: Monthly Review.

Shakespeare, William (1959) *The Merchant of Venice*, ed. John Russell Brown. The Arden Shakespeare. Cambridge, MA: Harvard University Press.

Shell, Marc (1979) 'The wether and the ewe: verbal usury in *The Merchant of Venice*', *Kenyon Review*, n.s. 1 (4): 65–92.

Spenser, Edmund (1949) *A View of the Present State of Ireland*, ed. Rudolf Gottfried. Vol. 9 of *The Complete Works of Edmund Spenser: A Variorum Edition*, ed. Edwin Greenlaw et al., 10 vols. Baltimore, MD: Johns Hopkins University Press.

Walvin, James (1971) *The Black Presence: A Documentary History of the Negro in England, 1555–1860*. New York: Schocken.

Whigham, Frank (1979) 'Ideology and class conduct in *The Merchant of Venice*', *Renaissance Drama*, n.s. 10: 93–115.

Bottom's Up

Annabel Patterson

Annabel Patterson's article on A Midsummer Night's Dream *situates the play within the context of Elizabethan popular protest and festivity. Developing C. L. Barber's theories of comedy's roots in the festive calendar, she outlines the debate between views of carnival entertainments as essentially containing or subversive. Patterson's account historicizes and politicizes views of laughter and festivity, and interrogates the relationship between laugher and laughed-at, particularly in terms of social status. The mechanicals' play and the on-stage aristocratic audience of Act V of* A Midsummer Night's Dream *are offered as a metonym of the relations between comedy and audience. Elsewhere in her study, Patterson considers* Henry V, Hamlet *and* The Tempest *as products of, and contributors to, particular social moments and tensions.*

Annabel Patterson, 'Bottom's Up: Festive Theory', in *Shakespeare and the Popular Voice* (Oxford: Blackwell, 1989), pp. 52–70.

Even though chronology places regularity above permanence, it cannot prevent heterogeneous, conspicuous fragments from remaining within it. To have combined recognition of a quality with the measurement of the quantity was the work of the calendar in which the places of recollection are left blank, as it were, in the form of holidays.

Walter Benjamin, *On Some Motifs in Baudelaire*

On 29 September, Michaelmas Day, 1662, Samuel Pepys recorded in his diary a characteristically guilty moment:

This day my oaths for drinking of wine and going to plays are out, and so I do resolve to take a liberty to-day, and then to fall to them again. To the King's Theatre, where we saw 'Midsummer's Night's Dream,' which I had never seen before, nor shall ever again, for it is the most insipid ridiculous play that ever I saw in my life. I saw, I confess, some good dancing and some handsome women, and which was all my pleasure.[1]

The psychological conflicts for which Pepys's diary is famous have in this instance an ideological quotient – the conflict between the Restoration court's support of the stage and the Puritan principles he had incorporated[2] – a conflict which descends, obviously, from the Elizabethan theater's relation to governmental allowance and control. And lest we should doubt that this conflict, in Pepys, was serious, we should take note of his 'Observations' at the New Year, 1662: 'This I take to be as bad a juncture as ever I observed. The King and his new Queen minding their pleasure at Hampton Court. All people discontented; some that the King do not gratify them enough; and the others, Fanatiques of all sorts, that the King do take away their liberty of conscience'.[3] The moral embarrassment in which Pepys finds himself is especially signified by the contradictory function of 'liberty' in these two entries, the Nonconformist liberty of conscience threatened by the Act of Uniformity dialectically opposed to the festival liberty that Pepys resolves to allow himself (one of many such suspensions of his private rules) for Michaelmas Day.

Pepys's critical reaction also speaks to the theater history of *A Midsummer Night's Dream*, which already, one can tell from his mention of 'good dancing', had succumbed to operatic or balletic impulses. These impulses dominated all productions from 1692, when it was rewritten as a spectacular opera with music by Henry Purcell, through 1914, when Harley Granville-Barker produced the uncut text 'in a world of poetic and dramatic rather than scenic illusion'.[4] For over two centuries, then, the play that Shakespeare wrote was rendered invisible by conspicuous display; and its most striking metadramatic feature, the concluding amateur theatricals of Bottom the weaver and his colleagues, lost both its structural and social force. In 1692 'Pyramus and Thisbe' was moved to the middle of the performance, and in 1816 the Covent Garden performance had as its grand finale a pageant of 'Triumphs of Theseus'. The result was a performance whose last word, in the year after Waterloo, was the extravagant celebration of monarchical and military power.

The *Dream* has also tempted literary critics to subordinate Bottom and his colleagues, or to neutralize the impact of the play-within-the-play. The temptation is posed by the speech of Theseus that both summarizes the erotic experiences of the young Athenians on midsummer night, and serves as the aristocratic prologue to the artisan's playlet:

> More strange than true. I never may believe
> These antique fables, nor these fairy toys.
> Lovers and madmen have such seething brains,
> Such shaping fantasies, that apprehend
> More than cool reason ever comprehends.
>
> The poet's eye, in a fine frenzy rolling,
> Doth glance from heaven to earth, from earth to heaven,
> And as imagination bodies forth
> The forms of things unknown, the poet's pen
> Turns them to shapes, and gives to airy nothing
> A local habitation and a name.
>
> (V. i. 2–17)[5]

Like the stage history, the tradition of privileging this Thesean aesthetic as the locus of Shakespeare's intentions had the effect of making the *Dream* an 'airy nothing', unaccountable to social or political realism, while at the same time giving to Theseus an exegetical authority that his own behavior scarcely justifies. And though this critical tradition has been roundly challenged, most notably by Jan Kott's counter-privileging of Bottom and his fellows[6] (the academic equivalent of Peter Brook's famous 1970 production) it probably retains its dominance in the classroom.

In fact, even as within this speech imaginative process requires the assistance of things known – bodies, names and local habitations – Shakespeare gave the *Dream* a 'local habitation' so historically specific that the play would make no sense (as Pepys discovered) when performed outside its own cultural environment. The evidence occurs in two passages, close neighbours to each other, in the second act, where the story of Oberon's quarrel with Titania over the changeling boy is told from its beginnings and given a new impetus. In planning his revenge on Titania for her refusal to give up the child into his retinue, Oberon describes to Puck where he may find the 'little western flower', that will be the instrument of her enchantment. Quite gratuitously in terms of plot or strategy, he explains the origins of the flower's erotic capacities as an instance of displaced energies:

> That very time I saw (but thou couldst not),
> Flying between the cold moon and the earth,
> Cupid all arm'd. A certain aim he took
> At a fair vestal, throned by the west,
> And loos'd his love-shaft smartly from his bow
> As it should pierce a hundred thousand hearts.
> But I might see young Cupid's fiery shaft
> Quench'd in the chaste beams of the watery moon;

> And the imperial votress passed on,
> In maiden meditation, fancy-free.
>
> (II. i. 155–64)

Missing its target, the shaft strikes the flower, which is thereby transformed from milk-white to purple, from mere flower to concept, 'love-in-idleness'. The erotic drive is displaced into the territory of the symbolic, producing an excess of textual energy that seems to require special attention. The original andiences would certainly have recognized its galvanic source in the implied presence of Elizabeth herself. As H. H. Furness remarked in 1895,

> That there is an allegory here has been noted from the days of Rowe, but how far it extended and what its limitations and its meanings have since then proved prolific themes. According to Rowe, it amounted to no more than a compliment to Queen Elizabeth, and this is the single point on which all critics since his day are agreed.[7]

Was it, however, so clearly a compliment? Increasingly as she aged, the problems posed by Elizabeth's status as unmarried female ruler were either finessed or exposed to critical scrutiny by the motif of virginity as power. As the moon goddess, Diana, Cynthia or Phoebe, she was celebrated as the Belphoebe of Spenser's *Faerie Queene*, and the Cynthia of Ben Jonson's *Cynthia's Revels* and Ralegh's *The Ocean's Love to Cynthia*, all texts of the 1590s when Elizabeth was approaching or in her sixties.[8] And as *A Midsummer Night's Dream* is in one sense a play about moonshine, the lunar presence invoked in its lines is far from a positive force: 'O, methinks, how slow / This old moon wanes!' cries Theseus, 'She lingers my desires.'

Further, as the title of Spenser's poem indicates, the myths of the classical moon-goddess also merged, for the unique moment of Elizabeth's reign, with fairy legends of Titania and Oberon. Even in Ovid's *Metamorphoses*, Titania was another name for Diana (III, 173); during a royal progress of 1591 the 'Fairy Queen' presented Elizabeth with a chaplet that she had received from 'Auberon, the Fairy King';[9] and after her death Thomas Dekker referred to Elizabeth as Titania in his *Whore of Babylon* (1607). This alternative mythology also appears in the *Dream*, and with equally problematic resonance. For Titania, far from remaining chastely aloof, engages in a struggle for domestic power with Oberon that, however we attribute the fault, has had a disastrous effect on the environment.

Titania herself rehearses these natural disasters, in the other passage of topical significance:

> The ox hath therefore stretch'd his yoke in vain,
> The ploughman lost his sweat, and the green corn

> Hath rotted ere his youth attain'd a beard;
> The fold stands empty in the drowned field,
> And crows are fatted with the murrion flock;
> The-nine-men's-morris is fill'd up with mud,
> And the quaint mazes in the wanton green
> For lack of tread are undistinguishable.
>
> (II. i. 93–100)

And on the basis of this passage, and our knowledge that the one season in Shakespeare's career that was notorious for its bad weather and bad harvests was 1595–6, a consensus has developed for dating the *Dream* at some point in 1596. This dating alone might have generated speculation about the frontal presence of a group of artisans, whose amateur theatricals contribute the play's conclusion, if not its resolution. It was not until 1986, however, that Titania's lament and the artisanal presence were connected, by Theodore Leinwand, to the abortive Oxfordshire rising of November 1596, when Bartholomew Stere, a carpenter, and Richard Bradshawe, a miller, had planned an anti-enclosure riot of distinctly violent proportions.[10] Depositions concerning this event were still being heard in London by the Privy Council during January 1597; it was said that Stere's 'owtward pretense was to . . . helpe the poore cominaltie that were readie to famish for want of corne, But intended to kill the gentlemen of that countrie . . . affirming that the Commons, long sithens in Spaine did rise and kill all the gentlemen in Spaine, and sithens that time have lyved merrily there.'[11] The handful of leaders were all artisans; and although the rising literally came to nothing (the leaders could find no followers), the Privy Council took the matter extremely seriously.

To write seriously about comedy can unfortunately give the impression that one has no sense of humor. Yet it is not implausible to see an allusion to a time of hardship not only in Titania's speech, but also in the name of one of Shakespeare's artisan actors, Robin Starveling. Titania's speech, with its invocation of natural rhythms and cosmic distress, invites large and complex notions of drama's relation to festivity and ritual action, traditionally connected with the seasonal cycle and the socialization of fertility; but Starveling's name and artisanal status reminds us that harvest cycles have social and economic correlatives. Their intersection in Shakespeare's play needs to be warily described, not least because certain theorists of popular culture, especially in France, have emphasized how easy it was for festival or carnival events to get out of control and become riots, or, conversely, as in the notorious Carnival at Romans, to serve as the pretext for organized class warfare.[12]

It cannot now be erased from our consciousness that when Shakespeare committed himself to write *A Midsummer Night's Dream* his environment was, if anything, even more disturbed than it had been in 1591–2. Nor do we need to posit his knowledge of the puny Oxfordshire rising, late in 1596. According to Brian Manning, there were at least thirteen disturbances in 1595 alone in London and suburbs, of which twelve took place between 6 and 29 June,[13] that is to say, in that same Midsummer season that the Privy Council had seen as part of the problem in 1592. Of these, one was initiated by a silk-weaver who reproached the mayor for misgovernment, and was rescued from confinement in Bedlam by the intervention of the crowd. Another, on 29 June, involved 1,000 rioters, a mixture of artisans and apprentices (including silk-weavers), took several days to suppress, and concluded, on 24 July, with the execution of five persons.[14] A pamphlet published to explain the severity of the punishment insisted that the insurgents were precisely not to be excused by the concept that carnival behavior had gotten out of hand:

> But it may (by some) be here objected, sedition and rebellion are unfit tearmes to be used in the case I am now to handle: for the Prentises of London had no seditious purpose, no intention of open rebellion. Truely I perswade me, a headlong wilfulnes continued by a custome of abused libertie, gave first fyre to this unadvised flame: but he that shall dout, that a most trecherous resolution, and dangerous purpose followed, shall make question at a most apparent truthe . . .[15]

On 5 November 1595, the Stationers' Register listed *The poor mans Complaint*, and on 23 August 1596, *Sundrye newe and artificiall Remedies against famyne . . . uppon the occasion of this present Dearthe*. Well before November 1596, then, when Stere staged his sequel to these events Shakespeare would have seen the social and cultural signs of unusual, economic distress; and he might even have noticed how frequently weavers were featured in the more public and violent protests. As Buchanan Sharp observed,

> Most of the symptoms of social distress are to be found in the words and actions of artisans in general and clothmakers in particular . . . they made the loudest complaints about food prices and unemployment by means of riot, attempted insurrections, and frequent petitions to local justices and to the Privy Council . . . it was to their complaints above all that the authorities listened and responded in the formulation of policy.[16]

All this being said, and all the more clearly for its admission, Shakespeare's play evidently staged its own resistance to social pessimism, and especially, perhaps, to the argument that festival liberty leads to violence. Shakespeare did not, however, close his eyes to the social scene. By invoking the dangerous Midsummer season in his title, by featuring a group of artisans as his comic protagonists, by making their leader a weaver, by allowing class consciousness to surface, as we shall see, in their relations with their courtly patrons, and especially in the repeated fears expressed by the artisans that violence is feared from them ('Write me a prologue, and let the prologue seem to say we will do no harm with our swords' [III. i. 15–17]), he faced his society squarely; and instead of the slippage from carnival to force, he offered it a genuinely festive proposition. Bartholomew Stere's assertion that rebellion was the only route to 'a meryer world'[17] is countered (whether before or after its utterance) by Shakespeare's promise that 'Robin shall restore amends'. The *Dream*, therefore, seems to have aspired to the role of legitimate mediation that, in *Henry VI, Part 2*, only an aristocratic counsellor was authorized to perform.

Of all the comedies, this one offers the most powerful invitation to explain it by some theory of festive practices. The question is, which branch of festive theory? There are three main branches to which the *Dream* has hitherto been tied, directly or implicitly. All have support from some part of the text, but none by itself can explain the whole. Indeed, they tend partially to contradict each other, or perhaps to repeat a contest that was actually occurring in Shakespeare's day. The first is based on Shakespeare's allusion to Elizabeth's lunar presence in Oberon's speech, which, as in Rowe's theory of compliment, has been used to argue that she must have been present in the original audience: and this assumption, combined with the fact that *within* the play a marriage is celebrated, has produced an 'occasionalist' argument: that the *Dream* was itself written to celebrate an aristocratic wedding.[18] This occasionalist theory relies, primarily, on the *Dream*'s opening and closing emphasis on a season of 'merriment' ordered by Theseus, in order to change the tone of his courtship of Hippolyta from conquest to celebration, and on his goodnight speech after the artisans' play is ended:

> . . . Sweet friends, to bed,
> A fortnight hold we this solemnity,
> In nightly revels and new jollity.
> (V. i. 369–72)

Despite the difficulty that critics experience in finding an appropriate marital occasion during 1595–6, and an uneasy recognition that the play seems rather to *problematize* than celebrate marriage, it is somewhat alarming to see how readily this hypothesis has been absorbed as fact into texts designed for students; Sylvan Barnet, in the Signet edition, for example, states categorically that the *Dream* 'was undoubtedly intended as a dramatic epithalamium to celebrate the marriage of some aristocrat' (p. xxv). And the occasionalist premise also associates the reader with the courtly circle around Theseus, and therefore with the Thesean aesthetic. Yet this framing festive plot actually represents a strategy by which popular drama was increasingly brought, involuntarily, under court control. By identifying Philostrate (in the list of Dramatis Personae) as 'Master of the Revels' to Theseus, the Folio text of the *Dream* alludes to an office created by Elizabeth in 1581 as an instrument for ensuring high quality in her own entertainment, for initiating the recentralization of the theater under court patronage, and for keeping it under surveillance.[19] Although the office did not become as influential under Elizabeth as later under James, and the theater in the 1590s continued to be alternatively tolerated and regulated by local authorities, with the Privy Council and the Lord Chamberlain intervening as little or as much as court policy dictated, its very title designates a much smaller, more tightly supervised and essentially courtly concept of dramatic entertainment than Shakespeare's theater generally assumes. Rather, Shakespeare's own situation as a member of the Chamberlain's company would situate him somewhere *between* the court and amateur popular theatricals, with the occasional 'command performance' bringing him closer to Bottom and his colleagues than to those, frequently themselves aristocrats, who created the royal entertainments. The artisanal hope of being 'made men', with 'sixpence a day' for life, is a parodic version of that discontinuous patronage relation; but the play speaks more to its uneasiness than to its rewards, as well as to Shakespeare's self-consciousness about how the popular theatrical impulse was in danger of being appropriated to hegemonic ends.

The second branch of festive theory refers not to courtly revels but to popular rituals, and assumes that the play was motivated less by the social needs of the Elizabethan court than by instincts and behavior usually interrogated by anthropologists. When C. L. Barber published his ground-breaking *Shakespeare's Festive Comedy* in 1959,[20] he connected Shakespeare with a large and today still expanding intellectual movement that includes the work of Durkheim, Van Gennep and Victor Turner. Barber's innovation was to set Shakespeare's early comedies in the socio-historical context of English popular games, entertainments and the rituals accompanying Easter, May, Whitsun, Midsummer, or Christmas holidays, or the harvest home. Some of these festive occasions, like the annual excursions from rural parishes to bring in the May, which Robert Herrick's gorgeous *Corinna's Going a Maying* and Phillip Stubbes' virulent *Anatomie of Abuses* both, though from opposite points of view, represent as an excuse for feminine defloration, were vestiges of ancient pagan fertility rites. In the *Dream*, Theseus assumes that the four young lovers whom he has found asleep in the forest 'rose up early to observe / The rite of May' (IV. i. 135–6). Others, like the lord of Misrule festivities primarily associated with the twelve days of Christmas, were secularized versions of the religious Feast of Fools, which enacted the Christian inversions of exalting the low and humbling the proud. In *Twelfth Night*, this temporary misrule is epitomized in the name of Olivia's 'allowed fool', Feste, and in Feste's antithesis to Malvolio the puritan, who would unduly narrow the space permitted to fooling in a courtly household and so becomes its victim. But misrule was also adapted to and merged with the country feasts and improvized in taverns, a social fact that Shakespeare explores in *Henry IV*. Morris dances, too, like May Day rituals with their phallic Maypoles, were genetically connected to fertility rites, as well as to the legends of Robin Hood with their theme of social outlawry. The morris, as a mixture of sexual energy and political subversion, was extremely interesting not only to Puritan writers like Stubbes but also to Elizabethan and Jacobean dramatists. While Titania's reference to the 'nine-men's-morris . . . fill'd up with mud' is a pun (within a lament for infertility) that overrides an alternative etymology,[21] Shakespeare alludes to the transgressive aspects of the morris in *Henry VI, Part 2*, where Jack Cade is described by Richard of York, who plans to exploit his energies, as capering 'like a wild Morisco, Shaking the bloody darts as he his bells' (III. i. 346–66). In *Henry V* the Dauphin, assuming that Henry is still in his tavern phase, mocks the English preparations for war as a 'Whitsun morris dance' (II. iv. 25); and Hamlet compares his dead father to the morris-dancer's hobby-horse, 'whose epitaph is "For O, for O, the hobby-horse is forgot"' (III. ii. 140–1); his mother's disloyalty and the failure to commemorate his father participates in the broader betrayal of drama's roots and his country's ancient customs.[22] These instances carry important valences, national, cultural and political, which seem to privilege the past and the primitive even as they are registered as such.

In Barber's view, however, all of these festive or folk elements in Shakespeare's plays were part of a cultural migration in which the archaic and amateur forms of dramatic representation and ritual were absorbed by the mature national theater. Claiming that saturnalian impulse, 'when directly expressed, ran head on into official prohibition', Barber concluded that the transfer of festive impulses to the theater was an enforced 'shift from symbolic *action* towards *symbolic* action'.[23]

> Shakespeare's theater was taking over on a professional and everyday basis functions which until his time had largely been performed by amateurs on holiday. And he wrote at a moment when the educated part of society was modifying a ceremonial, ritualistic conception of human life to create a historical, psychological conception. His drama, indeed, was an important agency in this transformation . . . In making drama out of rituals of state, Shakespeare makes clear their meaning as social and psychological conflict, as history. So too with the rituals of pleasure, of misrule, as against rule: his comedy presents holiday magic as imagination, games as expressive gestures.[24]

This is the move that aestheticizes; that seeks to distinguish between 'art' and 'life', between literary and non-literary texts; and that therefore, in its invocation of the unexaminable (Thesean) term, 'imagination', begs the very questions that cultural historians must attempt to answer. Barber's strongest message was that both the archaic festivals and their Elizabethan echoes functioned to reaffirm, through reconciliatory symbolic action, the hierarchical structure of society.

If Barber represents the idealist version derived from social history, its equivalent in anthropology is found in the work of Victor Turner, himself much influenced, however, by Barber. In a late work, *From Ritual to Theatre*,[25] Turner admitted that his own thinking had been shaped by 'early exposure to theatre', specifically *The Tempest*, which Turner had seen as a child of five. In *The Ritual Process* (1969), Turner developed his theory of *communitas*, or the individual's sense of belonging, voluntarily, to a larger, cohesive and harmonious social group, on the idealist model of ritual action inherited from Durkheim and Van Gennep. Thus Turner argued initially that 'cognitively, nothing underlines regularity so well as absurdity or paradox. Emotionally, nothing satisfies as much as extravagant or temporarily permitted illicit behavior.' This regulatory motive accounts for the fact, he thought, that inversion rituals occur most often 'at fixed points in the annual cycle . . . for structural regularity is here reflected in temporal order'.[26] However, in the later *Dramas, Fields, and Metaphors*, inversion rituals were seen rather as motivated by some natural disaster or 'public, overt breach or deliberate non-fulfilment of some crucial norm', which requires remedial intervention rather than regulatory confirmation.[27] And *communitas* was reconceived as running *counter* to the stratified and rule-governed conception of society, in the space that Turner called *liminality*, in which social distinctions are temporarily suspended. In liminal situations, the lower social strata become privileged, and bodily parts and biological referents, conceived as the source of regenerative energy, are revalued; hence the ritual use of animal disguises, masks and gestures. An exchange takes place, Turner argued, between the normative or ideological poles of social meaning, which dictate attitudes to parents, children, elders and rulers, and the physiological poles or facts of life (birth, death, sexuality) which the norms exist to regulate; and in this exchange 'the biological referents are ennobled and the normative referents are charged with emotional significance',[28] which renders them once again acceptable.

By proposing this ritual exchange between rules and energies as demanded by natural disasters or unusual breaches in social relations, Turner's model seems more promising than Barber's for interrogating the most ritual components of the *Dream*, the breach between Oberon and Titania that has resulted in crop failure and disrupted the natural cycle, and the manner in which that breach will be healed. But even in its late form Turner's festive theory remains idealist, in the sense that the purpose of festive rituals is, in the last analysis, reconciliation, getting the social rhythms running smoothly once more.

There is, of course, an alternative possibility: that popular festival forms and inversion rituals were actually subversive in intent and function all along. This position is represented in Shakespeare studies by Robert Weimann, and more generally by Mikhail Bakhtin's study of Rabelais, preceded as it was by a social history of carnival forms. Weimann's magisterial study established the possibility of a class-conscious analysis of popular traditions, and, by extending the inquiry to the tragedies, discovered the levelling implications of Shakespeare's fools, clowns and grave-diggers.[29] Bakhtin, to whom Victor Turner acknowledged a debt, provided our most powerful explanation of carnival's emphasis on the material grotesque, or the 'lower bodily stratum', belly, buttocks and genitals. This movement of festive impulse downwards, or degradation, Bakhtin argued, was intended as social fertilization: 'to bury, to sow, and to kill simultaneously, in order to bring forth something more and better . . . Grotesque realism knows no other level; it is the fruitful earth and the womb. It is always conceiving.'[30] But he also insisted that fertilization was essentially a social myth of populist self-definition and incorporation:

> We repeat: the body and bodily life have here a cosmic and at the same time an all-people's character; this is not the body and its physiology in the modern sense of these words, because it is not individualized. The material bodily principle is contained not in the biological individual, not in the bourgeois ego, but in the people, a people who are continually growing and renewed . . . the collective ancestral body of all the people.[31]

Yet, though both of these influential studies assume a Marxist theory of history, neither finally provided a radical solution to the old polarities that have plagued aesthetic debates since their first beginnings: high versus low culture, mind versus body, consciousness versus material practise. Weimann's book was as deeply influenced by Barber as by Marx, producing in effect a version of the Thesean aesthetic, by which the festive and ritual elements that Shakespeare recorded were seen as the raw material for a new formal synthesis of the natural with the conventional, of primitive with learned humanist materials; and Shakespeare himself, working at a transitional moment when social change made visible the very concept of archaism, appears as the genius at the end of evolutionary trail. Leaning on the modern preference for a disinterested art, Weimann praised 'Shakespeare's universal vision of experience' as 'more comprehensive and more vital . . . in . . . its skepticism and its freedom', than either of the traditions it drew from;[32] and even his own insights into the subversiveness of topsy-turveydom were constrained by the conviction that class consciousness was not fully available as a category of thought in Shakespeare's time. The echoes of folk misrule in the plays were, he thought, 'playfully rebellious gestures', and 'the contradictions between the popular tradition and the culture of the ruling classes were to some extent synthesized with the needs and aspirations of the New Monarchy and were overshadowed by an overwhelming sense of national pride and unity.'[33]

Bakhtin could equally be charged (and indeed has been) with universalism, for insufficiently specifying the historical vectors of carnival events.[34] For while he situated Rabelais in a 'history of laughter' from the middle ages to the nineteenth century, with occasional references to Marxist historiography, Bakhtin explicitly rejected Veselovsky's nineteenth-century theory of clowning as a populist defence against feudal values: 'No doubt', wrote Bakhtin, 'laughter was in part an external defensive form of truth':

> It was legalized, it enjoyed privileges, it liberated, to a certain extent, from censorship, oppression, and from the stake. But . . . laughter is essentially not an external but an interior form of truth . . . Laughter liberates not only from exterior censorship but first of all from the great interior censor; it liberates from the fear that developed in man during thousands of years; fear of the sacred, of prohibitions, of the past, of power . . . The seriousness of fear and suffering in their religious, social, political, and ideological forms could not but be impressive. The consciousness of freedom, on the other hand, could be only limited and utopian.[35]

'It would therefore be a mistake', Bakhtin concluded, to presume that festive and carnival forms expressed 'a critical and clearly defined opposition'.[36]

In what follows, I propose to create a gargantuan mingle-mangle of the strongest and boldest suggestions that these different festive theories proffer, while pushing them beyond their own aesthetic or procedural inhibitions. I rely for conceptual support on Shakespeare himself, who within the text of *A Midsummer Night's Dream* seems to have recognized much of the thinking I have just described and the conflicting interests it represents (then and now); and, by making the different versions of festive theory modify and correct each other, produced in the end a more capacious proposal. Within the aristocratic premise of 'revels', for instance, certain surprises are introduced. Theseus's selection of the 'tragical mirth' of the artisans' play is carefully articulated as a rejection of learned, humanist entertainments:

> 'The battle of the Centaurs, to be sung
> By an Athenian eunuch to the harp.'
> We'll none of that;
> 'The riot of the tipsy Bacchanals,
> Tearing the Thracian singer in their rage.'
> That is an old device
> 'The thrice three Muses mourning for the death
> Of Learning, late deceas'd in beggary'?

That is some satire, keen and critical,
Not sorting with a nuptial ceremony.

(V. i. 44–55)

What does sort with a nuptial ceremony, apparently, includes the ribald: the by-play on Wall's 'stones' (a vulgarism for testicles) 'chink' and 'hole', through which Pyramus and Thisbe try to make physical contact. 'My cherry lips', complains Thisbe to Wall, who is of course a man, 'have often kiss'd thy stones, / Thy stones with lime and hair knit up in thee' (V. i. 190–1). It is noteworthy that neither the Quarto nor the Folio text authorizes the stage direction 'Wall holds up his fingers', a bowdlerizing intervention added by Edward Capell in 1767 and now a standard feature of modern editions, running counter to the text's bawdry, and discouraging a producer from having Pyramus and Thisbe bend to reach each other through the open legs of Snout the tinker.[37] Yet this interpretation, and the kind of laughter it would provoke, would have 'sorted' well with the sexual ambience of Renaissance wedding festivities, as well as with their archaic precedents in bedding rituals; 'in which', remarked George Puttenham in his *Arte of English Poesie* (1589), 'if there were any wanton or lascivious matter more then ordinarie which they called *Ficenina licentia* it was borne withal for that time because of the matter no lesse requiring.'[38] Even the main festive plot, therefore, requires the *Dream*'s audience, then and now, to consider the relationship between broad sexual humor and the social construction of the audience; for by making his courtiers enjoy this 'palpable gross' entertainment Shakespeare precludes the argument that his obscenity was really beneath him, designed only for those convenient receptacles of critical discards, the 'groundlings'. In Bakhtin's terms, the boundary between courtly and popular entertainment is broached by the material grotesque, by the laughter that drives the festive imagination downwards to the lower bodily stratum.

On the other hand, the festive plot that most attracted Barber's attention, the May game that takes the four young lovers into the forest, cannot be explained merely in Barber's terms, as one of those archaic fertility rituals absorbed and contained by the transforming imagination; not, at any rate, unless that imagination is as defined by Theseus. It is, after all, only Theseus who, finding them asleep after the confusions of identity and erotic attraction are resolved, assumes 'they rose up early to observe / The rite of May' (IV. i. 131–2), whereas in fact the motive for the transgressive excursion was escape from parental and patriarchal oppression. Barber's account of the magical doings in the forest underestimates the severity not of the 'sharp Athenian law' (I. i. 162) by which marital arrangements were based on dynastic as opposed to erotic imperatives, but of Shakespeare's treatment of it; a law administered by Theseus, and manifestly intended to be felt by the audience as unjust, while reminding them of its correlative in Elizabethan England. At the very least, then, we need for this part of the *Dream* a festive theory that, like Victor Turner's, admits the political or ideological dimension of festive actions, some sense of the norms of 'respect for elders' and 'obedience to political authorities' that ritual will again render acceptable. But if we look to Turner for a model for the way this plot is handled we shall still be disappointed. There is no exchange between rules and energies in this tale of adolescent silliness, underlined by the very ease with which the young people's emotions are rearranged. Even Shakespeare's calendrical vagueness (is it May or Midsummer?) which evidently worried Barber,[39] is naughtily incompatible with Turner's original theory that the festival calendar mimics and hence reinforces social order. The callowness of the young escapees, moreover, remains when the parental and societal inhibitions have been finessed away, not by a genuine reconciliation, but by magical legerdemain. It expresses itself in their mockery of the very play that speaks to what their own predicament was, and what its ending might have been. When Bottom leaps up to 'assure' his courtly audience that 'the wall is down that parted their fathers', and that burials are therefore unnecessary (V. i. 337–8), he marks, as they themselves are incapable of doing, the sociological seriousness that their own festive plot implied. Once again, the courtly and the popular seem to change places; and it only adds to the complexity of the exchange that the artisans do *not* present an entertainment with its roots in folk tradition; rather, they struggle to give the courtiers what they might be supposed to admire, an Ovidian legend in the high rhetorical and hence self-parodying mode.

But more transgressive still is the third festive plot – Titania's quarrel with Oberon over the changeling boy, which results in disastrous weather and crop failure, and which can only be resolved by the most extreme example of status inversion and misrule that Shakespeare's canon contains, the infatuation of the Queen of Fairies with a common artisan who is also, temporarily, an ass. This is the plot, also, that Louis Montrose has marvellously related to psychoanalytic conceptions of gender and power in Elizabeth's reign, and, under the aegis of Theseus's phrase for imaginative work, 'Shaping Fantasies', suggested that within the fantasy of Titania's liaison with Bottom lies 'a discourse of anxious misogyny' precipitated by the myth of the Virgin Queen and the pressures it exerted on male sensibilities.[40] Montrose put vital pressure on aspects of the play that Barber's benign thesis overlooked – the dark pre-history of Theseus as betrayer of women, the repressed myth of Amazonian independence that Hippolyta represents, the harshness of Theseus's treatment of Hermia (even during his own festive season), Titania's elegiac account of her friendship with the changeling boy's mother, who died in childbirth, even the subjects of the rejected entertainments, with their allusions to eunuchs and Centaurs, rape and dismemberment.

While Montrose's approach is true to the *Dream*'s mixture of light and dark, and subtle in its handling of the Elizabethan semiotics of gender, his psycho-analytic reading does not give Shakespeare his due. It implies that these darker resonances in the play rose up from its author's and the national (male) uncon-scious, as distinct from being part of a conscious analytic project. Assuming that the *Dream* in its conclusion both 'reaffirms essential elements of a patri-archal ideology', and 'calls that reaffirmation in question', Montrose determines that those contradictory projects occur 'irrespective of authorial intention'.[41] And Montrose's psychoanalytic theory also distracts attention from the socio-economic component in the episode that he reads as the male's revenge – the amazing suggestion not only that a queen could be made by magic to mate with a male from the bottom stratum of society – as well as from the fact that its results are positive. For thanks to Bottom the weaver, the crisis in the natural cycle and the agricultural economy is resolved, albeit by restoring male author-ity. In Montrose's essay, Titania's liaison with Bottom is related not to festive inversions, but rather to the dream of Simon Forman, professional physician and amateur drama critic, who fantasized that the queen had made herself sex-ually available to him; and it is only a detail, over which Montrose does not pause, that his dream rival for the queen's affections is 'a weaver, a tall man with a reddish beard, distract of his wits'.[42] In *both* dreams, fortuitously, Forman's and Shakespeare's, there is staged a contest for significance, for exegetical control, between critic and weaver, high and low culture. But in Shakespeare's *Dream*, the weaver (who is also a dreamer) wins.

Let us now return to Turner's proposal that rituals of status inversion or revitalization frequently make use of animal masks, and imagine with new eyes what the Elizabethan audience might have seen when Bottom appears on the stage with an ass's head replacing his own. Weimann had noted 'the surpris-ing consistency of the ass' head motif from the *mimus* down to *A Midsummer Night's Dream*'; but he assumed that it, like the calf's hide which the Eliza-bethan fool still wore in the Mummer's Play, the coxcomb, antlers, horns, and foxtail, was merely 'the survival of some kind of mimetic magic, which, after having lost its ritual function, became alienated from its original purpose and hence misunderstood as a comic attribute'.[43] But in the *Dream*, the ass's head distinguishes itself from comic props and animal masks in general, and becomes part of a complex structural pun, by which the ritual exchange between rules and energies does after all take place, and the lower bodily parts are, as in Turner's theory, ennobled. Bottom is not only the bottom of the social hierarchy as the play represents it, but also the 'bottom' of the body when seated, literally the social ass or arse. It is typical of the *Oxford English Dictio-nary*'s conservativism that it does not sanction this meaning of the word in Shakespeare's day, with the result that generations of editors have been satisfied with 'bottom' as a technical term for the bobbin in weaving. Yet as Frankie Rubinstein observes in her dictionary of Shakespeare's sexual puns,

Shakespeare and his contemporaries took for granted that *ass*, as the vulgar, dialectical spelling of *arse*, was the meeting point of a powerful set of linked concepts: 'Shakespeare . . . used "ass" to pun on the ass that gets beaten with a stick and the arse that gets thumped sexually, the ass that bears a burden and the arse that bears or carries in intercourse.'[44] And she cites in analogy the Fool's rebuke to Lear that speaks to a male humiliation by the female, paternal by filial: 'When thy clovest thy crown i' th' middle, and gav'st away both parts, thou bor'st [barest] thine ass on thy back o'er the dirt: thou hadst little wit in thy bald crown when thou gav'st thy golden one away . . . thou gav'st them the rod, and putt'st down thine own breeches' (I. iv. 167–71, 180–1). Here exposed bodily parts, top and bottom, crown and arse, unite in a political allegory of status inversion and corporal punishment. And in the 1640s, John Milton made the same set of meanings converge in a metaphorical beating of one of his opponents: 'I may chance not fail to endorse him on the backside of posterity, not a golden, but a brazen Asse';[45] thereby including in the multiple pun, for good measure, *The Golden Ass* of Apuleius.

In the *Dream*, the structural pun on *ass* is anticipated by Puck's gratuitous 'bottom' humor, his account of pretending to be a stool that removes itself from under the buttocks of 'the wisest aunt telling the saddest tale' being an early warning signal of popular fundamentalism:

> Then slip I from her bum, down topples she,
> And 'tailor' cries . . .
>
> (II. i. 51–4)

Here the play on *tale / tail(er)* is one of the puns that Howard Bloch, himself influenced by Bakhtin, explored in his rule-breaking study of the French medieval *fabliaux*.[46] Bloch argued that these jokes are ultimately metacritical and serve to theorize the jongleur's profession. The Old French homophony between *con* (cunt) and *conte* (tale) 'or, in English, the tail and the tale . . . signifies the closeness of physical and linguistic longings'; postmodernist theory fuses 'the desire so often expressed in sexual terms on the level of theme and the desire for the story itself'.[47] But because Bottom is also an ass, the structural pun in the *Dream* has a still more complex resonance, one that requires precisely those social categories from which Bloch's deconstructive work, regrettably, would liberate popular obscenity.

In the great medieval encyclopaedia of Bartholomaeus Anglicus, translated in 1582 by Stephen Batman as *Batman upon Bartholome*, the ass is defined as a creature in whom coalesce the meaning-systems implied by Shakespeare's puns: 'The Asse is called Asinus, and hath that name of Sedendo, as it were a beast to sit upon . . . and is a simple beast and a slow, and therefore soone overcome & subject to mannes service' (XIX: 419). The theme of servitude symbolized by the ass was, of course, rendered fully allegorical by Apuleius, whose episode of Lucius's period of slavery in the bakery has been recognized as 'the only passage in the whole of ancient literature which realistically . . . examines the conditions of slave-exploitation on which the culture of the ancient world rested.'[48] And Bakhtin, who claimed that the ass is 'one of the most ancient and lasting symbols of the material bodily lower stratum, which at the same time degrades and regenerates', connected *The Golden Ass* with the 'feast of the ass' which commemorates the Flight to Egypt, and also with the legends of St Francis of Assisi.[49]

As visual pun and emblem, therefore, Bottom stands at the fulcrum of Shakespeare's analysis of the festive impulse in human social structures. Is he merely a comic figure, the appropriate butt of Thesean critical mockery, and his liaison with Titania the worst humiliation an upstart queen could suffer? Or does his (im)proper name, in symbolic alliance with his ass's head, invoke rather an enquiry into the way in which the lower social orders, as well as the 'lower bodily stratum', function, and suggest that the service they perform and the energies they contain, are usually undervalued? Hinting as to how this question might be answered, Shakespeare included a brilliant gloss on the multiple pun that is Bottom, keying his festive theory into the most impeccable source of ideology available to him. At the moment of his transformation back into manhood, Bottom implicates his own ritual naming in the central act of interpretation that the *Dream* demands:

> Man is but an ass if he go about to expound this dream. Methought I was – there is no man can tell what. Methought I was – and methought I had – but man is but a patched fool if he will offer to say what methought I had. The eye of man hath not heard, the ear of man hath not seen, man's hand is not able to taste, his tongue to conceive, nor his heart to report, what my dream was. I will get Peter Quince to write a ballad of this dream: It shall be called 'Bottom's Dream,' because it hath no bottom. (IV. i. 205–15)

It has long been recognized that this passage contains an allusion to I Corinthians 2: 9 ('Eye hath not seen, nor ear heard, neither have entered into the heart of man, the things which God hath prepared for them that love him'). But so quick have most commentators been to denigrate Bottom that they focus only on his jumbling of the biblical text, rather than on its context of profound spiritual levelling. Even Weimann, who connected it to his theme of popular topsy-turveydom,[50] does not pursue the biblical context to its logical conclusion, in I Corinthians 12: 14–25, where the metaphor of the body is developed more fully in terms of a Christian *communitas*:

> If the whole body were an eye, where would be the hearing? If the whole body were an ear, where would be the sense of smell? But as it is, God arranged the

organs in the body, each one of them, as he chose. If all were a single organ, where would the body be? As it is . . . the parts of the body which seem to be weaker are indispensable, and those parts of the body we invest with greater honor, and our unpresentable parts are treated with greater modesty, which our more presentable parts do not require. But God has so adjusted the body, giving the greater honor to the inferior part, that there may be no discord in the body, but that the members may have the same care for one another.

In the *Dream* which has no bottom because Bottom dreamed it, the 'unpresentable parts' of the social body are invested with greater honor by their momentary affinity with a utopian vision that Bottom wisely decides he is incapable of putting into words, at least into words in their normal order. Shakespeare's warning to the audience is unmistakable; prudent readers, especially those who are themselves unprivileged, will resist the pressure to interpret the vision. Yet its inarticulate message remains: a revaluation of those 'unpresentable' members of society, normally mocked as fools and burdened like asses, whose energies the social system relies on.

But how far did this social criticism intend to go? How much are we really to make of the artisans' fears of frightening the ladies, and the constant need to break the dramatic illusion lest the courtly audience think that their mimic swords are drawn in earnest? What is to be made of the prologue actually written for the playlet, that 'tangled chain [of being]; nothing impaired, but all disordered' (V. i. 124–5) which, as Leinwand observed, 'teeters back and forth between deference and offensiveness',[51] creating in its *double entendres* the very sociopolitical apprehensions that the artisans most wished to avoid? And what was the London theatrical ambience in 1595–6? In September 1595 the Mayor wrote to the Privy Council 'Toutching the putting doune of the plaies at the Theater & Bankside which is a great cause of disorder in the Citie', and specifically proposed a connection between this and the 'late stirr & mutinous attempt of those few apprentices and other servantes, who wee doubt not driew their infection from these & like places'.[52] This record connects with the Privy Council's embargo in 1592, as also with the memory of that 'Play at Windham' that had actually, if the historians of Kett's uprising were to be believed, served as the occasion for a major social upheaval. Yet in 1595–6, if *A Midsummer Night's Dream* is to be believed, Shakespeare was willing to argue, with Montaigne, that there could be 'honest exercises of recreation', that plays acted 'in the presence of the magistrats themselves' might actually promote 'common societie and loving friendship'. The *Dream* imagines a festive spirit deeper and more generous than the courtly revels that seemed, in the 1590s, to be appropriating plays and actors; an idea of social play that could cross class boundaries without obscuring them, and by those crossings imagine the social body whole again; and a transgressive, carnival spirit daring enough to register social criticism, while holding off the phantom of 'the Play at Windham', the dramatic scene of violent social protest. It would not be until after *King Lear* (Shakespeare's darkest experiment in role-reversal and carnival exposure), and not until after the Midlands Rising (the country's gravest social crisis since 1549) that Shakespeare was forced to admit that the popular voice had grievances that the popular theater could no longer express comedically. In 1595–6, it only 'rehearse[d] most obscenely and courageously' (I. ii. 100–1) for that later, more demanding project.

There is, however, one qualification to this otherwise genial thesis. In 1549, we remember, the worst of the grievances listed by the ventriloquist was the rebels' sense that their case was the subject of mockery: 'their miserable condition, is *a laughing stocke to most proud and insolent men. Which thing . . . grieveth them so sore, and inflicteth such a staine of evill report: as nothing is more grievous for them to remember, nor more injust to suffer.*'[53] Economic deprivation and physical hardships, in other words, are deemed less oppressive than the mockery that makes of those same sufferings a 'laughing stocke'. In relation to the *Dream*, this part of the story is potent. When Bottom and his fellows are mocked by the aristocratic audience, the audience outside the *Dream* has the opportunity to consider whether or not to laugh themselves, which sort of festive spirit to select for their own enjoyment. If laughter is necessary to mediate social tensions, Shakespeare's festive theory seems to argue, then let it be a laughter as far removed as possible from the red-hot iron of social condescension.

Notes

1   *The Diary of Samuel Pepys*, ed. Robert Latham and William Matthews, 11 vols (Berkeley and Los Angeles, 1979), vol. 3, p. 208.

2   Although Pepys's editors conclude that by 1660 he was 'clearly an Anglican by habit and sentiment' (*Diary*, vol. 1, p. xviii), he was educated first at Huntingdon grammar school (of which Oliver Cromwell was an alumnus) and subsequently, following the path of John Milton, at St Paul's School and at Puritan Cambridge. One of his cousins, Richard Pepys, became Cromwell's Lord Chief Justice of Ireland; and Pepys himself recorded in his *Diary* for 1 November 1660 his embarrassment when one of his old school-fellows 'did remember that I was a great roundhead when I was a boy' (vol. 1, p. 280).

3   Pepys, *Diary*, vol. 3, p. 208.

4   See R. A. Foakes (ed.), *A Midsummer Night's Dream* (Cambridge, 1984), pp. 12–17.

5   References are to the New Arden edition: *A Midsummer Night's Dream*, ed. Harold Brooks (London, 1979).

6   Jan Kott, *The Bottom Translation* (Evanston, IL, 1987), pp. 29–68.

7   H. H. Furness (ed.), *A Midsommer Nights Dreame*, New Variorum Edition (1895, repr. New York, 1966), p. 75. How prolific were the efforts of the old historical allegorizers can be seen from the seventeen pages of annotation that Furness had to provide for this single passage.

8   See also Louis Montrose, '"Shaping fantasies": figurations of gender and power in Elizabethan culture', *Representations*, 2 (1983), p. 80, on the 'last and most extravagant phase' of the cult of virginity. Montrose mentions the 'sacred Temple of the Virgins Vestal' that was featured in the 1590 Accession Day pageant.

9   See ibid., p. 80, citing John Nichols, *Progresses and Public Processions of Queen Elizabeth*, 3 vols (1823; repr. New York, 1966), pp. 118–19.

10   Theodore Leinwand, '"I believe we must leave the killing out": deference and accommodation in *A Midsummer Night's Dream*', *Renaissance Papers* (1986), pp. 17–21.

11   *Calendar of State Papers Domestic*, 1603–10, vol. 28, art. 64, p. 373 (misplaced and misdated). For accounts of the Oxfordshire rising, see Buchanan Sharp, *In Contempt of All Authority: Rural Artisans and Riot in the West of England, 1586–1660* (Berkeley, 1980), pp. 39–40; John Walter, 'A "rising of the people"? The Oxfordshire rising of 1596', *Past and Present*, 107 (1985), pp. 90–143.

12   See Yves-Marie Bercé, *Fête et Révolte: Des mentalités populaires du XVIe au XVIIIe siècle* (Paris, 1976), especially pp. 55–92, 'Les fêtes changées en révolte'. The fullest description of the Romans happening is by Le Roy Ladurie, *Carnival in Romans*, trans. Mary Feeney (New York, 1979). Reversing Bercé's thesis, François Laroque argued, in relation to *Henry VI, Part 2*, that Jack Cade's *jacquerie* turned into a carnival. See 'Shakespeare et la fête populaire: le carnaval sanglant de Jack Cade', *Réforme, Humanisme, et Renaissance*, 11 (1979), pp. 126–30.

13   Brian Manning, *Village Revolts: Social Protest and Popular Disturbances in England, 1509–1640* (Oxford, 1988), p. 208.

14   See ibid., pp. 209–10. Apparently here too, reversing the situation in 1592, one of the authorities sided with the insurgents; in this instance it was Sir Michael Blount, lieutenant of the Tower, who resisted Mayor John Spencer's attempts to restore order, and who was later accused of conspiring to support the Earl of Hertford's claim to the throne.

15   *A Students Lamentation that hath sometime been in London an Apprentice, for the rebellious tumults lately in the Citie hapning: for which five suffred death on Thursday the 24. of July last. Obedientia servi Corona* (London, 1595), B1r. Significantly, this pamphlet cannot help connecting the apprentice riot to 'peasant ideology': 'Of Jacke Straw, Will Daw, Wat Tiler, Tom Miller, Hob Carter and a number more such seditious inferiour ringleaders . . . what hath been the end . . . All these at the beginning would be Reformers, & wrongs forsooth they went about to right: but when they had got head, what wrong did they not count right?' (B2v–3r).

16   Sharp, *In Contempt of All Authority*, p. 31. See also p. 37, for the indictment of a weaver for seditious words in November 1596. The plight of the weavers in 1595 was protested by Thomas Deloney in a published letter. See Frances Consitt, *The London Weavers Company* (Oxford, 1933), pp. 312–16. I owe this reference to Arthur Kinney.

17 See Walter, 'A "rising of the people"?'
18 See, for instance, John W. Draper, 'The queen makes a match and Shakespeare a comedy', *Yearbook of English Studies*, 2 (1972), pp. 61–7; Steven May, '*A Midsummer Night's Dream* and the Carey–Berkeley wedding', *Renaissance Papers* (1983), pp. 43–52; and, for a non-marital occasion, Edith Rickert, 'Political propaganda and satire in *A Midsummer Night's Dream*', *Modern Philology*, 21 (1923), pp. 53–153, who connected the play to an entertainment given for the queen by Edward Seymour, earl of Hertford, and hence to the problem of the earl's secret marriage to Lady Katherine Grey, whose child, declared illegitimate by the angry queen was, Rickert thought, obliquely represented in the changeling boy.
19 On the office of the Master of the Revels, see Virginia Gildersleeve, *Government Regulation of the Elizabethan Drama* (1908, repr. Westport, CT, 1975).
20 C. L. Barber, *Shakespeare's Festive Comedy: A Study of Dramatic Form and its Relation to Social Custom* (Princeton, NJ, 1959).
21 Compare Edmond Malone, *The Plays and Poems of William Shakespeare*, 10 vols (London, 1790), vol. 2, p. 464: 'Some, however, have thought that "the nine men's morris" here means the ground marked out for a morris dance performed by nine persons.'
22 On the hobby-horse, compare Malone (ibid., vol. 9, p. 307): 'Amongst the country may-games there was a hobby-horse, which, when the puritanical humour of those times opposed and discredited these games, was brought by the poets and ballad-makers as an instance of the ridiculous zeal of the sectaries.'
23 Barber, *Shakespeare's Festive Comedy*, p. 57.
24 Ibid., p. 15.
25 Victor Turner, *From Ritual to Theatre* (New York, 1982), p. 9.
26 Victor Turner, *The Ritual Process: Structure and Antistructure* (Chicago, 1969), p. 176.
27 Victor Turner, *Dramas, Fields, and Metaphors: Symbolic Action in Human Society* (Ithaca, 1974), p. 35.
28 Ibid., p. 55.
29 Robert Weimann, *Shakespeare and the Popular Tradition in the Theater*, ed. Robert Schwartz (Baltimore, 1978, 1987).
30 Mikhail Bakhtin, *Rabelais and his World*, trans. Helene Iswolsky (Boston, 1968, Bloomington, 1984), p. 21.
31 Ibid., p. 19.
32 Weimann, *Shakespeare and the Popular Tradition*, p. 251.
33 Ibid., pp. 24–5.
34 See Peter Stallybrass and Allon White, *The Politics and Poetics of Transgression* (London, 1986), pp. 12–22.
35 Bakhtin, *Rabelais and his World*, pp. 94–5.
36 Ibid., p. 95.
37 For an extended defense of this as the intended staging, see Thomas Clayton, '"Fie what a question's that if thou wert near a lewd interpreter": the wall scene in *A Midsummer Night's Dream*', *Shakespeare Studies*, 7 (1974), pp. 101–23.
38 George Puttenham, *The Arte of English Poesie* (London, 1589), p. 43.

39 Barber, *Shakespeare's Festive Comedy*, p. 120: 'Shakespeare does not make himself accountable for exact chronological inferences.'

40 Montrose, '"Shaping fantasies"'.

41 Ibid., p. 74.

42 Ibid., p. 62.

43 Weimann, *Shakespeare and the Popular Tradition*, pp. 50, 31.

44 Frankie Rubinstein, *A Dictionary of Shakespeare's Sexual Puns and their Significance* (London, 1984), p. 17.

45 John Milton, *Colasterion*, in *Complete Prose Works*, ed. D. M. Wolfe et al. (New Haven, CT, 1953–82), II. ii. 57.

46 See R. Howard Bloch, *The Scandal of the Fabliaux* (Chicago and London, 1986): 'In the counting of the vagina and the anus we recognize the accounting of the poet who plays upon the homophone of *con* [cunt] and *conte* [tale] . . . The debate between adjacent body parts is, at bottom, that of the jongleur who, in addressing his audience, manages to make *cons* and *culs* speak' (p. 106).

47 Ibid., p. 109.

48 See Jack Lindsay (trans.), *The Golden Ass* (Bloomington and London, 1932), p. 22; and, for an extension of Shakespeare's interest in Apuleius, J. J. M. Tobin, *Shakespeare's Favorite Novel* (Lanham, MD, 1984), especially pp. 32–40.

49 Bakhtin, *Rabelais and his World*, p. 78.

50 Weimann, *Shakespeare and the Popular Tradition*, p. 40.

51 Leinwand, 'Deference and accommodation', p. 22.

52 E. K. Chambers, *The Elizabethan Stage*, 4 vols (Oxford, 1923), vol. 4, p. 318.

53 Alexander Neville, *Norfolkes Furies, or A View of Ketts Campe: Necessary for the Malecontents of our Time, for their instruction, or terror; and profitable for every good Subject*, trans. R[ichard] W[oods] (London, 1615), B2r (italics added).

6

Performance

The history of modern performance criticism is usually traced to the work of Arthur Colby Sprague. In his *Shakespeare and the Actors* (1944), Sprague traced the accumulated stage business of the plays' theatrical history from the Restoration to the beginning of the nineteenth century, arguing that 'Shakespeare's plays were written for performance, and surely, through performance, light has been shed on many dark places in them' (Sprague, 1944: xxv). Since Sprague, approaches to Shakespeare in performance have diverged to include accounts by theatre practitioners, theoretical discussions of the dynamics of theatre and, latterly, film, stage histories showing how individual plays have changed over a long period of productions, reviews and interpretations of current individual performances or productions, reconstructions of the contexts of historical productions, speculative accounts of theatrical possibilities, and theories of intention and reception.

In *Moment by Moment by Shakespeare* (1985), Gary Taylor attempts to analyse Shakespeare in performance from the perspective of the spectator and to investigate the pleasure of theatre-going through a sophisticated 'study of response' (Taylor, 1985: 3). Taylor argues that plays in performance unfold as a series of moments, not a static whole. One of his extended examples is from *Twelfth Night*, and Taylor concludes his study:

> The dramatist's manipulation of emphasis might therefore be described in terms of his control of the direction, distance, velocity, mass, and impact of a hypothesis moving through a very particular kind of space. At least, any adequate description of how an audience responds to particular moments in that movement must take account of all these factors, and must at the same time resist all of the associated occupational prejudices of the academic reader. I believe that anyone who could achieve such a description would indeed have succeeded in catching Shakespeare 'in the act of greatness'. (Taylor, 1985: 236)

In *The Shakespeare Revolution* – the title refers to his argument that 'the initiative in recovering Shakespeare has shifted to the theatre' (Styan, 1977: 232) – J. L. Styan argues that both page and stage are needed for the fullest appreciation: 'the scholar will modify the actor's illumination, the actor will modify the scholar's, a process of infinite adjustment' (1977: 237). The book discusses different eras in twentieth-century Shakespearian production. In his *Perspectives on Shakespeare in Performance* (2000), however, Styan proposes a more antithetical relationship between criticism and theatre:

> Criticism is inevitably a generalizing activity, whereas the theatre experience is always particular; criticism is reflective and docile, whereas perceptions in the theatre are wild and immediate and alive. Yet by performance, notions and theories can at least be tested, and the ultimate question can be asked – 'Does it work?' (Styan, 2000: 5–6)

H. R. Coursen's *Shakespearean Performance as Interpretation* (1992) sides with this approach:

> A Shakespearean script exists only in performance. Period. Performance sharpens 'the text' necessarily in this or that direction. We are free to debate or enjoy the choices a director and his actors make. But the debate has relevancy only as it responds to performance. Otherwise, 'the text' becomes a spaceship filled with tinkerers and dial-watchers, but with no destination. (Coursen, 1992: 15)

Harry Berger's *Imaginary Audition: Shakespeare on Stage and Page* (1989) takes issue with the proponents of what he dubs 'New Histrionicism': 'that reading is irresponsible unless it imitates playgoing' (Berger, 1989: xii). Instead, through a critique of the limited methodology of current performance criticism, including Styan (1977) and Taylor (1985), he proposes the practice of 'imaginary audition' as:

> an attempt to reconstruct text-centered reading in a way that incorporates the perspective of imaginary audition and playgoing; an attempt to put into play an approach that remains text-centered but focuses on the interlocutionary politics and theatrical features of performed drama so as to make them impinge at every point on the most suspicious and antitheatrical of readings. (Berger, 1989: xiv)

Richard Levin's 'Performance-critics *vs* Close Readers in the Study of English Renaissance Drama' (1986) also proposes that both schools of criticism can learn from each other:

> one of the most valuable contributions that performance-criticism might make would be to curb the excesses of the close readers of the thematic and ironic

schools, whose interpretations of the plays of this period are often so far removed from theatrical experience that they could not be conveyed in any performance . . . Once we acknowledge that the plays of Shakespeare and his fellow dramatists were written for the stage, then it necessarily follows that any interpretation of them that cannot be conveyed on the stage could not have been intended by the author and so must be rejected. (Levin, 1986: 545, 547)

Opposed to such deference to the theatre, Martin Buzacott, in his *The Death of the Actor*, questions the 'current social and aesthetic supremacy of *actors* in general' (1991: 7). Following Barthes's proleptic declaration of 'the death of the author', Buzacott announces the death of the actor as 'a body devoid of any cultural authority', instead arguing that 'Shakespearean texts speak regardless of the individual who presumes to be their mouthpiece' (Buzacott, 1991: 142). *Shakespeare Quarterly*, volume 36 (1985) includes a special issue 'Reviewing Shakespeare', with essays by Cary Mazer, Alan Dessen, Robert Speaight and H. R. Coursen. Thompson and Thompson (1989) gather a collection of essays on performance criticism which review its methodology and practice, including a useful bibliography. W. B. Worthen's (1989) discussion of performance criticism usefully reviews a number of different positions, arguing for the need to locate the claims of these approaches as criticism, and to integrate performance with other theoretical and methodological enquiries. Alan Sinfield's essay in Dollimore and Sinfield's *Political Shakespeare: New Essays in Cultural Materialism* (1985) offers one example of this integration: in 'Royal Shakespeare: Theatre and the Making of Ideology' Sinfield discusses the ideological work of the Royal Shakespeare Company in Britain since the 1960s and argues for a more incisive critique of that '*Shakespeare* – the whole aura of elusive genius and institutionalised profundity' (Dollimore and Sinfield, 1985: 178) which is sustained through theatrical means. In 'Thatcher's Shakespeare?' (1989), Isobel Armstrong extends Sinfield's analysis in her discussion of the relationship between 'radical academic critique and the performing arts', and in his Afterword to *The Shakespeare Myth*, edited by Graham Holderness (1988), Terry Eagleton criticizes the theatre practitioners represented in the volume, including Jonathan Miller and Sam Wanamaker, for failing to take up the challenge of radical Shakespeare critics: their 'bland Hampstead bohemianism' promotes 'depressing' 'liberal pluralism' and 'depoliticising eclecticism', and their 'dismally regressive opinions' are at odds with avant-garde political scholarship (Holderness, 1988: 206–7). Other essays on the theory of performance criticism are gathered in James C. Bulman's *Shakespeare, Theory, and Performance* (1996).

A recent growth in performance criticism has been in published diary accounts by actors of particular roles or productions, giving the practitioners' perspective. In *Clamorous Voices: Shakespeare's Women Today* (1988), Carol

Rutter mediates interviews with a number of Shakespearian actors: the chapter on *The Taming of the Shrew* is reprinted below. The 'Players of Shakespeare' series offers commentary by Royal Shakespeare Company actors. Volume 1 includes Patrick Stewart and Sinead Cusack on their roles in *Merchant*, Donald Sinden on Malvolio, John Bowe on Orlando and Gemma Jones on Hermione; there are essays on characters from *As You Like It, Measure for Measure* and *The Merchant of Venice* in volumes 2 and 3, on *Love's Labour's Lost* and *Twelfth Night* in volume 2 and *Much Ado About Nothing* in volume 3. In volume 4, *Love's Labour's Lost, As You Like It* and *The Winter's Tale* are discussed. Barton's (1984) volume *Playing Shakespeare* reports on workshops in which actors discuss and experiment with different readings of Shakespeare's language; Janet Suzman (1996) discusses *Acting with Shakespeare: Three Comedies*. Recent stage productions of *The Taming of the Shrew, A Midsummer Night's Dream* and *The Tempest* are analysed in H. R. Coursen's *Shakespearean Performance as Interpretation* (1992); screen versions of *The Comedy of Errors* and Kenneth Branagh's film of *Much Ado About Nothing* are covered by the same author's *Shakespeare in Production: Whose History?* (1996). In his *Shakespeare: The Two Traditions* (1999), Coursen discusses Shakespeare in the cinema, including the 'almost insuperable difficulties of communicating this script [*Twelfth Night*] through a medium that does not ask us to suspend our disbelief' (1999: 200).

Several series take individual plays and discuss their stage histories. Titles in the 'Text and Performance' series include Lois Potter on *Twelfth Night* (1985), who pays particular attention to stage versions in the period 1969–81; David Hirst on *The Tempest* (1984); Pamela Mason on *Much Ado About Nothing* (1992); Bill Overton on *The Merchant of Venice* (1987); Ronald Draper on *The Winter's Tale* (1985); Graham Nicholls on *Measure for Measure* (1986); and Roger Warren on *A Midsummer Night's Dream* (1983). The 'Shakespeare in Performance' series includes James Bulman on *The Merchant of Venice* (1991), which discusses the play's changing impact on the stage from the Elizabethan period to the BBC television production and culturally self-conscious versions from the 1980s, with a focus on the question of anti-Semitism. Jay Halio's volume on *A Midsummer Night's Dream* (1994) gives extensive coverage of Peter Brook's landmark production and its consequences for subsequent directors. On *Love's Labour's Lost* (1993) Miriam Gilbert analyses a number of twentieth-century productions for stage and television in Britain and America. For the 'Shakespeare in Production' series, John Cox's edition of *Much Ado About Nothing* (1997), Trevor Griffiths's *A Midsummer Night's Dream* (1996) and Christine Dymkowski's *The Tempest* (2000) combine an extensive introduction to the stage history with a specifically performance-annotated edition of the play text. A new series, 'Shakespeare at Stratford', focusing exclusively on Royal Shakespeare Company productions, currently has titles on *The Merchant of Venice* by Miriam Gilbert (2002) and Patricia Tatspaugh on *The Winter's Tale* (2001). Roger Warren's book *Staging Shakespeare's Late Plays* (1990) looks at productions by Peter Hall, among other recent directors. Dennis Kennedy's *Looking at Shakespeare: A Visual History of Twentieth-century Performance* (1993) combines methodological and descriptive commentary, and the contributions to his collection *Foreign Shakespeare: Contemporary Performance* (1993) shift the focus away from British theatre.

By contrast with these studies, which usually favour culturally central productions in Stratford-upon-Avon, London and Hollywood, John Russell Brown's polemic *Free Shakespeare* (1997) argues that 'seeing the usual kinds of Shakespeare production will not help the reader to advance further' (Brown, 1997: 3). Brown suggests that directors may impose 'a confinement, a cutting down of a work founded on something other than an intellectual idea' (1997: 14), and advocates 'radical experiment', much of it based on Elizabethan staging practices such as cue-scripts for actors, the same lighting for stage and audience, and stressing 'the explorative and fluid engagement for which they were written' (1997: 83, 82). The most developed account of recreated Elizabethan staging is Pauline Kiernan's *Staging Shakespeare at the New Globe* (1999), which reflects on the early findings of the rebuilt Globe theatre on London's Bankside. Standard works on the Shakespearian theatre are by Gurr (1992) and Thomson (1992). Gurr's work on *Playgoing in Shakespeare's London* (1996) and *The Shakespearian Playing Companies* (1996) develop this field. G. E. Bentley's article in *Shakespeare Survey*, 'Shakespeare and the Blackfriars Theatre' (1948), discusses the connection of the late plays with the particular staging conditions of Blackfriars. A good deal of work on the historical conditions of the performance of Shakespeare's comedies has been focused on the implications of all-male acting companies: see chapter 4 on 'Gender and Sexuality' for a discussion of this critical trend.

The discussion of Shakespeare in recent performance has flourished in the area of film and television productions of the plays. Pioneering studies by Manvell (1971) and Ball (1968) on silent versions were followed by Jorgens (1979), who usefully divided Shakespearian film into: the 'theatrical', in which film is used to record a performance designed for theatrical representation; the 'realist', which uses film's mimetic qualities to situate the play in a realist context; and the 'filmic', where the director is a 'film poet, whose works bear the same relation to the surfaces of reality as poems do to ordinary conversation' (Jorgens, 1979: 10). *Watching Shakespeare on Television* (1993) by H. R. Coursen develops some of the specifics and the implications of the reduced format of Shakespearian film on video and small screen. Susan Willis (1991) discusses the BBC television Shakespeare series. Deborah Cartmell's *Interpreting Shakespeare on Screen* (2000) includes material on films of *Much Ado About Nothing* and *The Tempest*. Samuel Crowl discusses Shakespearian comedy on film in his *Shakespeare Observed* (1992), with particular reference to Zeffirelli's *Taming of the Shrew* and Hall's *A Midsummer Night's Dream*. Contributors to *The Cambridge Companion to Shakespeare on Film*, edited by Russell Jackson (2000) consider specific genres and plays, including Michael Hattaway on 'The Comedies on Film', who concludes 'perhaps a truly great film of a comedy has yet to be made' (Jackson, 2000: 96).

Much recent work on performance integrates stage-readings with other critical approaches. For example, Laurie Osborne's (1996) analysis of performance editions of *Twelfth Night* unites textual and stage approaches to illuminate the different cultural forms in which an apparently singular play has flourished, and Penny Gay (1994) combines gender criticism and stage history in her *As She Likes It: Shakespeare's Unruly Women* (see her chapter on *As You Like It* reproduced below).

References and Further Reading

Armstrong, Isobel (1989) 'Thatcher's Shakespeare?', *Textual Practice*, 3: 1–14.
Ball, Robert Hamilton (1968) *Shakespeare on Silent Film: A Strange Eventful History*. London: Allen and Unwin.
Barton, John (1984) *Playing Shakespeare*. London: Methuen.
Bentley, G. E. (1948) 'Shakespeare and the Blackfriars Theatre', *Shakespeare Survey*, 1: 38–50.
Berger, Harry (1989) *Imaginary Audition: Shakespeare on Stage and Page*. Berkeley, CA: University of California Press.
Berry, Ralph (1989) *On Directing Shakespeare: Interviews with Contemporary Directors*. London: Hamish Hamilton.
——(1993) *Shakespeare in Performance: Castings and Metamorphoses*. Basingstoke: Macmillan.
Brown, John Russell (1966) *Shakespeare's Plays in Performance*. London: Edward Arnold.
——(1997) *Free Shakespeare*. London: Applause.
Buchman, Lorne M. (1991) *Still in Movement: Shakespeare on Screen*. Oxford: Oxford University Press.
Bulman, James C. (1991) *The Merchant of Venice* (Shakespeare in Performance). Manchester: Manchester University Press.
——(ed.) (1996) *Shakespeare, Theory, and Performance*. London: Routledge.
Burnett, Mark Thornton and Wray, Ramona (2000) *Shakespeare, Film, Fin de Siècle*. Basingstoke: Macmillan.
Buzacott, Martin (1991) *The Death of the Actor: Shakespeare on Page and Stage*. London: Routledge.
Cartmell, Deborah (2000) *Interpreting Shakespeare on Screen*. Basingstoke: Macmillan.
Collick, John (1989) *Shakespeare, Cinema and Society*. Manchester: Manchester University Press.

Coursen, Herbert R. (1992) *Shakespearean Performance as Interpretation*. Newark: University of Delaware Press.

——(1993) *Watching Shakespeare on Television*. Rutherford: Farleigh Dickinson University Press.

——(1996) *Shakespeare in Production: Whose History?* Athens: Ohio University Press.

——(1999) *Shakespeare: The Two Traditions*. Madison, NJ: Associated University Presses.

Cox, John F. (1997) *Much Ado About Nothing* (Shakespeare in Production). Cambridge: Cambridge University Press.

Crowl, Samuel (1992) *Shakespeare Observed: Studies in Performance on Stage and Screen*. Athens: Ohio University Press.

Dawson, Anthony B. (1988) *Watching Shakespeare: A Playgoers' Guide*. Basingstoke: Macmillan.

Dollimore, Jonathan and Sinfield, Alan (1985) *Political Shakespeare: New Essays in Cultural Materialism*. Manchester: Manchester University Press.

Draper, Ronald P. (1985) *The Winter's Tale* (Text and Performance). Basingstoke: Macmillan.

Dymkowski, Christine (2000) *The Tempest* (Shakespeare in Production). Cambridge: Cambridge University Press.

Gay, Penny (1994) *As She Likes It: Shakespeare's Unruly Women*. London: Routledge.

Gilbert, Miriam (1993) *Love's Labour's Lost* (Shakespeare in Performance). Manchester: Manchester University Press.

——(2002) *The Merchant of Venice* (Shakespeare at Stratford). London: Arden Shakespeare.

Griffiths, Trevor R. (1996) *A Midsummer Night's Dream* (Shakespeare in Production). Cambridge: Cambridge University Press.

Gurr, Andrew (1992) *The Shakespearean Stage 1574–1642*, 3rd edn. Cambridge: Cambridge University Press.

——(1996a) *Playgoing in Shakespeare's London*, 2nd edn. Cambridge: Cambridge University Press.

——(1996b) *The Shakespearian Playing Companies*. Oxford: Clarendon Press.

Halio, Jay L. (1994) *A Midsummer Night's Dream* (Shakespeare in Performance). Manchester: Manchester University Press.

Hirst, David L. (1984) *The Tempest* (Text and Performance). Basingstoke: Macmillan.

Holderness, Graham (ed.) (1988) *The Shakespeare Myth*. Manchester: Manchester University Press.

Jackson, Russell (ed.) (2000) *The Cambridge Companion to Shakespeare on Film*. Cambridge: Cambridge University Press.

——and Smallwood, R. L. (1988) *Players of Shakespeare: Further Essays in Shakespearian Performance*. Cambridge: Cambridge University Press.

——and——(1993) *Players of Shakespeare 3: Further Essays in Shakespearian Performance*. Cambridge: Cambridge University Press.

Jorgens, Jack J. (1979) *Shakespeare on Film*. Bloomington, IN: Indiana University Press.

Kennedy, Dennis (ed.) (1993a) *Foreign Shakespeare: Contemporary Performance*. Cambridge: Cambridge University Press.

——(1993b) *Looking at Shakespeare: A Visual History of Twentieth-century Performance.* Cambridge: Cambridge University Press.

Kiernan, Pauline (1999) *Staging Shakespeare at the New Globe.* Basingstoke: Macmillan.

Levin, Richard (1986) 'Performance-critics vs close readers in the study of English Renaissance drama', *Modern Language Review,* 81: 545–59.

McKernan, Luke and Terris, Olwen (1994) *Walking Shadows: Shakespeare in the National Film and Television Archive.* London: British Film Institute.

Manvell, Roger (1971) *Shakespeare and the Film.* London: Dent.

Mason, Pamela (1992) *Much Ado About Nothing* (Text and Performance). Basingstoke: Macmillan.

Mazer, Cary M. (1985) 'Shakespeare, the reviewer, and the theatre historian', *Shakespeare Quarterly,* 36: 648–61.

Nicholls, Graham (1986) *Measure for Measure* (Text and Performance). Basingstoke: Macmillan.

Osborne, Laurie E. (1996) *The Trick of Singularity: Twelfth Night and the Performance Editions.* Iowa City: University of Iowa Press.

Overton, Bill (1987) *The Merchant of Venice* (Text and Performance). Basingstoke: Macmillan.

Potter, Lois (1985) *Twelfth Night* (Text and Performance). Basingstoke: Macmillan.

Rutter, Carol Chillington (1988) *Clamorous Voices: Shakespeare's Women Today,* ed. Faith Evans. London: Women's Press.

Smallwood, R. L. (1998) *Players of Shakespeare 4: Further Essays in Shakespearian Performance.* Cambridge: Cambridge University Press.

Sprague, Arthur Colby (1944) *Shakespeare and the Actors: The Stage Business in his Plays (1660–1905).* Cambridge, MA: Harvard University Press.

Suzman, Janet (1996) *Acting with Shakespeare: Three Comedies.* London: Applause.

Styan, J. L. (1977) *The Shakespeare Revolution: Criticism and Performance in the Twentieth Century.* Cambridge: Cambridge University Press.

——(2000) *Perspectives on Shakespeare in Performance.* New York: P. Lang.

Tatspaugh, Patricia (2001) *The Winter's Tale* (Shakespeare at Stratford). London: Arden Shakespeare.

Taylor, Gary (1985) *Moment by Moment by Shakespeare.* London: Macmillan.

Thompson, Marvin and Thompson, Ruth (eds) (1989) *Shakespeare and the Sense of Performance: Essays in the Tradition of Performance Criticism in Honor of Bernard Beckerman.* Newark: University of Delaware Press.

Thomson, Peter (1992) *Shakespeare's Theatre,* 2nd edn. Theatre Production Studies. London: Routledge.

Warren, Roger (1983) *A Midsummer Night's Dream* (Text and Performance). Basingstoke: Macmillan.

——(1990) *Staging Shakespeare's Late Plays.* Oxford: Oxford University Press.

Willis, Susan (1991) *The BBC Shakespeare Plays: Making the Televised Canon.* Chapel Hill, NC: University of North Carolina Press.

Worthen, W. B. (1989) 'Deeper meanings and theatrical technique: the rhetoric of performance criticism', *Shakespeare Quarterly,* 40: 441–55.

Kate: Interpreting the Silence

Carol Rutter

Carol Rutter's unobtrusively edited narrative comprises the comments of three Kates from different productions between 1978 and 1987. Drawing on actors' comments about their preparation for their roles and the productions in which they took part, this gives a unique insight into the performance history of The Taming of the Shrew. *Rather than smoothing over differences of emphasis, Rutter makes these the subject of the chapter, including such issues as the historical location of the production, the attitude to the induction scene, and the characterization of the major figures. Part of the challenge of this approach to more conventional critical writing, including performance criticism, is its register: sometimes colloquial, emotional and, perhaps, less constrained by big critical questions such as authorial intention, historical contextualization and characterization. Elsewhere in Rutter's volume,* Measure for Measure, As You Like It, Macbeth, All's Well that Ends Well *and* Cymbeline *are discussed through a similar lens. Other accounts by actors of their performances in Shakespeare's comedies can be found in the 'Players of Shakespeare' series (see above).*

Carol Rutter, 'Kate: Interpreting the Silence', in *Clamorous Voices: Shakespeare's Women Today*, ed. Faith Evans (London: The Women's Press, 1987), pp. 1–25.

Surely we're trying to find out at the beginning what we mean by 'shrew'. Supposing we said 'shrew' equals 'noisy one'. Along comes a man to tame the noisy one. And for almost five acts we never hear her speak. *Fiona*

I wanted the play to be about Kate and about a woman instinctively fighting sexism. But I don't really think that's what the play is about. It's not the story of Kate: it's the story of Petruchio. He gets the soliloquies, he gets the moments of change. All the crucial moments of the story for Kate, she's off stage. *Paola*

I think the play is about Kate being liberated. At the end that so-called 'submission' speech is really about how her spirit has been allowed to soar free. *Sinead*

Kate has a very strong watching brief. *Sinead*

Kate has eyes everywhere. *Paola*

I felt very watchful. *Fiona*

The play is a love story. *Paola*

The play is a problem play. *Sinead*

The play really isn't clear enough to deal with the hot area it's handling. It's underwritten and over-endowed. *Fiona*

Three Kates – Paola Dionisotti, Sinead Cusack and Fiona Shaw – talking about *The Taming of the Shrew* agree as often as they disagree, and contradict not just each other but themselves. But they reach consensus on this: the play is full of traps, and there are many *Shrews* inside *The Shrew*.

The story of Petruchio wooing, wedding and finally winning Kate can be played as a romping farce or as social satire, as legitimising the title or interrogating it. It can be dismissed as an apprentice work – perhaps Shakespeare's first play – that bears little relation to his mature comedies, which are structured around female viewpoints. Or perhaps it should be seen as deceptively sophisticated, subverting the conventions of inherited shrew literature. The conventional taming story ends with the unruly woman silenced, but in Shakespeare's version, 'noisy' Kate, silent throughout, is invited at the end to speak; this 'tamed' shrew talks and talks and talks.

Some *Shrews* negotiate an uneasy truce between the clamour of Kate's story and the whimsy of her sister Bianca's, and most use the drunken tinker, Christopher Sly, to frame and fictionalise the story. Sly's function is to tell us that *The Taming of the Shrew* is, after all, only a play, performed for his benefit when he wakes from his stupor.

Directors, all of them male on the main RSC stage, have mapped various routes through the play. In 1978 Michael Bogdanov put *The Shrew* in modern dress and began the action in the audience. A drunk came reeling down the aisle. Shoving aside the usherette, he jumped on to the stage, wrecked the set and then passed out. As the dust settled, men in hunting pinks appeared dragging a dead vixen, which they dumped on his body. The drunk was, of course, Christopher Sly, and when he roared in again on a motorbike Bogdanov's strategy was clear: this *Shrew* was being played as Sly's dream, a male supremacist's fantasy of revenge upon women. The usherette was Paola Dionisotti. She would be Kate to Sly's Petruchio, and the dead vixen would predict the relationship between man and wife. But for Paola, the director's decisions were problematic:

He was very keen that the whole thing was Sly's dream, that Kate was really a figment of Sly's imagination. Which is the kind of statement to which you reply, 'Right, sure, okay,' then you go away thinking, 'How on earth do I act a figment of someone's imagination?' It's the kind of information you wish directors would keep to themselves, because it is of no use to any actor.

She felt that putting the play into modern dress gave her Kate no room to manoeuvre, because in 1978 someone as angry as Kate would have been at the forefront of the women's movement; she certainly wouldn't have behaved as the play requires her to.

> Kate has to have a context that the audience can instantly identify as one that represses her, confines her. If what one is watching is someone who represses and confines *herself*, I think one ends up going against what Shakespeare's written. I don't believe he has written a woman who's self-destructive. Mike, our director, wanted to create a wealthy, western European world, with British aristocracy and Italian mafioso imagery thrown in. Now the women in a true mafioso society are often magnificent and powerful but they have terribly clear-cut areas in which they can operate. My tension in the production was that I kept finding myself internalising; I kept wondering why I didn't just get up and go. And it shouldn't be an internal thing. The point is that she *can't*. Kate can't get up and go.

In this production the 'world of the Minolas was monied and cynical', while Petruchio was a 'no-hope outsider who's used by that society to get Kate off their hands'. As Paola observes, 'They were really quite glad to see the back of both of them.'

> Jonathan [Pryce] played Petruchio as that kind of classic man who comes strolling into a society bragging like hell; he is terribly competitive because he has this *need* to be accepted, though he never will be. He's an outsider. She's an outsider. And she's a problem. It's an embarrassment for Baptista to have that kind of daughter, a daughter who can run rings round people, and can do it in public. After they're married, Baptista doesn't give a damn how Kate is getting on with Petruchio. She is completely abandoned.

In the 1982 production Barry Kyle again used Sly as a fictionalising device, opening his production in a cosily realistic Elizabethan Warwickshire at Christmas. This 'real world' disappeared when the taming story began, in a Padua that was disconcertingly fantastic. Sinead Cusack played Kate in a dress she describes as 'Elizabethan Zandra Rhodes'; Petruchio – Alun Armstrong – wore jack boots, and Bianca's suitor Lucentio turned up in a striped blazer and boater. There was a bicycle built for four, a black wedding dress, a water trap and endless invention that came to annoy Sinead:

> I think our production was overwritten with images. They were such an inventive company that all of them came up with wonderful ideas, but the mistake we made was that we didn't throw out the dross. We hung on to so much, whereas what we needed to do was to distil the essence of the play and to find its savagery. The invention clouded the production and a lot of the time I felt I was working against the text.

One image, though, she did like: for Bogdanov, Kate's journey had been prefigured by the dead vixen; for Kyle it was predicted by a female falcon, a live haggard. Petruchio brought it on, hooded, for the famous soliloquy in Act IV, scene 1, 'My falcon now is sharp', which outlines his taming strategy.

> Then he would lift the hood and she would shake her bells. The imagery there was very clear and it was very pure, the way he gentled the falcon. What I felt strongly was that the falcon would be free: it was liberating her to a role that she was going to enjoy playing. And that's what I felt Petruchio was doing with Kate.

At the end, these two productions pointed towards very different futures for their Kates: Sinead's was liberated 'from the carapace she'd built to protect herself from the brutal world of men', while Paola's ended up as a casualty of male power games.

Jonathan Miller, in 1987, saw another Kate. He cut Sly, making Kate's world the only world of the play. This meant the audience confronted her story direct, and it allowed a clear presentation of the difficult issues, the domestic politics that are raised by the taming story and Kate's apparent submission. Kate's final speech is only the final articulation of these issues, and the production was designed to make that speech intelligible, to make sense of words like 'hierarchy', 'supremacy', 'duty', 'content'. Miller set the play in Elizabethan dress. And he cast Fiona Shaw as Kate.

> I like to believe that I was cast because in the past few years I've become really excited by trouble-shooting. I think it's a difficult role to cast. On the face of it, Kate doesn't seem to drive the play: you have to listen to what other people say about her with really sensitive ears.
>
> I found the play difficult to read, not at all what I was used to. I had come from playing Portia and Beatrice – who on the page are so vibrant: they leap up and all you've got to do is act them – to this rather obscure woman, a woman who's not very witty, or so I thought when I read it, just reactive. A woman who, *when* she speaks, speaks in a kind of merry-go-round language, in jangly rhythms, dum-de-dum-de-dum:
>
> > Iwis it is not half way to her heart.
> > But if it were, doubt not her care should be
> > To comb your noddle with a three-legged stool,
> > And paint your face, and use you like a fool.

Not great stuff! And yet the journey of the play leads Kate from that to this:

> > But now I see our lances are but straws,
> > Our strength as weak, our weakness past compare,
> > That seeming to be most which we indeed least are.

The pure rhythms at the end of the play are so beautiful.

Fiona Shaw describes *The Shrew* as 'a difficult play full of traps', one of which is 'received notions of what Elizabethan expectations of marriage were. I find that very unrevelatory, because in any kind of diachronic relationship between then and now it's so easy to fail to understand what they were about.' And she defends Jonathan Miller against any charge that his interpretation of *The Shrew* 'merely' substantiated Elizabethan attitudes:

> The status quo isn't necessarily a dirty word for Miller. He's very challeng-ingly anti-liberal in that way. He's more complicatedly conservative. His feeling about the play historically – he kept on using history, or his notion of history, as a touchstone – was that the mid-Elizabethan period had included such hopelessness in relation to marriage. Men, like Petruchio and Bianca's suitors, did buy women; many women were unhappy, and men were too, and so the expectation of marriage was rather low. But as the middle-class economy changed, so did expectations about marriage. The potential for making marriage pleasant included a duty on the part of the parents to try to make sure that the couple liked each other. That was a big step.
>
> Now Miller says, to substantiate this new view of happy marriage, that there are many Elizabethan portraits of happy, smiling women, and a lot of graves all over Warwickshire – where he thinks the play is really set – with two bodies carved in stone, clearly people devoted in life and in death. He feels that's a real clue: that men and women did resolve the difference in status by making marriages based on mutuality.
>
> But I, like Jane Austen, have a little bias in favour of my own sex. To me those images may be far more indicative of the way women allowed the system to function: by aligning themselves, rather than by mutual align-ment, in marriage. The cost of making a marriage work seems to me to be very one-way. Clearly there has been a system at work which modern feminist theory has brought brilliantly to light: a double-think, where men have described the reality and women have conformed to that description of it.

If Jonathan Miller is 'complicatedly conservative', Fiona Shaw is complicatedly radical, but they didn't know this about each other until they met on the rehearsal floor.

> We all came as strangers, which was difficult. I'd never worked with Brian Cox – Petruchio – or with Jonathan before. I felt very protective of womankind in relation to the play, and certainly I found myself in rehearsal being watchful.
>
> Jonathan's interest in the play was to make sense of it, and he acknowl-edged the difficulties by saying that Kate behaves like many children who are unloved. I have a slight problem with that because I don't think Kate

is a child. She's a woman, and I think that to make her a child is to under-estimate her.

He also didn't think she's a particularly intelligent woman (maybe Shakespeare's heroines sometimes aren't; I've always thought they are) and he thought that she reacts like children do who are unloved: she behaves badly, really younger than she is, like a ten-year-old. Until this man comes, who takes her on. And without beating her up – which is the usual way in productions of *The Shrew* – he very non-violently disorientates her by not accepting anything she says. Jonathan says that's what doctors do with aggressive children. I think he was translating the 'taming' of the shrew into 'therapy', the realignment of the delinquent.

That's a heavy imposition, because once you commit yourself to that statement, you could go a step further and have Petruchio in a white coat.

It took Fiona a year of playing *The Shrew* to 'know the play terribly well and to hear the heartbeat of it', and to be persuaded that Miller's disturbed child was misconceived.

The heartbeat isn't of a quiet, sullen delinquent, but of a woman who's raging. She's everything she's described as. She's a fright. She's a real shrew. She does bang about. I can imagine a Kate who *enjoys* behaving as badly as she does; that in itself is enjoyable. My Kate was very unhappy. She radiates unhappiness, and that's an odd first beat to conjure up. Look at Shakespeare's other heroines and you'll see that, when they come on, they're often in a state of crisis, but they always express themselves in such a way that you can really hear the soul of who they might be were they not in crisis.

Fiona's first entrance as Kate made that crisis explicit. She showed her to be a woman who had no standing in Padua. Shakespeare sets the play in a town among town preoccupations – merchandise, markets and marriage – and town pressures. To have a termagant daughter in Padua is not just a personal mis-fortune but a public nuisance. Miller's production defined this context: his Padua was both affluent and feudalistic, its high gold-washed walls enclosing a public place where self-exposure was always imminent.

The Shrew is also about upstarts and outsiders, an unruly woman and a sub-versive suitor who affront decorum and knock Padua off its level footing. Miller's set demonstrated this too. It put Padua on a steep slope, its street a vertiginous rake. Whoever entered Padua came as if over the top of a ha-ha, pitched forward and having to back-pedal to brake a fall.

Into this scene came Baptista Minola with two daughters and two suitors. Except for the numbers, everything was wrong. The suitors were twits, the father a ninny. Both suitors were haggling over Bianca; neither was interested in Kate, but Baptista wouldn't hear their suit, he said, until his unmarriage-able elder daughter was off his hands. Bianca, who in this production moved as if on oiled wheels, stood ignored on the sidelines while Baptista was assailed by the suitors. As so often in this play, a scene that seemed to be about a woman turned out to be about the men. In *The Shrew*, women are marginalised. None more so than Kate.

She finally appeared, behind the rest, self-absorbed, teetering down the steep edge of the steep verge, arms outstretched like a tightrope walker. On one side was High Street Padua, on the other, a sheer drop. This woman was on the brink. While the suitors bickered, Fiona's Kate ranged behind them, flashing her embroidery scissors, gouging initials into the walls and hacking off handfuls of hair.

I wanted to give the effect of a woman mutilating herself like some women in prison do. I wanted to use the scissors to cut my arm – I thought about women in crisis who, far from being aggressive towards other people, are very often aggressive towards themselves. I was going to try to do tattoos, but on the big stage you've got to make choices that are seeable. I have a tendency as an actress to come on and make a strong statement so the audi-ence know who I am and then get on with it. For me in this scene, the point was that Kate doesn't fit the group. Physically she is a misfit.

Is she a shrew? Or has she been made a shrew? Miller was very clear about Kate's case history – from the age of three or whatever. Her mother may have died in childbirth, with Bianca perhaps; Bianca was always more conformist, Kate always difficult.

After a while, when people are calling you a shrew, you start living the name. If you're told you're ugly, you start acting ugly. Kate has started acting 'shrew', and the reputation gives her an amazing amount of power: she tyrannises everybody, she radiates disapproval, she makes uncontrollable noise, and it's always massively at her own cost. She'll make noise, lose status, but create a stir. So by the time we meet her she is somebody whose identity is linked to her behaviour.

But the problem with expressing any of this is that Kate doesn't have the language, she doesn't have the lines. So you have to hear Kate's silence and to interpret the clues of the silence. I think Shakespeare is making a point of it. This man comes to tame Kate and speaks through the whole play. But surely we're trying to find out at the beginning what we mean by 'shrew'. Supposing we said 'shrew' equals 'noisy one'. Along comes a man to tame the noisy one. And for almost five acts we never hear her speak. The noisy one is not speaking! So we must interpret the silence.

Why is Kate silent? Well, she doesn't *choose* to be silent. She's not let speak. Petruchio deprives her of her usual noise. But of course action is also language, and Kate does have that language. She goes whack, bang, whack! That's language too.

In Kate's opening scene (Act I, scene 1) she has to endure the sniping comments of Bianca's suitors, but for Fiona it was less the suitors than her father who made Kate wretched.

> Baptista is so unkind. He's focused on Bianca all the time. At the end of the scene, he's told her to go in and he's dismissed the suitors. He turns to Kate. In our production we made an acting choice here – Baptista hesitated as if he'd forgotten her name before saying, 'Katherina, you may stay,' meaning, 'You may stay outside in the street.' Kate has to demand her right to go into the house: 'I trust I may go too, may I not?'
>
> It seems to me that when people are as unhappy as Kate they are the voice of something that the whole community should be responsible for. I met a doctor the other day who was talking about dementia in South Africa. When South African whites go loopy their dementia is always about black men coming over their walls and beating them up and killing them. Dementia is a very good mirror of what's going on in the subconscious of a community. There's a corporate identity of which the disturbed individual is but a part.
>
> I'm not removing from Kate the responsibility for behaving as she does, but there's no doubt that she is the voice of pain in the community. You don't go very far off the centre of a community to appear like a maniac. It's not easy to do everything wrong as constantly as Kate does! When you do everything wrong you really aren't happy.

Kate's next scene (Act II, scene 1) shows both her pain and her anger. It begins with her binding Bianca – she is pumping her sister for information about her suitors – and ends with her being bound to Petruchio.

> Shakespeare is showing Kate in action, behaving very badly to her sister. There's no doubt that she's causing pain, and the pain is written in: 'bondmaid', 'slave', 'unbind my hands'. Kate has tied her up! But it also hints at the state that Kate is in. She seems to be spiralling out of control. She's now got to tying up her sister, and in a moment we hear why.
>
> Bianca, either inadvertently or because of the astuteness that siblings often have about each other, says, 'Is it for him' – a suitor – 'you do envy me so?' The point is that Kate does envy her. She doesn't envy *Bianca*, but in that awful nightmare world of lack of clarity – the inability to be outside one's own situation – there are things she envies *about* Bianca, even though she can't stand her. To my mind this scene screams desperation, with its rather dirty-mac desire to hear who Bianca's keen on. This is surely the

voice of someone who herself hasn't registered what men are, but senses that her sister has. The scene is humiliating; it must have cost Kate a lot.

Is it also pathetic, given the idiocy of Bianca's suitors? Maybe. But I know a lot of idiots who are also very dangerous men to be with. What we've got to see is the potential of men in a community, and we've got to believe that Kate and Bianca could be married to those men.

The scene shows a Kate who is remarkably different from her sister but who is also significantly interested in marriage.

I'm sure they look different. The text hints at it. People always dress to say something about themselves, and I think Shakespeare intended that polarisation. Bianca wears 'gawds'. She's a decorated creature. And the implication is that Kate isn't. Besides, Bianca is such a good operator. When their father enters, Bianca's not weeping because Kate has hurt her: it's an extra weeping because he's come in. Part of Kate's rage is at the unfairness of it all.

Kate talks a lot about marriage and seems to want to get married, but she wouldn't marry those snot-rags Gremio and Hortensio, Bianca's suitors, and she knows they wouldn't marry her either. But you've got to believe that she's not mad, that she would marry someone who was marriageable.

When Petruchio arrives from Mantua, however, Kate gets a suitor she doesn't anticipate. Petruchio is outrageous, 'mad', he affronts social decorum. His marital objectives are mercenary: 'I come to wive it wealthily in Padua.' But so, too, are the other suitors' – it's Petruchio's bluntness that astonishes everyone. He is a man who speaks half-lines: he has no time, nor words, to waste. He is, they say, 'marvellous froward'. And 'froward', like 'mad', is a word that's been used on Kate in Act I, scene 1: 'That wench is stark mad or wonderful froward.'

Brian Cox played him grizzled and square, a man who had lived his lines:

> Have I not in my time heard lions roar?
> Have I not heard the sea, puffed up with winds,
> Rage like an angry boar chafed with sweat?
> Have I not heard great ordnance in the field . . .

This was no man to fear 'a woman's tongue'. His manservant Grumio handed him a stiff drink while Baptista hurried off to fetch Kate. But in Miller's production the ominous preliminaries were a joke on the audience's expectations, for the wooing that ensued was no knock-down fight. For all his ruggedness, Petruchio was no bully. And that disconcerted Fiona Shaw.

Originally I had the idea that because Kate herself didn't have a lot of language, she was very physical. I wanted to do weightlifting and so on. I'd planned it that I would make as big a racket physically as I normally make verbally. I would love to have come in and been very difficult for him to handle. People have criticised my Kate for not putting up more of a fight. I'm dying to put up a fight but look at the text – it ain't there!

And Cox, almost in defiance of theatrical tradition, insisted on playing the text straight, a text that in spite of the swagger makes Petruchio gentle, courtly, accommodating. And dominant. As Fiona points out, 'There's more than one way to batter a woman . . .'

Her Kate was shoved through the door into this wooing.

All she sees is a back. She doesn't know how to behave alone with a man, and this is clearly going to be a wooing. But she has never been led to believe that anyone would marry her. This is going to be at best an embarrassing situation and at worst an appalling one. She comes in – and is *talked to* by a man for the first time; that's what disorientates her. Not his violence but his gentleness. He seems to be talking in riddles. He's a bit peculiar, this man. She hasn't heard people talk like that ever!

Indeed, Petruchio's tactics are linguistic rather than physical. His strategy is to subvert language: 'Say that she rail, why then I'll tell her plain / She sings as sweetly as a nightingale.' And he starts with Kate's own name. 'Good morrow, Kate – for that's your name, I hear.' She corrects him: 'They call me Katherine that do talk of me.' But he answers:

> You lie, in faith, for you are called plain Kate,
> And bonny Kate, and sometimes Kate the curst.
> But Kate, the prettiest Kate in Christendom . . .

'You lie' is outrageous: it wipes out her identity. Or it just might be the opening gambit in a mutual process of realigning language that will cancel out labels like 'shrew'. Fiona's Kate was intrigued.

Kate starts enjoying the conversation. They fire off each other, they banter. He doesn't seem appalled by her – that's pretty novel. But then she makes to leave, and he blows it by saying, 'With my tongue in your tail?' I feel that's below the bottom line. She doesn't mind a bit of rude talk, she's up to that, but nobody speaks to her obscenely. She walks down, he apologises, and she wallops him. I think she is really appalled. That slap is the first clue that Kate's behaviour is, ironically, a plea for dignity.

I think that's something of what the play's about. Being a shrew in a community – it's like being a loose woman, people can treat you any way they like. Kate lays herself open to that kind of violation. So she hits him

– she gains that one – and instead of breaking her arm or kicking her out, he engages in an exchange that absorbs both of them.

Then he tells her he's going to marry her. And she says nothing. The problem is how to occupy that silence. I think she's stunned. He is doing what all men in that society can do, which is to deprive her of all freedom. Why should a man who talks to someone for five minutes then be able to say, 'And will you, nill you, I will marry you'? All the banter is undermined by that moment.

Nor can Kate have any reply, for Petruchio is controlling and distorting reality through language. He tells Baptista on his return that her ranting 'is for policy'. When Baptista expresses doubts that Petruchio has succeeded with Kate, since she has just sworn to see him 'hanged' rather than marry him, Petruchio mildly assures him:

> 'Tis bargained 'twixt us twain, being alone,
> That she shall still be curst in company.
> I tell you 'tis incredible to believe
> How much she loves me . . .

This is enough for Baptista. He declares the marriage made. But in the next scene (Act III, scene 2) he's nonplussed. It is Kate's wedding day and she has been stood up. The whole town is milling about, waving nosegays with less and less enthusiasm.

> When Petruchio doesn't turn up for the wedding, it's just cripplingly embarrassing. Nothing has ever been right for Kate, including her wedding day. Even that's wrecked. There are certain expectations in one's life, like your first communion or your wedding, when it's your day and everyone has to dress up for you. For a fellow not to turn up for a wedding is the biggest let-down of all.

Yet her humiliation had the ironic effect of realigning Kate with her community. For the first time she was standing centre stage, surrounded by a Padua sympathetic to her enraged tears, edgy at its own complicity in the débâcle. And when Petruchio did finally appear wearing 'monster' apparel, Padua was offended. The man they had introduced into the community to eliminate their social problem was now humiliating them: he was a 'devil', she a 'lamb'. Fiona feels that Petruchio's costume should be an affront:

> It isn't merely comic; Kate ought to see a man dressed like a maniac. Petruchio is undermining the values of her society, and she ought to see that too. His costume should be monstrous, insulting, threatening – and a mirror for Kate to see herself in.

But Fiona wasn't satisfied that it did mirror her appearance, because her own costume was too elegant.

> I don't think Kate should be in any way glamorous. I think she should have spit down her front: she's beginning to appear the way people look at her. I couldn't work out the story of my costume. Did Kate choose that gold material, or did someone else? If somebody else did, then I'd probably be wearing what Elizabethan men thought women should wear, and I suspect that would be a rather dull tapestry. That's why I wear my costume with a distaste for it: Kate doesn't fit it. It's not her dress. Petruchio gives her a wedding all right, but at what cost! He violates all her basic expectations.

He doesn't allow her to attend her own bridal dinner. He's in a hurry: 'I must away today.' The company demurs. Then Kate tries: 'Let me entreat you.' Petruchio is 'content'; and Fiona's Kate, mild for the first time in public, was transformed into someone erect, gracious. Until Petruchio adds, 'I am content you shall entreat me stay – / But yet not stay, entreat me how you can.' Kate explodes.

> Do what thou canst, I will not go today,
> No, nor tomorrow – not till I please myself . . .
> For me, I'll not be gone till I please myself.

She issues her own invitation to Padua:

> Gentlemen, forward to the bridal dinner.
> I see a woman may be made a fool
> If she had not a spirit to resist.

Padua starts to snicker, Petruchio appears cowed: 'They shall go forward, Kate, at thy command.' But then he deftly turns the tables on her: 'For my bonny Kate, she must with me.' Brian Cox made the scene ludicrous but dangerous by addressing most of the famous 'goods and chattels' speech not to Kate but to the crowd, who had no intention of seizing his property:

> Nay, look not big, nor stamp, nor stare nor fret,
> I will be master of what is mine own.
> She is my goods, my chattels, she is my house,
> My household stuff, my field, my barn,
> My horse, my ox, my any thing,
> And here she stands. Touch her who ever dare!

Kate got the message. 'They shall not touch thee, Kate!' was both a threat and a promise.

And in our production, instead of throwing her over his shoulder and running off (there's a hint that that should happen in the text because Kate has no time to say anything; they simply exit), Petruchio hands me a *bible*! I flick through this missal, and it dawns on me, this is what I've inherited as an Elizabethan woman. People like Kate who are purely reactive sometimes get a flash of analytic clarity; it's a tough revelation to discover that your protection, the bible, is also your danger – a book telling you you're nothing. Grumio is standing there with a sword to keep back people who aren't coming forward; Petruchio is talking nonsense – 'They shall not touch thee, Kate' – when nobody has tried to help, not even her father.

And that's why I throw the bible down and *choose* to go with Petruchio. It was one of those moments when I had an effect on this production. I think women often do choose destinies that aren't best for them, and I think Kate chooses to go with him. Little does she know what she's in for.

Even Kate's one moment of resistance, 'I see a woman may be made a fool / If she had not a spirit to resist,' is to Fiona's ears more petulant than persuasive.

She's actually saying, 'Nanny, nanny, nanny! You're not going to catch *me* out!' There's a rhythm in it that is slightly less than philosophic.

But if you're not going to be made a fool of, you often make a fool of yourself. So she reaches for her dignity – and once again Petruchio disorientates her. When he says, 'Look not big,' it's absurd because she's not, but the sub-text to it is, 'That's married life and how it's going to be, it's going to be a rough ride all the way.'

Petruchio is having a go at all of them. But he isn't against spirit. He's not daunted by it; he has plenty of it himself. And that's why he likes Kate. And why he takes her away from Padua, from where she's functioned with that social identity 'shrew'.

Petruchio takes her home to Mantua (Act IV, scene 1), to a house that is like a bizarre hostel, where she is the only woman in the place and she is stripped of all power to tyrannise.

She's not given a chance to restart that old cycle in the new place. For Kate, it becomes a very dangerous play in the second half. The audience are of course delighted with Grumio's story about the appalling journey home – how the horse fell on her, how Petruchio beat Grumio, how she waded through the mire to pluck him off and 'prayed, that never prayed before'.

The possibilities of the homecoming scene are so interesting because this is the point when Kate starts being really tamed. She comes in wrecked from the journey, still in her wedding dress, and what happens next is that her expectations of normal life are totally undermined. She who has been characterised by violence now has to observe what violence really is.

Petruchio at home looks mindlessly violent.

> He shouts at the servants, then the next moment tells Kate, 'Relax!' He
> beats them up and says, 'Nay, Kate, be merry!' It's wonderful! It's a night-
> mare. Because the tamer is a man who says, 'You want violence? Look at
> this, what d'you think of this? Bang!' So much so that the only lines Kate
> speaks in that scene are defending the servant! 'Patience, I pray you, 'twas
> a fault unwilling.' For the first time she is the one who's tempering. For the
> first time Petruchio makes contact with her civilisedness.

Is Petruchio really violent, or is it only a ploy?

> Petruchio's violence has got to be real *to Kate*, so that we can see who she's
> dealing with. It puts Petruchio on the line: he's really got to say, 'I know I
> hit my servant, but I'm doing it to show you something,' so that when he
> then says, 'Come, I will bring thee to thy bridal chamber,' it's not carry-on-
> up-your-trousers time, it's this man who beats servants now taking her to
> bed. I don't want to be earnest about it, but this is the reality of the situa-
> tion that Kate thinks she is in. And that's marriage.

Petruchio takes her to bed, but not to consummate the marriage. Instead, he
makes 'a sermon of continency' to her. Again, the violence is all verbal; again,
Kate's expectations are staggered: Petruchio

> rails, and swears, and rates, that she, poor soul,
> Knows not which way to stand, to look, to speak,
> And sits as one new-risen from a dream.

Whether the tactics are verbal or physical, Fiona thinks Petruchio in love is
violent to Kate.

> Men are violent to women. Maybe Shakespeare is showing us the enacted
> metaphor of being 'violently in love' – you know, 'I love you so much I'm
> gonna beat you if I see you talking to anybody else.' What's that about? It's
> possession, it's hunting. You desire something. And you kill it!

But hunting and killing were not what this Petruchio had in mind. When
Brian Cox returned on stage to outline his taming strategy, 'My falcon now is
sharp,' the soliloquy emerged from an Elizabethan context. To tame a falcon
involved a sequence of endurance tests, a 'warring' that was mutual: neither
falcon nor falconer ate or slept until they both did. Implicit in the transaction
was the belief that a broken falcon is a better bird. But then breaking a falcon
might not be an exact model for breaking a wife, so Cox's Petruchio was taking
a risk. Underlying the process was the implication that it might not work.

Cox played it over a basin of washing water, his shirt pulled half over his head, his nakedness partly exposed. He looked vulnerable. His appeal, 'He that knows better how to tame a shrew / Now let him speak – 'tis charity to show,' was a *cri de coeur* from an exhausted man at his wits' end.

His bewilderment anticipated Kate's in her next scene (Act IV, scene 3). Grumio sat impassively sewing as Kate, now in a white smock, as though her clothes had been confiscated, dragged from surface to surface looking for somewhere to curl up, but someone always prodded her back into alertness.

She hasn't been allowed to sleep, and she's dizzy. The rhythms, the pressure of her speech, seem to be awake; it's that kind of vibrant exhaustion where you're trying to keep your head awake, and you're almost hyperactive, you're so tired.

And now for the first time we hear her view of things. It's her first long speech, the nearest thing to a soliloquy in the play for her. She is saying, 'I have no idea what's happening to me. What's he trying to do? Did he marry me to starve me?' She asks Grumio for food and he plays cat and mouse with her hunger: he takes a kind of sadistic delight in having been given the reins of power for half an hour. But the pace of the game has to be relentless, Kate's got to be dizzy with disorientation, so as Grumio finishes on her Petruchio comes in smiling. 'Darling! I've brought you lunch!' He offers it to her, takes it away, offers it to her, and *makes her thank him*. There's something pornographic about it: 'I thank you, sir.' *He* is teaching her a lesson in politeness!

Then, having said she can eat at last, Petruchio distracts her. He says, 'And now, my honey love, / Will we return unto thy father's house,' and that's wonderful, because she's dying to get out of this madhouse, but when she turns back to her plate the food is gone! And then suddenly a hat's thrust under her nose. They're going home. Petruchio's ordered new clothes. So in comes the hat, in comes the haberdasher. Speed, speed, speed. Look at the hat, a great hat, a wonderful hat. It's the hat Petruchio has ordered, but he says 'terrible hat', 'frightful hat', and she says, 'It's a wonderful hat!' She is crossing him – rightfully, because it *is* a nice hat! It's a hat of the times, it's a hat for her, a lady's hat so it's not his place to . . . and they're back into a rigmarole again. It's very dizzy – until she reaches a point where she must speak. She's got to elbow the room, to break the frenzy of what we sense has been about twelve hours of complete nightmare, and say something that she hadn't even intended to say, which is that she can't spend her life not speaking:

> Why sir, I trust I may have leave to speak,
> And speak I will. I am no child, no babe.
> Your betters have endured me say my mind,

And if you cannot, best you stop your ears.
My tongue will tell the anger of my heart,
Or else my heart concealing it will break,
And rather than it shall, I will be free
Even to the uttermost, as I please, in words.

It's a beautiful speech. The metre is utterly regular, implacable. She's tried everything. She's tried not speaking. She's tried understanding. And now she's saying, 'I'm furious, and if I can't let my fury out, my heart might break, "And rather than it shall, I will be *free* . . . in *words*."' She's claiming language. And if that's shrewish, that's shrewish. But she can't keep in what she feels.

Now that's a *natural* disposition, and that's what interests me about the Elizabethan model. She's a voice. Every now and again there's a character who really isn't Shakespeare's most interesting heroine but who nevertheless says something of primary importance, which is that part of the problem of our whole society is that women have been *told* they may not speak. And every now and again there's a victim of that who says, 'I can't manipulate my way around it: I am *by nature* a speaker. We've been born with these things – legs, arms, voices – and we've got to use them.'

But Petruchio's response to her plea is: 'Why, thou say'st true – it is a paltry cap.'

That's outrageous. Outrageous! It takes your breath away. He trivialises her. Wipes her out. Which I think should resonate, because people do it all the time. And it's a plumb line in the play. Petruchio has pushed it too far.

He has made her a cipher, and the scene proceeded to make her a tailor's dummy. Dismissing the haberdasher, Petruchio summoned the tailor. Kate was hoisted on to what might have been a scaffold or a pedestal and folded into yet another version of a dress she would not wear. 'What's this?' Petruchio bellowed, 'A sleeve?' It came away in his hand, and Kate looked as though she was being dismembered. The violence to the dress summarised all the violence in the play; and when the men began arguing among themselves Kate stood on her pedestal, silent, ignored, watching another demonstration of her own style of behaviour.

The reversal of expectation was as devastating as on her wedding day. The tailor might have been dressing her for a triumphant homecoming; instead, Petruchio had stripped her to her smock – a gown of humility perhaps, except that it had been dirtied by the manhandling.

We really are reaching the bottom line now. We're down to granite. Petruchio has brought things to chaos. The tailor, a servant, is humiliated, and that's wrong. The tailor doesn't know it's a game. And anyway, it's not right that servants should be abused. Petruchio abuses a servant to teach her that the abuse of servants isn't right. It's a mock scene that uses real abuse.

Kate smiled wryly, pulled off her wedding ring, peered through it, and fixed it back on to her finger. When the stage cleared, Petruchio sat down beside her and talked to her unresponding back.

> Well, come my Kate, we will unto your father's
> Even in these honest mean habiliments.
> Our purses shall be proud, our garments poor,
> For 'tis the mind that makes the body rich . . .

He went on talking until she began to listen. And one of the things she heard was that he would take risks on her.

> What, is the jay more precious than the lark
> Because his feathers are more beautiful? . . .
> Oh no, good Kate, neither art thou the worse
> For this poor furniture and mean array.
> If thou account'st it shame, lay it on me.

Petruchio's nonsense is puckered by a wonderful clarity. And that, presumably, is what cumulatively clicks with Kate. She still doesn't know what he's on about, but eventually the whole lot will make sense! Ripping the gown has a point: Petruchio is saying, outsides don't matter, names don't matter, because ''tis the mind that makes the body rich.' That's a huge statement! And if you're reproached, 'Lay it on me,' that's huge risk!

But then, at the end of the tailor scene, Petruchio hits her with a new low. He says it's seven o'clock. Kate frowns. She knows it's two. Petruchio says, 'It shall be what o'clock I say it is.'

God, what a line! Shakespeare is sailing so close to the wind. The line looks like a stamp of approval for male dominance – 'Whatever I say goes!' – but I don't think it is. I hope it's not. I think Petruchio is playing another of those word games that haven't yet quite clicked with Kate. Understandably, she is blind to the freeing possibilities of conceding anything, having become a barnacled custodian of reaction. Petruchio's line is really about language, and about how language works. Once again he's trying to show her names don't matter, *externals* don't matter. Essentials do.

It is not until the next scene (Act IV, scene 5) that Kate finally does see. They are on their way home to Padua. Kate still has on her wrecked wedding dress, walking not riding, and they stop for a rest in the middle of nowhere. Petruchio looks up at the sun, and calls it the moon.

You can understand Kate hanging on to one of the few things she can be sure of. She can't resist saying, 'The moon? The sun! It is not moonlight now.' And his response is, 'If that's what you think, we're going home.' Stalemate. And then someone appeals to her, 'Say as he says, or we shall never go.'

It's wonderful and an awful moment for Kate. For the first time, the responsibility of that whole group of people is in her hands. One word from her and they go back. Or one word from her and they go forward. Her dilemma is that she can control the situation, but only by seeming to lose control over her own sense of reality: she has to call the sun the moon. But then what she recognises at that point is that instead of always saying 'no', she can try 'yes' – she may as well, she's got nothing to lose. Try saying, 'Yes, I'll call the sun the moon, because it doesn't matter.' 'Yes' matters, names don't.

It's freedom. It's power. And it's a wicked, terrible play because she's got to render herself up before she gains herself. In losing her life she wins it. What a dilemma. What a gamble.

The scene isn't about humiliation. Or about Kate falling in love with Petruchio. It's about a third thing. It's about being given a chance, for the first time in her life – like Helen Keller working out what water was when she could neither hear nor see, finally making the connection, when her nanny took her arm and said, 'Water, water,' that the sound she was being made to say linked to something else. This man who has seemed to be her tormentor has given her, or has allowed her to take, the step that will save the rest of her life.

That's why it's so wrong if the play is about dominance and a broken spirit. It's about someone on the brink – you recall that first image, a woman on the brink – who found a way of saying 'yes' without being compromised. At the end of the play, Kate wins. She can say anything now and she's still Kate. Interestingly enough, every night the audience is silent at that moment.

There are, it seems, moments that belong so essentially to the play that they transcend whatever interpretation actor, designer or director imposes on them. For Sinead and Paola too, this scene was an epiphany that transformed both Kate and the play. 'Just listen to her!' says Paola:

> Forward, I pray, since we have come so far,
> And be it moon, or sun, or what you please.
> And if you please to call it a rush-candle,
> Henceforth I vow it shall be so for me.

She's saying, 'I can go further in this game than you.' She's on top of the language. It's absolutely balanced. And then they have that exchange:

> *Petruchio*:   I say it is the moon.
> *Katharina*:   I know it is the moon.
> *Petruchio*:   Nay, then you lie. It is the blessèd sun.
> *Katharina*:   Then, God be bless'd, it is the blessèd sun.
>   But sun it is not, when you say it is not,
>   And the moon changes even as your mind . . .

Kate picks up all those images of sun and moon and intensifies them. She *dances* with it. The beauty of the speech becomes like an escape from the situation. The images are warm and the meshing of the lines gives the feeling that they're writing a love poem together, or playing a game. She has finally discovered that it *is* a game, and that they can play it together.

As Kate and Petruchio arrive back in town, Padua is in uproar. Strangers are pounding on doors and being refused admittance. Servants are pretending to be their masters, and Bianca has eloped with what everybody thinks is her tutor. Kate watches from the sidelines as the outrageous discovery is made. But whatever triumph she may feel at seeing Bianca transformed into a black sheep she caps in the final act by the coup she pulls off at Bianca's wedding dinner.

Jonathan Miller set it as a street party. A huge table loaded with bread and fruit straddled the stage, and everyone was there, even the tailor and the haberdasher. Fiona Shaw thinks that when Kate and Petruchio come in they ought to look exhausted.

> She should be in her muddy wrecked wedding dress. One look at them and everybody ought to think, 'Wooo, it's been the disaster we thought it was going to be!' And she should have the hat – the hat they rowed over . . . They're muddy; that should be shaming, but now she knows who she is. She burns from within.

The scene around the trestle table was solemn, celebratory – until male jibes began elbowing their way around it. Bianca stalked out; Kate followed.

> It's important that the women don't separate. In a minute she makes a statement, not on behalf of how great men are, but on behalf of our inability to change things. And that speech is going to take on board what she sees here: yet another table of men making noise. The men – as soon as the women have gone, the men behave like men do: they start betting on women.

Each of the newly married men lays a wager on his wife: that she will obey his summons to return to the table. And Kate wins the wager. More than that, she is invited to instruct the fractious wives in obedience.

So what is Kate's final speech about?
Sinead Cusack saw it as a declaration of independence.

At the end of the play I was determined that Kate and Petruchio were rebels and would remain rebels for ever, so her speech was not predictable. Having invited her to speak, he couldn't know what form her rebellion was going to take. He was very shaky indeed in the scene, not knowing what was coming. This so-called 'submission' speech isn't a submission speech at all: it's a speech about how her spirit has been allowed to soar free. She is not attached to him. He hasn't laid down the rules for her, she has made her own rules, and what he's managed to do is to allow her to have her own vision. It *happens* that her vision coincides with his. There's a privately shared joke in the speech. And irony. And some blackness. The play is dark, savage sometimes. But I enjoyed the last speech. They're going to go on to a very interesting marriage. Petruchio was on his knees. I was standing.

Paola Dionisotti saw it as a statement of utter disillusion.

We came out of the previous scene having kissed. I had called him husband. 'Now pray thee, love, stay,' was an attempt to say, 'We've arrived, we're about to be husband and wife with my family.' I had called him 'love', and that was an attempt to get him to talk to me, *me*, not to that woman he was trying to dominate, but to *me*. And he responded. Suddenly, everything was possible. I used to feel, 'I think I know what game I'm playing. I think it will be all right. I think I can actually enjoy this.'

For Bianca's wedding I'd been to the hairdresser, had my nails done. I was done up to the nines. We were coming from a meal. Bianca's husband Lucentio was slightly pissed – you know that sense of family gatherings. The last scene was set around a huge green baize table. The men were slouched around it drinking brandy, gambling, playing cards. When Bianca got angry – it was her party and they weren't playing her games – I followed her out, so when Petruchio summoned me into what turns out to be the wager scene, I knew something was up.

When I entered, I saw someone quite high, quite flushed, proving something to the blokes. He is playing poker – the outsider is playing poker with the boys – and he's got this huge need to win. So when I come in, he is so triumphant. He's been able to bring me back, doll me up, *and* get me to win the wager for him. When he tells me to 'swinge' Bianca and the widow soundly, I pause, trying to suss out . . . we're part of a game and I want to know what it's about. But the game he is playing is just a traditional macho power game. What I find impossible is, having been through all that stuff over Bianca's elopement, having watched all that rubbish, that 'ado' in the previous scene, I then discover that Petruchio *still* has a need to prove me – just one more test – in front of all of them.

They aren't worth it, Petruchio! We know that. We've *watched* them. But he has a need. He will always have a need. He will always be competitive because he will always feel threatened. So that last speech: he is so chuffed about his triumph that he is more relaxed towards me than probably anywhere in the play, so he listens properly. He makes the mistake of encouraging me to say something. *So I say it all.*

I used to find it very moving – that speech is so full of affection for women. Kate is completely in control of her language in this speech. What she is feeling inside, she deals with and rises above with the language. However desperate her situation, her articulacy never really fails her, which is why it's so wrong that her voice should be strangled – mine often was.

She's talking to different people. To the women she's saying, 'This is what our role is, girls – really explore it; it's like an acting exercise. *Investigate the realities*: thy husband is thy lord. Your life is in his hands.' That's the reality. For many women that's the reality. To Petruchio she's saying, 'Is this what you want? Is this what you're asking me to do? Give us your foot ... The man I was having gags with in the street, does that man want me to do this? *Who* is it who wants me to do this?' He was triumphant, so he listened; for the first time, he listened properly. And what he heard was somebody saying, 'A woman should lick a man's arse. She should wipe her face under his shoe. Because she loves him. Men are everything. They are our gods. They make all the right decisions' – that, given the history of what's just happened in the play! And she ended up with, 'And I'll do it. Because that's what you want. I'll do it.'

My Kate was kneeling and I reached over to kiss his foot and he gasped, recoiled, jumped back, because somehow he's completely blown it. He's as trapped now by society as she was in the beginning. Somewhere he's an okay guy, but *it's too late*. The last image was of two very lonely people. The lights went down as we left – I following him, the others hardly noticing we'd gone. They'd got down to some hard gambling. They just closed ranks around the green baize table.

For Fiona Shaw, Kate's last speech is about 'a choice that has dignity'. In a curious way, it emerges from the wager itself. Fiona has no illusions about it being an easy speech.

When Petruchio lays a bet on Kate, maybe that's where he renders himself up: he takes a chance on her. She took a chance on him, she rendered herself up in the sun/moon scene. Now *he* takes a chance on her. Even so, the soliloquy seems to go off into a terrible area – it's a pattern of this play. You think, 'We're lost, we're lost, this is a spirit broken.' And yet it comes back at the point of no return. It starts out directed to those two women – Bianca and the widow – but it's in the presence of all those men. It's not a speech he told her to speak. It's clearly her own language. It's new-minted. Petruchio releases her in some way, and so she does speak. She speaks, and says everything she wants to say, more beautifully than anybody else has said it.

Fiona's Kate was not merely articulating the status quo and falling in line with the patriarchy, she was handing back the challenge of that status quo.

Kate makes the men take themselves on. She is saying, 'I acknowledge the system. I don't think we can change this' – which is a terrible indictment of a system of patriarchy that is so strong it is unchangeable *even for its own good*. To say 'I see . . . Our strength as weak' in front of men is terribly strong. She's saying, 'I concede it. You own the lot. Feel good about it, boys? Feel good about it? I don't mind whether you feel good about it or not. You own the world. Right, the only thing that's left for us women to do is to follow a duty according to the model of our whole society. And our duty to our husband is to "do him ease".'

Kate had been standing alone, mid-stage. Gradually, though, she moved around the table to the corner where Petruchio sat. She sat down next to him, still talking, now to him, as one by one the other men at the table stopped eating and began listening. On 'Place your hands below your husband's foot . . . my hand is ready,' she wiped her hands – it wasn't resignation; she was getting the crumbs off – then offered Petruchio her hand. He clasped it, and shook it, an equal partner in a marriage whose interwined fingers signalled an intelligent peace.

It's the first step towards saying, 'Let our marriage be about marriage first.' And he takes another chance and says, 'Kiss me, Kate.' And she goes another step further and kisses him.

Then Kate and Petruchio walked out of the play, in this production side by side. They abandoned the table of gawpers to their own futures and makeshift exits. For Fiona,

the play lands back in Kate's hands. It's her play at the end. It's a very serious play. It's terribly fundamental, almost transcendental. These two people have to rise, through their pain, above the usual territory of negotiation. They're not down in the mud. 'I'm not slugging you down here. We're going up there. We're going to slug it out on the roof.' But when they get to the roof, they don't have to slug any more. Somehow they've climbed all that way, and now they're skating. It's almost medieval in that – it's like all those journeys of people who go through a terrible ordeal.

What about the other women? What about Bianca at the end? Does she take over where Kate left off?

Not at all. The thing's far more interesting than our desire to unify plays neatly at the end. As Kate symbolises those few who get away, Bianca symbolises the many who stay. And Bianca is in for the fight now. Not that she deserves it. There's no such thing as goodies and baddies in that chaos.

And what about that quirk of English etymology: was Fiona's shrew *shrewd*?

Not at all. Not at all shrewd. She was absolutely, stupidly *raw*. But she's learnt. She seems to go through the valley of men and come out the other side a woman. She has learnt the most brilliant lesson. She's going to be able to handle anything after this.

Cast Lists for *The Tami ng of the Shrew*

First performance 19 April 1978

Katherine	Paola Dionisotti
Bianca	Zoë Wanamaker
Petruchio	Jonathan Pryce
Lucentio	Anthony Higgins
Grumio	David Suchet
Tranio	Ian Charleson
Baptista	Paul Brooke
Curtis	Juliet Stevenson
Directed by	Michael Bogdanov
Designed by	Chris Dyer

First performance 7 October 1982

Katherine	Sinead Cusack
Bianca	Alice Krige
Petruchio	Alun Armstrong
Lucentio	Mark Rylance
Grumio	Pete Postlethwaite
Tranio	John Bowe
Baptista	David Waller
Curtis	William Haden
Christopher Sly	Geoffrey Freshwater
Directed by	Barry Kyle
Designed by	Bob Crowley

First performance 3 September 1987

Katherine	Fiona Shaw
Bianca	Felicity Dean
Petruchio	Brian Cox
Lucentio	Alex Jennings
Grumio	Barrie Rutter
Tranio	Bruce Alexander
Baptista	George Raistrick
Curtis	Derek Hutchinson
Directed by	Jonathan Miller
Designed by	Stefanos Lazaridis
Costumes by	Martin Chitty

As You Like It

Penny Gay

Penny Gay surveys productions of As You Like It *from the second half of the twentieth century as a way of discussing the play's impulses towards gender liberation and containment. Extensive quotation from contemporary reviews establishes audience reception of the play's gender politics in different productions as crucial to its continuing reinvention in the theatre. The chapter gives a sense of directors' changing priorities as they envisage the social and erotic relationships between the main characters. Penny Gay's book also offers similarly detailed chapters on other comedies, including* Twelfth Night, Measure for Measure, The Taming of the Shrew *and* Much Ado About Nothing.

Penny Gay, '*As You Like It*: Who's Who in the Greenwood', in *As She Likes It: Shakespeare's Unruly Women* (London: Routledge, 1994), pp. 48–85.

Pretty pastoral or exploration of the dark recesses of the psyche? Or damning indictment of a power-hungry urban society? The conventions of pastoral, which Shakespeare drew on so extensively in *As You Like It*, allow for all these interpretive emphases, and more. The play's social framework is clear, but in commentaries it tends to take second place to the fantasy of transformation in the greenwood – self-sufficiency, sudden conversions, and above all, a marvellously fluid sexuality, independent of conventional gender signs and embodied in the image of the free woman in love, Rosalind. Recent critics have stressed the way the powerful fantasy of liberation, particularly sexual liberation, is contained by a reassertion of the patriarchal system, which is always there in the greenwood anyway (in a fantastically benign version) in the exiled Duke's 'court'. Rosalind's last two speeches in the play's narrative are a ritual of voluntary re-entry into the patriarchy:

> (*To the Duke*) To you I give myself, for I am yours.
> (*To Orlando*) To you I give myself, for I am yours.
> . . . I'll have no father, if you be not he.
> I'll have no husband, if you be not he.
>   (V. iv. 114–15, 120–1)

But as Valerie Traub argues, this submission does not take place until after Rosalind has led the play 'into a mode of desire neither heterosexual nor homoerotic, but both heterosexual *and* homoerotic'.[1] Her last line before the teasing epilogue is the provocative reminder to Phoebe: 'Nor e'er wed woman, if you be not she.'

Rosalind's elaborate courtship game with Orlando throws into question not only the regulation and organisation of desire, but also the construction of gender.[2] What *is* the proper behaviour for a young woman in love? 'You have simply misused our sex in your love-prate', says Celia (IV. i. 189); yet Celia herself is of just such a 'coming-on disposition' when occasion finally arises in the person of Oliver – and so too is Phoebe, taking 'Ganymede's' outward signs of masculinity as a licence to desire. *As You Like It* effects, through Rosalind's behaviour, the most thorough deconstruction of patriarchy and its gender roles in the Shakespearean canon; yet it is a carnival licence allowed only in the magic space of the greenwood. At the end, all must return to the real world and its social constraints – though we can read Rosalind's epilogue as a liberating reminder of a world of alternative possibilities: is she/he finally boy or girl?[3] By comparison, *Twelfth Night* seems the more troubled and troubling play, since no exit from Illyria is implied for the characters, despite Feste's reminders to the audience of *their* real world.

Stephen Greenblatt comments that Rosalind belongs to 'a social system that marks out singularity, particularly in women, as prodigious, though the disciplining of singularity is most often represented in Shakespearean comedy as romantic choice, an act of free will, an expression of love.'[4] Greenblatt's second clause has been privileged over the first in the critics' response to Rosalind in performance: she is thought of as *society's* ideal young woman,[5] on the verge of marriage – and when an actress presents Rosalind's 'singularity' as disruptive of social norms, there is often considerable unease in the ranks of critics. The play's history at Stratford over the last forty years reflects most strongly our culture's fascination with this figure of the marriageable daughter;

inevitably also it responds to a changing view of the nature of social bonds, in the depiction of the two Dukes' courts, and most notably in the figure of Jaques.

1952–57

The 1952 production by Glen Byam Shaw has all the hallmarks of post-war glamour that are typical of this period.[6] The lovers were the youthful and attractive Margaret Leighton and Laurence Harvey. The sets and costumes by Motley were elaborately pretty – 'the scene is France', the programme tells us – and had the look of tapestries from the court of Louis XIII, though some critics found the foliage 'sub-tropical'. The greensward extended beyond the proscenium arch, and included a fake rock-pool (33 years later the water would be real, a stream across the front of the stage, and much use would be made of it, from narcissism to ritual cleansing). Tellingly, the commonest critical epithet for Motley's greenwood was 'Neverland' – with Margaret Leighton clearly recognisable as Peter Pan; her boyish looks and figure made this a natural association (she played Ariel in the same season at Stratford). In Arden, she was comfortably dressed in a floppy shirt, breeches, and short jacket, and seemed quite at home in her role as commander of various Lost Boys (and girls). She was not reluctant to sit inelegantly on the ground, and many critics commented on her 'sprightliness', her vitality, her 'tomboyish fun and high spirits'. This quality in the performance was perceived by the critic of the *Western Daily Press* (1 May 1952):

> Livened by the sprightly personality of Margaret Leighton, this 'As You Like It' . . . bubbled up to an enchanting make-believe of Spring song. Miss Leighton was a gay deceiver of infectious spirit, boyish and girlish together in swift changing moods that rippled like a babbling brook through the still beauty of Motley's Arden.

Others, however, found all this energy somewhat exhausting, even unladylike:

> Perhaps Miss Leighton's interpretation would be even more satisfying if her apparently inexhaustible vitality were subjected to firmer control. Her gestures sometimes gave the impression of restlessness. (*Birmingham Post*, 1 May 1952)

> Margaret Leighton had taken her pattern of a boy from an attractive but underfed, over-excitable *gamin*, rather than from the sturdy English adolescent, who can be among the most beautiful of living creatures. She was, it is true, hampered by the clothes designed for Ganymede, for, in an effort to get away from the hackneyed (but becoming) doublet and hose, Motley provided her with an adaptation of the costume affected by girl cyclists on long, dusty tours. This

> scruffy attire could not obliterate the actress' great beauty, but 'heavenly Ros-
> alind' was almost too well disguised. (Ruth Ellis, *Stratford Herald*, 2 May 1952)

Clearly there were some members of the audience who didn't care for the image of the modern young woman in her freedom-bestowing pedal-pushers. Another aspect of ladylikeness which Leighton flouted came under the heading of 'reserve' or 'poise'. Philip Hope-Wallace thought that she 'ha[d] not the aristocratic sense of comedy of the greatest Rosalinds . . . she was obliged to work too hard, in order to save the play, to allow for many of those contrasts of silent happiness which can so well set off the raillery' (*Manchester Guardian*, 30 April 1952). Such vitality and independence might even bring on social disaster:

> If she conceives the part as Shakespeare wrote it, for an Elizabethan boy, her
> straddle-legged disguise as Ganymede looks right. If she supposes this Princess
> of Harden [*sic*] to be of courtly breeding, such inelegant posturing is of old-maid
> inclination. (Kenneth Pearson, *Manchester Daily Despatch*, 30 April 1952)

Perhaps the oddest of these observations from those who have seen the writing on the wall and realise, with fear, that the day of the dutiful, charming daughter is passing came from the critic of *The Sunday Times* (4 May 1952):

> Miss Leighton does not have that bubbling gaiety that Dame Edith Evans
> brought to the part. She is younger, sadder; she is paler, thinner; dressed as a
> boy, she is too short in the coat, too long and flimsy, frail and wasted in the leg.
> What an actress Miss Leighton would be, if only she could be persuaded to
> transfer her reverence for Stanislavski to steak-and-kidney pie!

It's the foreignness, the un-Englishness of this new image of women that is such a threat to conservative critics: the transatlantic girl bicyclist or androgynous French *gamine* look, lacking feminine curves; intellectual, even. The critics were of Margaret Leighton's parents' generation, and they were not reassured (though often, despite themselves, charmed) by what they saw.

Laurence Harvey's Orlando, on the other hand, was perfectly acceptable: adjectives such as handsome, sturdy, virile, manly and romantic were applied to him, and he was particularly congratulated on his wrestling. He was evidently secure about both his status (despite the play's opening scenes) and his sexuality. Did Leighton's Rosalind, however, perhaps find him a little dull? Ivor Brown reported that 'confronted with the double affection of Rosalind, love of Orlando in his simplicity and of her own wit in its complexity, [she] throws the more emphasis on the latter' (*Observer*, 4 May 1952).

Other aspects of the production brought general approval. Though *The Times* did not care to be shown 'Arden in winter', others welcomed the response to the text's suggestions that it was not always summer in an ideal-ised pastoral greenwood (though the play did in fact move from winter through spring to final summer). Similarly an unusually 'chirpy' Celia (Siobhan McKenna), obviously responding to Leighton's spiritedness, brought enthusi-astic comments, particularly as 'Miss McKenna controlled her performance with such tact that the competition was never serious' (*Birmingham Post*, 1 May 1952) – *she* remained a lady. Michael Hordern's Jaques was commended for his 'sad, gentle music' (*Western Daily Press*, 1 May 1952) in a generally admired performance of the conventional melancholic.

Five years later Byam Shaw undertook another production at Stratford, again with Motley as designers; the show was a vehicle for Peggy Ashcroft, then in her forty-ninth year (she had first played Rosalind in 1932 at the Old Vic). The blocking was much the same as in Shaw's earlier production; what was missing, however, was Margaret Leighton's energising sprightliness. Motley's designs did not help matters: still 'French' in general style, the period was moved back to the early sixteenth century; the costumes were heavy, the Forest of Arden was wintry, then very thinly clothed with obviously artificial leaves on Rosalind's arrival. Stage pictures were reminiscent of a Book of Hours, clear and uncluttered to the point of sparseness.

Reactions to Ashcroft's Rosalind were mixed. This star of the English stage was not just a lady, she was a Dame; she had royal approval. 'Triumphant' though many thought her performance to be, 'She could never be an arch young woman, a thigh-slapper. She is an actress whose gaiety is born of truth, and who can speak to us when she is silent . . . She does not romp and rage' (J. C. T[rewin], *Birmingham Post*, 3 April 1957). The fact that she went on on the first night with a throat infection may have exacerbated the general impression of this Rosalind's 'sadness', which 'overflows into almost every line she speaks, the result being that it is barely possible to believe in her love for Orlando' (R. B. M[arriot], *Stage*, 4 April 1957). Rosemary Ann Sisson found her 'gentle and affectionate rather than high-spirited, as befits a girl first in sorrow for her father's banishment, and later altogether overcome by love' (*Stratford Herald*, 5 May 1957). [. . .]

Some critics expressed nostalgia for Margaret Leighton's bubbling youth-fulness; others, and Dame Peggy herself, looked forward to her Imogen in the same season – 'a character worth at least a pair of Rosalinds', said J. C. Trewin in the *Illustrated London News* (13 April 1957). In fact, according to Michael Billington, 'Rosalind . . . has never been one of her favourite Shakespeare parts. It is amusing to find her writing to George Rylands in the course of rehearsal: "Rosalind is a wonderful girl but I wish she didn't talk *quite* so much." '[7] This sounds like the judgment of a 49-year-old woman on the behav-iour of the young, and her envy of their irrepressible energy. Byam Shaw's attempt to regain the high ground of conservative theatrical practice by correcting the daring modernity of Leighton's Rosalind – replacing her with a mature 'star' – had missed its mark, receiving faint praise as 'safe, sensible, and good-natured' (*Birmingham Mail*, 3 April 1957). The tide had turned, and what critics wanted to see now was a Rosalind who, as well as displaying the familiar traits of warmth, tenderness, and humour, created the thrill of sexual readiness.

1961–73

Almost thirty years after Vanessa Redgrave's barefoot, denim-capped Rosalind stepped onto the Stratford stage, critics were still recalling her with wonder and delight. Julian Holland of the *Evening News* (5 July 1961) was one of several reviewers who declared themselves 'madly and desperately in love' with Redgrave, who at 24, tall and slim, had no need of heavy stage makeup to give her beauty. Overwhelmed critics attempted to convey the essence of her charismatic performance: it was 'sunny', 'luminous', 'radiant'. *Punch* managed a slightly more telling analysis:

> she is immensely natural, and her gentle mockery is always near the surface, so that even in the extravagance of adoration she is never mawkish. Of course she is an entirely modern Rosalind. She might be any of our daughters, bowled head over heels, and it is a pleasure to watch her. (Eric Keown, *Punch*, 12 July 1961)

Redgrave's 'modernity' was a matter of her personal style and presence. Her costume (by Richard Negri, as were the sets) was quite remarkably similar to that of Margaret Leighton nine years earlier – floppy shirt and breeches (called 'jeans' by some confused critics, just as Leighton's were), worn with an air of comfort and gaiety. Where Leighton was berated for sitting inelegantly on the ground, Redgrave's naturalness was expressed in her *lying* on the greensward next to Orlando, chatting animatedly, at times grabbing hold of him quite unselfconsciously. 'Prone or supine, kneeling or crouching, hugging her knees, or flinging herself backwards before Orlando when in "a more coming-on disposition", she is exquisite,' said Felix Barker (*Evening News*, 11 January 1962). Some critics thought her 'gawky', but to none of them did this seem a disadvantage; on the contrary,

> Miss Redgrave had the audience in the hollow of her hand. Perhaps it is not playing fair to Shakespeare to turn his Rosalind into a twentieth-century gamin, a fantasticated Bisto kid, a terror of the lower fifth. Miss Redgrave's Rosalind is like all these things. It may be, on the other hand, that 'As You Like It' has had to wait until the 1960s for someone to appreciate that this is what Rosalind is. (*Birmingham Mail*, 11 January 1962)

'She achieved something rare in acting – she was at once timeless and contemporary': Julian Holland's tribute to Redgrave's quality is typical of the
critics' capitulation. No longer are they prescribing ladylike behaviour, describing their own ideal girl: they have been forced to recognise that the part of
Rosalind is there to be filled out by an actress who can put into it her own
sense of what it is to be a young woman 'fathom deep' in love. But she is also
a character thrown on her own resources when exiled by an authoritarian state.
It seems entirely appropriate that Redgrave, between the Stratford season and
the London revival, became a political activist, for what she was demonstrating on the Stratford stage was literally 'actresses' liberation'.[8]

Michael Elliott's production was a breakthrough on many levels. A minor,
but not insignificant, point was that the play had only one interval, rather than
the two that were *de rigueur* at the time: going to the theatre was no longer
quite so dominated by social considerations – rather, the audience members
were expected to concentrate on the play for over an hour and a half before
resuming their social selves. The first half of the play took place in winter, the
second in summer (the evocative lighting, by Richard Pilbrow, was much
admired). For the first time, also, a 'movement director', Litz Pisk, was
credited in the programme; many reviewers found this idea somewhat risible,
but henceforward no production of a Shakespearean comedy would be complete without its dances. For both these developments the publication of C.
L. Barber's *Shakespeare's Festive Comedy* in 1959 may have been partly responsible; by the later 1960s, Barber's influence was clearly acknowledged in Peter
Hall's and other directors' work on the comedies.

Richard Negri's set was another departure from tradition: a single, stylised,
huge tree placed on a steepish rising mound. The only changes were in lighting, props, and backcloth. Reviewers complained, not for the last time, about
the lack of a forest, but by eschewing picturesqueness Elliott and Negri obliged
the audience to concentrate on the characters' relationships and on the symbolic significance of the pastoral. 'At the opening', one critic pointed out,
the director 'underlines the tension and violence which is often ignored as a
mere prelude to the pastoral sweetness to come . . . the early scenes uncover
moments of unexpected force' (*Leamington Spa Courier*, 7 July 1961). Similarly, life in the forest was not, for once, an unalloyed 'golden time': 'The
lugubrious tone in which "This life is most jolly" is uttered suggests that most
of the banished Duke's followers are thoroughly fed up with picnics and the
pastoral life, and will welcome their return to court' (*The Daily Telegraph*, 6
January 1962). Jaques was played by Max Adrian, whose wry, rueful, stylish
performance emphasised the character's role as cynical commentator on pastoral fantasies; no longer could the actor of Jaques get away with being either
slightly daffy or a sonorously venerable court philosopher. Most strikingly, the
killing of the deer became a crucial symbolic set-piece which acted as a cri-

tique of naive pastoralism and affected the characterisation of the court-in-exile: 'By staging the stalking of the prey, its killing amid bestial cries from men momentarily turned to wolves, Mr Elliott gives point to Jaques' wincing – and suggests a reason for his melancholy, the old nightmare of the horns' (J. W. Lambert, *The Sunday Times*, 9 July 1961). Thus Elliott brought into question the 'naturally superior' attributes of the male on which a patriarchal social order is based.

This questioning of received ideas about masculinity was also evident in the Orlando of Ian Bannen, who had recently played a neurotic, slouching Hamlet. He at first eschewed the role of romantic hero, taking refuge in a self-burlesquing style. 'He is too complex a character to convey simplicity', said T. C. Worsley (*The Financial Times*, 5 July 1961); and J. C. Trewin admitted unselfconsciously that Bannen 'has not been my idea of Orlando. He is a lank figure with a weary eye, [looking] like someone from a contemporary novel who has lost his way in the forest' (*Birmingham Post*, 5 July 1961). This mod-ernist consciousness allowed Bannen to explore a possibility in Orlando's char-acter that has been generally ignored – a hint of bisexuality, which, according to Lambert, made him 'respond much more eagerly to the apparent boy than to the dream of the lost girl'. By the time the production moved to London, either Bannen had become more extrovert or the critics had adjusted their spectacles to the contemporary emotional world, for there were no further complaints about miscasting.

The final scene of the play focused on Rosalind, a shining image spotlighted in her white dress, surrounded by flickering torches and the dark night. The irradiating power of the young woman's personality was here most strikingly presented, a challenge to the darkness of the patriarchal system which the young couples are about to re-enter, and to the symbolic winter which inevitably will come again. The adjectives 'sunny', 'radiant', and so forth, describing Redgrave's presence, chimed with Michael Elliott's apparent inten-tion to encourage the audience to receive, however subliminally, a symbolic reading, rather than just another lovely night in the theatre.

'Director's theatre' was underway, and *The Times*'s reviewer was canny enough to comment on it:

> Mr Elliott sees clearly into the double game that Shakespeare was playing. His production reflects both sides of it. We are made to feel both how pleasant it may be for courtiers to seek release from themselves in dreaming of Arcady in Arden, and how preposterous is their dream. Human nature in Arden is still human nature. (*The Times*, 11 January 1962)

This critic went on to commend Patrick Wymark's Touchstone, 'at the centre of the play . . . the natural gross man who blurts out in every crisis just those undesirable facts, even those touching his own affairs, which it is the whole object of romance to refine away'. In none of the previous productions had Touchstone had such an accolade (Wymark replaced Colin Blakely from the Stratford production), and his role as counterweight to Jaques – deflating the pastoral from a low-life perspective rather than that of the court – is increasingly emphasised hereafter. Elliott's production thus became the first theatrically self-conscious reading of the play, recognising the court–country opposition as a metaphor enabling exploration of the human psyche in its social construction.

In the next production at Stratford, directed by David Jones in 1967, the programme carried a number of quotations from literary critics on the role of Touchstone (and Elizabethan fools in general), and the contrasting figure, Jaques. Touchstone was played by the variety comedian Roy Kinnear. Critics were amazed at how funny Touchstone's tedious jokes could be when 'delivered straight across the footlights like a true clown' (B. A. Young, *The Financial Times*, 16 June 1967), that is, acknowledging the theatrical pleasure available in a non-naturalistic reading of the part: 'It is very physical, but this suits well his wickedly accurate verbal timing . . . He stresses Shakespeare's comic fool, the zany jester, the joker we've often longed for in the long procession of Touchstones with white faces and a secret grief up their motley' (Gareth Lloyd Evans, *Guardian*, 16 June 1967). Alan Howard's Jaques more closely resembled this latter type, and developed the characterisation initiated by Max Adrian – 'sour-mouthed, pale and obviously motivated by a cynicism near to hatred' (Doreen Tanner, *Liverpool Post*, 3 October 1967); 'a white-faced, haunted apparition of walking pain, whose view of the world is amply justified by the Darwinian jungle of slaughter and mating he finds around him' (Ronald Bryden, *Observer*, 18 June 1967).

This *As You Like It* was the first Shakespeare production by the young David Jones, and he was keen to show his intellectual credentials; as well as passages from literary critics, the programme contained extracts from Jones's rehearsal notes – 'The forest only helps those who help themselves' – and a page of 'Sightlines', random quotations to help the audience 'read' the production correctly. Yet it struck Irving Wardle as merely 'a middling actors' show', that is, lacking in strong direction; he found in it 'echoes of past productions that take the place of original invention; quantities of awkward moves and a general uncertainty of comic tone' (*The Times*, 16 June 1967). It is possible that casting might have been at the root of the problem: the programme also contained a double-page photographic spread celebrating the fact that the Rosalind, Dorothy Tutin, was playing her tenth role for the RSC. It is hard to avoid the inference that the production was mounted as a star vehicle for Tutin, at that point 36 years old and presumably keen to do 'her' Rosalind on the national stage before she was much older. If this was the case, the intention backfired at several points: uncertain direction, a Rosalind 'in the shadow of Vanessa Redgrave' (Wardle), and a Celia, Janet Suzman, who in youth and vitality was a much more likely successor to Redgrave.

Reviewers were not uncomplimentary about Tutin's Rosalind, but the compliments tended to be on her technique rather than her presence; and her performance emphasised Rosalind's 'femininity' rather than a more modern complex sexuality:

> [Miss Tutin] never allowed her clothes to distract us from her basic femininity. Her gauche walk, the awkward movement of her hands into her trouser pockets, the timorous way in which she bunched a fist, were there to remind us that she was first and foremost a woman in love. (Milton Shulman, *Evening Standard*, 16 June 1967)

> Dorothy Tutin plays Rosalind in the disguise scenes with an air of bewildered self-mockery; her comic timing is superb, especially in her deliciously funny attempts to play the man. (Doreen Tanner, *Liverpool Post*, 3 October 1967)

Most striking is the extent to which Suzman's Celia is noticed: B. A. Young thought her 'just as gay and hoydenish as her cousin, and never retreating into nonentity as she so easily may', and Wardle found Celia 'an enchanting combination of self-mocking dignity and sheer fun, which redoubles the comic delight of the Rosalind scenes. If Oliver had arrived in the forest as soon as Orlando, Miss Suzman could clearly have conducted an equally brilliant courtship.'

Tutin's costume as Ganymede had a curiously old-fashioned air. Designed by Timothy O'Brien, it comprised boots, breeches, long-sleeved shirt, a fastened jerkin with loose belt, and a straw hat. Nothing except her hands and face was bare, in contrast to Redgrave's bare feet and short-sleeved shirt: the effect was of a buttoned-up, cautious woman in her mid-thirties rather than a very young woman exploring the freedom masculine (or 'unisex') dress could give her. When the inevitable happened and Janet Suzman took over the role in a revival of the production in the following year, her change of style was immediately obvious in her costume. She was barefoot, with an open-neck shirt, the sleeves rolled up, and an unbuttoned jerkin which was removed for some scenes, leaving the shirt loosely tucked into her breeches. Like Redgrave, she wore a soft worker's cap (which happened to be fashionable in the late 1960s). Suzman simply looked like a modern young woman, enjoying the freedom of her body and flirtatious games with an almost identically dressed Orlando (Michael Williams, whose costume also loosened up between the 1967 and 1968 productions). Among the intelligent young, the production seemed to suggest, gender differences and the power-structures based on them were simply irrelevant.

The *Oxford Mail*'s critic noted the difference between Tutin's and Suzman's performances:

> Miss Tutin played Rosalind as a coy eager sixth-former wilting bashfully from the pangs of calf-love. Miss Suzman plays her – as she played Celia last year – as a young woman of enormous intelligence and sensitivity who falls head over heels in love. And not unnaturally her performance gives a tremendous lift to Michael Williams's warm-hearted, tousle-haired portrayal of Orlando. (Don Chapman, *Oxford Mail*, 22 May 1968)

A number of critics were happily reminded of Redgrave's performance; a few others found Suzman somewhat over-emphatic (were they still hoping for 'feminine' behaviour – from a young woman in 1968?). But all considered that she lightened a production which, in its revision, had become even darker.

> David Jones never once lets us forget the play's reliance on the disruptive yet sustaining natural world . . . This Arden is black and cold; we first see the Duke and his compatriots shivering in sheep-coats, stamping upon the ground in order to forget the discomforts of exile. Jones makes a great deal of the deer-hunting scene which he transforms into a frightening ritual in which the men of Arden stain each other with blood. (Peter Ansorge, *Plays and Players*, July 1968)

Jones, like Elliott in 1962, but now more emphatically, seized the opportunities offered by the text to explore the values of 'masculinity' embedded in the patriarchy. He was to meet with critical resistance: B. A. Young complained, 'Surely Duke Frederick's orchard was not such an austere mausoleum of black slate last year, or the Forest of Arden such a land of perpetual night? This excessively dim ambience hardly suits such a happy comedy' (*The Financial Times*, 22 May 1968). 'While agreeing that the play contrasts the romantic pastoral ideal with the sometimes harsh rural reality', wrote Michael Billington, 'one has to admit that there are reserves of gaiety and lyricism in the play that this production leaves untapped' (*The Times*, 22 May 1968). He went on to comment on Alan Howard's Jaques, a lynchpin of David Jones's directorial concept:

> [Howard] builds up a remarkably complete portrait of a diseased cynic, conceivably suffering from the pox and unable to look anyone squarely in the face. This reading turns the Seven Ages of Man speech, for example, from a mellow poetic recital into an expression of misanthropic disgust, but at times I feel the part can barely support the weight of the interpretation.

Jones's programme note told the audience that Jaques and Rosalind represent 'polar opposites . . . the creative optimistic mind of Rosalind and the destruc-

tive pessimistic mind of Jaques . . . Rosalind's innocence is quite inaccessible
to Jaques; Jaques' maimed cynicism is beyond the aid of Rosalind. But the attitudes they represent echo throughout the play' – as they echoed, of course,
through the world of the late 1960s, with its rebellious youth and disgruntled
elders.

Nineteen-sixty-seven was also the year of a curiosity in the annals of *As You
Like It*, the National Theatre's all-male production at the Old Vic. Directed
by Clifford Williams (who the previous year had directed the RSC's first
sexually self-conscious *Twelfth Night*), it claimed to be an attempt to recreate
the atmosphere of the Elizabethan theatre. The programme carried pictures
of 'The Drag Tradition' (hedging its bets for a non-Elizabethan audience), and
Williams contributed an essay:

> The examination of the infinite beauty of Man [*sic*] in love – which lies at the
> very heart of *As You Like It* – takes place in an atmosphere of spiritual purity
> which transcends sensuality in the search for poetic sexuality. It is for this reason
> that I employ a male cast; so that we shall not – entranced by the surface reality
> – miss the interior truth.

J. C. Trewin was sarcastic about these anti-theatrical pretensions: 'What a relief
it is not to be entranced by the surface reality!' (*Illustrated London News*, 14
October 1967). While praising many of the performances, including Ronald
Pickup's Rosalind, he found the casting distracting in a twentieth-century
context. The National Theatre's theory-based experiment attempted to divorce
theatre from its cultural context – the audience of a particular time and place,
who have certain 'natural' (i.e., culturally conditioned) interpretations of what
they see on stage. What this audience of the late 1960s saw was 'a bard for
this season's King's Road silhouette of girlish boyishness' (Ronald Bryden,
Observer, 8 October 1967), rather than the abstract purity aimed for by
Williams – the costumes, by Ralph Koltai, were entirely contemporary, as was
the set of perspex tubes and screens.

Some critics made a superhuman effort not to be distracted by the camp
associations of the production. Peter Lewis in the *Daily Mail* (4 October 1967)
spoke of 'a conception of the play so different, so strange, so visually and aurally
hypnotic that the fact that all the girls are really men takes its place as merely
one of the elements in a dream-like total experience, which you accept along
with the rest.' Shakespeare as Strindberg? But if so, it was Strindberg without
the erotic passion, the soul-destroying emotion:

> [Pickup's Rosalind] is completely non-erotic. It begins demurely with a few well-
> observed female gestures, and takes on character only during the Ganymede
> scenes. It is a blank that comes to life under the stress of intense platonic feeling.
> (Irving Wardle, *The Sunday Times*, 4 October 1967)

Its real effect turns out to be that it puts eroticism, whether ambiguous or straightforward, out of the theatre altogether. (Harold Hobson, *The Sunday Times*, 8 October 1967)

The conclusion, at this distance, must be that the experiment was divided against itself: was its intention to reproduce Elizabethan conditions – a symbolic last stand by the male theatrical establishment to claim a special 'historical' right to Shakespeare? Or did it truly want to speak to a contemporary audience of Jan Kott's fashionable 'thesis that absolute love is absolutely neuter' (Milton Shulman, *Evening Standard*, 4 October 1967), the intellectual version of the late 1960s' ideology of polymorphous sexuality? The experiment might have been more convincing had the performers been in Elizabethan dress, or had they allowed homosexual eroticism a place. Of the other women's roles (Charles Kay as a bespectacled Celia, Anthony Hopkins as a Wagnerian Audrey), Irving Wardle said 'the result is entirely comic: and the comic variety seems very much a temperamental reflex of the different actors'. Jeremy Brett's 'very masculine' Orlando, Derek Jacobi's cockney Touchstone ('prettier than any of the girls', said Wardle) were generally admired; as was Robert Stephens's Jaques – 'a white-suited, fastidious, apparently sour old man, fundamentally lonely and kindly, [who] picks his way through the plastic wood with a civilised disdain . . . out of touch with his time' (Frank Marcus, *Plays and Players*, December 1967). Apart from this characterisation, no sense of the play's commentary on contemporary social mores emerges, as indeed it could hardly do, given its determined avoidance of anything sexual.[9]

The RSC's success with a modern-dress approach to *As You Like It* had to wait until 1973, the so-called 'Hair' production directed by Buzz Goodbody and starring Eileen Atkins. Sally Beauman describes Goodbody as

> the most promising young RSC director; she was also the one person within the company who in background and experience bridged the polarities of Seventies theatre. She had been educated at Roedean and Sussex, and had joined the RSC in 1967, aged twenty, as John Barton's personal assistant. Barton had seen and admired a production she directed while at university. Like her fellow male directors she was deeply interested in working on classical texts, and gained experience within the RSC working on both TGR [touring] and large-theatre Shakespeare. She was also a communist and a committed feminist; she had sympathy and connections with alternative theatre work, and in 1971 had helped to start the first feminist theatre company, the Women's Street Theatre Group.[10]

Goodbody's style, in her first major production at Stratford, was relentlessly anti-traditional and defiantly feminist, an attempt to reclaim the play for women after the National's reactionary experiment. The production was contemporary rather than 'timeless'. The design by Christopher Morley echoed

Koltai's abstract ideas: a 'forest' of tubing, with some realistic props – armchairs and a somewhat incongruous log. Everyone wore the fashionable gear of 1973: flared jeans, fringed jerkins, silk scarves, headbands and stacked heels for the men (including 'Ganymede'), Laura Ashley-style frills for the women. Critics complained that there was no distinction between court and country, between aristocrats and the local peasantry. To this Goodbody replied that in Arden 'Hardly anyone seems to do any work: the shepherds and shepherdesses . . . are not really country people. I see them as art college students – drop-outs who live in the country and have mummies and daddies in town with large incomes' (interview, *Birmingham Post*, 9 June 1973). For Goodbody, the play's comment was on modern society as a whole, rather than on polarisations within it. Both poster and programme indicated that the production would be making points about 'a woman's place' in society. The poster showed a back view of Eileen Atkins in jeans, accompanied by a provocative quotation from Luther: 'Men have broad shoulders and narrow hips, and accordingly they possess intelligence. Women have narrow shoulders and broad hips. Women ought to stay home . . . for they have . . . a wide fundament to sit upon, keep house and bear and raise children.' The programme contained, as well as the usual educational essay on the pastoral, a stage history of the presentation of the forest, and Anne Barton's essay 'A Woman's Place', with illustrative material from Erasmus to Virginia Woolf. The intention of the poster, presumably, was to provoke thought about whether there is any real difference, physical or intellectual, between men and women; to remind us that the play's central character is a young woman who leaves home with her 'sister' and triumphantly makes her way in the world – through a male-dominated wildwood to marriage and a return to the bosom of her father. This final irony (from a feminist point of view) was not in fact explored by the production, which thus rather lost its point: Michael Billington remembers, 'They had great problems with the final scene, because Buzz Goodbody said "I don't believe this". How do you direct something if you don't fundamentally subscribe to that ideal?' (interview with the author, December 1990).

The ideological gap was filled with 'business': one-off gags and easy hits at contemporary fashions:

> a Polonius would have to describe Miss Goodbody's version as farcical-metallurgical-sartorial-stereophonical. In no way does it penetrate to the essence of Shakespeare. The play isn't recognisable as a preworking of *The Tempest*, an alluring picture of a world which (if occasionally cruel) offers new perspectives to the perspicacious, restores values as well as health, couples the young and reconciles the old. Still less does the production make fresh, interesting points about 'a woman's place' in society . . . A sort of factitious urban glee constantly intrudes, getting in the way of anything sensitive, trenchant or true. (Benedict Nightingale, *New Statesman*, 22 June 1973)

This critic has his own essentialist view of the play, but he is willing to accept 'fresh, interesting points' – if the production makes them. Ultimately the success of the production (and it was successful with audiences) depended not on a directorial concept, but on Atkins's playing and a general air of contemporary pleasure represented by the rock settings of the songs and a final rain of paper hearts onto the audience – a recreation of the ambience of *Hair* for those who had been too nervous, or too snobbish, to go.

Eileen Atkins was 39 in 1973 – rather old for a representative of modern youth. Goodbody obviously wanted a strong female lead with a distinctly contemporary air – an anti-romantic – and could not find such a figure among younger actresses, who, presumably, would have attempted to emulate the still-potent Rosalind of Vanessa Redgrave, 'a marvellous memory from your reviewer's early adolescence', sighed W. Stephen Gilbert in *Plays and Players* (August 1973) – 'a melting with love which invited the audience to share in it'. Goodbody's gamble, on the whole, paid off:

> fascinating actress though she is, Eileen Atkins is no exponent of springtime romance. With those swivelling eyes and sceptical cadences she expresses the wary defensiveness of someone who has seen too much to have Rosalind's emotional confidence. She is at her best in the Ganymede scenes – jaunty, critical, turning on joke voices and coupling brazen outward assurance with inner confusion. (Irving Wardle, *The Times*, 13 June 1973)

> [Eileen Atkins] makes light of the cliches and finds comedy in places where no-one has found it before. She struts, she rolls her big eyes, she enjoys the ironies which she lifted from the text. (David Isaacs, *Coventry Evening Telegraph*, 13 June 1973)

> Her evident depression and boredom at her uncle's court marks her out as a woman of more than average capacity for feeling: she proves it when she falls in love. Try as she will, she can't always prevent that bony, spiky face from breaking into a look of extraordinary longing, as if she might suddenly do something unexpected and embarrassing, like clutch Orlando by the bicep or buttock and kiss him. I can't imagine many actresses putting as much covert sexuality into the part. (Benedict Nightingale, *New Statesman*, 22 June 1973)

It was an uncomplicated heterosexuality, modern and uninhibited: 'any hint of sexual equivocation is knocked on the head by Eileen Atkins's minimal attempt to disguise her femininity as Rosalind. Indeed, with her headband, fringed blouse, and crutch-hugging jeans, she seemed even more seductive as Ganymede than before' (Michael Billington, *Guardian Weekly*, 23 June 1973). Several critics complained about how hard it is for anyone – male or female – to look romantic in 'drab' jeans. David Suchet's Orlando was distinctly plebeian (he had stepped in for an injured – and much more conventionally good-looking – Bernard Lloyd), though his honesty and directness were admired. The unisex contemporary costuming in fact had the effect of 'normalising' the sexualities, and the general behaviour, of the lovers in the audience's perception, since jeans are the one twentieth-century costume which is virtually free of both gender and class specificity.

Much more interesting to the reviewers was Richard Pasco's Jaques, in a crumpled white suit; as Nightingale described him:

> half-crazed with old desires and guilts, as contemptuous of himself as of the world: he blinks, twitches, hiccoughs, screws round his shoulders, and half-lopes, half-stumbles across the stage, seizing the Duke by the lapels and scrabbling at his chest. Words like 'p-pleasure' get sneering emphasis, and every speech is likely to end with a tiny, cracked laugh, as if nothing mattered anyway.

According to Robert Cushman, 'In Richard Pasco's hands, Jaques becomes almost the central character of the play – paradoxically, really, since he spends most of his time prowling its periphery, peering at the action with beady distaste through rimless glasses' (*Observer*, 17 June 1973). As in most productions since 1961, Jaques represented the production's built-in critique – here the old cynic watching the young moderns' 'love-in' and reading them all as fools in the forest, who forget the inevitability of the last four ages of man in the illusory euphoria of the Age of Aquarius.

Goodbody's attempts to emphasise the contemporary in the play's relationships and ignore the pastoral conventions (which among other things question the 'proper' behaviour of lovers) delighted audiences but dissatisfied critics, who felt that Shakespeare was being lessened ('*As You Like It* is not about courtship as a developing relationship, but about Courtly Love, which Shakespeare did not invent', argued John Elsom in the *Listener*, 21 June 1973). The effect on the university-educated male hierarchy at Stratford – directors such as Trevor Nunn and Terry Hands – was, one suspects, to make them feel that *As You Like It*'s literary conventions had to be reinstated. Yet the play must entertain a contemporary audience: how was this to be done?

1977–80

Nunn's solution, in his 1977 production, was to create a seventeenth-century operatic extravaganza. Turning a play into a musical had worked extremely well with his *Comedy of Errors*: the artificialities of farce could easily be stopped for a song. But *As You Like It* is a later work than the *Comedy*, and it required a more obviously intellectual approach. Nunn took his cue from the seventeenth-century tradition of masque, which frequently contrasted such things as court and country, or celebrated allegorical figures; there is just such a celebratory masque in Act V of *As You Like It*. Nunn actually began the play with another masque – a ten-minute sung debate between Hymen, Nature and Fortune (words by Ben Jonson, Edmund Spenser, Thomas Carewe, and others, music by Stephen Oliver). At various points throughout the play – not just where Shakespeare specified a song – characters broke into Purcellian recitative or aria. Touchstone and Audrey's mock-wedding was accompanied by a 'Puritan hymn', words by assistant director John Caird, of which this is a fair sample:

> O God, in whom we trust
> Look on these twain with grace
> Who leave their filthy thoughts and lust
> To come before thy face.

Sets and costumes, the design of John Napier, were extravagantly French, all frills and bows, with a false proscenium arch and sky-pieces in the manner of baroque theatre. That is, the play was presented by the director as a commentary on the dominance of French culture in England in the mid-seventeenth century – thus solving the dual problems of entertainment and intellectual respectability. But the latter point seems to have gone over the critics' heads. For John Peter, typical of most reviewers but more clear about his reasons,

> *As You Like It* is quite enjoyable and thoroughly baffling. There was poor old Shakespeare applying all his skill and sophistication to turning the rigid pastoral form into warm human drama; and here comes Trevor Nunn and turns it back into elaborate artifice . . . Shakespeare meant the Forest of Arden to be a healing and civilising place: so why turn it into a dotty fairyland of toy bridges, painted brooks with round holes for fishing, and daintily gartered shepherds? The final masque is a poetic conclusion towards which the play gently and delicately grows: so why add an opening masque which gives the story a sense of unreality from the start? (*The Sunday Times*, 11 September 1977)

It's a *play*, not an opera or a ballet or a musical called 'Kiss Me Ros', the critics insisted, unanimous for once. Gareth Lloyd Evans commented,

> The frequent recourse to individual and choral singing with music that lacks lyrical resonance tends to generalise and mechanise the human responses of the characters . . . [T]hough there are a number of excellent performances, nobody really connects . . . [F]or all its virtues . . . it wasn't really a performance of Shakespeare you were seeing. (*Stratford Herald*, 16 September 1977)

What Lloyd Evans means here by 'Shakespeare' might be read as '*contemporary* Shakespeare': a production which 'connects' (his significant word) with itself and the audience; a production that answers the question, who is Rosalind and what is this society she flees, then returns to?

Kate Nelligan's Rosalind, resplendent in lace and ruffles, floppy boots, and huge feathered hat, was, in Robert Cushman's words, 'a natural, able with her superb whole-heartedness to rule a scene, but not to govern this stage, this language, and this over-complicated production' (*Observer*, 11 September 1977). The consensus of critical opinion was that although hers was a high-energy performance, full of infectious gaiety, Nelligan was somewhat lacking in complex (modern, ironical) passion – the production did not allow her to explore this possibility. Felix Barker called it a 'Madcap of the Lower Fourth approach' (*Evening News*, 9 September 1977). 'Miss Nelligan', said a delighted John Barber,

> combines a splendid athleticism with a disturbing ardour. At first sight of Orlando, she is disgracefully, shamelessly smitten . . . But, unrecognised in her boys' clothes, she teases him with so much mischief, laughs at him with so much delight, brims over with so much fun, her whole being becomes a frolic of happiness which it is impossible not to share. (*The Daily Telegraph*, 9 September 1977)

But the ambiguities of the part that critics were beginning to expect in the sexually exploratory 1970s were missing: 'Kate Nelligan's romping, energetic Rosalind changes not a whit with the donning of male attire, and the sexual subtleties of the trial wooing . . . remain at a pantomime level of meaning', said Gordon Parsons (*Morning Star*, 15 September 1977).

Peter McEnery's performance as Orlando had a similar fresh-faced quality: 'This Orlando is still young enough to have no beard, to rush off spontaneously after new ideas . . . and to play silly games with the teenage kid Ganymede that he meets in the forest' (B. A. Young, *The Financial Times*, 8 September 1977). Nunn's directorial concept did not even allow for the now common individual characterisations of Celia, Touchstone, or Jaques. Celia (Judith Paris) was most remarked upon for her ability to skate on the wintry set; Touchstone (Alan David) was costumed as a Watteauesque Pierrot, and had to work hard for his laughs; Jaques (Emrys James), 'in puritan black, laughs a great deal and his final decision to leave the woodland merrymaking and avoid a return to the court shocks, after his having taken a full part in the preceding song-and-dance sequences' (Parsons).

'What then do I miss?' asked Billington:

> The sense that the trip to Arden is a voyage of discovery where every man finds his true self; the very pulse and rhythm of this comedy, undermined by turning minor figures like Sir Oliver Martext into an excuse for another aria; and a basic trust in the given material. (*Guardian*, 10 September 1977)

This last point indexes the final loss of directorial innocence which is the hall-mark of most modern productions. In our postmodern culture, directors know that there is no such thing as a simple 'trust in the given material'; it has no intrinsic life, and it must be read in such a way as to engage an audience which itself reads intertextually. Nunn's 'historical' concept could have been more interesting than it was; it needed to go a lot further than the surface enter-tainment that he patronisingly offered. A basic trust in the actors and actresses to do their work, to perform as *adults*, exploring their roles within the histor-ical framework, might have produced more challenging results.[11]

Terry Hands, in 1980, continued his personal exploration of the meaning of 'Shakespeare's festive comedy' for today (his *Twelfth Night* had opened in 1979), offering a structural contrast between a wintry and pessimistic opening and spring's optimism in the second half. But the actors were not swamped by the directorial concept; instead, they were encouraged to respond to it by flam-boyant self-presentation. The outstanding quality of this production was, in Irving Wardle's words, that it was

> a performance. From the opening quarrel which erupts over the whole down-stage area, and the wrestling match where Rosalind and Celia join in with hisses and hair-pulling, it is an evening of fearlessly extrovert animation by a company who have clearly been told never to be afraid of going over the top. It is fast, passionate, and tightly controlled . . . the show is irresistible. This play is sup-posed to be about the force of fertility and that is what the company deliver direct.[12] (*The Times*, 5 April 1980)

Billington, with his own quasi-directorial ideas about the play, thought that it was a bit much:

> everyone behaves as if he were in a nineteenth-century Surrey-side melodrama . . . The problem is that all this wild-eyed frenzy pre-empts the key point: that Cupid was, in Rosalind's words, 'conceived of spleen and born in madness.' If everyone behaves as if he were a bit touched, it undercuts the lovers' especial dementia . . . this is a production that throughout looks stunning and that builds to a climax of real festivity. But the bold, frontal, declaratory style of acting that suited Hands's production of the Histories looks slightly forced in a comedy about inter-relationships. (*Guardian*, 5 April 1980)

Most critics, however, thought that the up-front physicality of the per-formers gave greater force to the inter-relationships. For example, Jaques, in his dialogue with 'Ganymede' in Act IV, scene 1, folded 'him' in his bear-like grasp and presented 'him' with a red rose. This puzzled Sally Aire (and many other critics): 'but I am glad the moment happened, and grateful that a pos-sible new dimension to the play was revealed to me by it' (*Plays and Players*,

May 1980). The point was, presumably, that even the cynical Jaques is not immune to desire, and that the multi-gendered Rosalind/Ganymede, for this play, embodies it. By the same token, Sinead Cusack's Celia, a close and loving companion to Rosalind, was 'a sexual competitor for Orlando' (Billington) until she realised she was outrun, though this did not sour her relationship with Rosalind; Cusack remained 'a very obvious and determined and available Celia . . . [sitting] centre stage',[13] a silent commentator on her cousin's excesses.

Susan Fleetwood's Rosalind and John Bowe's Orlando were notably well-matched, and clearly displayed the electric current of physical desire running between them by a vocabulary of kisses, hugs, and romps.[14] 'This Rosalind', commented Eric Shorter,

> is of such a breathless coming-on disposition that as Ganymede . . . she seems to throw to the winds all pretence of being a boy and simply itches to get her hands on her pupil. He in turn . . . steals kisses and embraces in such a way that tends to contradict the plot, but since they are both evidently so many fathoms deep in love that their romantic games seem even sillier than usual, who could really object? (*The Daily Telegraph*, 7 April 1980)

Sally Aire added (and most critics agreed), 'John Bowe's Orlando is totally free of the narcissism all too often seen in this role. He is a raw, energetic force, a "nature's gentleman", and on the moral and psychic level is a worthy suitor for Rosalind.'[15] Fleetwood's Rosalind produced greater enthusiasm among the critics than anyone had for twenty years – the bright memory of Vanessa was at last beginning to be displaced. 'Radiance' is no longer thought of as Rosalind's intrinsic quality; this one was rather, said Gareth Lloyd Evans, 'an essentially physical, sexy young woman whose authority lies not in any mysterious spiritual femininity (the accustomed emphasis put on the role) but in the potent example of her own capacity to love' (*Stratford Herald*, 11 April 1980). 'I have not seen Rosalind better played', said Sally Aire:

> I don't expect to see her better played for a very long time, if ever. Informed by a deep intelligence, this performance ranges from the sublimely ingenious to the overtly sexual. There is bubbling humour and that human warmth which has always been Susan Fleetwood's greatest natural quality as an actress.

Perhaps one might expect this response from a modern female critic, delighted to see a woman as such a positive, vital, intelligent centre to a production (certainly it was mine as a member of the audience); but even the doyen of male critics, J. C. Trewin, gave her his accolade: 'Let me say, without pausing, that Susan Fleetwood is the most persuasive Rosalind I have known in four decades. Fathoms deep in love, never arch, she rules her Arden of the spring with a gaiety that has nothing of the principal-boy swagger' (*Birmingham Post*, 7 April 1980).

This production refused to countenance cynicism. Touchstone and Jaques had a positive role in the play: according to Wardle,

> the love-action is supervised by the two counter-clowns Touchstone and Jaques. As at the National Theatre [where a production by John Dexter, with Sara Kestleman and Simon Callow, was concurrently showing] a close bond develops between these two from the moment when Derek Godfrey, instead of simply reporting his meeting with a fool in the forest, launches into his own clown routine.

As the reviewer for the *Oxford Mail* commented, 'It is amazing what a difference focusing hard on the young lovers makes to the play. Superbly as Derek Godfrey plays him no longer is there any risk of the melancholy Jaques casting a long dark shadow across the comedy' (D. A. C., *Oxford Mail*, 8 April 1980).

The play ended with a riotous fertility feast, with huge corn dollies, deer-horn head-dresses, and flowery garlands everywhere. Memories of the court, which in Farrah's design had been a cold and threatening prison (eight metal stakes across the centre of a black-and-white stage), were obliterated in a joyous dance celebrating the healing power of sex. The play inhabited the audience's folk-memory rather than any specific historical period. It was a vision of an England, and an uncomplicated sexuality, that were about to disappear. Hands's directive to the cast had been that *As You Like It* was 'a fairy tale'.[16]

1985–90

Adrian Noble's 1985 production took the perhaps inevitable next step and psychoanalysed the fairytale in a contemporary (modern-dress) reading, set in the country of the modern mind. Here court and country were but flipsides to each other, both metaphors of the prisons/landscapes we construct for ourselves out of our desires and their repressions. Designed by Bob Crowley, the play began in an 'attic' filled with shapes of furniture draped in white material – here Rosalind and Celia had come to escape the oppressive court, but (of course) it pursued them. The move to Arden simply involved the lifting of the covers, with a huge piece of white silk pulled up in the centre of the stage to suggest a tree-trunk, and, eventually, a green silken canopy. 'We wanted something that was genuinely plastic, that would change shape according to what the actors did, according to the moment in the play, because the Forest of Arden in *As You Like It* changes shape, dimension, character, according to the perception of each person.'[17] Over all loomed a huge moon: we were clearly in the realm of the unconscious ('Within the Forest/the Forest within', as the programme directed us). In the Stratford version, much play was made with a large carved looking-glass, through which characters entered and exited, and a clock, which began ticking only when the play was over. In the transfer to London these perhaps over-insistent symbolic props disappeared, and 'key moments of transition [were] reserved for a great luminous port-hole in the back wall, where figures poised for flight or return appear[ed] in silhouette' (Irving Wardle, *The Times*, 18 December 1985).

Instead of the usual educational material on the pastoral, the programme contained poems and prose related to the thematic idea that to enter the 'wood' is to enter a dream or fantasy. It quoted Heinrich Zimmer: 'it is only after . . . a journey in a distant region, in a new land that . . . the inner voice . . . can make itself understood by us.' There were also quotations relating transvestism to the Jungian animus/anima, and the query 'What is love *anyway*?' Juliet Stevenson, the Rosalind, in an interview in *Plays and Players* (May 1985), explained that the play is 'a vital exploration of gender, the male and the female within us all. Rosalind is very released when her masculine aspect is allowed release.' Arden is 'a realm where you can dress up and change your gender, change your way of life'. Bob Crowley's set, she went on to explain, 'is mostly to do with colours, and space, and different moons. These moons get larger and larger as you get into the forest.' Jung's symbolism has probably never had such a thorough outing in the Shakespearean theatre. In another example, the deer-hunt became Celia's dream of defloration:

> Adrian Noble had equated the deer with the virginal Celia, who lay asleep beneath the towering, white, lingam-like mountain of silk that dominated the stage for the forest scenes. Her body had been caught by a snaking, blood-stained trail of cloth, pulled across the stage as she slept . . . and she would awaken to fall in love with Oliver. (Barry Russell, *Drama*, 3, 1985)

The critics' response was astonished but on the whole quite enthusiastic; some made complimentary comparisons with the effect of Peter Brook's revolutionary *Midsummer Night's Dream* of 1970. John Barber thought that the design 'had the effect of cleansing the text . . . of the greasy fustian of painted scenery and the varnish of old conventions gone stale' – an *As You Like It* for this generation (*The Daily Telegraph*, 25 April 1985). Benedict Nightingale's review is typical – resistant but fascinated despite his principles:

> I dislike seeing texts strongly slanted by a director . . . I dislike being violently and superfluously reminded of a play's contemporary 'relevance' by performers wearing bowlers, braces, tuxedos, donkey-jackets, as happens here . . . And yet there are times at Stratford – for instance, when Juliet Stevenson's marvellously bright, buoyant and sexy Rosalind becomes marvellously grave, melancholy and

sombre too – when [Noble] achieves a complexity and, yes, a depth I don't recall
seeing in any previous production of the play. (*Listener*, 25 April 1985)

Michael Billington was not so convinced of the success of the production's
dealings with the erotic; for him, it was

> a highly original reading but one that undercuts the play's sheer Mozartian joy
> . . . [Noble's] chief conceit is to suggest that the court and the forest are not con-
> tinents apart but simply opposite sides of the same human coin . . . I don't mind
> the absence of real trees . . . But Arden is also a place of discovery filled with the
> 'madness' of love and what I find missing in this production is transforming
> human ecstasy . . . [Hilton McRae and Juliet Stevenson] embody the Jungian
> animus and anima (hello Jung lovers wherever you are), each having something
> of the other's sexual nature . . . But rarely in their encounters did I feel I was
> witnessing the marriage of two minds or even two souls. (*Guardian*, 26 April
> 1985)

'Better a production with a concept than a bland retread; and Mr Noble's intelligence shines through', he concluded, '[b]ut I would beg him to remember
that *As You Like It* is still billed as a comedy.' What Noble may well have intu-
ited, however, is that his working definition of comedy as 'a ceremony or
initiation leading towards matrimony'[18] is not necessarily in this age a recipe
for joyous laughter or sexual delight. Rather such an 'initiation' might be the
opportunity for an examination of power-structures within the community and
within the individual psyche (for example, the 'doubling' of the two Dukes'
courts indicated two 'aspects of the same person' for each actor).[19]

Juliet Stevenson is an actress ever willing to explore the intellectual issues
raised by the character she is playing. She obviously followed Noble's directorial concept with enthusiasm (see her comments in *Plays and Players* above);
but she also found herself going beyond Noble to discover a strong feminist
reading of the play. For Stevenson, 'what happens to [Orlando] is classically what happens to women in Shakespeare. His love is tested.
Rosalind/Ganymede uproots his idea of the wooing process. Not only is
Orlando being wooed, not wooing, but his hopelessly romantic notions of
wooing are deconstructed in the process.'[20] Further, Stevenson together with
Fiona Shaw, who played Celia, considered that an important aspect of the play
is the story of the friendship between the two women:

> Armed with this resolve to jettison stereotype, we began work . . . To liberate
> Shakespeare's women from the confines of literary and theatrical tradition
> requires an analysis of the nature and effects of those social structures which
> define and contain them – the opening of this play sees Rosalind and Celia
> already contained within a structure that is oppressive and patriarchal, namely

the court of Duke Frederick, Celia's father. The modern dress decision served to remind us that such structures are by no means 'ancient history', and that the freedom and self-definition that the two girls are seeking remain prevalent needs for many of their contemporaries today.[21]

This insistence on the contemporary reality of the women's emotional and psychological experience produced a compelling and admirable performance from Stevenson. Irving Wardle's review describes the effect:

> Rosalind begins as a prisoner of a stifling court and discovers her real powers through playing games . . . She begins as a rather plain downcast girl, very much the house guest of Fiona Shaw's sharp-eyed Celia; then she gets into a white suit and begins to discover herself, first in . . . clown routines with Hilton McRae's Orlando, and then entering deeper waters where neither she, her lover, nor the audience can tell truth from masquerade. I have never seen their later dialogue played with equivalent erotic force; nor seen the mock-marriage take on such sacramental qualities. (*The Times*, 24 April 1985)

What was evidently lost in this reading of Rosalind was the comic vitality with which actresses have traditionally been able to imbue the role. Stevenson was intense and sincere rather than naturally playful (none of the production pictures shows her laughing or smiling, in strong contrast to the photos of virtually all earlier productions). Nicholas Shrimpton commented on this quality in her performance: 'Juliet Stevenson's Rosalind is touching in her vulnerable moments but desperately unconfident when she is required to be witty, flirtatious or high-spirited. Possibly she is weighed down by the psychological lumber of the interpretation. More probably this gifted actress is . . . simply not a comedienne' (*Times Educational Supplement*, 10 May 1985). Nor need Rosalind be, in such a reading of the play as this; and 'Fortunately', Shrimpton continues, 'the production reminds us that the play has not one but two heroines, and supplies a superb Celia to take up the slack.' Fiona Shaw's Celia brought many appreciative comments, most notably Billington's sense that the production's 'one igniting spark of passion . . . was when Fiona Shaw's Celia (beautifully played as a slightly woozy Mitfordesque deb who turns to mantras and meditation in the forest) exchange[d] instant glances with Bruce Alexander's transformed Oliver' (*Guardian*, 26 April 1985). The archival videotape confirms this observation: Celia and Oliver's long, hypnotised stares at each other, ignoring Rosalind's faint, and their comically awkward, mutually absorbed exit, brought a round of applause.

The play's male characters were less complex, except for the directorial concept of doubling the Dukes and their courts (a practice followed by John Caird in the 1989 production). Alan Rickman's Jaques was an arrogant but vulnerable lone intellectual: 'He did not care who married whom, nor who was in power. He had been there and seen it, and cared for it no longer' (Barry Russell, *Drama*, 3, 1985). Hilton McRae's Orlando, according to Michael Ratcliffe, 'is the sole reference to any resolved humanity warming the cerebral chill of the [play's] first half . . . Into the world of hatchet faces and long over-coats at the start, [he] erupts scruffy, humorous, brave and enormously like-able, if in need of a bath' (*Observer*, 24 April 1985). His wrestling match was a comic epic in the manner of television's rock 'n' roll wrestling, with McRae in a very fetching G-string; at one crucial point he released himself from the grunting Charles by giving him a hearty kiss. 'One might even say', wrote Barry Russell,

> that this Orlando was used as the 'token male'. He took his clothes off, showed us his body, was pretty, long-haired and attractive. He was the romantic dreamer who spent much time in thought, but actually seemed incapable of achieving very much if left to his own devices. Rosalind, by contrast, looked strong and played strong.

So the production achieved its aim of presenting the feminine in the masculine, the masculine in the feminine. But, according to Stevenson, this deconstruction of gender roles presented problems as the play approached its end – a magical, joyous celebration which insists on the characters' return to the patriarchal 'hierarchies of the structured world', which is also the 'real world'. Stevenson and Noble argued about the staging of the ending:

> Having spent three hours challenging notions of gender, we couldn't then end with a final stage picture which was clichéd and stereotypical, which threw the whole play away. Adrian did point out to me that, whether I liked it or not, Shakespeare was a monarchist, a reactionary, a bourgeois and a conservative, but I said, 'I think it's irrelevant what Shakespeare was. The fact is the *play* asks the most anarchic questions. It doesn't attempt to resolve them, so why should we?[22]

Eventually, by the time the production came to London, the actors and direc-tor had re-worked the ending so that the play continued its challenge to the audience:

> the dance culminated in a moment of still suspension, as the characters took in the Arden they were about to leave, and absorbed the *consequences* of the return to the ordered world. They then exited, through a moon-shaped hole in the backdrop, which both told the story more clearly and laid emphasis on the fantastical nature of the whole event . . . These changes meant that the issues explored were no longer smothered, at the end, by excesses of 'merry-making', and we no longer felt obliged to abandon ourselves on the stage to some imposed inevitability.[23]

Stevenson hoped that 'the audience would go out of the theatre talking to each other', that the production's serious re-thinking of this comedy would in some way affect the lives of the spectators:

> I don't expect audiences to go skipping out of *As You Like It* humming the tunes, because the play isn't about that. It isn't about confirming cosy opinions or settled stereotypes. It isn't about a woman in search of romantic love. The search is for knowledge and for faith, and in that search Rosalind is clamorous.[24]

This clarion call from one of the new generation of feminist classical actresses was, astonishingly, ignored in subsequent RSC productions of the play. Nineteen eighty-nine brought John Caird's new production, and a question from a somewhat weary Michael Billington: is *As You Like It* being done too often? (*Guardian*, 15 September 1989). Stewart McGill found the production 'a major disappointment':

> As the theatre world awaits the announcement of a successor to Terry Hands, the focus of the debate must be on what kind of Shakespeare should this company be doing as we move toward the 1990s . . . Caird, his designer Ultz and composer Ilona Sekacz have destroyed the play in a quest for yet another way of reviving Shakespeare for today's audiences. The RSC production is loud, expensive, spectacular and utterly heartless. (*Plays and Players*, November 1989)

Caird clearly had a 'concept' for the play: an even more radical questioning of the power of the comic paradigm than Noble's. The problem lay in the communicating of these ideas. A case in point is the opening scene, as striking a directorial imposition as Nunn's operatic masque in 1977. The audience entered the theatre to find a 1930s' cocktails-and-tango party going on on stage. The effect was overwhelmingly funereal, not to say sinister. These were the bored, idle, and corrupt rich; no one smiled; the men grimly challenged each other in toreador postures; Duke Frederick's heavies eyed the auditorium; and no one danced with Rosalind. Yet for the two male critics quoted above, 'The aim, I take it, is to build up a party atmosphere' (McGill); 'Why, if Duke Frederick's court is an incipient tyranny, is everyone having such a good time?' (Billington). Billington incorrectly describes the event as a 'tea-dance' – apparently unaware that people don't wear black and diamonds, and dance with cold formality, at a *tea*-dance. The brutalist mood continued with a wrestling match in which Orlando appeared to be badly injured, spitting blood, and which he finally won by fighting dirty. The Duke's henchmen pulled guns on him when he revealed whose son he was: this 'court' was the home of a tough, loveless gangster, whose conversion is never remotely likely.

The 'forest' was created by the same henchmen (with a change into brown overcoats; the Dukes too were doubled, by the actor Clifford Rose) simply pulling up the black boards of the floor, to reveal a small patch of wintry ground, which was gradually enlarged, as the forest ethos took over. All this provided a strong moral contrast between court and country – or rather, as Caird was clearly reflecting the ethical concerns of the 1980s, between the City and those who try to escape its circle of power – while at the same time indicating, as Noble did, that the two are inextricably linked. It was, however, the image of Arden which most worried the critics – an alien, vaguely sinister world in the play's first half, all piles of planks and swirling mist, and in the second half, a pool surrounded by surrealistic bullrushes; no trees (again). Its inhabitants, most notably Silvius and Phoebe, behaved very oddly indeed, pursuing their courtships in underwear (eventually, in the 'summertime', the court in exile was also reduced to boxer shorts). The audience was clearly invited to take a patronising view of the absurd behaviour of these pastoral types ineptly aping their betters (by contrast, an admired aspect of Noble's production was that the yokels were treated with respect as people, not caricatures). As Irving Wardle commented, 'they, no less than the courtiers, are giving a performance . . . the forest has no claims to reality' (*The Times*, 15 September 1989) – as opposed to the all-too-grim reality of the court.

The programme was little help: it carried a number of Blake's *Songs of Innocence and Experience* which reflected the production's ambivalence about the relation between the loveless adult world and 'the echoing green', but it was hard to tell what value was placed upon the green world. Perhaps the portrayal of Rosalind as a bored young sophisticate released into her true self, a tomboyish schoolgirl, was meant to present an image of Blakean energy which might transform the oppressive social world. Certainly Sophie Thompson's performance offered an excess of manic vitality. But if this was Caird's intention, it was somewhat skewed in performance by Thompson's comic genius. She used the role of Rosalind to create a highly inventive and amusing study of the tomboy schoolgirl in love. For Michael Coveney this was enough:

> a performer of blazing comic personality, powerful voice, dimpled, darting radiance and quixotic charm . . . Sophie Thompson joins an exalted company of tomorrow's Denches and Smiths in a performance that ripples with invention, bubbles with high spirits and delights at every turn. (*The Financial Times*, 15 September 1989)

Others were less enchanted:

> Sophie Thompson's Rosalind emerges as a simpering St Trinian's schoolgirl, dressed in shorts, gym shoes, straw hat and a satchel. Eschewing any hint of androgynous appeal Miss Thompson runs a gamut from bawling declamation to the doleful quaver, whose nasal stresses are reminiscent of Maggie Smith. (Nicholas de Jongh, *Guardian*, 13 April 1990)

As one might expect from such a characterisation the production was short
on sexual excitement, a lack which disappointed de Jongh: 'there is small hint
of sexual pathos, flirtatious mockery or erotic tension in her larkish, gamey
performance when set against Jerome Flynn's morose Orlando, a youth whom
you almost feel would prefer to be otherwise engaged.' Hugo Williams of the
Sunday Correspondent (17 September 1989) offered a more generous judgement – which also reminded theatre-goers of the ephemerality of the art they
support, dependent on performers and performances:

> As usual, the play's success depends on Rosalind, with a little help from Touch-
> stone. It is almost thirty years since Vanessa Redgrave's Rosalind, and yet one
> goes on comparing succeeding Rosalinds to her lanky principal boy. Sophie
> Thompson could not be more different: short, knock-kneed, Chaplinesque, it is
> a knockabout characterisation which takes some getting used to because of its
> lack of physical allure, but which finally triumphs by radical conviction and
> wholeness . . . Though never 'luminous', she is finally loveable.

As, one might add, small children or clowns are loveable. Thompson's
Rosalind and Mark Williams's red-nosed Touchstone provided between them
many laughs; but it might be argued that this directorial emphasis suggests a
curious desperation: does 'comedy' now only mean a brilliantly performed
joke? Has it, at the end of the twentieth century, lost its power to reconcile
and renew? Ultz's design for Arden had created a surrealist dream-world –
Wonderland, or a return to the Neverland of the 1950s. Now, however, it is a
dream-escape from an extremely unpleasant contemporary real world. Perhaps
the biggest clue to the production's perspective is given by the poster adver-
tising the show. Rosalind and/or the greenwood are nowhere to be seen;
instead, Charles the wrestler throws Orlando, in front of a grim-faced male
courtier. The sources of power and energy are not to be found in Rosalind or
the greenwood, but in the world of macho games ruled by the men in suits
(these games were grimly parodied in the deer-killing, whose primitivism disgusted the cold dandy Jaques). The same pessimism underlay the uncomfortably jokey 'business' surrounding the Epilogue: Orlando stepped forward to
speak it, had a fit of stage-fright, and Rosalind came to his rescue – she was
not *in herself* an authoritative figure, just a Blakean 'happy child'. One won-
dered how these children of the greenwood would survive on the outside,
lacking even the empowerment of sexual desire.[25]

Notes

1 Valerie Traub, *Desire and Anxiety: Circulations of Sexuality in Shakespearean Drama*
   (London: Routledge, 1992), p. 124. She quotes James Saslow, *Ganymede in the*

Renaissance (New Haven, CT: Yale University Press, 1986): 'the very word *ganymede* was used from medieval times well into the seventeenth century to mean an object of homosexual desire' (p. 2). Traub argues that 'the erotics of *As You Like It* . . . are diffuse, non-localized, and inclusive, extending to the audience an invitation to "come play" – as does Rosalind-cum-boy-actor in the Epilogue. Bypassing a purely scopic [phallic] economy, *As You Like It* possesses provocative affinities with the tactile, contiguous, plural erotics envisioned by Luce Irigaray as more descriptive of female experience' (p. 142).

2   Jean E. Howard offers an illuminating commentary on this matter: 'In my view, the figure of Rosalind dressed as a boy engages in playful masquerade as, in playing Rosalind for Orlando, she acts out the parts scripted for women by her culture. Doing so does not release Rosalind from patriarchy but reveals the constructed nature of patriarchy's representations of the feminine and shows a woman manipulating those representations in her own interest, theatricalizing for her own purposes what is assumed to be innate, teaching her future mate how to get beyond certain ideologies of gender to more enabling ones': 'Crossdressing, the theatre and gender struggle in early modern England', *Shakespeare Quarterly*, 39: 4 (1988), pp. 410–40, p. 435.

3   '[W]hen in the Epilogue the character playing Rosalind reminds us that she is played by a boy, the neat convergence of biological sex and culturally constructed gender is once more severed. If a boy can so successfully personate the voice, gait, and manner of a woman, how stable are those boundaries separating one sexual kind from another, and thus how secure are those powers and privileges assigned to the hierarchically superior sex, which depends upon notions of difference to justify its dominance?' (ibid., p. 435). In modern performance by a woman, these ontological confusions are even more present: from what gender position can she possibly be speaking?

4   Stephen Greenblatt, *Shakespearean Negotiations* (Oxford: Clarendon Press, 1988), p. 91

5   For the history of this cultural appropriation of Rosalind, see Mary Hamer, 'Shakespeare's Rosalind and her public image', *Theatre Research International*, 11: 2 (1986), pp. 105–18: 'In the course of two centuries, as the play from 1741 onwards became ever more firmly established in the popular taste, the presentation of its heroine became fixed in a predictably idealizing mode. Play and heroine acquired a special status in the non-academic imagination. They came to constitute a sort of group fantasy' (p. 107), which, Hamer argues, was reinforced by actresses' 'willingness to display [their] femininity in a particularly appealing and unthreatening way' (p. 115).

6   '*As You Like It* was just the play for the 1950s. Its air of liberation, its informality of style, its delight in "happenings" and eccentricity, above all its "image of life triumphing over chance", which Susanne Langer dubbed the essence of comedy, all chimed in with the mood of the 1951 Festival of Britain': M. M. Mahood, 'Shakespeare's middle comedies: a generation of criticism', *Shakespeare Survey*, 32 (1979), p. 8.

7   Michael Billington, *Peggy Ashcroft* (London: Mandarin, 1988), p. 170. Two further

reviews quoted by Billington indicate the limitations of Ashcroft's 'feminine' reading of the role: Derek Granger in *The Financial Times*: 'The shades of fancy and wonder which cross her face at the moment of falling in love are as sweetly defined as the light and shower of April weather; and, even in between the lines, her little starts and hesitations as her heart sways her carry the charming import of a woman becoming *joyfully enslaved*' (my emphasis). Kenneth Tynan found her 'too daughter-of-the-late-colonel-ish' (p. 170).

8   'As I had made a leap as an actress [in Rosalind], I took an irrevocable decision to make a leap into political life as well. Bertrand Russell and members of the Committee of 100 were arrested and charged with incitement to break the law when they spoke at a rally in Hyde Park in September 1961. John Morris, a member and organiser in the Committee, rang me and asked if I would join the Committee to take the place of those who had been arrested. I agreed.' She wrote to her father, the actor Michael Redgrave, explaining her position on unilateral nuclear disarmament: 'I want to act as well and as continuously as possible all my life, no holds barred . . . But in the present situation I have to realise that there may not *be* another season at Stratford . . . [M]y awareness of all the life around me, political, personal, natural or theatrical, and my love for that life which is *why* I act after all, had been doubly *increased* since becoming more aware and involved with the present political situation' (*Vanessa Redgrave: An Autobiography* [London: Hutchinson, 1991], pp. 95, 96, 99).

    Some idea of Redgrave's performance of Rosalind can be gleaned from the Shakespeare Recording Society's record of 1962 (Caedmon Cassette CDL 5210). In the wooing scenes she is passionately involved: the voice is womanly, warm, seductive, seduced, quavering before reverting to brave boyishness. All the 'court' roles are, by modern standards, extremely well-spoken – including Stanley Holloway's Touchstone, today routinely a cockney. Max Adrian's Jaques is a particularly arresting vocal characterisation, elegant yet full of pain.

9   There was in this year another 'Swinging Sixties' production, by Peter Dews for the Birmingham Rep, which transferred to London in the summer of 1967 and was very successful: 'the contemporary version of pastoral is the fancy dress of King's Road and Carnaby Street . . . designed for no real weather or public occasion one can imagine in Britain . . . [rather] an Arcadia of youth, an androgynous, perpetually sunlit Arden of huge paper blossoms' (Ronald Bryden, *Observer*, 18 June 1967).

10 Sally Beauman, *The Royal Shakespeare Company: A History of Ten Decades* (Oxford: Oxford University Press, 1982), p. 320.

11 The most famous *As You Like It* of 1977 was Peter Stein's at the Schaubühne in Berlin. This was a production in a huge film studio, in which the audience walked 'through a ten-minute woodland labyrinth' to an Arden with 'real trees . . . shrubbery, a sprawling pond, huts, a herbal stall, butterfly displays, an astronomical laboratory and an Elizabethan globe above it all'. The action was played above, below, behind, and in the midst of the audience, and became more and more fanciful, or 'unhistorical', as the play proceeded. Many of Stein's postmodernist ideas seem to have permeated the consciousness of RSC directors of the 1980s (for a full

description of the production see *Plays and Players*, December 1977: interestingly, this article does not once mention Rosalind).

12 John Bowe (the Orlando) records, 'Terry's simple solution to lovers' games was circles: histories and tragedies have straight lines, comedies and romances have circles. If you had a map of our footprints in the two major scenes of the second half, you would have a picture of spirals all over the stage': 'Orlando in *As You Like It*', in *Players of Shakespeare*, ed. Philip Brockbank (Cambridge: Cambridge University Press, 1985), p. 73.

13 Sinead Cusack in Carol Rutter, *Clamorous Voices: Shakespeare's Women Today* (London, The Women's Press, 1988), p. 115.

14 Susan Fleetwood, interviewed in 1990 as she prepared to open as Beatrice in Bill Alexander's *Much Ado About Nothing* [. . .] recalled 'It was a gift of a production, it was the chemistry of everyone in it that made it so alive and loving. People still come up to me, touch me and say "Oh, I saw your *As You Like It*. Thank you." Emotive about it still, as if it touched something very warm in them. Isn't that marvellous?' (Unidentified cutting [*Daily Telegraph*?], Shakespeare Centre Library).

15 John Bowe thought of his character as 'this energetic but shy young man, suppressed by his eldest brother, Oliver, since his father's death. No bad thing, perhaps, since it meant his life was spent nearer to Nature. Throughout rehearsal and performance I felt more and more that this was of importance to the balance of Rosalind and Orlando's relationship' (in *Players of Shakespeare*, ed. Philip Brockbank, p. 68).

16 Bowe in ibid., p. 67.

17 Noble adds, 'We had not designed that production on the first day of rehearsals. We designed it during rehearsals. And that wasn't a totally successful concept', being very impractical for the actors (Noble interviewed in Ralph Berry, *On Directing Shakespeare* [London: Hamish Hamilton, 1989], p. 163). See also his remarks in '"Well, this is the forest of Arden": an informal address', *Images of Shakespeare*, ed. Habicht et al. (London: Associated University Presses, 1988).

18 Noble in *Images of Shakespeare*, ed. Habicht et al., p. 337.

19 Ibid., p. 338.

20 Juliet Stevenson in Rutter, *Clamorous Voices*, p. 105.

21 Fiona Shaw and Juliet Stevenson, 'Celia and Rosalind in *As You Like It*', *Players of Shakespeare 2*, ed. Russell Jackson and Robert Smallwood (Cambridge: Cambridge University Press, 1988), p. 57. Shaw commented elsewhere, 'For that play we were probably more fuelled, as a lot of women were, by the excitement of a new sense of who they were in society. We were exploring – very honestly, not trying to map anything on – the possibility of women's friendships . . . We didn't play a received notion of what women's friendships were . . . We played it that those two girls betray each other left, right and centre. That's in the text but it does need the colouring of where you are at the time, to see it': 'Fiona Shaw talks to Helen Carr', *Women: A Cultural Review*, 1: 1 (1990), pp. 67–80, p. 77.

22 Stevenson in Rutter, *Clamorous Voices*, pp. 119–20.

23 Shaw and Stevenson in *Players of Shakespeare 2*, ed. Jackson and Smallwood, p.

71. The appearance of Hymen also changed: in Stratford 'a flickering silhouette on a lighted screen, placed upstage, obliging the actors to turn away from the audience to perceive him'; in London 'a mere beam of light whose source was *behind* the audience . . . in this way, the audience was able to focus not on the god, but on the face of those whose future he is deciding. This afforded each of us the opportunity to play against the "happy ever after" element, if we chose' (p. 70). Despite these developments, Susan Carlson quotes a 1986 letter from Stevenson in which she says, 'for 18 months I played a Rosalind that I never felt I'd been allowed to make truly my own' (*Women and Comedy: Rewriting the British Theatrical Tradition* [Ann Arbor: University of Michigan Press, 1991], p. 66).

24 Stevenson in Rutter, *Clamorous Voices*, p. 121.

25 Fiona Shaw played Rosalind in an Old Vic production by Tim Albery in 1989. It was not well received, owing largely to an awkward design and the interesting suggestion of a lesbian relationship between Rosalind and Celia (which the girls then 'grow out of'). Like the other late 1980s' productions, Albery's was dispirited and humourless; as Michael Billington commented, 'it's a play we can't deal with very easily at the moment, for various reasons. Productions . . . are getting more frenetic, darker, gloomier, colder, and unable to embrace two things . . . the marital conclusion . . . and a sort of pastoral vision, because we don't seem to believe in that either' (interview with the author, December 1990).

David Thacker's 1992 RSC production of *As You Like It* did not expand the play's meaning for the audience of the 1990s, and won faint praise as clear but unadventurous: 'Samantha Bond's Rosalind, stronger on languishing than on mischief, settles for a leisurely rhythm that fails to ignite the Orlando scenes. Last year's Cheek By Jowl [all-male] version of the play released an emotional charge nowhere approached in this production' (Irving Wardle, *Independent on Sunday*, 26 April 1992). Benedict Nightingale found Bond 'a kind of androgynous elf or sprite, part Ariel and part Peter Pan' (*The Times*, 24 April 1992). Michael Coveney (*Observer*, 26 April 1992) commented, 'If an audience does not love its Rosalind, and is not heard to be falling in love with her, the play simply fails to catch alight.' He sensed 'a complete indifference to the intellectual and sexual climate of the comedy'.

Index